The Irish World Wide
History, Heritage, Identity

Volume 6 **The Meaning of the Famine**

The Irish World Wide
History, Heritage, Identity

Edited by Patrick O'Sullivan

Volume 1 Patterns of Migration
Volume 2 The Irish in the New Communities
Volume 3 The Creative Migrant
Volume 4 Irish Women and Irish Migration
Volume 5 Religion and Identity
Volume 6 The Meaning of the Famine

The Irish World Wide
History, Heritage, Identity

Volume 6

The Meaning of the Famine

Edited by Patrick O'Sullivan

Leicester University Press
London and Washington

Leicester University Press
A Cassell imprint
Wellington House, 125 Strand, London WC2R 0BB, England
P.O. Box 605, Herndon, VA 20172, USA

First published 1997
© Editor and contributors 1997

British Library Cataloguing in Publication Data
A catalogue record for this book is available from the British Library.

ISBN 0 7185 1426 2

Library of Congress Cataloging-in-Publication Data
The meaning of the famine / edited by Patrick O'Sullivan.
        p. cm. — (The Irish World Wide ; v. 6)
    Includes bibliographical references and index.
    ISBN 0-7185-1426-2
    1. Famines — Ireland — History — 19th century. 2. Ireland —Emigration
and immigration — History — 19th century. 3. Ireland— History—1837–1901.
I. O'Sullivan, Patrick, 1944– .
II. Series
DA950. 7.M43 1997
941. 50841—dc20   96–44980

Typeset by Patrick Armstrong, Book Production Services
Printed and bound in Great Britain by
Creative Print and Design Wales, Ebbw Vale, Gwent

In memory of Mae O'Sullivan

Contents

List of tables

List of contributors

Francis Costello holds a doctorate in Modern Irish History, and is a regular contributor of articles on Irish history and current events to newspapers and historical journals in the United States. He is the author of the biography of Terence MacSwiney, *Enduring the Most*, has recently completed a history of the Irish Revolution and its aftermath, and is now finishing a study of Michael Collins. In his professional life, Francis Costello works as an economic development consultant in the USA and in Ireland: he is chairman of the Boston-based International Creative Strategies.

Graham Davis is Course Director of the MA in Irish Studies at Bath College of Higher Education, Bath, England. He is the author of *The Irish in Britain 1815–1914*, and of numerous articles on aspects of Irish experience. He is currently working on a major study of the Irish in Texas.

Ruth-Ann M. Harris is visiting professor at Boston College, USA. She is editor of the 15-volume series *The Search for Missing Friends: Irish Immigrant Advertisements in the Boston Pilot, 1831–1916*, and her latest book is *The Nearest Place that Wasn't Ireland: Early Nineteenth Century Labor Migration*. She is currently working on a study of emigrant letters by Irish women in North America.

Christine Kinealy is a Research Fellow of the Institute of Irish Studies, within the University of Liverpool, England. Her major study of the Irish Famine, *This Great Calamity*, was published in 1994. She is now working on further studies of British policy in Ireland during the Famine years.

Richard Lucking, originally a research physicist who moved into the economic and social sciences, is based at the Development and Project Planning Centre, at the University of Bradford, England. He has been involved in development projects in many countries, including Indonesia, Sri Lanka and Namibia. He is currently Director of *Phare*, a European Union Project offering advice and support to independent Latvia.

Christopher Morash is based at St. Patrick's College, Maynooth, Ireland. He is the editor of *The Hungry Voice: the Poetry of the Irish Famine* and co-editor of *'Fearful Realities': New Perspectives on the Irish Famine*. He is the author of *Writing the Irish Famine*, published by Oxford University Press, 1995.

Frank Neal is Professor of Economic and Social History in the European Studies Research Institute, within the University of Salford, England. His principal research interests include Irish immigration into Britain and maritime history. He is the author of *Sectarian Violence: the Liverpool*

Experience, 1819–1914, numerous articles, and a forthcoming book, *Black '47: Britain and the Irish Famine.*

Patrick O'Farrell holds a personal chair in History at the University of New South Wales, Australia. Among his published works are the standard works on Irish Australia, including *The Catholic Church and Community: an Australian History* and *The Irish in Australia* and two books on Anglo-Irish relations.

Marianna O'Gallagher is Director of Carraig Books, Quebec, Canada. Her continuing research into the experiences of the Irish in Canada includes a major study of the quarantine station at Grosse Île.

Patrick O'Sullivan is editor of *The Irish World Wide.*

Acknowledgements

A project like *The Irish World Wide* gains new friends and incurs new debts everyday. I have therefore waited until the last possible moment to record my thanks to all those who made the project possible.

First and foremost I thank my wife Alison, without whose love and friendship this project would not have been possible. I thank my sons, Dan and Jake. I think all three cope remarkably well with the problems of living with a writer.

I thank all our friends and neighbours in Bradford, especially Marguerite Sobol and Stephen Sobol. What would we have done without them? I thank Tom Gallagher, Richard Lucking, Tony Ward, and Karyl Woods.

I thank all my friends for their long-term support and encouragement, especially Sheridan Gilley, Robert Hewison, and Ann Rosenberg – the 'three godparents' to this project.

Leicester University Press, formerly an imprint of Pinter Publishers, is now an imprint of the Cassell group. I thank all those who have worked at Leicester University Press over the years.

In particular I thank the original commissioning editor, Alec McAulay, who had the vision to understand the project when it was first discussed. It was Alec McAulay who said, 'It will have to be many volumes, won't it?' and who did not flinch when I changed the original plan, from five volumes to six. (That was when I decided that we had to tackle questions around the relationship between migration and creativity, in what has become *The Creative Migrant*, Volume 3 of *The Irish World Wide*.)

I thank Patrick Armstrong, Stephen Butcher, Lucy Culshaw, Ludo Craddock, Vanessa Harwood, Colin Hutchens, Catherine Johnston, Elizabeth Leroy, Janet Joyce, Ray Offord, Anne O'Neill, Frances Pinter, Marilyn Turner, Bee Whilems, Sara Wilbourne and Alan Worth.

At the University of Bradford, I especially thank Russell Murray, the project's advisor on research methodology. If part of the agenda of *The Irish World Wide* project has been to teach research methodology to the Irish diaspora then there are scholars throughout the world who have benefited from his calm and wise advice.

I thank the University of Bradford, and especially the Department of Applied Social Studies and the Department of Interdisciplinary Social Studies, for providing me with an academic base and support. I thank all past and present colleagues within those Departments, and within the University of Bradford, especially John Allcock, Pauline Baird, Malcolm Chapman, Maurice Colgan, Roger Fellows, Mike Fisher, Jeff Hearn, Reg Hindley, Danny Kennally, Ruth Lister, Eileen Moxon, James O'Connell, Hilary Rose, and K. E. Smith.

I thank Peter Ketley, and his colleagues at the J. B. Priestley Library at the University of Bradford; Janet Wallwork, and her colleagues at the John Rylands Library, University of Manchester; the staff of the Brotherton Library, University of Leeds; and the staff at the Bodleian Library, Oxford.

A project like this depends on the creation of networks, and the creation of networks depends on there being kind and helpful people in the world. I thank past and present officers and organizers of: the American Conference for Irish Studies; the British Association for Irish Studies; the Canadian Association for Irish Studies; the Centre of Canadian Studies, Edinburgh; the Conference of Irish Historians in Britain; *Fortnight* Educational Trust; the International Association for the Study of Anglo-Irish Literature; the Institute of Irish Studies, Dublin; *Ireland Worldwide*; the Irish-Australia Conference; the Irish Diaspora Project, Dublin; *Irish Literary Supplement*; *Irish Studies Review*; the Irish Studies Workshop, Leicester; and the Lipman Seminars on Ireland,

I thank Donald Akenson, Bo Almquist, Bernard Aspinwall, Shelia Baird, John Barry, John Belchem, Kevin Boyle, Sarah Briggs, R. H. Buchanan, Patrick Buckland, Philip Bull, Bob Burchell, Eleanor Burgess, Mervyn Busteed, Philip Butterss, Bernard Canavan, Angela Carter (Irish Books, New York), Seamus Cashman, George J. Casey, Sean Connolly, Deborah Cottreau, Martin Croghan, Mary Daly, Mary Daniels, Graham Davis, Philip Deacon, James E. Doan, Luke Dodd, James S. Donnelly, David Noel Doyle, Owen Dudley Edwards, Marianne Elliott, Charles Fanning, Burt Feintech, Roy Foster, Laura Fuderer, Finn Gallagher, Thomas Gallagher, William Gillies, Maurice Goldring, Leo Gooch, Ruth-Ann Harris, Mary Hickman, Jackie Hill, Eamon Hughes, Tess Hurson, Seán Hutton, Paul Hyland, Toni O'Brien Johnson, David Kavanagh (Irish Film Institute), Leon Litvack, Robert G. Lowery, James White McAuley, John McGurk, Donald MacKay, William J. McNally, Ged Martin (Centre of Canadian Studies, Edinburgh), Patrick Meany, Robert Miles, Kerby Miller, Austen Morgan, Don Mullan (Concern Worldwide and Afri), Chris Myant, James P. Myers, Frank Neal, Éilís Ní Dhuibhne, Robert O'Driscoll, Patrick O'Farrell, Cormac Ó Gráda, Tom Paulin, Greville Percival, Bob Purdie, Ann Rossiter, Richard L. Rubenstein, Neil Sammells, Joe Sheeran, W. J. Smyth, Eileen Sullivan (Irish Educational Association, Florida), Roger Swift, Mary Helen Thuente, David Tipton, Nigel Todd, Mike Tomlinson, Blanche M. Touhill, Pauric Travers, Virginia Valentine (Semiotic Solutions, London), Norman Vance, Bronwen Walter, James Walter, Peter Way, Tjebbe Westendorp, Anna Whitworth, Charles W. J. Withers, and many, many others.

I thank all those who discussed possible contributions to the project with me, and shared their time and their thinking. I especially thank David Storey and Christie Davies.

For words of encouragement at a difficult time I thank Mary Robinson, President of the Republic of Ireland; Donal Mooney, Brendan Mac Lua and their colleagues at *The Irish Post*, London; Niall Gallagher and his colleagues at AIB, Bankcentre, Britain; Kevin Cassidy and his colleagues at AIB, Leeds; Paul Murray and his colleagues at the Irish Embassy, London.

And lastly, I thank all the contributors to *The Irish World Wide.* Everything that everyone else listed here has done, they have done. They have offered words of encouragement, they have networked, they have been patient when patience was needed, they have worked hard when hard work was needed, they have shared their scholarship with the world. They deserve our thanks.

Patrick O'Sullivan
Bradford
September 1996

Introduction to Volume 6: the meaning of the Famine

Patrick O'Sullivan

I begin writing this Introduction to *The Meaning of the Famine*, aware that this is the last volume of *The Irish World Wide*, and that a seven-year task nears completion. Let me explain why *The Meaning of the Famine*, the most closely focused volume in the series, is placed at the end. You will be aware of the ways that these academic, multi-authored volumes are brought together. There is a certain amount of broadcast appeal, but that is only one part of the creation of networks of personal contacts and of negotiations, as potential contributors are identified, matched to specific topics, commissioned and coaxed towards delivery.

When I planned the series, in the early 1990s, I had expected to be inundated with offers of material about the relationship between the Irish Famine and Irish migration. Well you would, wouldn't you? Indeed, I feared that the Famine might dominate the entire *Irish World Wide* project: for one thing, I felt that understanding of Irish migration generally would help towards a better understanding of the relationship between famine and migration. I decided to give the Famine its own volume. I expected to be able to place the Famine within the broad sweep of the chronology of Irish migration, and I had accordingly planned that the volume on the Famine appear at about the mid point of *The Irish World Wide* series. I thought that I would be able to pick and chose from a wealth of famine-related material to create a coherent volume. I decided to call that volume 'The Meaning of the Famine'.

My strategy turned out to be absolutely correct: but for all the wrong reasons. In my first world-wide trawl I was offered virtually nothing on the Famine. There seemed to be little new research. In a way (and I put this in an extreme form for dramatic effect) it was as if there was a world-wide academic conspiracy to ignore the Irish Famine. I can regard the difficulty I have had in creating a volume on the Famine as itself a research finding of the project, and confirmation of Cormac Ó Gráda's observation of a 'paradox' within Irish historiography.[1]

We can, like Ó Gráda, think of reasons for this neglect of the Irish Famine by Irish historians. Generally in these islands we are looking for reasons to love one another rather than reasons for hate. The Famine is a controversial subject: and formal academic careers, at least in their initial stages, are not helped by controversy. Some of that controversy has focused around Cecil Woodham-Smith's book, *The Great Hunger*.[2] But that book is in turn, as far as its publishers are concerned, the most successful Irish history book ever: and, very likely, simply the most successful history book ever. We have to put academic neglect alongside a public wish to know. There is thus another, and in a sense related, controversy around certain other books about the Irish Famine and migration.[3]

Some accounts of the Irish Famine are, of course, 'oppression history', pure and simple, and accounts of the Famine migrations become subsumed into the larger 'oppression, compensation, contribution' continuum.[4] Disadvantaged groups may well wish to see their experiences in terms of 'oppression', as an indication that, at the very least, they frighten those in power: rather than in the terms that the powerful might wish to use, which suggest that the disadvantaged simply do not matter. It has long been evident that we are studying here not only events but the meaning attached to events; these are links with all those philosophies and theologies which strive to find a meaning in the individual life, and which strive to demonstrate that history has a direction – or ought to have a direction.[5] It is not absurd to talk about 'the meaning of the Famine' when, in the 150 years since the beginning of Irish famine, people throughout the world have tried and are still trying to find 'meaning' in those events. This is 'the public wish to know', of which I spoke earlier.

So, here I was, planning my volume on 'the meaning of the Famine', a volume which must acknowledge that wish to know, but which must also extend the debate, fitting in within the patterns of *The Irish World Wide* series. I was aware of gaps in the Famine historiography, and the ways that these gaps affect our understanding of the relationship between famine and migration. At one point I wrote to a contributor, 'Do we have to fill every gap in the Famine historiography in order to bring together a volume called *The Meaning of The Famine* for a series called *The Irish World Wide*?' Well, clearly we could not. I moved *The Meaning of the Famine* to the end of the series, in order to maintain momentum with the other five volumes of the series, and to give me more time to think through these problems and find solutions.

The solutions involved patience and work. Patience, because I was aware that the approaching anniversary, in 1995, of the beginning of the Irish Famine, might trigger new interest within the academic communities and within the wider community: I kept track of developments, mapping the ways that any new famine research impinged on our understanding of Irish migration. And work, clearly, because I had to travel, and 'network', even more intensively, if I were to bring together that coherent volume on the Famine and migration that I had envisaged. It follows that, even more than any of the other volumes of *The Irish World Wide*, this volume on the Irish Famine is based on one-to-one contacts throughout the world. Every chapter in this book was especially commissioned for this volume, sometimes drawing on a larger work in progress.[6]

As 1995 approached there was, indeed, renewed interest in the Famine.[7] New popular books of synthesis, and a BBC television series, appeared.[8]

But without new research there is a danger that any synthesis will simply rehash lockjawed arguments and familiar (usually secondary) sources. Those outside the academic community need to be aware of how expensive and time-consuming real research is, and how brave researchers, and those who support them, have to be to commit themselves to this controversial subject – here I should especially mention Peter Gray and Christine Kinealy.[9] If new interest in the meaning of the Famine is to lead to new research, that research cannot be produced overnight.

Let me then record my gratitude to the contributors here, who saw the five earlier volumes of *The Irish World Wide* published, who were themselves patient when patience was needed, and who worked hard when hard work was needed, as we laboured to bring together our volume on *The Meaning of the Famine*. My task in all the Introductions to the volumes of *The Irish World Wide* has been an unusual and unusually interesting one: to fill the gaps, clarify the background, make connections, and open up debates. While striving to do that here, I have, at the same time, kept this Introduction to *The Meaning of the Famine* as brief as possible – because our contributors needed the space. In any case, much of my own thinking about the Irish Famine has been subsumed into the last chapter in the volume.

'The Potato Famine'

The Famine in Ireland, 1845–50, is sometimes referred to as 'the Potato Famine': that is the chapter title in Salaman's classic work.[10] This term annoys some: the argument being that the Irish died, not because they lacked potatoes, but because they lacked food. Indeed – as, for example, Patrick O'Farrell's chapter below makes clear – that question was raised by commentators at the time of the Famine: how could the loss of one food-stuff cause famine?

Ever since the Spanish conquerors first came across the potato in 1537, in the mountains of Peru – 'the most important if less acclaimed of all the Spanish discoveries and conquests' – the potato has moved across the world.[11] If the potato itself is a migrant then so is the potato blight, *Phytophthora infestans*.[12] The blight travelled from its original home in the Americas, to discover sites of intensive cultivation of potato varieties with little resistance to infection.[13] The potato blight thus presages other pests, like the aphid, *Phylloxera vastatrix*, which struck down the vines of Europe, especially in France, during the 1860s, and the blue mildew, *Peronospera viticola*, which attacked the vines in the 1880s. The blight and mildew are still with us, and the first cure for both, discovered in 1882, is to spray with copper compounds, 'Bordeaux mixture'. In the twentieth century Irish scientists and agriculturalists played a significant part in untangling the mystery of the blight: the key figure was Professor Paul Murphy, at the Albert Agricultural College, Glasnevin, Dublin.[14]

The long-term use of fungicides and pesticides itself causes concern: such chemicals may affect human health, the blight seems to be becoming resistant to the chemicals, and there is now the danger of new forms of blight through genetic mutation.[15] In the longer term the solution seems to be to strive to produce disease-free seed, and more disease-resistant varieties, though we do not know how precisely this endeavour will affect the potato as a human foodstuff.[16]

That is the first way that the Irish Famine was a phenomenon with world-wide significance – it was, in part, a consequence of the spreading of the potato, itself part of world-wide changes in human diet, changes which are by no means over.[17] Changes in human diet can bring wider social change, sometimes with affinities to the Irish pattern.[18] And, 'the great Irish failure of 1846 is the classic example of an outbreak of blight...'.[19] The place of the potato within Irish nineteenth-century peasant diet, where it became not only a staple but *the* staple, is still cited as a cautionary tale. If, as the chapter by O'Sullivan and Lucking in this volume suggests, Ireland has a curious, privileged place within 'the discourse of famine', then Ireland has a similar, curious place within 'the discourse of the potato'.[20]

Reading the Famine

News of the Irish Famine was spread throughout the world, by private letters and by the newly emerging mass mediums.[21] The news was greeted with appalled horror by the pre-Famine migrant Irish communities, and with a certain grim satisfaction by the enemies of the smug British Empire. News of the Famine was soon followed, in some parts of the world, by the fleeing Famine victims themselves, bringing with them, written on their own bodies, the evidence of catastrophe.

Within Ireland there have been attempts to bring some sort of solidity to our understanding of the vanished communities that were devastated by the Famine: I am thinking of the Famine Museum at Strokestown, County Roscommon; the Cobh Heritage Centre, County Cork; and the Ulster-American Folk Park at Omagh, County Tyrone. Yet the Famine sites in Ireland remain as much places of mystery, or dread, as of knowledge. In part, this connects, I think, with the nature of our existing research methods, and the need for new kinds of research. I am intrigued, therefore, by the approach of historical archaeologist, Charles Orser, and his groundbreaking (in every sense) work at Strokestown.[22] In the long term I would hope that forensic archaeology would be allowed to bring us new insights into the lives and the deaths of the Famine Irish, to add that extra dimension to William P. MacArthur's 'Medical History of the Famine'.[23] Christopher Morash speaks of the dead 'being silenced' and 'claimed' by subsequent writers.[24] Can the dead be allowed to speak for themselves?

World-wide understanding of the Famine is shaped by three texts: Charles Trevelyan's account of the Irish famine, 'The Irish Crisis', the review article which first appeared in the *Edinburgh Review* of 1848, and which was later published twice in book form; John Mitchel's *The Last Conquest of Ireland (Perhaps)*, first published in book form in 1861; and Cecil

Woodham-Smith's *The Great Hunger*, first published in 1962.[25] The reader will find much discussion of these texts later in this volume: I will simply remind scholars that Mitchel should be read as a counterblast to Froude, and to Trevelyan. It was, I think, Patrick O'Farrell who first pointed out the way that a very small number of texts were shaping the 'discourse' of the Famine.[26]

Our volume on *The Meaning of the Famine* begins with two chapters that help us grapple with this fact, that, to an extraordinary extent, the Irish Famine was and remains a 'paper event' – something heard of and written about rather than experienced.[27] Continuing with that theme of 'discourse', and to help us in our reading, these two chapters are both, in different ways, about 'writing the famine'. First, a starting point that we had to have, is Graham Davis's chapter on the historiography of the famine, and the implications of that historiography for the Irish diaspora. It is a part of the scholarly enterprise that Davis and I have looked at the same famine historiography, and our conclusions differ.[28] And we have agreed to differ.

If, as W. B.Yeats famously remarked, 'passive suffering is not a theme for tragedy...' then the problems of 'writing the famine' for popular markets become a little clearer.[29] For, as one commentator on Yeats goes on: 'In general, passivity does not invite empathy. What does invite it – what enables one to project oneself into someone else's world and see it as continuous with the one that one knows oneself – is anything that permits one to see the other as an agent.'[30] The pattern of anger is long established, anger with or anger on behalf of those who suffered passively: the two kinds of anger are two sides of the same coin. Michael Davitt could find no excuse for 'the wholesale cowardice of the men who saw food leave the country in shiploads, and turned and saw their wives and little ones sicken and die, and who "bravely paid their rent" before dying themselves.'[31] In popular accounts of the Irish Famine we can see attempts to move away from the 'passive suffering' of starving Irish peasants, to find the agents, the actors, the rebellious.[32]

Jean Drèze and Amartya Sen re-emphasize, at the conclusion of their important book, *Hunger and Public Action*, 'our focus on public participation – collaborative and adversarial – in eradicating famines, undernutrition and deprivation. It is, as we have tried to argue and illustrate, essential to see the public not merely as "the patient" whose well-being commands attention, but also as "the agent" whose actions can transform society.' Anger is energy, of course, and we must sympathize with activists like Don Mullan of Concern Worldwide, who try – collaborative and adversarial – to direct Irish energy, and 'memory' of the Famine, towards solutions of wider subsistence problems in our world today.

Christopher Morash's chapter for us here begins with a meditation on 'memory': his chapter on 'writing the famine', serves as an introduction to his sensitive methods, and to the lengthier exposition in his recently published book.[33] Some of our problems in 'reading the famine' must arise, in part, from problems within the craft of writing, the limitations of the written word – and I know of no better explorer of those limitations than

Morash. An earlier book by Morash, *The Hungry Voice*, collected and presented the poetry of the Irish Famine.[34] In his Introduction to that volume Morash made the connection, which many others have made, between the Irish Famine and Auschwitz.[35]

The Famine and the diaspora

We now turn to case studies, showing how news of the Famine – soon followed by the fleeing Famine refugees – reached four major centres of the English-speaking Irish diaspora: Britain, Canada, the United States of America and Australia.

Frank Neal offers the first comprehensive survey of the experiences of Famine refugees in England and Wales. This is an extraordinarily detailed study, full of new insights. Note that we are observing not simply panic-stricken flight. There was panic-stricken flight, but we also see rational responses not only to famine but to seemingly unresolvable social conflict in Ireland. Again and again in Neal's study, the Famine refugees are trying to reach other members of their family, earlier pre-Famine migrants settled in England and Wales: a pattern also observed by Marianna O'Gallagher in her chapter on the Famine refugees in Canada.

In my General Introduction to *The Irish World Wide* I drew attention to 'the lost Irish', people of Irish heritage who might, for any one of a number of reasons, be invisible to our research.[36] Michael Palin, that quintessential Englishman, television performer, film actor and writer, has a fascination with his own family history. And, as with most English people, a little family history soon finds an Irish ancestor. Palin's Irish ancestor was a Famine orphan, Brita or Bridget Gallagher, who arrived in New Jersey in 1847, aged about 5. Brita was adopted by a wealthy widow, Caroline Watson. Some years later Brita and Caroline journeyed to Europe, where they met another Palin ancestor, the then-celibate Oxford don: this encounter is the subject of Michael Palin's film, *American Friends*.[37] It is sometimes said that we, the living Irish, are all descendants of Famine survivors. This is nonsense. And it is the lives of the scattered orphans of the Famine, within Ireland and beyond Ireland, that show most clearly that this is nonsense.

The next chapter is part of Marianna O'Gallagher's continuing study of Grosse Île, the quarantine station on the St. Lawrence River, Canada.[38] In her chapter on the orphans of Grosse Île – a chapter that is full of sadnesses – O'Gallagher finds some comfort, the story of the Irish orphans who were adopted by French-Canadian families, and whose ancestors now celebrate this dual heritage. And certainly one image stays in the imagination, of the priest from Grosse Île setting out with his cartload of children, the little ones on his knee, to find homes for the orphans.

Francis Costello is a scholar, a politician and a businessman: these roles are not incompatible in Boston.[39] His chapter is a message from the heart of Catholic Irish America. But it is a complex message. For example, here we see, as we have seen many times in *The Irish World Wide*, the Famine,

and the realities of Irish migration, wrong-footing simplistic Irish nationalism – as the young Thomas D'Arcy McGee takes it upon himself to direct
the concerns of the Boston Irish away from famine relief.[40]

In my own thinking about our volume on 'the meaning of the Famine'
I should acknowledge the influence of a chapter by Laurence Geary on the
Australasian response to the 'Irish Crisis' of 1879–80, when it was feared
that famine would return to Ireland.[41] I shared these thoughts with Patrick
O'Farrell.[42] In a sense what O'Farrell offers us here now is a prelusion to
Geary's work, showing the Irish, and Ireland's sympathizers, in Australia
at the time of the Great Famine, trying to understand what was going on,
and wishing to help. Oddly we and they seem to be placed in the same
relationship with events in Ireland, we by time, they by distance.

Philanthropy

The next two chapters amplify themes present in those four focused studies of Britain, Canada, the United States and Australia. Continuing with
that theme of 'wishing to help', Christine Kinealy chronicles the philanthropic responses to the Irish Famine, and lists those, sometimes themselves in the most desperate circumstances, to whom the Irish have cause
to be grateful: the convicts on the prison hulks, the Choctaw people on
their reservation, the newly freed slaves in the Caribbean. And, above all,
the Quakers. The complexities of Queen Victoria's contribution to famine
relief are clarified. If Kinealy's chapter reassures us, with its accounts of a
kindly, human wish to help, then it must also, like the Quakers, stress the
limitations of simple private charity.

Ruth-Ann Harris's chapter picks up that theme, of philanthropy in
response to the Famine. Through her detailed study of Vere Foster's emigration schemes we see emigration, as a response to the Famine, being
built into the fine detail of Irish family life. Notice how it is the young
women who are to be removed – or saved, depending on your point of
view. So that even a staunch nationalist, and opponent of emigration, like
John Boyle O'Reilly, might wish for a better life for his sisters, and seek the
help of Vere Foster.

The Famine world wide

The last chapter in this volume, the last chapter in the entire *Irish World
Wide* series, by Patrick O'Sullivan and Richard Lucking, looks at the place
of the Irish Famine within the development of famine policy and famine
theory on our little planet. One starting point for my own thinking here
was certainly a paragraph, first read long ago, in which Thomas P. O'Neill
in the 1956 Edwards and Williams volume, *The Great Famine*, directed
attention to India under British rule, the 1880 Indian Famine Commission
and the success of the Indian Famine Codes.[43] Through my interest in
'Third World' and development issues I already knew of the importance of

the Famine Codes. For some 12 years I have been seeing if it was possible to integrate the study of the Irish famine within developments in famine theory in our own time.[44] And I had discovered that the matter was not as straightforward as might have been hoped. In the very first paragraph of my General Introduction, in Volume 1 of *The Irish World Wide*, I asked, 'How are we to share our experiences, and understanding, with others?'[45] Finding answers to that question is one of the great challenges facing the scholar of the Irish Famine.

I shared my thoughts with my friend, neighbour and colleague, Richard Lucking, whose work requires a knowledge of economic and resource problems in many parts of the world.[46] Informal discussion led to formal co-operation, the co-authorship of our present chapter, linking the Famine in Ireland with British famine policy in India throughout the nineteenth century, and with developments in famine theory in our own century. We were prevented – by considerations of space – from continuing the discussion with studies of famine in Africa, where the patterns of new subsistence crops and new cash crops bear similarities to the nineteenth-century Irish pattern. It is undoubtedly true that the Irish Famine was 'no ordinary subsistence crisis'.[47] That does not mean, sadly, that the Irish Famine lies quite outside the continuum of human experience, and offers no lessons or guidance. Yet, some of the observations made by O'Sullivan and Lucking are worth stressing – that, for example, 'common knowledge' about the Irish Famine may have mis-led the British elite in India, and may, if we are not careful, mis-direct discussions of famine in our own time. That would be the last ignominy for our Famine dead. And that is further argument for new research.

There is support for Cormac Ó Gráda's suggestion that the Famine Irish were 'desperately unlucky'.

> Far from being inevitable, the series of massive and lasting fungus-induced crop failures that produced the Great Famine was utterly unpredictable. In the decades before 1845 the country had been learning how to cope with serious crop failures, not without hardship, though without massive excess mortality. But nothing quite as horrific as *Phythopthora* [sic] *infestans* had appeared before, in Ireland or anywhere else. Moreover, had the fungus arrived either some decades earlier or later, the damage inflicted would not have been so horrific. Earlier, reliance on the 'accursed potato' would have been less, the pressure on resources less, and governments (like that of 1822) less constrained by ideological scruples.[48]

Thus the nature of that 'ill luck' has to be explored. So that, elsewhere, Ó Gráda discusses the claim that 'to expect any mid-nineteenth century government to have behaved like a decent twentieth-century social-democratic one is a historical or anachronistic.' [49] Yet it is important to acknowledge – as Ó Gráda does – that the British government's famine policy in Ireland was opposed by many decent people at the time. They expressed distress that in a time of profound peace the starving should be left to die 'on political economy'.[50] In 1849 the Quaker, Jonathan Pim, pointed out in a letter to Charles Trevelyan, that 'the Government alone could raise the funds, or carry out the measures necessary in many districts to save the lives of the people...'[51]

And, as the chapter by O'Sullivan and Lucking shows, within 30 years, in another part of the Empire, within the lifetimes of many of those involved in the implementation of famine policy in Ireland, famine policy changed. An active policy of famine prevention was launched, was fine-tuned, and was highly successful. The Irish nationalists of the late nineteenth century would sometimes wonder what Ireland's fate might have been if the country had been conquered by another Empire, rather than by that Empire centred on the neighbouring island. The history of famine policy within the British Empire shows that this was an unusual Empire among Empires: the British Empire was an Empire capable of shame.

Patrick O'Sullivan
Bradford
June 1996

Notes

1. 'The Famine is the main event in modern Irish history, as important to Ireland as, say, the French Revolution to France or the first Industrial Revolution to England. Yet, at least until recently, secondary references to the Famine were out of all proportion to the amount of fresh research published. Irish historians tended to shy away from the topic...' Cormac Ó Gráda, *Ireland: A New Economic History, 1780 –1939*, Clarendon Press, Oxford, 1994, p. 174. See also Ó Gráda, *Ireland Before and After the Famine: Explorations in Economic History, 1800 –1925*, Manchester University Press, Manchester, 1988, p. 78. Ó Gráda's observations are discussed by Graham Davis, Chapter 1, below. The fact that it seems possible to study Irish migration without much reference to the Irish Famine may well be a research discovery of *The Irish World Wide* project.

2. Cecil Woodham-Smith, *The Great Hunger: Ireland 1845–49*, Hamish Hamilton, London, 1962, and many times reprinted. The reader is directed to the extensive discussion of Woodham-Smith in the chapters by Graham Davis, Chapter 1, and by O'Sullivan and Lucking, Chapter 9, below. For the controversy around Woodham-Smith, *The Great Hunger*, see Ó Gráda, *Ireland Before and After the Famine*, p. 80.

3. I think, for example, of Thomas Gallagher, *Paddy's Lament: Ireland 1846–47; Prelude to Hatred*, Harcourt Brace Jovanovich, New York, 1982 (reprinted, Ward River Press, Swords, 1985) and the book whose bibliographic classification confuses librarians, but which should most probably be: [Robert Sellar], *Gerald Keegan: Famine Diary*, edited by James J. Mangan, Wolfhound, Dublin, 1991.

   To anticipate much discussion later, Donald Akenson, *The Irish Diaspora: A Primer*, P. D. Meany, Toronto/The Institute of Irish Studies, Belfast, 1993, p. 10, cites Gallagher's book as 'a particularly unfortunate Irish American example' of John Mitchel's long-term influence. On the scandal surrounding the 'Keegan' volume see: Christopher Morash, Chapter 2, below; Akenson, *Irish Diaspora*, p. 16; Jacqueline Kornblum, 'Mixing History and Fiction', *Irish Literary Supplement*, Vol. 11, No. 1, Spring 1992, p. 10; Jim Jackson, 'Famine Diary – the making of a best sellar', *Irish Review*, 11, Winter 1991/1992, pp. 1–8. Both

Gallagher and 'Keegan' use the devices of the novel: Gallagher intersperses chapters of history with chapters of fictionalized narrative.

I must express sympathy with this public wish to know, and the wish to hear some authentic Irish voice speak of Irish experience. It is, in part, the problem of sources, which bedevils all Irish Studies and Irish Migration Studies, and not only studies of the Irish Famine: Cormac Ó Gráda speaks of 'unsympathetic and uninformed outsiders', 'numerous travellers' accounts' drawing 'unfavourable comparisons' (Ó Gráda, 'Poverty, population, and agriculture, 1801–45', in W. E. Vaughan (ed.), *Ireland Under the Union*, Volume V of *A New History of Ireland*, Clarendon Press, Oxford, 1989, p. 125, p. 109).

4. For the applicability of the terms 'oppression, compensation, contribution' to the historiography of the Irish migrations, see my 'General Introduction to the Series', pp. xviii–xx, in Patrick O'Sullivan (ed.), *Patterns of Migration*, Volume 1 of *The Irish World Wide*, Leicester University Press, Leicester & London, 1992, and my 'Introduction', pp. 4–6, in O'Sullivan, ed. *Irish Women and Irish Migration*, 1994, Volume 4 of *The Irish World Wide*, Leicester University Press, London, 1995.

5. This continues the discussion in my 'Introduction', in O'Sullivan (ed.), *Religion and Identity*, Volume 5 of *The Irish World Wide*, Leicester University Press, London, 1996.

6. And I have had my failures. I was not able, despite strenuous efforts, to secure a chapter on the Famine refugees who went to France. We know such refugees existed, through family lore in Brittany, and, for example, the story of Eliza Lynch (see my 'Introduction', p. 8, p. 19, in O'Sullivan (ed.), *Irish Women and Irish Migration*). I was not able to secure a chapter on the wider European understanding and of comment on the Irish Famine.

7. Don Mullan (ed.), *A Glimmer of Light: An Overview of Great Hunger Commemorative Events in Ireland and Throughout the World*, Concern Worldwide, Dublin, 1995, is a helpful survey of that renewed interest.

8. For example, Peter Gray, *The Irish Famine*, Thames and Hudson, London, 1995; John Percival, *The Great Famine: Ireland's Potato Famine*, BBC, London, 1995 (this book accompanies the BBC television series); Helen Litton, *The Irish Famine: An Illustrated History*, Wolfhound, Dublin, 1994.

9. Peter Gray, 'Potatoes and Providence: British Government's Responses to the Great Famine', *Bullán*, Vol. 1, No. 1, Spring 1994; Christine Kinealy, *This Great Calamity: the Irish Famine, 1845–52*, Gill & Macmillan, Dublin, 1994.

10. Redcliffe N. Salaman, *The History and Social Influence of the Potato*, Cambridge University Press, Cambridge, 1949, reprinted 1970, Chapter XVI, pp. 289–316.

11. Salaman, *Influence of the Potato*, pp. 35–6. See also, for example, Ó Gráda, *Ireland Before and After the Famine*, p. 8 onwards, or Ó Gráda, *The Great Irish Famine*, Macmillan, Basingstoke, 1989, p. 22 onwards.

12. Woodham-Smith, *The Great Hunger*, p. 95, is forced to dismiss the 'pleasing theory', that blight had to wait for the coming of steam to cross the Atlantic.'

13. Salaman, *Influence of the Potato*, p. 291; Ó Gráda, *The Great Irish Famine*, p. 39 onwards.

14. Salaman, *Influence of the Potato*, p. 180, p. 332; Woodham-Smith, *The Great Hunger*, p. 97.

15. It is now believed that *Phytophthora infestans* originated in the Toluca Valley of Mexico where two types of pathogen have been identified, A1 and A2. For reasons which are not understood the A1 type escaped from its homeland some 150 years ago, while the A2 type remained. In the 1970s the A2 type was unintentionally exported to Europe, most probably on tomatoes, and began to contaminate seed potatoes. There is now the danger that, when types A1 and A2

meet, new forms of blight will emerge. (Information supplied by the International Potato Center (CIP), Lima, Peru; Department of Horticulture at Purdue University, Indiana; Irish Department of Agriculture, Food and Forestry; US Department of Agriculture, Maryland.)

16. Jennifer A. Woolfe, *The Potato in the Human Diet*, Cambridge University Press, Cambridge, 1987, p. 170.

17. Massimo Livi-Bacci, *Population and Nutrition: An Essay on European Demographic History*, translated by Tania Croft-Murray and Carl Ipsen, Cambridge University Press, Cambridge, 1991, p. 95 onwards.

18. Woolfe, *The Potato in the Human Diet*, p. 19, citing C. von Fürer-Haimendorf, *The Sherpas of Nepal: Buddhist Highlanders*, University of California Press, Berkeley, 1964, suggests that the introduction of the potato into the Sherpa region stimulated population growth and provided the agricultural surplus necessary for the rise of an elaborate Buddhist civilization.

19. Woodham-Smith, *The Great Hunger*, p. 102.

20. Indeed, to anticipate the discussion in Chapter 9 by O'Sullivan and Lucking, below, at times the two discourses precisely meet. 'Viewing the potato as an exclusive monocrop or "mono-food" will not encourage its viability in the long run. Single-mindedness can cause disaster just as single-minded dependence on potatoes reduced the Irish population by half in the nineteenth century.' Woolfe, *The Potato in the Human Diet*, pp. 220–1. Her source is Woodham-Smith, *The Great Hunger*.

21. To acknowledge that we should consider mass medium evidence other than the printed word, see Margaret Crawford, 'The Great Irish Famine, 1845–49: image versus reality', in Brian Kennedy and Raymond Gillespie (eds), *Art into History*, Town House and Country House Publishers, Dublin, 1992. The famous Mahoney illustrations for the *Illustrated London News* are put helpfully into context by Patrick Hickey, 'Famine, mortality and emigration: A profile of six parishes in the Poor Law Union of Skibbereen, 1846–7', in Patrick O'Flanagan and Cornelius G. Buttimer, *Cork: History & Society*, Geography Publications, Dublin, 1993.

22. Historical archaeology is, broadly, the application of archaeological methods to the history of the more recent past, periods about which we may have much documentation and an existing written history based on that documentation. Historical archaeology may, then, be intrinsically critical of that existing history, giving a voice to the 'muted' and the undocumented. A good introduction to themes and methods is Charles E. Orser, Jr. and Brian M. Fagan, *Historical Archaeology*, HarperCollins, New York, 1995. Charles Orser has already made two distinctive contributions to Irish Migration Studies, 'The Illinois and Michigan Canal: historical archaeology and the Irish Experience in America', *Eire-Ireland*, Winter, 1992; and 'Can there be an Archaeology of the Great Famine', in Christopher Morash and Richard Hayes (eds), *'Fearful Realities': New Perspectives on the Irish Famine*, Irish Academic Press, Dublin, 1995.

23. I am aware that this suggestion may offend some, but the suggestion arises out of discussions within the greatly respected Department of Archaeology at the University of Bradford. For the medical and nutritional aspects of the Irish Famine see William P. MacArthur, 'Medical history of the Famine', in R. Dudley Edwards and T. Desmond Williams, *The Great Famine: Studies in Irish History, 1845–52*, Browne & Nolan, Dublin, 1956; Peter Frogatt, 'The response of the medical profession to the Great Famine', and E. Margaret Crawford, 'Subsistence crises and famines in Ireland: A nutritionist's view', both in E. Margaret Crawford (ed.), *Famine: The Irish Experience, 900–1900*, John Donald, Edinburgh, 1989.

24. Christopher Morash, *Writing The Irish Famine*, Oxford University Press, Oxford, 1995, p. 180 onwards.
25. Trevelyan, 'The Irish Crisis', *Edinburgh Review*, Vol. 87, No. CLXXV, 1848, pp. 229–320, reprinted as *The Irish Crisis: Being a Narrative of the Measures for the Relief of Distress Caused by the Great Irish Famine of 1846–7*, Longmans & Co., London, 1848, and reprinted by Macmillan & Co., London, 1880; John Mitchel, *The Last Conquest of Ireland (Perhaps)*, *The Irishman* Office, Dublin, 1861 [there are many later editions: the publication history of this text needs clarification]; Cecil Woodham–Smith, *The Great Hunger*.
26. I am thinking of Patrick O'Farrell, 'Whose Reality?: the Irish Famine in history and literature', *Historical Studies* (University of Melbourne), Vol. 20, No. 78, April 1982.
27. It is fairly easy to experience hunger: it is more unusual to experience starvation in conditions in which we can report, or observe, the effects on mind and body and take this knowledge into our understanding of famine history. See the discussion in Livi-Bacci, *Population and Nutrition*, Chapter 3, 'Famine and want', p. 40 onwards, which recalls, p. 41, 'two tragic and well-documented historical cases: the death in 1920 of 'the Irish nationalist Mac Swiney, mayor of Cork', and the deaths in 1981 of 'ten young Irish nationalists, headed by Bobby Sands...'. Livi-Bacci then goes on to look at the famous Minnesota experiment in the 1940s, when volunteers explored a condition of semi-starvation in controlled conditions and after six months, 'showed the classical signs and symptoms of famine victims, namely edema, anaemia, polyuria, brachycardia, weakness and depression.'
    The most recent biography of MacSwiney, Francis J. Costello, *Enduring the Most: the Life of Terence MacSwiney*, Brandon, Dingle, 1995, movingly tracks the process towards death by starvation. On Bobby Sands and his companions see, for example, David Beresford, *Ten Men Dead: The Story of the 1981 Irish Hunger Strike*, Grafton, London, 1987; Padraig O'Malley, *Biting at the Grave: The Irish Hunger Strikes and the Politics of Despair*, Blackstaff, Belfast, 1990; Brian Campbell, Laurence McKeown and Felim O'Hagan (eds), *Nor Meekly Serve My Time: The H-Block Struggle, 1976–1981*, Beyond the Pale Publications, Belfast, 1994. Is it the Irish Famine that makes the hunger strike seem so resonant a political gesture to the Irish; or is the hunger strike a way of retrospectively giving meaning to the death by starvation of the Famine dead?
28. I have suggested that the difficulties I have had in creating a volume on *The Meaning of the Famine* for *The Irish World Wide* project is itself a research finding of the project. Where I see 'gaps', Davis sees 'fragments'. Davis certainly makes me look back at my own experiences: how far were my difficulties simply a consequence of this fragmentation of the historiography?
29. W. B. Yeats, 'Introduction', *Oxford Book of Modern Verse*, Clarendon Press, Oxford, 1936, p. xxxiv.
30. John Fraser, *Violence in the Arts*, Cambridge University Press, Cambridge, 1974, p. 60.
31. Michael Davitt, *The Fall of Feudalism in Ireland*, Harper & Brothers, London, 1904, p. 48.
32. Ó Gráda, *Ireland, A New Economic History*, p. 204, sees here 'ample scope' for further research by cultural, social, and local historians.
33. Christopher Morash, *Writing the Irish Famine*, cited in Note 24.
34. Christopher Morash, *The Hungry Voice: the Poetry of The Irish Famine*, Irish Academic Press, Dublin, 1989.
35. Morash, 'Introduction', *The Hungry Voice*, p. 37. See also, Richard L. Rubenstein, *The Age of Triage: Fear and Hope in an Over-crowded World*, Beacon

Press, Boston, 1983, a book which sees the Irish Famine as part of the patterns of genocide. Rubenstein, p. 124, acknowledges his debt to Woodham-Smith, *The Great Hunger*, but disagrees with her conclusions.

36. See my, 'General Introduction', in O'Sullivan (ed.), *Patterns of Migration*, p. xx.
37. Michael Palin, private communication. See the 1991 Millennium/Mayday film, *American Friends*, written by Michael Palin and Tristram Powell, directed by Tristram Powell – based on the travel diaries of Michael Palin's great-grandfather, the film becomes a sensitive exploration of survivor guilt, and the ambivalence of gratitude. (Note that in this fictional film some character names have been changed.)
38. The island's name is variously spelt, in the nineteenth-century sources, and by historians: 'Grosse Isle', or correctly in the French manner, 'Grosse Île', with the circumflex indicating the lost S. It is, simply, the largest island in a little archipelago (Donald MacKay, *Flight from Famine: The Coming of the Irish to Canada*, McClelland & Stewart, Toronto, 1990, pp. 134–5.)
39. In his professional life, Francis Costello works as an economic development consultant in the United States and in Ireland, and is Chairman of the Boston-based International Creative Strategies. He has worked as Chief of Staff to Congressman Joseph Kennedy, and Director of foreign trade development for the City of Boston under Mayor Raymond Flynn, when he also served as the Mayor's liaison to the Irish community. It was in that latter role that Francis Costello began the work that will lead to the re-dedication in 1998 of the grave of the Irish Famine victims at Deer Island.
40. Note too that in Costello's chapter we have *The Irish World Wide*'s second encounter with the American writer, Henry Thoreau: see James P. Myers, jun., 'Till their... bog-trotting feet get *talaria*: Henry D. Thoreau and the immigrant Irish', in O'Sullivan (ed.), *The Creative Migrant*, Volume 3 of *The Irish World Wide*, Leicester University Press, Leicester & London, 1994, (significantly, this chapter on Thoreau is the only study specifically of anti-Irish prejudice that I have allowed into the series).
41. Laurence M. Geary, 'The Australian response to the Irish Crisis, 1879–80', in Oliver MacDonagh and W. F. Mandle (eds), *Irish-Australian Studies*, Australian National University, Canberra, 1989.
42. There is no more respected scholar in world wide Irish Studies than Patrick O'Farrell. His *Ireland's English Question: Anglo-Irish Relations, 1534–1970*, Schocken, New York, 1971, is one of those books whose very title changes perspectives; his *The Irish in Australia*, New South Wales University Press, Sydney, 1986, second edition 1993, is the most complete and satisfying book in Irish Migration Studies.
43. Thomas P. O'Neill, 'The organisation and administration of relief, 1845–52', in Edwards and Williams, *The Great Famine*, p. 259, p. 468.
44. My first attempt was written for my own purposes, a little, unpublished essay, which I have in front of me now: 'Explanations of famine', dated May 1985. That essay is, in the main, a discussion of the wider applicability, to 'Third World', development and poverty issues, of the arguments and the methods of Joel Mokyr. *Why Ireland Starved: A Quantitative and Analytical History of the Irish Economy, 1800–1850*, George Allen & Unwin, London, 1983. I should record, too, that it was with some relief that I found that I was following in the footsteps of Cormac Ó Gráda, who had noted too that here was this gap in the historiography of the Irish Famine: see Ó Gráda, *Ireland Before and After the Famine*, p. 79.
45. 'General Introduction', in O'Sullivan (ed)., *Patterns of Migration*, p. xiii.
46. Richard Lucking's current role, directing the European Union's economic

liasion with the government of Latvia, has meant that he has not been able to be as involved in the writing and research of this chapter as we would have liked. But he has been involved in the discussion of every draft.

47. Peter M. Solar, 'The Great Famine was no ordinary subsistence crisis', in E. Margaret Crawford (ed.), *Famine: The Irish Experience*.

48. Ó Gráda, *The Great Irish Famine*, p. 76: Ó Gráda also uses the word 'unlucky' in Ó Gráda, *Ireland: A New Economic History*, p. 189.

49. Ó Gráda, *Ireland: A New Economic History*, p. 175.

50. William Thomas, a mining captain from Cornwall, cited in Patrick Hickey, 'Famine, mortality and emigration', p. 912.

51. Jonathan Pim to Charles Trevelyan, 5 June 1849, *Transactions of the Central Relief Committee of the Society of Friends during the Famine in Ireland in 1846 and 1847*, Hodges and Smith, Dublin, 1852, Appendix XXIV, p. 454.

1 The historiography of the Irish Famine

Graham Davis

'Between the 1930s and the 1980s, the Irish academic profession sought fit to address the subject of the Famine on only occasion'.[1] This charge, laid against Irish historians by Dr Brendan Bradshaw, forms part of an attack against 'revisionism' in Irish history. Why was the central event of nine-teenth-century Irish history virtually ignored by professional historians? To Bradshaw, it is only the most glaring example of historians evading the 'catastrophic dimension' in Irish history by adopting a value-free and past-centred approach, and attempting to 'purge Irish history of its myths and of its nationalist bias'.[2] Where the revisionists have failed, according to Bradshaw, is in convincing Irish people of their version of the past. An alarming gap has opened up between academic and popular history. Bradshaw sees it as the failure of professional historians to be morally engaged with their subjects that has produced what is essentially 'bad' history.

A similar charge that the Famine has been the subject of little serious academic research has also been made by the economic historian Cormac Ó Gráda.[3] Furthermore, the published studies by Irish historians, the collection of essays, *The Great Famine: Studies in Irish History*, edited by Dudley Edwards and Williams in 1956 and Mary E. Daly's, *The Famine in Ireland* (1986) are described as examples of 'generosity and restraint' in avoiding the emotive excesses of nationalist propaganda and in not attaching blame to the British government of the day.

With the commemoration of the 150th anniversary of the beginning of the Famine in 1845 being marked by a series of lectures, conferences, new Famine centres and new publications over a period of several years in the 1990s, at least part of the past neglect of the Famine is being addressed. If it is remarkable that most Famine scholars have come from outside Ireland, it is also worth noting that they have been attracted by pursuing their own research in economic history, demography or in the study of social policy with reference to the Irish Poor Law. While outsiders may feel less constrained in writing about what is still a painful subject in Ireland, they may also be less bound by the academic conservatism of Ireland's historical profession.

The study of history in Britain and North America has been enlarged by the growth of a set of sub-disciplines that have developed their own specialist jargon and methodology. While this process is capable of offering fresh insights, it can also, through fragmentation, produce barriers to effective communication. In particular, the quantification of data in measuring long-term trends in the Irish economy and in the patterns of marriage and fertility in nineteenth-century Ireland have, for some authorities, appeared to reduce the importance of the Famine to the role of accelerating existing trends. This contrasts with narrative accounts of the Famine that describe the despair and distress of the victims of starvation and disease or of those caught up in the headlong rush to the emigrant ship. To some degree, different methodologies produce different interpretations and meanings of the Famine.

A further development of importance lies with the study of the interplay between the contemporary ideological framework and the rationalization of the tragic events of the Famine years. A revision of the Malthusian interpretation of the Famine challenges a number of assumptions about the way British ministers thought about Ireland and raises questions about popular versions of the Famine story.

Where Bradshaw and Ó Gráda make an important point is in identifying the gap between academic history and popular understanding. This would not be confined to Irish history and does not necessarily invalidate either version of the past. It does, however, provide a useful question in setting out to explore the historiography of the Famine. Why does the traditional, nationalist version still command a powerful hold over the popular imagination? Why have 'revisionist' historians failed to persuade the public in qualifying the importance of the Famine? An historiographical survey opens up these questions and reflects on the merits of competing claims.

The Mitchel thesis

Popular understanding of the Famine did not arise spontaneously from the Famine period. As Patrick O'Farrell has argued, the idea of the Great Famine was largely the creation of the journalist-historian John Mitchel (1815–75) whose enduring influence may be traced to two works: *Jail Journal of Five Years in British Prisons* (New York: 1854), and *The Last Conquest of Ireland (Perhaps)* (New York: 1860).[4]

In the 'Introduction' to *Jail Journal*, Mitchel produced a version of Irish history in which everything was subordinated to a diatribe against the tyranny of England. In a powerful polemic, Mitchel constructed the history of Ireland from Cromwell to the 1848 rising as a catalogue of English oppression of the Irish people. Mitchel's withering prose created an image of the 'Famine' as starvation in the midst of plenty. He presented the bitter prospect of thousands of Irish people starving to death while Ireland sent its surplus produce to feed the population of England. Mitchel's account transformed the events of the Famine into a terrible indictment of English 'colonial' rule and by a masterly stroke of propaganda the tragedy became harnessed to the bandwagon of Irish nationalism.[5]

Mitchel claimed that the Famine was no mere historical accident. With the establishment of the Devon commission in 1843, Mitchel saw the sinister intention of the British government to rid Ireland of its 'surplus' population. What was set down in the commission report in 1845 as a straightforward analysis of the size of holdings and the need to make them more economically viable (albeit in the interests of the landlords and 'strong' farmers) Mitchel interpreted as a plot to murder the cottiers and the labouring poor of Ireland.[6]

The theme developed in Mitchel's *The Last Conquest of Ireland (Perhaps)*. Here the religious context of the times was accepted but neatly turned into a deadly political weapon: 'The Almighty, indeed, sent the potato blight, but the English created the Famine'.[7] Mitchel explained the seemingly unintelligible sequence of events in the Famine years as a sinister conspiracy to exterminate the Irish people. After pointing out how the idea of 'surplus' population in Ireland had become axiomatic in English political circles prior to the Famine period, the charge of genocide was laid like a slowly ticking bomb at the door of the Imperial government:

> the potato blight and consequent famine, placed in the hands of the British government an engine of state by which they were eventually enabled to clear off not a million, but two millions and a half of the 'surplus population' – to 'preserve law and order' in Ireland (what they call law and order) and to maintain the integrity of the Empire for this time.[8]

O'Farrell makes a convincing case that Mitchel's charge of genocide lifted the tragedy of the potato blight to the status of high drama, with 'villains in the highest political places' constructing a monstrous inhuman plot, 'designed to achieve racial extermination, emigration and land clearances in the interests of economic principles and power'.[9]

Historically, the importance of the Mitchel thesis lay not only in its early acceptance among Irish emigrants, especially in North America, but also in the influence it was to exercise over later historians and in popular fiction. Mitchel's charge of starvation amidst plenty became a standard theme in the work of O'Rourke (1872), Charles Gavan Duffy (1882), P. S. O'Hegarty (1952), Cecil Woodham-Smith (1962), Robert Kee (1972), Thomas Gallagher (1982) and of Christine Kinealy (1994).[10] While Mitchel, Duffy, O'Rourke might be understood as either being involved in the events themselves or committed to Irish nationalism, the pervasive influence of the Mitchel thesis over a period of more than 100 years is reflected in the work of popular historians of the last 30 years. The continuing success of Woodham-Smith's, *The Great Hunger*, still the best narrative account of the Famine, pinpointed the failure of the administration of famine relief in the person of the Treasury official, Sir Charles Trevelyan. In doing so, Woodham-Smith put a face to the conspiracy identified by Mitchel, and although the tone is politer than the emotive rhetoric employed by Mitchel, the unfolding drama retains the moral imperative in condemning the ideological blindness shown by British ministers.

An even wider audience was gained for the Mitchel/Woodham-Smith view with the television series based on Robert Kee's *Ireland: A History*, in 1982, based on his earlier work, *The Green Flag* (1972). Once more, Trevelyan was made the villain of the piece, and the British government charged with failing in the fundamental responsibility of protecting its own citizens.[11]

The popular tradition was maintained with Thomas Gallagher's, *Paddy's Lament: Ireland 1846–1847; Prelude to Hatred*, first published in 1982 and produced in paperback in 1985. The book aims to speak for the victims of the Great Famine and to explain how centuries of hostility turned into undying hatred on the part of their descendants. The Mitchel thesis is endorsed and re-worked as Gallagher contrasts the distress found in Ireland with the satisfying-superior tone of complacency found in England. In building on targets identified by Mitchel, Gallagher amplifies the nationalist case with stomach-churning descriptions, designed to make an emotive appeal to a popular readership.

Alongside reportage on 'the skeleton forms of the living' drawn from *The Cork Examiner*, Gallagher quotes *The Times*, as representative of English indifference to the plight of a starving Irish peasantry. To the editors of *The Times*, here was a picture of appalling squalor caused by a people apparently removed from civilized sensibilities. The Famine was no natural disaster but the result of idleness and dependence on public money. In a damning analogy with disease, using language more normally associated with the potato blight itself, the moral corruption of the Irish peasantry was proclaimed:

> Deep, indeed, has the canker eaten. Not into the core of a precarious and suspected root – but into the very hearts of the people, corrupting them with a fatal lethargy, and debasing them with a fatuous dependence!... Thus the plow rusts, the spade lies idle, and the fields fallow.[12]

Christine Kinealy's acclaimed study of the Famine, *This Great Calamity*, is a highly professional and scholarly work that focuses on the administration of the Poor Law in Ireland during the Famine years. Dr Kinealy rejects the revisionist tradition dating from Raymond Crotty in the 1960s and exemplified, most notably, in the 1980s with Roy Foster.[13] Pride of place is given to the way relief policies were conceived and implemented and to the reaction of the British authorities which she found to be 'patently inadequate'. She argues that the 'challenge posed by the Famine could have been met successfully and many of its worst excesses avoided, had the political will existed'. Her fundamental conclusion is that:

> there was no shortage of resources to avoid the tragedy of a Famine. Within Ireland itself, there were substantial resources of food which, had the political will existed, could have been diverted, even on a short-term measure to supply a starving people. Instead the government pursued the objective of economic, social and agrarian reform as a long-term aim, although the price paid for this ultimately elusive goal was privation, disease, emigration, mortality and an enduring legacy of disenchantment.[14]

Put starkly, the Mitchel case against England in its handling of the Famine crisis was a charge of moral neglect – a failure on the part of a great imperial power to feed its people in time of want. Even if we discount the claim of a deliberate policy of genocide, now no longer regarded seriously, the moral imperative remains. If the Famine had struck Cornwall instead of Cork would appropriate measures have been taken to prevent starvation and death? At the heart of Mitchel's 'sacred wrath' was the humanitarianism and egalitarianism that formed part of both the English and Irish radicalism of the period.

Set against Mitchel's philosophy that the food of Ireland belonged morally, if not legally, to the people of Ireland, and that the life of a peasant was worth as much as the life of a lord, the prevailing ideology in the English government rested on free-market economics, the protection of propertied interests, and a deeply gloomy view of the moral condition of the lower orders. Trevelyan's response to reports of heart-rending scenes of death and pestilence in famine-torn Ireland was to point to the character of the people: 'The great evil with which we have to contend, is not the physical evil of the famine, but the moral evil of the selfish, perverse and turbulent character of the people'.[15] It was no use to send more food, as this would undermine the free play of the market. Private enterprise had to be protected: 'We attach the highest public importance to the strict observance of our pledge not to send orders abroad, which would come into competition with our merchants and upset all their calculations'.[16] Local landowners were urged to contribute to the relief of their own people, on the principle that Irish property should provide for Irish poverty.

To Mitchel, the stark contrast between good and evil, humanitarianism versus political economy, people before property, was essential to the nationalist case against British rule. However, three recent works of political history reveal the complexity of the ideological debates in Britain and in Ireland and how unfortunate was the timing of the dominant orthodoxy in government circles in relation to the administration of the Famine.

Peter Gray has argued that classical political economy was an inadequate scapegoat for the failure of famine policy in the Russell administration. More significant was the doctrine of Christian Providentialism which saw the Famine as a means of curing Ireland's intractable poverty and dependence on the potato. By way of example, Commissary-General Routh is quoted in arguing for the diffusion of a taste for a higher kind of food and better habits of industry among the Irish. 'Even in the most afflicting dispensations of Providence there was ground for consolation, and often even occasion for congratulation.'[17]

Donal Kerr has presented a reassessment of the Russell government and the role of the Catholic Church in the famine period.[18] Ironically, in terms of what followed, the Whigs were welcomed as a potential improvement on Peel's ministry. Lord John Russell, himself, had a distrust of Irish landlords, formed part of a radical tradition that espoused 'justice for Ireland' and was pledged to provide equality of treatment for Irish Catholics. As it turned out the promised era of prosperity for Ireland was shattered by the Famine deaths and the failure of each temporary expedient attempted by the Whig government. Traditionally, the Catholic clergy have earned an heroic reputation for their involvement and personal sacrifice in Famine relief. While the Catholic hierarchy was regarded as strangely silent about the loss of life among the Irish peasantry, Kerr's explanation for the lack of protest was that the bishops were too divided among themselves and they were silenced by the government and press association of protest with rebellion. Critically, the murder of Major Denis Mahon of Strokestown, in Co. Roscommon, following the eviction of over 3,000 of his tenants, was used to intimidate the Catholic hierarchy which also clung on to the prospect of better treatment from a Whig government. Indeed, in 1848, the offer of state payment of the clergy was made and refused. When the bishops did protest in the form of a memorial presented to Lord Clarendon, the Lord Lieutenant of Ireland, in October 1847, they boldly rejected the government's insistence on property rights as subordinate to those of human life: 'The sacred and indefeasible rights of life are forgotten amidst the incessant reclamations of the subordinate rights of property'.[19] If the bishops went beyond a strictly religious sphere to condemn government policy, to criticize the social order and to champion social justice, there was an uneasy feeling that the Church was closely allied to the economic interests of the strong farmers and emerging Catholic middle class who benefited from the amalgamation of holdings at the expense of cottiers and smallholders.

Thomas A. Boylan and Timothy P. Foley have argued that the Irish establishment employed the language of political economy to defend the existing social order in Ireland and demonstrate how orthodox economic ideas were disseminated in the National Schools. The Anglican Archbishop of Dublin, Robin Whately, was the crucial influence in this movement to pacify Ireland through a process of assimilation into British ways of thinking. The schools were to be the vehicles of this cultural transformation, and Whately as chair of the National Education Board wrote the basic texts for the official curriculum. He also founded the first chair in political economy at Trinity College Dublin and from this subsequent chairs followed in the Queen's Colleges, so extending the ideology of the 'Dublin School' of economics throughout Ireland.[20]

What these three works address in different ways is the complexity of the ideological debate conducted in Britain and Ireland. Different strands of opinion competed for supremacy within the realm of political economy, between government ministers and officials in Ireland and between factions within the Catholic Church. While Mitchel's moral claim on the British government to feed the people of Ireland found echoes among the Catholic bishops, the political interest of the Church in extracting concessions from the Whig government limited the strength of protest in defence of the starving peasantry.

With hindsight, the tragedy of the Great Famine was widely interpreted as the inevitable consequence of too great a population, fatally dependent on a subsistence agriculture. The writings of the Rev. Thomas Malthus appeared to offer a seductively simple explanation of the poverty of Ireland. Population growth was ultimately limited by the availability of resources. When population began to outstrip resources, a number of 'Malthusian checks' to further population growth would come into play – war, famine, disease – to restore the natural equilibrium. Malthus's theory of population growth implied that natural law would not tolerate 'overpopulation' indefinitely and, where it occurred, a proper corrective to the relationship with resources was inevitable. While Malthus did not write much about Ireland and did not predict a dramatic fall in population, his recipe for the 'overpopulation' of Ireland implied that 'a great part of the population should be swept from the soil'.[21] His 'overpopulation' thesis fitted well with the dominant orthodoxy of the day and took on a powerful credibility with the scale of death and emigration of the Famine period in Ireland. Significantly, the Malthusian view became not only the conventional wisdom in Victorian England, completely accepted by Trollope who knew Ireland well,[22] but it has remained a dominant influence for most of the twentieth century.

The importance of Joel Mokyr's work lies in the subjection of the 'overpopulation' thesis to a series of statistical tests. Mokyr finds that the results are at best inconclusive. First, he argues that the behaviour of the Irish economy, after the Famine, lends little support to the Malthusian approach. The standard of living of those who survived increased as a result of a rise in agricultural prices and was due to structural changes in the economy, not because of the loss of population. Second, it is by no means proven that Ireland was more densely populated than other countries. For instance, Belgium had a higher density of population than Ireland. If there had been no Famine and economic circumstances had been more favourable, Mokyr concurs with Blacker's prediction in 1834 that Ireland could have sustained a population of around 17 million people by the end of the century. He concludes that there appears to be no statistically significant relation between poverty and population pressure variables in pre-Famine Ireland. He further calls into question whether emigration acted as a Malthusian check. Since pre-Famine emigration emanated from the more advanced counties of Ireland, it was unlikely that there was any reduction of pressure on the poorest province of Connaught. The technical nature of Mokyr's work and his fondness for counterfactual techniques may explain why he has been relatively neglected by mainstream historians.

Famine and emigration

It has to be recognized that popular understanding of the impact of the Famine on Ireland's population and on emigration from Ireland has not kept pace with the work of a generation of scholars over the last 30 years. Traditionally, the haunting images of the Great Famine and the spectre of thousands of emigrants fleeing overseas are linked together, and in a sense, there is a very real connection between the incidence of famine and the mass exodus of Irish people in the 1840s. The population of Ireland fell dramatically by some 20 per cent between the censuses of 1841 and 1851 and a million and a half people emigrated during the seven years of the potato blight from 1845 to 1852.[23] In another sense, many other factors need to be taken into account.

It is now clearly established that Ireland's population increase in the pre-Famine period, 1785 to 1841, when it doubled from 4 million to 8.2 million, disguised extensive emigration, and after the Famine period, further waves of emigration continued through to the end of.the century and beyond into our own time. A pattern of continuous emigration from Ireland was established before the Famine, was accelerated by the experience of the Famine, and remained firmly in place long after its immediate influence. By 1911, the population of Ireland, at 4.4 million, was approximately half the level it had been on the eve of the Great Famine.[24]

Not merely the scale of mass emigration but the complex nature of its economic and social context is under review. A more precise recognition of regional variations in population trends and in patterns of migration weaken the old assumptions made about the universal impact of the Famine period.

Brenda Collins has argued that despite a continuous increase in population until the mid-century, a slowing down of regional rates of growth is discernible from the last quarter of the eighteenth century.[25] Furthermore, regional variations in the incidence of migration from the northern counties of Ireland can be traced to the growth and contraction of the Irish linen industry. The domestic nature of the manufacture of linen, integrated with the possession of land and the growing of flax on the family plot, encouraged a growth of population from the middle of the eighteenth century but also formed a barrier to the establishment of an industrial economy. Subsistence agriculture, with its reliance on the cultivation of the potato was therefore prolonged until technological change in the British textile industry brought about a de-industrialization of the Irish linen industry. Collins more than hints that potato harvests were less important than the changing economic developments within the British Isles in promoting Irish emigration in the pre-Famine era.[26]

Collins also demonstrates how Irish weavers clung to their familial work patterns in migrating to the textile areas of Scotland and the north of England. In the 1820s and 1830s, Irish weavers continued their craft in Lancashire, Yorkshire and in the Scottish cities of Aberdeen and Dundee, both centres of coarse linen production. When the potato harvest failed in successive years in the 1840s, a stream of migrants from north-central Ireland found their way via Drogheda to Dundee. The dependence on Irish labour in Dundee was so great that the familial patterns transported intact to the east coast of Scotland.

The importance of textiles in early nineteenth-century Ireland is echoed by Eion O'Malley in a study of the decline of Irish industry.[27] He estimates that one-third of Irish counties in 1821 had a greater number employed in manufacture, trade or handicraft than in agriculture and that, as late as 1841, one-fifth of the labour force were occupied in textile manufacture. O'Malley argues that the phenomenon of general industrial decline and a concentration of industry in Ulster can be explained by the advantages of the early development of large-scale, centralized production and proximity to markets.[28] The decline of the Irish woollen industry in the 1820s and 1830s was comparable to the decline of the smaller British centres, such as East Anglia and the south-west, in the face of the growing strength of the Yorkshire woollen industry.[29] In Ireland, as in England, it was the peripheral areas that suffered a dramatic reduction in both production and employment.

The consequences of the decline in the woollen industry and the concentration of linen spinning in Belfast were most acutely felt by the rural poor. For landless labourers, cottiers and small farmers, spinning had contributed a vital additional income, particularly in Ulster and in Connaught. With agriculture also becoming less labour intensive, with the expansion of beef relative to other agricultural products, there were fewer opportunities for employment on the land.[30] So the migration already evident in the 1820s and 1830s was a response to the shortage of industrial and agricultural employment in Ireland.

The relationship between poverty and migration from Ireland, highlighted by the devastating loss of population during the Great Famine, retains some interesting features. Kerby Miller has shown that migration was less evident among the poor than among farmers and tradesmen in the period of 1815 to 1835, and something of this pattern persisted in the second half of the century.[31] Also S. H. Cousens has shown that the poorest districts of Ireland lost most population during the Famine crisis, but this was more the result of extensive mortality than through excessive migration.[32] Moreover, despite the devastation of the 1840s, the demographic pattern of the pre-Famine era survived from the 1850s to the 1880s.[33] Whereas the population of Ireland as a whole continued to fall, population continued increasing in the poorest and least fertile parts of the west of Ireland. With the exception of urban areas, the marked disparity in population growth between the east and west of Ireland persisted until 1881. Further crop failures in the late 1870s and early 1880s prompted exceptionally heavy migration from the western counties.

What has to be explained is both the persistence of the pre-Famine pattern of population increase until late in the century and a sudden exodus from the western counties in the 1880s. The different rates of rural population growth between the east and the west of Ireland were bound up with the availability of land. The population density of the western coast in 1871 was three times as high as in the south east of Ireland.[34] High population densities inevitably meant smallholdings and the continuation of a subsistence agriculture largely dependent on the potato crop. Contemporary opinion had it that a holding of 10–15 acres was insufficient to support a family on poor western soils, yet half the holdings in nineteen western unions in 1861 were in this category. What appeared to be a reduction in the size of holdings that was already insufficient to support an increasing population, spelt imminent trouble should there be further failures in the potato crop. Whereas improvements were taking place in the condition of Ireland as a whole, the west of Ireland remained dangerously dependent on subsistence agriculture.

Sustaining the east/west division in population growth was the regional variation in marriage rates in Ireland, and despite the intervention of the Great Famine, these actually widened between 1841 and 1871. The relatively high propensity to marry, and at an early age, was closely related to the opportunities for occupying land in the western counties. There, the presence of wasteland enabled people to throw up a cabin and to cultivate potatoes, on tiny plots near the coast, manured with the application of seaweed. Also, the common holding of land under the rundale system, as in County Mayo in the west, allowed an increase in the number of dependent households through the subdivision of plots. In the more fertile east of Ireland, the comparative absence of wasteland and the difficulty of subdividing tenancies under leaseholding agreements, meant that occupation of the land had to wait on natural inheritance.

The impact of the Great Famine on the availability of land served to accentuate the differences between the east and west of Ireland. In the east, the drive to amalgamate smallholdings into substantial farms led to the systematic removal of the smaller tenants but a continual cultivation of the land. In the west, the peasantry, who were unable to pay their rent, were evicted and landlords threw down their cabins, leaving large areas of wasteland available for letting as smallholdings. The increase in the number of holdings below 30 acres was a western phenomenon of the 1850s which continued into the 1870s. Once it became difficult to obtain holdings in the western counties, the demographic patterns of the pre-Famine era came to an end. Conditions in the west began to approximate to those of the east and the trend towards a more uniform age of marriage throughout the country.[35] Cousens concludes that the poverty of western Ireland had the effect not of promoting but of restricting migration between 1861 and 1881.

How those poor smallholders were able to cling on to their plots, for a generation after the Great Famine, is explored more fully by Cormac Ó Gráda, in the importance he attaches to seasonal migration in the subsistence economy of the western counties.[36] Ó Gráda argues that the extent of seasonal migration to Great Britain was greater than has been recognized and increased in scale between the 1840s and the 1860s, facilitated by the provision of special trains by the Midland Great Western Railway, transporting harvesters from the west to the east coast ports. In the 1860s, some 60,000 seasonal passengers were carried by the railway en route to the harvest fields of Scotland and the north of England, and Ó Gráda estimates the annual total of seasonal migration was of the order of 100,000 for the whole of Ireland.

Seasonal migration on this scale, most prominently from those western counties furthest from mainland Britain, requires explanation. Ó Gráda argues that there was a close association between the continued poverty experienced in the subsistence agriculture of the west, specifically the need to find the annual rent to maintain the family plot, and the pattern of seasonal migration to Britain. Seasonal work could add about £10 to the family budget, amounting to a third of its income – sufficient to pay the annual rent.

Dependence upon seasonal migration leads Ó Gráda to suggest that the drying up of demand for harvest labour in Britain contributed, along with the near-famine conditions of 1879–83, to permanent migration from the west of Ireland. The crisis in British agriculture from the late 1870s, when a series of disastrous harvests coincided with the importation of cheap American wheat, reduced the demand for seasonal labour from Ireland. The mechanization of agriculture gradually took hold accompanied by a reduction in cereal growing as a structural change in British agriculture took place in the closing decades of the century. The American inventions of mechanical reapers in the 1850s and 1860s ultimately contributed to a lower demand for Irish seasonal labour as machines became more common in British harvest fields from the 1870s. This, in turn, led to a substantial migration from the western counties to the United States in the 1880s.[37] The number of seasonal migrants from Ireland to Britain subsequently halved between the 1880s and the 1910s. What demand remained was largely for picking potatoes and turnips which were more difficult to mechanize.

David Fitzpatrick poses the problem of why 'backward' migrants should have chosen the more expensive destination of America rather than Britain.[38] He speculates that many more migrants fled from the western counties, in the generation after the Great Famine, than have been recorded, supported by generous remittances received from America which largely financed a chain migration. The accident that the Great Famine in Ireland coincided with industrial recession in Britain also encouraged dispossessed westerners to struggle across the Atlantic, often taking advantage of cut-price passages from British ports. Such an argument lends weight to the case that Ireland's economy and patterns of migration were strongly influenced by external pressures but also helps to explain that mass migration to America, the principal destination, was self-sustaining.

Folklore

In pursuing an explanation of the gap between popular understanding and academic history, it is ironic that the evidence drawn from folk memory appears to qualify Mitchel's popular thesis that the Famine was the fault of the British government. The surviving evidence, compiled by Roger McHugh, points to a predominantly religious explanation of the potato blight.[39] Contemporaries believed that the very abundance of the crops in good years had made people careless of their good fortune and wasteful of the Lord's bounty. People scarcely knew what to do with their surplus potatoes and wasted them. Potatoes were stacked in heaps and left to rot, were burnt or buried, or even used to fill up gaps in fences. Such waste created a foreboding of retribution, and as famine spread over the land, it was assumed to be a scourge from God, a punishment for the abuse of plenty. Reinforcing this belief was what McHugh described in biblical terms as:

an ominous season of mist, or storms of rain and wind alternating with periods of vast and terrible stillness; of the names of fields where the blight first appeared and of men who first noticed the heavy smell of decay or saw the brown spots spreading on the leaves, the blackened stalks leaning over the potato-pits ominously sagging. [40]

Folk memory also records how people survived the Famine through the miraculous appearance of food. The most popular of such stories featured the 'charitable woman' who embodied the traditional Irish virtue of sharing what little she had with poor neighbours, only to find that food given away was miraculously replaced. Such stories are found in a variety of forms in Mayo, Galway, Cork and Wexford. Others emphasize the virtues of hospitality in the shape of the stranger who is welcomed by poor people and, in turn, rewards them by making food appear. Others still have the miraculous appearance of food in response to prayer. The enduring belief in these tales, long after the Famine years, is a tribute to the power of religious and communal values among surviving Irish-speaking people, especially in the south and west of Ireland.

The corollary of the belief in supernatural power to save life was the often bitter memory of evictions from hearth and home and the very real hatred of landlords and rapacious neighbours who acquired the land of the unfortunates who became evicted. Cathal Póirtéir cites this example of folk memory recalled from County Cork in 1945:

> In my young day I used to hear old people discuss the awful cruelty practised by farmers who were fairly well off against the poorer and less comfortable neighbours. The people who were old when I was young, I'm sixty six, were never tired of discussing how some of those, taking advantage of the poverty of their neighbours, used to offer the rent of their farms to the landlord, the rent which the owners could not pay, and grab their farms adding some to their own farms.
>
> Several people would be glad if the Famine times were altogether forgotten so that the cruel doings of their forbears would not be again renewed and talked about by the neighbours.[41]

Successive failures of the potato crop by early 1847 had induced a condition of hysteria in particular communities. Oliver MacDonagh cites the newspaper stories about people suddenly making feverish arrangements to leave, of fights for contract tickets at the ports, of deliberate felonies being committed in the hope of transportation – an emigration driven by panic and the contagious example of neighbours. Emigration rates varied considerably between parishes in the same district, suggesting that a reverbatory effect had occurred in some places and not others. MacDonagh sensed the beginning of a profound social disintegration, prompting a fatal loss of morale among respectable farmers and tradesmen, whose flight left the peasantry scrambling in imitation to get out of the country. Further disastrous crop failures, and the fiasco of the 1848 Rising, brought on a 'deep mood of staleness and defeat' that was to last through the next three seasons.[42]

Patrick O'Farrell, in seeking to define the mood of people suffering the most profound psychological shock in the Famine years, argues that for a time Ireland went mad as the country was in the throes of 'lunatic disorder and irresponsible anarchic social dissolution'.[43] Yet, O'Farrell suggests that neither history nor literature have fully conveyed what Carleton called 'the insanity of desolation'. While there is an echo in the novels of Carleton and O'Flaherty, did the condition of madness exist beyond the form of a dramatic device, as an historical reality? 'Was peasant Ireland mad – crazed, demented, bereft of all rational hope, driven by rage and despair, reduced to animal survival patterns, then apathy – in the Famine period?' O'Farrell's affirmative answer draws on the evidence of the contemporary *Journals* of Mrs Elizabeth Smith. As the Famine approaches, the tone becomes increasingly apocalyptic – moving from descriptions of peasant excitability and violence to wild fearful passions until in May 1846, the *Journals* speak of 'a nation of lunatics! Everyone of them stark staring mad from the peer to the peasant'. By 1847 the madness plays itself out, consumed by widespread misery and apathy.

The state of Famine madness that brought about a revolutionary change in Irish society also beckoned the end of the old peasant order. The brutal shock of starvation and famine hastened the longer-term process of the modernization of Ireland. While the Irish peasantry was reduced by death and emigration, the survivors were weakened as a political force in post-Famine Ireland. It was left to Mitchel and the intellectuals who led the nationalist movement to construct a meaning out of revolutionary change. Ironically, the nationalist dream rested on an anti-modern ideology, incorporating the virtues of an old peasant economy that was fatally damaged by the Famine. It employed a 'vengeful rhetoric' and offered the escape route of continuous emigration. If O'Farrell's argument is accepted it goes some way to restore the Famine to its traditional role as a crucial watershed in Ireland's history.

Famine relief

At every level of society, the devastating impact of the successive failure of the potato crops in 1846, 1847 and 1848 brought not only starvation and eviction for labourers and cottiers, but spelled economic ruin for many farmers and landlords in the worst affected districts. While landlords faced greatly increased burdens from poor rates and were being pressed to relieve the distress among the labouring population by providing employment on a much greater scale, they were suffering a decline in income from farm rents collected.

Bitterness and conflict grew as each sectional interest sought to protect itself in the face of the economic blizzard of the Famine years. The failure to pay farm rents was followed by landlord seizure of tenants' goods. A collective resistance to the distraint of goods by large hostile crowds prompted landlords to enforce a distress notice with a strong force of constabulary. Where landlords were intent on securing their rents at all costs, many tenants sold their crops and stock and disappeared.[44] The law was disregarded by both sides.

Similar attempts to evade the law arose from the implementation of the notorious quarter-acre clause.[45] A provision of the Poor Law Amendment Act of June 1847, it attracted widespread hostility in promoting enforced starvation and the clearance of paupers from estates. Pauper tenants were evicted and their cabins levelled. Evasive action was taken by tenants, transferring their holdings to friends or relatives, on the understanding that they would reclaim the land once out of the Workhouse. Such collusion was common to districts with a high proportion of smallholders who clung on to tiny plots and sent wives and children into the Workhouse. Vigilant Poor Law Guardians tried to preserve the workhouse test by rejecting such applications.

Because towns were the centres for administering poor relief and public works, the famine-stricken rural poor flocked to them, so creating tensions between the towns and country districts. 'On an average', *The Cork Constitution* reported in April 1847, 'about 300 of these miserable creatures come into the city daily, who are walking masses of filth, vermin and sickness'.[46] The authorities feared being swamped by a horde of refugees. After some 20,000 paupers had invaded the city and an estimated 500 were dying each week, 22 special constables were armed to guard the city entrances and turn the famine victims away.

A more sympathetic response was evoked from the young Marquis of Sligo when thousands of rural poor descended on the town of Westport in County Mayo in the spring of 1847. As chairman of the Westport Guardians and of the Westport Relief Committee, he was sensitive to the extent of distress in the area and along with some of the local clergy (Catholic and Protestant), he was able to offer some relief to the starving population. He chartered a ship, the *Martha Washington*, to sail from New Orleans to Westport with 1,000 tons of flour on board. The ship arrived in June 1847, and its cargo was sold at half price, with Lord Sligo bearing most of the loss incurred, amounting to £3,012. His personal contribution to support relief meant that he had to borrow to pay the rates, close the family home and move into town.[47]

The operation of the Poor Law, already under strain before the Famine period, encountered severe difficulty especially in the worst affected southern and western counties. Christine Kinealy's study of the Poor Law in County Mayo makes a case for regional diversity.[48] Opposition to rate collectors was widespread and in the Ballina, Swinford and Castlebar Unions, the Guardians received no rates and were without funds. Following the assault on rate collectors in the Ballina Union, the Commissioners allowed the presence of a magistrate and the military to enforce collection.

The onset of the Famine exposed the Poor Law as totally incapable of providing relief on the scale required. In Mayo, the Workhouses had a capacity of 4,400 inmates and when funds were exhausted, the Guardians were compelled to turn paupers away. Yet, on one day in 1847 2,000 paupers applied for relief at Ballina, when the Workhouse was full, and the

Guardians could only provide them with a meal. During the same year, the weekly expenses of the Poor Law Unions were met by private donations by the Earl of Lucan at Castlebar and by the Marquis of Sligo at Westport. Despite the Commissioners' insistence on local distress being met by local taxation, the severe financial difficulties experienced by all the Mayo unions forced the government to provide additional relief.

The prolonged distress in the western counties diverted the Government from its ideological stance over the Poor Law in Ireland. While the situation was improving in Ulster and other parts of Ireland, the distress in Mayo, Galway, Clare and parts of Kerry was at its greatest in 1849. So in those areas external financial assistance continued to supplement what could be collected from the poor rates. The government introduced Rate-in-Aid as a national rate designed to compel the wealthier unions to subsidize the poorer ones.

Accompanying the inadequacy of poor relief and a desperate migration to the towns, food riots and the stealing of food assumed unprecedented proportions. In February 1847, an armed mob of labourers broke through the outer gate of Cork city and attacked the bread shops, and only after a long struggle were they dispersed by police, charging with fixed bayonets. Over the succeeding months such scenes were to be repeated in towns throughout the south of Ireland. Soup depots, corn mills, provision stores and even cars laden with Indian meal, under police escort, were targets for attack by mobs of starving people in the summer of 1847. James Donnelly concludes that only the forbearance of the police and military authorities prevented bloodshed among potentially violent crowds.[49] No doubt, the price of restoring order on behalf of the property owners of Cork was paid by the deaths of a desperate, starving peasantry from the surrounding rural area.

In rural districts, the forbearance of magistrates, in dismissing cases against labourers of stealing turnips, brought local objections from the farmers, some of whom took the law into their own hands by protecting crops with shotguns. Not surprisingly, intimidation through warning shots directed against potential theft, occasionally, led to loss of life in defence of property interests. More serious was the marked increase in the stealing of cattle, sheep and poultry, as widely reported in the *Cork Examiner* from late 1846 to early 1849.[50] Farmers, in addition to being subjected to raids on their stock by the starving population of rural districts, also faced serious losses from gangs of thieves roaming the county.

Sheep and cattle stealing were regarded as serious offences and convicted labourers, even when driven by starvation, were sentenced to transportation to Australia for between 7 to 15 years. Transportation from Ireland rose from 600 to 2,000 a year during the Famine years. While this represented a draconian policy by magistrates to protect the property of farmers, it also probably included many labourers who saw transportation to Australia as preferable to destitution in Ireland. Self interest and survival became the rule. In County Cork and Leitrim, the most distressed counties in Ireland, the Great Famine created an opportunity for landlords to clear their estates of bankrupt middlemen, for the larger farmers to increase the size of their holdings, and for tenants to flee the country without paying their rents. As a result, class antagonisms were sharpened and conflicts arose between farmers and magistrates, landowners and Poor Law officials, and between merchants, shopkeepers and the labouring poor.

The severity of the Famine varied between different parts of Ireland and continued longer in the poor southern and western counties than in other parts of the country. Landlord reaction also varied, ranging from the selfless and humane to the cynically opportunist. While some landlords impoverished their estates in relieving the distress of poor tenants, others exploited the situation by clearing their estates of poor cottiers and increasing the size of holdings. In the desperate scramble for survival, strong farmers, merchants and tradesmen looked to defend their economic interest, either at the expense of their neighbours or by fleeing the country to avoid having to shoulder the burden of widespread distress.

Migration as a means of preserving property is reflected in the variations between county levels of mortality and county levels of emigration. Five Irish counties, Cork, Kerry, Clare, Galway and Mayo – all on the Atlantic coast – had an average excess mortality above an eighth of the total population in the period 1846 to 1850. At the same time, the rate of emigration from the southern counties was relatively moderate in relation to other parts of Ireland. For instance, County Cork is estimated to have lost 10–12 per cent through emigration between 1841 and 1851, a rather lower proportion than the estimated 20 per cent who left Mayo, Roscommon, Sligo, Monaghan, Cavan, Longford, and Leix in the same decade. Of these, the midland counties had the highest rates of emigration where the small farmer, on holdings of 5–15 acres, possessed the means to emigrate and had the least incentive to stay.[51] S. H. Cousens explains the lower level of emigration from southern counties in relation to the heavy concentration of labourers within the region.[52] Put simply, the high level of poverty found in many of the southern districts meant that many people simply lacked the means to leave. Where there was a higher incidence of assisted emigration, as in Clare, Limerick and Kerry, more landless labourers did manage to emigrate. The most distressed areas of the south and west which experienced high levels of mortality attracted most public attention, but the midland counties from which there was the greatest exodus of population, were relatively ignored.

Certainly, there were glaring shortcomings in the provision and administration of relief. A failure to control the grain trade, and the inadequate wages available on the public works in the autumn of 1846, made all the more likely the widespread starvation and disease in early 1847. Yet, inspired by the success of private relief schemes, the government reversed policy, providing food relief from January 1847, free to the destitute, and directly to all distressed applicants outside the Workhouses. Stirabout (a thick soup made from Indian meal and rice) was sold cheaply or distributed free. Through the auspices of the Poor Law unions, relief committees set up soup-kitchens throughout the country and, by the summer of 1847 at the height of the operation, government kitchens distributed soup rations to over three million people throughout Ireland.

Distribution of food on this massive scale kept thousands alive and prevented a fearful mortality from rising still further. This was only made possible by huge imports of foreign grain, some 2.85 million tons during the first six months of 1847, resulting in a dramatic reduction in the price of Indian corn, from £19 a ton in February to £7 10s by the end of August.[53] Plentiful supplies at low prices enabled the relief committees to operate their soup-kitchens effectively. Although intended as a temporary form of relief until changes in the Poor Law could be introduced, it represented a triumph of pragmatism over dogma. Trevelyan's rhetoric and the fulminations of *The Times*, designed to appease propertied interests in England concerned about the cost of relief to Ireland, were at variance with some of the practical steps taken by the British government during the first two years of the Famine crisis.

The theme of starvation amidst plenty, a key part of Mitchel's nationalist propaganda, may also be seen as an oversimplification. Donnelly has shown that food exports from Ireland were affected severely during the Famine years. Drastic reductions occurred in the level of grain exports as grain was diverted to home consumption, partly to provide food for livestock to compensate for the deficiencies in the potato crop.[54] Before the Famine, about a third of the annual potato crop was consumed by livestock, and over half of that went to feed pigs. The potato blight severely reduced pig-breeding but the raising of cattle expanded as farmers turned to oats for cattle feed. Dairy farming also prospered and butter exports went on increasing through the late 1840s. The reduction in domestic consumption through poverty, death and emigration, had the effect of diverting butter on to the export market. Irish agriculture, like Irish industry, formed part of the wider British economy, and in the free play of market forces, the bigger cattle and dairy farmers not only weathered the storm but even prospered during the Famine years while the smaller farmers, dependent on cereals, pigs and sheep, faced adverse conditions.

The sheer scale of the shortage of food has been addressed by Austin Bourke, an agricultural meteorologist, in his interesting series of writings, entitled *The Visitation of God?, The Potato and the Great Irish Famine*, published in 1993. 'It is beyond question that the food deficiency arising from the loss of the potato crop in 1846 could not have been met by the simple expedient of prohibiting the export of grain from Ireland, even if the difficult practical problems of acquisition, storage, milling and distribution, could have been surmounted at short notice'. Grain exports in 1846 totalled 285,000 tons, which is the approximate food equivalent of a little over one million tons of potatoes: the shortfall in the potato crop of that year was well over ten times that figure. What was clear is that the grain crop of 1846, if it had been retained wholly in Ireland, could have contributed to bridging the starvation gap between the devastated potato crop in August and the arrival of imported maize in the winter months.[55]

The Miller thesis

Set against the Mitchel thesis of a deliberate policy of clearing a 'surplus' population out of the country, emigration from Ireland during the Famine and post-Famine period was not simply the result of a conspiracy by the British government. Kerby Miller in a major study of Irish emigration to North America, has argued that it was driven by 'push' factors in Ireland: changing economic conditions, social structures and cultural patterns.[56] Miller pinpoints three dominant social forces in nineteenth-century Catholic culture which spearheaded the process of modernization. He associates all three with the growing *embourgeoisement* of Catholic society: a middle class strengthened by the clearances of the 1840s and 1850s; the Catholic Church, which imposed through a 'devotional revolution', a coherent moral order on its followers; and Irish nationalism which found most of its support for constitutional change among strong farmers, the urban middle classes and village tradesmen. Commercialization created the right conditions for such groups to emerge the more powerful from the devastation of the Famine years.

In stronger-farmer families, the concentration of capital through impartible inheritance increasingly involved a prolonged adolescence and postponed marriage tied to the chance of succeeding the older generation. On smaller farms, where dowries were less likely for non-inheriting children, emigration for both sexes was commonly the only alternative. The Catholic Church in Ireland not only achieved a successful 'modernization', replacing old forms of worship with those prescribed by Rome but established a remarkable degree of clerical power over its parishioners. A reverence for celibacy and strict clerical injunction against sexual licence served to protect the planned marriages and inheritance in strong-farmer families. The Catholic clergy took over the allegiance that tenants had formerly given to their landlords, and an impressive control was exercised by providing 'psychic solace to the poor' and through their obscuring 'class and intergenerational conflicts within the Catholic community'.[57]

National ideology, supported chiefly by commercial farmers and tradesmen, also reinforced old habits of dependence and a lack of responsibility. In addition to a tradition-bound rhetoric, all Ireland's present woes were put down to external causes. In having the English to blame for Ireland's problems, the Irish absolved themselves of all responsibility. Miller offers a compelling explanation of this phenomenon in what he terms the 'culture of exile'. In reality, he argues, Irish emigration was surrounded by conflicting pressures and emigrants themselves possessed highly ambivalent attitudes. Many farmers and tradesmen believed it essential for the process of modernization, a process synonymous with increasing bourgeois dominance, and only made possible by a clearing out of the poor cottiers and landless labourers. Emigration reduced the fear of potential agrarian violence in resistance to the consolidation of holdings among the larger farmers. For parents on smallholdings, it eased the way for the painful disinheritance of children without the prospect of unbearable family conflict.

For the Catholic Church, emigration provided the opportunity for the faith to be spread abroad. Catholic freedom might be established not only in the United States but new settlements were consciously planned to rival those of earlier Protestant colonies in Australia and Canada. A well-documented example is the work of Bishop Quinn, the first Catholic bishop of Brisbane in Queensland. In an effort to relieve famine conditions in County Offaly and to build up a Catholic presence in his own diocese, Quinn established his own Queensland Immigration foundation which was financed by government land grants of up to £30 in value over two years to immigrants who had paid their own passages. Between 1862 and 1865, Quinn was able to bring over a total of 4,000 Irish immigrants in 12 ships. This individual piece of enterprise almost matched the government total of 5,000 migrants over the same period.[58]

Moreover, Irish emigrants abroad were seen as providing, through generous remittances, vital financial support for the building of Catholic churches and schools in Ireland. Emigrant money not only paid for passage across the Atlantic but also for farm rents and financed improvements for tradesmen at home. Likewise, Irish emigrants in Britain and America gave aid in the form of capital and arms, and exercised diplomatic pressure in favour of the nationalist cause. More obviously, emigration aroused considerable fears that the country was losing its brightest and best. Their loss could leave the people so pacified that the country would succumb to the English dream of a Protestant Ireland. The Church feared, too, that those who left for individual gain would violate the old values of family and faith. Parents would be abandoned to their fate as young people fled to a new life abroad.

To reconcile these conflicting tensions and anxieties, Miller suggests that a unifying theme of emigration as exile took hold in the popular imagery manifest in speeches, the press, and most especially in emigrant songs of the period. By explaining the phenomenon of emigration as enforced banishment, the result of continuing oppression and appalling neglect, England became the universally acknowledged scapegoat. This was both politically convenient in harnessing support for the nationalist cause, and also supplied an emotional need in coping with the sense of loss and defeat that emigration represented. More precisely, it diverted attention from the conflicting pressures within families and communities and in the hearts and minds of emigrants themselves. The idea of enforced exile absolved the emigrant from the charge of desertion in the pursuit of personal gain, and offered an external explanation of the personal agony that emigration commonly involved.

English radical support for Ireland

Just as emigrants might well have mixed feelings about the land they left behind, so English attitudes to Ireland extend beyond the usual caricature blend of superiority and condescension. In the early nineteenth century, Catholic Emancipation and reform in Ireland found widespread radical support in England. Not only was there a remarkably persistent commitment to the concept of social justice, uniting the labouring poor in Britain and Ireland, but the continuing plight of Ireland was seen as driving the Irish into flooding the British market with cheap labour. By removing Irish grievances, the need to migrate to Britain in search of work would also be removed. In supporting the Irish struggle for justice, radicals were also defending the living standards of the English working class. Political principle and economic interest were thus conjoined.

The force of sentiment and sense of common purpose against an exclusive, aristocratic system of government was most powerfully expressed in the writings of the great English radical journalist and editor of the Political Register, William Cobbett. His Irish writings confirm the vital link between English radicalism and the cause of Ireland.[59] Cobbett visited Ireland in 1834 and, after addressing Irish audiences in many towns, he wrote of his experiences in the form of a warning to the labourers of England:

> I saw the day before yesterday a mother with her four little children lying upon some straw, with their bodies huddled close together to keep themselves warm. I have written over to one of my labourers ... that if I find that George, the man who minds the cattle, should suffer them to have under them straw so broken and so dirty as that poor woman was lying upon, I would turn him out of the house as a lazy and a cruel fellow. (Cheers) ... The cause of the misery was, that those who work, and those were the majority of the people of every country, those who laboured had not what they ought to have, a due share of what they laboured for. (Hear)...[60]

The theme of starvation amidst plenty – one that developed into a powerful charge against England by the Young England movement and later by John Mitchel – was contrasted with a rosy picture of the well-fed English labourer. Cobbett argued that the only way Irish grievances could be removed was with the support of the English people, just as they had supported the Catholic Emancipation Bill and opposed the Coercion Bill. Prophetically, Cobbett anticipated tragedies and conflicts that were to hang over the condition of Ireland for the rest of the century. Famine, agrarian strife, the demand for Home Rule are all heralded in his warning of what was to come:

> Gentlemen, it is impossible that Ireland can be suffered to remain in its present state! What! vessels laden with provisions ready to sail for England, while those who have raised the provisions are starving on the spot where they raised them! What! Landlords living in England, having a 'RIGHT' to drive the King's subjects out of this island, on pain of starvation from hunger and from cold! What! call upon England for meal and money to be sent in charity to save the people of Ireland from starving, and make the relieved persons *pay rent the same year!* What! demand allegiance from a man whom you toss out upon the road, denying that he has any right to demand from any part of the community the means of sustaining life! ... What! give to 349,000 of the English people as many representatives in Parliament as you give to the whole Irish nation, and bid the latter be content![61]

References to charity instead of justice and to landlord exploitation of the poor united English radicals with Irish nationalists. The revolutionary overtones of class language and the humanitarian onslaught against political economy find common expression in the Chartist attacks against the cruelty of the industrial system.[62] It is no surprise that English political economists were deaf to the entreaties of the Famine Irish when they were equally unresponsive to the cries of the English labouring poor. Entirely separate ideological assumptions produced quite distinctive languages that were unable to communicate with each other. The following passage taken from the *Cork Examiner* may be understood as following William Cobbett and Feargus O'Connor, as well as echoing John Mitchel:

> AWFUL STATE OF SKIBBEREEN DISTRICT–DESTRUCTION OF PEOPLE–FAMINE DISEASE AND DEATH
> Without food or fuel, bed or bedding, whole families are shut up in naked hovels, dropping one by one into the arms of death – death, more merciful than this world or its rulers.
>
> What can private benevolence, what can private charity do to meet this dreadful case? – Nothing. It may release one from death, or two, or three; but hundreds and thousands are sunk in the profoundest depths of misery – they are wasting away in silent despair – 'dying like rotten sheep'.
>
> Government aid can alone be effective here. A vigorous effort can alone rescue our patient, uncomplaining people from destruction. Political economy has slain enough of victims; it has raised hecatomb upon hecatomb of fathers, mothers, children, to its cruel, bloody policy – Humanity alone can save the survivors.[63]

While the *Cork Examiner* pleaded for mercy to save the victims of famine, John Mitchel successfully pinned the blame for starvation and emigration on the British government. In a biting letter to Lord Clarendon, printed in the *United Irishman*, the power of his language, and the moral certainty of his case, remind us why the Mitchel thesis has maintained its hold on the public imagination:

> But the case is this: I assert and maintain that in the island of Ireland there is no government or law – that what passes for 'government' is a foul and fraudulent insurpation, based on corruption and falsehood, supported by force, and battening on blood. I hold that the meaning and sole object of that Government is to make sure of a constant supply of Irish food for British tables, Irish wool for British backs, Irish blood and bone for British armies; to make sure, in one word, of Ireland for the English, and to keep down, scourge and dragoon the Irish into submission and patient starvation.[64]

In linking together William Cobbett and John Mitchel, both savage critics of political economy, it is worth reminding ourselves that their joint commitment to humanity and social justice found limited support in the emerging Irish nationalism of the post-Famine era. Ultimately, the real victims of the Famine were the smallholders and landless labourers. The real beneficiaries, and long-term inheritors of the new Ireland, were the strong farmers and tradesmen. In practice, the influential, nationalist slogan that emerged from the Young Ireland Movement in 1848, 'the land of Ireland for the people of Ireland' did not extend to the poorest section of Irish society.

Far from evading the catastrophic dimension of Irish history, as Bradshaw has argued, the historiography of the famine incorporates it into a broader historical debate, a debate that moves beyond the sterile war of attrition between Ireland and Britain and between nationalism and revisionism.

Yet much remains to be done in extending our knowledge and in deepening our understanding of the meaning of the Famine. That can only be achieved in recognizing a methodology that is interdisciplinary in the path set by the pioneering work of Dudley Edwards and Williams in the 1950s and continued in the collective volume on Famine in Ireland, edited by E. Margaret Crawford in the 1980s and in the essays in *The Great Irish Famine*, edited by Cathal Póirtéir in the 1990s.[65] If ever there was a subject that cried out for an interdisciplinary approach among scholars, it is surely, the Famine. Yet, its treatment for the most part, has been securely confined within narrow specialisms. The specialist contributions of demographers and economic historians, of medical historians and historians of social policy, need to be brought together in a wide-ranging synthesis.

One example of the value of bringing together the knowledge and insights of separate disciplines may suffice. Dr Daniel Donovan in Skibbereen described the plight of starving people in 1848: 'In a short term the face and limbs become frightfully emaciated; the eyes acquire a most peculiar stare; the skin exhaled a peculiar and offensive foetor, and was covered with a brownish filthy-looking coating, almost as indelible as varnish. This I was at first inclined to regard as encrusted filth, but further experience convinced me that it is a secretion poured out from the exhalants on the surface of the body'.[66] Margaret Crawford, in explaining the physiological characteristics of victims of starvation, points to the condition of the skin becoming wrinkled and dry and assuming a deep brown pigmentation.

Here medical and scientific knowledge provides evidence for an explanation of the moral distancing from the Famine victims to be found in the reports of *The Times* newspaper which saw famine as self-induced, the result of idleness and fecklessness.

It was a moral distancing akin to that found among contemporary commentators on the slums of London. As François Barret-Ducrocq has observed,

> external appearance was an exact reflection of internal reality: both a sign and a consequence of the moral condition... The meaningless swarming of unknown beings in the rooms and courtyards evoked images of the irrational and the animal kingdom, while the mephitic stenches of rubbish and unwashed bodies could only indicate obscenity. In the moral symbolism of the nineteenth century foul air and evil blended together impartially polluting bodies and souls.[67]

A fear of a moral contagion subverting the existing social order was at the heart of the 'condition of England' question in Britain in the 1840s. These same moral fears, were applied by British ministers to Famine Ireland. Perhaps John Mitchel's denunciation of the British government's policy of 'death by political economy' should be amended to include 'death by moral distancing'. If that was the case, the mental divide between Britain and Ireland over the Irish Famine was based on class assumptions originating in fears of a social crisis in England. Not so much a case of England's difficulty, Ireland's opportunity, but of England's crisis, Ireland's tragedy.

Notes

1. Brendan Bradshaw, 'Revisionism revised', paper given at the Desmond Greaves Summer School, August 1991, in *Education Review*, November 1991 Vol. 1 , No. 3, p. 26.
2. Bradshaw, p. 25. See also the helpful collection, Ciarán Brady, *Interpreting Irish History: the Debate on Historical Revisionism*, Irish Academic Press, Dublin, 1994
3. Cormac Ó Gráda, *Ireland Before and After the Famine. Explorations in Economic History 1800–1925*, Manchester University Press, Manchester, 1988, p. 78.
4. Patrick O'Farrell, 'Whose reality? The Irish Famine in history and literature', *Historical Studies*, Vol. 20, 1982, pp. 1–13.
5. J. Mitchel, *Jail Journal of Five Years in British Prisons*, author's edition, Glasgow, 1876, p. 16.
6. Mitchel, *Jail Journal*, p. 15.
7. J. Mitchel, *The Last Conquest of Ireland (Perhaps)*, author's edition, Glasgow, 1876, p. 219.
8. J. Mitchel, *The Last Conquest of Ireland (Perhaps)*, p. 105. The charge of genocide revived Jonathan Swift's infamously satirical *A Modest Proposal* which recommended the eating of babies as a cure for over-population in Ireland.
9. O'Farrell, p. 3.
10. Canon J. O'Rourke, *The Great Irish Famine*, Veritas, Dublin, 1989, first published 1874, Charles Gavan Duffy, *Four Years of Irish History*, Cassell, Getter, Galpin, London, 1883; P. S. O'Hegarty, *History of Ireland under the Union*, Methuen, London, 1952; Cecil Woodham-Smith, *The Great Hunger*, Hamish Hamilton, London, 1962; Robert Kee, *The Green Flag*, Weidenfeld & Nicolson, London, 1972; Thomas Gallagher, *Paddy's Lament: Ireland 1846–47: Prelude to Hatred*, Ward River Press, Dublin, 1985; Christine Kinealy, *This Great Calamity: The Irish Famine*, Gill and Macmillan, Dublin, 1994.
11. R. Kee, *Ireland: A History*, Sphere, London, 1982, p. 90.
12. *The Times*, 26 March 1847, in Gallagher, *Paddy's Lament*, pp. 68–9.
13. R. Crotty, *Irish Agricultural Production*, Cork University Press, Cork, 1966; R. F. Foster, *Modern Ireland 1600–1972*, Penguin, Harmondsworth, 1989.
14. Christine Kinealy, *This Great Calamity*, pp. xv–xxi, p. 359.
15. Woodham-Smith, p. 156.
16. Woodham-Smith, p. 162.
17. Peter Gray, 'Potatoes and providence: British government responses to the Great Famine', *Bullán*, Vol. 1, No. 1, Spring 1994, p. 82.
18 Donal A. Kerr, *'A Nation of Beggars?' Priests, People and Politics in Famine Ireland 1846–45*, Oxford University Press, Oxford, 1994.
19. Kerr, *'A Nation of Beggars?'*, p. 82.
20. Thomas A. Boylan and Timothy P. Foley, *Political Economy and Colonial Ireland: The Propagation and Ideological Function of Economic Discourse in the Nineteenth*

Century, Routledge, London, 1992.

21. Joel Mokyr, 'Malthusian models and Irish history', *Journal of Economic History*, Vol. XL, No. 1, March 1980, pp. 159–66. See also, Joel Mokyr, *Why Ireland Starved: A Quantitative and Analytical History of the Irish Economy 1800–1850*, George Allen and Unwin, London, 1983, Revised 1985

22. A. Trollope, *Castle Richmond* (first published 1860), Oxford University Press, Oxford, 1989.

23. O. Macdonagh, 'The Irish Famine emigration to the United States', *Perspectives in American History*, Vol. X, 1976, pp. 257–446.

24. R. F. Foster, *Modern Ireland*, p. 323. For a discussion of the pre-Famine census figures for Ireland, see Joel Mokyr, *Why Ireland Starved*, pp. 30–8.

25. Brenda Collins, 'Proto-industrialisation and pre-Famine emigration', *Social History*, Vol 7, No. 2 , 1982, pp. 127–46.

26. Brenda Collins, 'Irish emigration to Dundee and Paisley during the first half of the nineteenth century', in J. M. Goldstrom and L. A. Clarkson, (eds), *Irish Population Economy and Society: Essays in honour of the late K. H. Connell*, Oxford University Press, Oxford, 1981, p. 201.

27. Eion O'Malley, 'The decline of Irish industry in the nineteenth century', *Economic and Social Review*, Vol. 13, No. 1, 1981, pp. 21–42.

28. O'Malley, p. 22.

29. L. M. Cullen, *An Economic History of Ireland since 1660*, Batsford, London, 1972.

30. R. Crotty, *Irish Agricultural Production*, Cork University Press, Cork, 1966.

31. Kerby Miller, *Emigrants and Exiles: Ireland and the Irish Exodus to North America*, Oxford University Press, Oxford, 1985, p. 198.

32. S. H. Cousens, 'The regional pattern of emigration during the Great Irish Famine 1846–51', *Institute of British Geographers*, Transactions and Papers, No. 28, 1962, pp. 126–9. Joel Mokyr claims that Cousens underestimates the level of Famine mortality whilst agreeing with regional variations. See Joel Mokyr *Why Ireland Starved*, pp. 263–8.

33. S. H. Cousens, 'The regional variations in population changes in Ireland 1861–1881', *Economic History Review*, Vol. 17, 1964, pp. 301–21.

34. Cousens, 'Regional variations', p. 310, fig. 4.

35. Cousens, 'Regional variations', p. 320.

36. C. Ó Gráda, 'Seasonal migration and post-Famine adjustment in the West of Ireland', *Studies Hibernia*, Vol. 22, 1980, pp. 48–6. See also Ruth-Ann Harris, *The Nearest Place that Wasn't Ireland: Early Nineteenth-Century Irish Labor Migration*, Iowa State University Press, Ames, Iowa, 1994. Seasonal migration is seen as a prelude to overseas emigration to America.

37. Ó Gráda, p. 60.

38. D. Fitzpatrick, 'Irish emigration in the late nineteenth century', *Irish Historical Studies*, Vol. 22, 1980, pp. 126–43.

39. Roger McHugh, 'The Famine in the Irish oral tradition', in R. Dudley Edwards and T. Desmond Williams, *The Great Famine: Studies in Irish History 1845–52*, Browne and Nolan, Dublin, 1956, pp. 391–436.

40. McHugh, pp. 395–6.

41. Cathal Póirtéir, 'Folk memory and the Famine', in Cathal Póirtéir, *The Great Irish Famine*, Mercier Press, Dublin, 1995, p. 230.

42. O. MacDonagh, 'Irish overseas emigration during the Great Famine', in Dudley Edwards and Williams, *The Great Famine*, p. 325.

43. Patrick O'Farrell, pp. 9–13.

44. James S. Donnelly Jnr, *The Land and the People of Nineteenth-Century Cork*, Routledge, London, 1975, p. 103.

45. Donnelly, p. 98.

46. *Cork Constitution*, 24 April 1847, in Donnelly, p. 87.

47. Paedar O'Flanagan, 'An outline history of the town of Westport, part IV, the Famine Years, its aftermath 1845–1855', *Cathair Na Mart*, Journal of Westport Historical Society, Vol. 6, No. 1, 1986, p. 105.

48. Christine Kinealy, 'The administration of the Poor Law in Mayo 1838–98', *Cathair Na Mart*, Journal of Westport Historical Society, Vol. 6, No. 1, 1986, p. 105.

49. Donnelly, p. 90: see also *The Mayo Constitution*, 4 May, 18 May and 26 June 1847.

50. Donnelly, p. 88.

51. O MacDonagh, 'The Irish Famine emigration to the United States', *Perspectives in American History*, Vol. X, 1976, p. 421.

52. S. H. Cousens, 'Regional death rates in Ireland from 1846–51', *Population Studies*, Vol. XIV, 1960–61, pp. 55–74.

53. Donnelly, p. 87.

54. Donnelly, p. 91.

55. Austin Bourke, *'The Visitation of God?' The Potato and the Great Irish Famine*, edited by Jacqueline Hill and Cormac, Lilliput Press, Dublin, pp. 164–5.

56. Kerby Miller, *Emigrants and Exiles.*

57. Miller, p. 126.

58. M. E. R. MacGinley, 'The Irish in Queensland: An Overview', in John O'Brien and Pauric Travers, eds, *The Irish Emigrant Experience in Australia*, Poolbeg Press, Dublin, 1991, p. 106.

59. Denis Knight (ed.), *Cobbett in Ireland: A Warning to England*, Lawrence and Wishart, London, 1984.

60. Knight, p. 73.

61. Knight, pp. 210–11.

62. *Northern Star*, 23 January 1847, in Graham Davis, *The Irish in Britain 1815–1914*, Gill and Macmillan, Dublin, 1991, p. 166.

63. *Cork Examiner*, 16 December 1846.

64. Quoted in P. S. O'Hegarty, *John Mitchel: An Appreciation with some Account of Young Ireland*, Maunsel, Dublin, 1917, p. 77.

65. R. Dudley Edwards and T. D. Williams (eds), *The Great Famine: Studies in Irish History 1845–52*, Browne and Nolan, Dublin, 1956; Margaret Crawford, *Famine: The Irish Experience 900–1900*, John Donald, Edinburgh, 1989; Cathal Póirtéir, *The Great Irish Famine*, 1995. Two recent works provide fresh insights into the literature of the famine: Christopher Morash, *Writing the Irish Famine*, Oxford University Press, Oxford, 1995 and Margaret Kelleher, *The Feminization of the Famine*, Cork University Press, Cork, 1996. And see the chapter by Morash, later in this volume.

66. D. Donovan, 'Observations on the peculiar diseases to which famine of the last year gave origin and on the morbid effects of insufficient nourishment', *Dublin Medical Press*, XIX (1848), p. 67, in Crawford, pp. 200–1.

67. François Barret-Ducrocq, *Love in the Time of Queen Victoria: Sexuality and Desire Among Working-Class Men and Women in Nineteenth-Century London*, translated by John Howe, Penguin, Harmondsworth, 1991, p. 8.

2 Making memories: the literature of the Irish Famine

Christopher Morash

Springs of memory

'It is an appalling picture, that which springs up to memory', writes Canon Sheehan of the Irish Famine in his 1905 novel, *Glenanaar*. 'Gaunt spectres move here and there, looking at one another out of hollow eyes of despair and gloom. Ghosts walk the land'.[1]

What is most remarkable about this statement is that Sheehan was born in 1852. The Famine, which even the most partisan observers admitted was over by 1851, could not 'spring up to memory' for Sheehan; he could not have witnessed it in the first place.

What, then, is he remembering? The simple answer to this question is that Sheehan is remembering other literary representations of the Famine. Having said that, however, the mechanisms by which literary texts become naturalized as memory are anything but simple. To begin with, we must define what we mean by 'literary representations' – a potentially daunting task perhaps best accomplished in structural terms. Many recent historical accounts of the Famine, such as the works of Joel Mokyr and Cormac Ó Gráda,[2] have relied heavily on statistical evidence, and as such have aimed at comprehensive representation. In other words, such historians attempt to enumerate all of those who died during the Famine, all of those who were confined to Poor Houses within a given county, and so on. In order for statistical evidence to be accepted as accurate it must be as inclusive as possible. Literary representation, by contrast, deliberately excludes all but a small, select group of details, and thus relies upon the related tropes of synecdoche, metonymy and metaphor.[3] The writer who depicts a lone, ragged figure starving by the side of a road is understood to represent more than just that single figure. The representation will be seen as existing both as an aesthetic object, complete unto itself, and as an iconic reference to thousands of other starving victims. Moreover, depending upon the context, the lone figure by the side of the road may, for instance, be identified with a Biblical type, such as the man 'stripped of his raiment...and left half dead'[4] who is helped by the good Samaritan. In another context, the starving figure may be identified with the nation, as when a poet writing in *The Nation* in the 1840s urges 'Rise, wretched Erin, from thy children's graves'.[5]

Hence, literary representation has meaning only when understood as part of a semiotic system which includes an archive of other texts, many of which will carry with them particular interpretations of the events to be represented. These other texts are, in Roland Barthes' often cited formulation, 'anonymous, untraceable, and nevertheless already read'.[6] This should remind us that no literary text is pure or autonomous – that is to say, literature is more (or less) than an unmediated transcription of experience. Furthermore, the literary text, by definition, cannot include a complete representation of the world – which means that from the very outset there is an element of exclusion involved in its construction. So it is worth remembering that, because literature participates in discourses other than literature *per se*, not all exclusions are based on purely aesthetic criteria.

A portable Famine

There is a further form of exclusion which must be considered in relation to literary representations of the Famine. Between 1847 and 1900, at least 14 novels and well over 100 poems were written which dealt with the Famine – to which can be added the numerous pamphlets, travel narratives, histories, journals, diaries, and other forms of writing which, when taken with an extensive oral tradition, form the archive of Famine literature. Yet, few of these texts are known today, and even fewer are in print. A reading of the literature of the Famine must begin by asking why some textual traces of the Famine have become so widely read that they constitute a form of memory, and why others have been confined to the obscurity of library shelves. In other words, we must address questions of textual transmission – the ways in which certain Famine texts appear to be portable, containing passages or structural elements which can survive when transplanted from the context in which they were written to other contexts, and sometimes even to other texts. The portability of literary representations of the Famine is of particular interest if we are to consider the ways in which textually generated memories of the Famine have been distributed and maintained throughout the Irish diaspora world wide.

Perhaps the most striking instance of a portable text is John Mitchel's *Jail Journal*, a work whose migratory nature is signalled in its full title: *Jail Journal, Commenced on board the 'Shearwater' steamer, Dublin Bay, continued at Spike Island – on board the 'Scourge' war steamer – on board the 'Dromedary' hulk, Bermuda – on board the 'Neptune' convict ship – at Pernambuco – at the Cape of Good Hope (during the anti-convict rebellion) – at Van Dieman's land – at Greytown – and concluding at No. 3 Pier, North River, New York. With an introductory narrative of transactions in Ireland.*[7]

Given the conditions of its composition, the *Jail Journal* might seem to be an unusual document to have achieved the status of a seminal eye-witness report of the Irish Famine. And yet, there is a structural feature of the *Jail Journal* which has given it a pre-eminence among accounts of the Famine, and which has allowed elements of the text to be incorporated into later works of Famine literature. As David Lloyd has noted, the *Jail*

Journal sets out to establish a complete identification between Mitchel as an authorial presence in his text, and the historical events he is describing:[8]

> The general history of a nation may fitly preface the personal memoranda of a solitary captive; for it was strictly and logically a *consequence* of the dreary story here epitomised, that I came to be a prisoner, and to sit writing and musing so many months in a lonely cell.[9]

In other words, Mitchel is saying that his personal history is synonymous with the history of Ireland; when Mitchel's own life is put on hold with his captivity, so too is the historical life of Ireland.

Mitchel develops this identification in the structure of the *Jail Journal* as a whole by bringing the history of Ireland outlined in his introduction to a stop at the point at which he leaves Ireland. The rest of the *Jail Journal*, written while he was 'a solitary captive' in 'lonely cell', is severed from the processes of history. 'There is more Irish history, too, this month', he laments at one point in his journal, 'if I could but get at it'.[10] Cut off from history as a living reality, it becomes an aspect of memory and 'impressions of the past grow vivid as the soul shuts itself from the present'.[11] Lost in memory, Mitchel leaves the public history of Ireland in a state of suspended animation; in the textual world of the *Jail Journal* it is forever 1848 in Ireland, and the Famine has never ended. It is possible to imagine a member of an Irish migrant community (particularly a member of a first generation community in the nineteenth century) encountering such a textual suspension of history, and finding that it emulates their own experience of Irish history, suspended at the moment of departure. For such a reader, the text would create an illusion of authenticity that was validated by experience; its claims to truth would be difficult to question.

Mitchel's later writings of Irish history could not, of course, exactly reproduce the structure of the *Jail Journal*, which depended for its effect on its unusual conditions of composition. Mitchel was able, however, to continue producing historical narratives which suspended history by re-using elements of the 'Introductory Narrative' of the *Jail Journal* in subsequent texts, and refusing to develop those texts beyond the point of his own departure from Ireland in 1848. Hence, neither his *Last Conquest of Ireland (Perhaps)* of 1861, nor his 1868 *History of Ireland From the Treaty of Limerick to the Present Time*[12] brings Irish history any further than 1851; in both cases, the treatment of the period after Mitchel's deportation in May of 1848 is cursory. By structurally creating a suspension of history, all three of these texts erase the 'pastness' of the Famine, thereby inscribing it in the present of his readers. The Famine not only existed: it continues to exist every time Mitchel's texts are read.

The horror and desolation of official red tape

A form of historical writing which emulates its reader's own experience has the potential to influence the way in which the past is interpreted –

and, as Patrick O'Farrell has argued, Mitchel's reading of the Famine as a deliberate act of genocide has shaped much contemporary Irish historiographic practice.[13] More recently, Graham Davis has argued that the idea of the Famine created by Mitchel provides the narrative structure for one of the most popular pieces of historical writing of recent years, Cecil Woodham-Smith's *The Great Hunger*, which went through six large editions between 1962 and 1980. 'Although the tone was politer than the emotive rhetoric employed by Mitchel', writes Davis, 'Woodham-Smith's narrative of the unfolding drama was equally forthright in condemning the ideological blindness demonstrated by the British government'.[14]

In Mitchel's writing of the Famine, true horror lies not in death from cholera or starvation – but in the increased amount of governmental control which such widespread deprivation occasioned. Indeed, a passage like the following, which places a representation of a Poor House in the context of gothic horror, suggests succinctly the ways in which Mitchel was capable of deploying literary conventions to invest the faceless processes of bureaucratic decision making with a mask of active evil:

> Rearing its accursed gables and pinnacles of Tudor barbarism, and staring boldly with its detestable mullioned windows, as if to mock those wretches who still cling to liberty and mud cabins – seeming to them, in their perennial half-starvation, like a Temple erected to the Fates, or like the fortress of Giant Despair, whereinto he draws them one by one, and devours them there: – the Poor-house.[15]

Mitchel's understanding of the function of the Poor House anticipates Foucault's analysis of 'The Great Confinement', the post-enlightenment need to incarcerate the 'other' of the emerging bourgeois society. 'The house of confinement in the classical age', writes Foucault, 'constitutes the densest symbol of that "police" which conceived of itself as the civil equivalent of religion for the edification of a perfect city'.[16] 'And, for the "institutions of the country,"' writes Mitchel, 'I loathe and despise them; we are sickening and dying of these institutions, fast; they are consuming us like a plague, degrading us to paupers in mind, body, and estate... from the top-most crown jewel to the meanest detective's note-book'.[17] For Mitchel, the 'institutions' which had been established by the state, ostensibly for the prevention of suffering, were in fact instruments of imperial hegemony. Later in *The Last Conquest*, when bringing his account of the Famine to a close, he writes: 'No sack of Magdeburg, or ravage of the Palatinate ever approached in horror and desolation to the slaughters done in Ireland by mere official red tape and stationery, and the principles of political economy'.[18]

An interpretation of the Famine which reads it as an aspect of state hegemony has the potential to be deployed by a subversive critique of hunger and political power. However, most later writers who have made use of Mitchel have done so in ways which neutralize the radicalism of his texts. A case in point is the Irish-American writer, D. P. Conyngham whose 1903 novel, *The O'Donnells of Glen Cottage: A Tale of the Famine Years in*

Ireland, makes use of Mitchel's accounts of the Famine in ways which bring Mitchel into line with the concerns of Conyngham and the Catholic Excelsior Press of New York, which printed the book. 'This potato blight and consequent famine were powerful engines of state to uproot millions of the peasantry, to preserve law and order,' says one of Conyngham's characters, paraphrasing Mitchel, 'and to clear off surplus population, and to maintain the integrity of the British empire'.[19] Indeed, Conyngham blends Mitchel's texts with his own novel so skilfully that it is difficult to see where one ends and the other begins. But then, Conyngham was well placed to do so, for he had already appropriated Mitchel for a Catholic reading of Irish history when he edited a massive one-volume history of Ireland made up of Abbé Mac-Geohegan's seventeenth-century account of early and medieval Ireland, Mitchel's *History of Ireland*, and Conyngham's own 'continuation' of Mitchel's history.[20] This 'continuation' included, along with accounts of the Irish Tenant League and the Fenian rising, a chapter dealing with the American Civil War, suggesting the degree to which Irish-Americans saw the history of the United States as a continuation of the 'unfinished' history of Ireland – a history which was seen as unfinished precisely because it was recorded in texts such as Mitchel's *Jail Journal* and *Last Conquest of Ireland (Perhaps)*, which present an historical narrative of incompletion.

In *The O'Donnells of Glen Cottage*, however, it is in the novel's attitudes towards social policy that we can see the usefulness of Mitchel for an Irish-American Catholic writer like Conyngham. Mitchel's attacks on the Poor Laws and their attendant apparatus (the Poor Houses, relief works, and soup kitchens) arose from his rejection of the scientific state *per se* – particularly in so far as that state was British:

> They [the Relief Acts] have always appeared to me a machinery for the destruction of an enemy more fatal, by far, than batteries of grape-shot, chain-shot, shells, and rockets: but many persons who pass for intelligent, even in Ireland, do believe yet that they were in some sort measures of *Relief*, not contrivances for slaughter.[21]

The ease with which this standpoint can be assimilated into a conservative Catholic social perspective can be seen by comparing this passage written by Mitchel in 1858 with the following passage from Conyngham, writing under vastly different social conditions for an American Catholic audience in 1903. Where Mitchel sees such institutions as the Poor House, the asylum, or government assistance to the poor as a means of limiting individual freedom, for Conyngham, government involvement in social welfare is seen as secular interference in what is properly the domain of the Catholic Church:

> The best legal enactments for providing for the maintenance of the poor seem somehow to clash against the wise dispensations of Providence; for even a casual observer must see that the best safeguards against extreme poverty lie in that charitable feeling planted by Nature in our bosoms...In fact the system has transformed the whole nature of charity...The poor laws are an encouragement

to vice; they support the unfortunate and her offspring, they take in the forsaken mother and her children... We see what good is effected in towns by pious communities.[22]

Conyngham recognizes that responsibility for the care of the poor is a form of power; moreover, he recognizes that it is a power which the Catholic Church was increasingly ceding to the state. By alluding to Mitchel, he equates social welfare with British imperialism, and sets in motion a complex set of antipathies to state controlled welfare *per se*. This allows him, in passages like the one above, to transform those antipathies into support for church-sponsored philanthropy.

Conyngham was not alone in using Mitchel in this way. In 1907, an Irish Jesuit, Fr. Joseph Guinan, S.J., delivered a lecture before a Co. Longford audience entitled *The Famine Years*, which was later published by the Catholic Truth Society of Dublin. Guinan's pamphlet makes extensive (although highly selective) use of Mitchel's accounts of the Irish Famine, reproducing passages from Mitchel's histories of the Famine, such as that referring to 'twenty steam-ships...carrying away food in the shape of corn, sheep, pigs or cattle' meeting ships from England carrying 'to Ireland 10,000 books and ledgers, fourteen tons of paper, and red-tape enough to stretch from Cork to Donegal'.[23] Guinan, like Conyngham, writing half a century after Mitchel and the Famine, is using Mitchel as an authenticating voice in a polemic against governmental control of social welfare, quoting Mitchel's description of the Poor House as a 'fortress of Giant Despair' with the comment: 'The Government of the country having failed to do its duty, there was no alternative but to appeal to the charitable all over the world', praising in particular 'the priests and doctors, nuns and nurses, and workhouse officers at home, who died of fever at the post of duty'.[24]

Our greater Ireland beyond the sea

> We'll put force against force, says the citizen. We have our greater Ireland beyond the sea. They were driven out of house and home in the black 47. Their mudcabins and their sheilings by the roadside were laid low by the battering ram and the *Times* rubbed its hands and told the whitelivered Saxons there would soon be as few Irish in Ireland as redskins in America. Even the grand Turk sent us his piastres. But the Sassenach tried to starve the nation at home while the land was full of crops that the British hyenas bought and sold in Rio de Janeiro. Ay, they drove out the peasants in hordes. Twenty thousand of them died in the coffinships. But those that came to the land of the free remember the land of bondage.[25]

If we take into account the prominence of James Joyce's *Ulysses* in Irish literary studies, this passage from the 'Cyclops' episode of the novel has probably been read by more students of Irish literature than any other considered in this study. Its distinctive details – the '*Times* rubbing its hands', the 'grand Turk' sending charity, and the mention of Rio de Janeiro – are paraphrases of well-known passages in Mitchel's writings.[26] By putting Mitchel's words in the mouth of the Citizen, who is identified with 'force, hatred, history, all that... the very opposite of that that is really life',[27] Joyce in effect accuses Mitchel of fostering hatred in the name of liberation. Indeed, the details which Joyce takes from Mitchel deal with race, particularly the mention of the 'grand Turk' and the 'redskins', thereby identifying Mitchel with the discourse of racial hatred which runs throughout the 'Cyclops' episode, culminating in an attack on the Jewish Leopold Bloom. Nor is this association without some justification, considering Mitchel's support for slavery, and his notorious comparison of the amount spent on Irish Famine relief and the 'twenty millions borrowed to turn negroes wild (set them "free" as it was called)'.[28]

This is not to say, however, that the nationalist use of Mitchel's Famine texts did not continue unabated, in spite of Joyce's critique. In the same year that Joyce completed *Ulysses*, 1919, Louis J. Walsh (with whom Joyce had debated Mangan's status as a nationalist poet when both were university students)[29] appropriated Mitchel's images of the Famine for his novel *The Next Time*. Walsh, an ardent nationalist even as a student, knew Mitchel's writings well, and was later to publish a hagiographic biography of Mitchel in 1934.[30] *The Next Time* suggests the degree to which he had assimilated a Mitchelite view of the Famine, for most of Walsh's descriptions of the Famine are taken, almost *verbatim*, from Mitchel's texts, but are not acknowledged as such. Hence, we find a chapter entitled 'Damn Their Economics', in which the novel's hero, Art O'Donnell, seeing men struggling with a relief project, asks: 'Wouldn't the greatest massacres in battle or even deaths at the stake have been pleasant compared with that slow torture!'[31] 'The horrors of war', wrote Mitchel of life during the Famine, 'were by no means so terrible as the horrors of peace'.[32]

Walsh's Art O'Donnell enacts Mitchel's desire 'to see blood flow' after witnessing his countrymen starve, joins the Young Ireland movement, and dies in the failed rebellion of 1848. Before he marches off to battle, however, he marries a peasant woman, Mary, whose heroism in caring for the victims of typhus is explicitly linked to Art's heroism in battle. This connection is important for a nationalist propagandist such as Walsh, for it allows him to treat the victims of the Famine as republican martyrs, whose passive deaths are equated with those who have died in military struggle. In making this association, his concerns intersect with those of a Catholic writer such as Guinan, who dogmatically asserts that the priests who died attending the Famine victims 'are known as the martyr priests'.[33] Similarly, the passive deaths of the Famine victims are read by Guinan as a triumph for religious faith:

> The calm, uncomplaining resignation with which they met death in its most terrible shapes was more than human. It was sublime. Their faith and the consolation of their religion lifted them above the utter misery of their earthly lot, while hope in their Father Who is in Heaven kept their dying eyes fixed on the shining path which led to the golden gates.[34]

In texts such as these we see the Famine, spiritual transcendence and nationalist martyrdom linked in an emotively powerful intertextual construct which is presented as an accurate representation of the past. Indeed, this use of the Famine, which transforms passive suffering into active triumph, may help to explain the resonance of the hunger strike in republican iconography.

It is worth noting that one of the most popular works of Famine literature, Liam O'Flaherty's *Famine* of 1937, functions as something of a corrective to the glorification of passive suffering that one finds in Guinan and other writers in the Catholic tradition. O'Flaherty, like the other novelists considered here, makes unacknowledged use of Mitchel, at one point quoting from a Royal Irish Constabulary 'Constable's Guide' of 1846 cited by Mitchel[35] commenting: 'In a word, the unfortunate people of Crom parish were treated as if they were in a state of criminal and armed insurrection, instead of their being on the point of destruction by famine'.[36] In O'Flaherty's writing of the Famine, however, starvation leads not to a self-effacing heroism, but to a brute struggle for survival. 'Under the pressure of hunger', he writes, 'as among soldiers at war, the mask of civilisation quickly slips from the human soul, showing the brute savage beneath, struggling to preserve life at all costs'.[37] Indeed, in his emphasis on struggle, O'Flaherty is closer to Mitchel's own radicalism than any of the more orthodox nationalists who have recycled Mitchel's texts.

The semiotics of starvation

In order for these appropriations of Mitchel's interpretation of the Famine as bureaucratic genocide to succeed, they must convince their readers of their accuracy as historical representations. *The Next Time*, for instance, is structured so that an experience of witnessing the Famine motivates Art O'Donnell to join the nationalist rising. Hence, if the novel is to function as propaganda, it must convince its readers that they too have witnessed the Famine. The passage in *The Next Time* which provides this experience (and acts as the turning point in the novel) occurs as Art is returning home to Gortnanan from Dublin at the height of the Famine:

> In fields, as the coach passed, he could see cowering wretches, almost naked in the savage weather, endeavouring to grub up roots that had been left in the ground when the crop was dug....In front of cottages you would sometimes see half naked children leaning against the fence – for they were too weak to stand...– their limbs fleshless, and their faces a sickening hue.[38]

This passage is able to function as an authentic representation of the Famine not because its author, Walsh, could claim that it is original, based on his own experience – such experience would clearly be impossible for a writer like Walsh, born in 1880. Instead, it reverses the conventional literary association of authenticity and originality, and lays claim to authenticity because it echoes a much more famous description of the Famine by 'the greatest Irishman, after O'Connell, of the nineteenth century',[39] Fr. Theobald Mathew. 'On the 27th of last month [July]', wrote Mathew in 1846:

> I passed from Cork to Dublin, and this doomed plant [the potato] bloomed in all the luxuriance of an abundant harvest. Returning on the 3rd instant [of August] I beheld with sorrow one wide waste of putrefying vegetation. In many places the wretched people were seated on the fences of their decaying gardens, wringing their hands and wailing bitterly the destruction that had left them foodless.[40]

Apart from the authority of its author, this particular passage has joined the vocabulary of Famine imagery because of its perspective. Mathew's view of Ireland through the window of a coach (the essential element repeated by Walsh) allows an accumulation of details without the necessity of narrative linkage. This montage-like structure is characteristic of much literature of the Famine – and, once again, it is Mitchel who provides the prototype in the introduction to his *Jail Journal*:

> There is no need to recount how the assistant barristers and sheriffs, aided by the police, tore down the roof-tress and ploughed up the hearths of village after village – how the quarter-acre clause laid waste the parishes, how the farmers and their wives and little ones in wild dismay, trooped along the highways – how in some hamlets by the seaside, most of the inhabitants being already dead, an adventurous traveller would come upon some family eating a famished ass – how maniac mothers stowed away their dead children to be devoured at midnight – how Mr. Darcy of Clifden, describes a humane gentleman going to the door of a house; 'and when he threw the crackers to the children (for he was afraid to enter), the mother attempted to take them from them' – how husband and wife fought like wolves for the last morsel of food in the house; how families, when all was eaten and no hope left, took their last look at the sun, built up their cottage doors, that none might see them die nor hear their groans, and were found weeks afterwards, skeletons on their own hearths...[41]

Reading this passage, one has the feeling that normal conditions – including the conventions of sentence structure – no longer apply. The syntax of the piece is fragmented, unrelated incidents are joined by dashes and commas, and there is no causal connection between one image and the next. Mitchel is able to make this unusual form of writing appear acceptable by telling his readers, in the passage's opening words, that 'there is no need to recount' what he is about to recount. In other words, he is telling his readers that they already know what they are about to hear – that these images are in the domain of public memory.

There is a striking structural similarity between this passage from Mitchel's *Jail Journal* and the paragraph from Canon Sheehan's 1905 novel, *Glenanaar*, with which this chapter opened:

> It is an appalling picture, that which springs up to memory. Gaunt spectres move here and there, looking at one another out of hollow eyes of despair and

gloom. Ghosts walk the land. Great giant figures, reduced to skeletons by hunger, shake in their clothes, which hang loose around their attenuated frames. Mothers try to still their children's cries of hunger by bringing their cold, blue lips to milkless breasts. Here and there by the wayside a corpse stares at the passers-by, as it lies against the hedge where it had sought shelter. The pallor of its face is darkened by lines of green around the mouth, the dry juice of grass and nettles. All day long the carts are moving to the graveyards with their ghastly, staring, uncoffined loads.[42]

Again, we have the opening statement that what follows is available through 'memory'; and again, although Sheehan uses conventional syntax, the sequence of images are not linked by any cause and effect narrative.

By the time that Sheehan was writing in 1905, each of the 'memories' in his Famine sequence has a literary genealogy. The dying mother and child, for instance, can be found in 'The Three Angels' of 1848, a poem by one of *The Nation*'s most prolific contributors, John De Jean Frazer,[43] as well as in an often anthologized poem written at the time of the Famine, 'The Dying Mother's Lament', written in the 1840s by John Keegan, whose collected *Legends and Poems* were reprinted in 1907.[44] Similarly, the 'gaunt spectre striding about the countryside' can be found in poems which date from the time of the Famine, such as the anonymous 'Spectre' of 1851:

Far west a grim shadow was seen, as 'tis said,
Like a spectre from Famine and Pestilence bred:
His gaunt giant-form, with pale Poverty wed...[45]

It is used again in 'The Funerals', a poem James Clarence Mangan wrote in 1849, the last year of his life, which creates an image of a countryside overwhelmed by walking skeletons.[46] Both the image of the dead mother and the stalking skeleton maintained their currency because of their metaphorical nature, the dead mother suggesting the dead (Mother) earth in the former, and the roaming 'spectre' of the latter suggesting the spread of the potato blight, typhus and cholera, as in Guinan's use of the image, when he writes that 'the dread spectre of famine had already set foot on the shores of Ireland, and was making ready to stalk through the fruitful land'.[47] Yet, at the same time that it is metaphorical, the image of the walking dead is historically 'true', in so far as it was put forward as a literal representation of reality at the time of the Famine. 'The streets of every town in the country', reported the *Mayo Constitution* in a report reprinted by Mitchel's *United Irishman*, 'are overrun by stalking skeletons'.[48]

The unnaturalness of both of these images – the dead mother suckling her child, and the 'stalking spectre' – is foregrounded in the image of the corpse with a mouth made green from having eaten nettles. This image also dates from the time of the Famine, and can be found in poems like 'The Boreen Side', first published in 1849:

A stripling, the last of his race, lies dead
In a nook by the Boreen side;

> The rivulet runs by his board and his bed,
>   Where he ate the green cresses and died.[49]

Or, again from a newspaper account of an inquest held in 1848, we find:

> A poor man, whose name we could not learn...lay down on the road-side, where shortly after he was found dead, his face turned to the earth, and a portion of the grass and turf on which he lay masticated in his mouth.[50]

We can see this process of self-perpetuating allusiveness at work if we imagine a reader of Sheehan's 1905 novel coming across Guinan's Catholic Truth Society pamphlet of 1908 (as well that reader might). In such a case, the reader would find that the following passage (an unaccredited paraphrase of the account of the grass-eating Famine victim from Mitchel's *United Irishman*) would have a ring of truth. And it would seem true not because it conformed to a lived experience of the Famine (which few readers would have had in 1908), but because it conformed to what had come to be accepted as a 'true' image of the Famine; that is to say, it made reference to other Famine texts:

> In Mayo a man, who had been observed searching for shell-fish on the seashore, was afterwards found dead, after vainly endeavouring to satisfy the cravings of devouring hunger with grass and turf.[51]

When we find an image repeated in a number of texts, we should keep in mind that it is not enough to document the 'influence' of one textual version of the image upon another. Because all of the texts containing the image exist simultaneously, they refer to one another synchronically, not diachronically. Moreover, in the case of certain images – such as the grass-eating man, the dead mother, and the walking skeleton – we find that they have acted as signifiers of 'famine' prior to the 1840s, as in this description of the Munster famine of 1580 by Edmund Spenser:

> Out of euerie Corner of the woodes & glennes they came crepinge forth vpon theire handes, for theire legges could not beare them, they looked Anotomies of death, they spake like ghostes cryinge out of their graues, they did eate of the dead Carrions, happye were they could fynde them...and yf they founde a plott of water cresses or shamrockes, there they flocked as to a feast for the tyme, yet not able longe to contynewe therewithall, that in shorte space there were none almost left.[52]

When we recall that Spenser used this image – which we have seen employed by nationalist writers – for the very unnationalistic purpose of proving that the native Irish were in fact little better than animals, we are given an indication of the ideological mutability of such images. Hence, we can say that although narratives of the Famine are almost never free from the structures of a particular ideological understanding of the past, individual images are open structures, capable of appropriation from a range of ideological positions.

By the turn of the century, the frequency with which such images had been repeated transformed them into a group of signs whose presence in a text signifies, in the first instance, 'famine'. The existence of such a semiotic vocabulary of anecdotes and images enabled writers like Sheehan to write of the Famine in an allusive shorthand, stringing together images with a multiplicity of referents whose genealogies extended back through a history of famines. Every time an image or anecdote from this fund was repeated it gained added credence. Every use of an image reinforces its place in the discursive world of the Famine, and increases the number of texts to which it makes silent reference.

Dismembered memories

The ability of such an intertextual web to maintain its claims to representational accuracy is not without limit, for once an image is repeated too many times its textual nature is recognized, and it becomes a cliché. However, two recent texts – Irish-American Alan Ryan's 1984 novel, *Cast a Cold Eye* and Irish-Canadian James J. Mangan's *Famine Diary* of 1991 – suggest that this point has not yet been reached with the key Famine signifiers when they are allied to literary representations of migration. The two works approach the experience of migration from opposite angles: Mangan writes of an emigration from Ireland in the nineteenth century, and Ryan tells of a third generation Irish-American visiting Ireland in the 1980s.

Ryan's novel, with its dust jacket endorsements by William Peter Blatty, author of *The Exorcist*, and Peter Straub, author of *Ghost Story*, follows the conventions of contemporary horror fiction. It deals with a writer, Jack Quinlan, who, having grown up in an Irish-American family in which 'a knowledge of Ireland is in the air',[53] arrives in Ireland to write an historical novel dealing with the Famine. On arriving in Ireland, he buys 'three dozen'[54] books, mostly dealing with the Famine, which he takes with him to a cottage outside Doolin, Co. Clare. Walking back to his cottage one dark night, however, he sees a vision of a Famine victim:

> He was as pale as a corpse in the windy moonlight, his head and face little more than a skull: eyes now hollow sockets, bony ridge of forehead protruding, parchment cheeks empty of flesh, white teeth exposed by withered lips. The lips and chin were stained and a dark saliva dribbled from one corner of his mouth and ran down onto his neck. Green, Jack thought, and leaned closer over the man's face to see better. The stains on the man's mouth and chin were green and the bubbling saliva on his lips was green. He'd been eating what? The weeds? He'd been eating the weeds?[55]

As Quinlan approaches the ghostly figure, it disappears. Later, as he tries to explain the apparition to himself, he recalls that 'the vision matched the very things he'd read'.[56] After several weeks, the experience is repeated when Quinlan sees a woman crouched in the road, who holds out to him 'a filthy bundle' which turns out to be an 'infant stretched out on its back, limp and lifeless, the head lolling back on a boneless neck, the legs dangling loose'.[57] In both cases the images – the man with the green mouth and the dying mother with her dead infant – are familiar from a range of Famine texts, including the passage which 'sprang to memory' for Canon Sheehan in *Glenanaar*. In *Cast A Cold Eye*, however, Famine 'memories' are represented as partially the product of a cultural inheritance carried by the Irish community throughout the diaspora, and partially the product of prior reading. This latter suggestion hints at a nascent awareness of the textual nature of memory; however, the text as a whole resists this awareness, which would challenge the assumption of a supernatural link bonding members of the 'Irish race' throughout the world.

This resistance is more graphically enacted in James J. Mangan's *Famine Diary*, published by Dublin's Wolfhound Press in 1991. Wolfhound published the *Famine Diary* as the diary of Gerald Keegan, a Sligo schoolmaster who migrated to Canada in 1847. It represents Ireland during the Famine in terms which are by now familiar, with 'the twin spectres, famine and pestilence, hold[ing] sway over the land'[58] – and, of course, there is a mention of men 'found dead with grass in their mouth'.[59] It also includes a narrative of a Famine migration to Canada, culminating in the narrator's death from typhus on arrival in Grosse Île, Quebec. This text is framed by an epilogue, which claims to tell how the manuscript was recovered after Keegan's death in 1847, and a preface which presents a De la Salle brother, James Mangan, as its modern editor. In his preface, Mangan mentions that the text had been published previously in 1895, 'but was apparently censored by the government'.[60]

However, as Jim Jackson points out in a recent essay in the *Irish Review*, when the *Famine Diary* was published by Carraig Books of Quebec in 1982 as *The Voyage of the Naparima*, it contained a number of pieces of vital textual apparatus omitted from the Dublin edition. In the first place, the 1982 Canadian edition makes it clear that the 1895 text which Mangan edited as the *Famine Diary* was not written by a Sligo schoolmaster in 1847. It was written by a Scottish-Canadian journalist, Robert Sellar, as one of a collection of tales entitled *The Summer of Sorrow, Abner's Device and Other Stories* which attempted, as its preface states, 'to convey in a readable form an ideal of an era in the life of Canada which has passed – that of its first settlement by emigrants from the British Isles'.[61] In other words, the *Famine Diary* is not an authentic transcription of migrant experience during the Famine: it is a work of historical fiction based on an earlier work of historical fiction. 'In editing and presenting Keegan's diary', writes Mangan in his preface, 'I wished to make it intelligible to readers who might not be familiar with the historical background of the mass emigration movement from Ireland in 1847'.[62] In rewriting Sellar's tale, Mangan included additional material taken from a number of sources, which were listed in a bibliography included in the 1982 Canadian edition, but omitted from the Dublin edition. This bibliography, which, as Jackson points out, 'provides interesting reading in itself,' was made up of Woodham-Smith's *The Great Hunger*, 'three 19th-centuries histories of Ireland and two historical novels published in the 1930s'[63] – including Mitchel's *History of Ireland*. The 1991 Dublin edition of the *Famine Diary*, by omitting this information, effectively erases the intertextual nature of the *Diary*, presenting it as a pure transcription of experience, an authentic act of memory.

The case of the *Famine Diary* provides a focus for the ethical problem which the Famine continues to pose. Canon Sheehan's claim that the Famine 'springs to memory' is analogous to the use of Mitchel's Famine writings by Conyngham, Guinan, O'Flaherty and Walsh: both textual strategies naturalize literary representation as memory. Like the more unusual steps taken by Mangan's Dublin publishers, these strategies attest to a need to have *real* memories of the Famine. The Famine – those thousands of lost lives and ways of life, those thousands of experiences of suffering beyond imagination – call out for some sort of memorial, much as the Holocaust does in the Jewish experience. And yet, an analysis of the literature of the Famine tells us that no narrative of the Famine is ever pure. Every Famine text partakes of other discourses, whether militant nationalism (Mitchel and Walsh), Catholic social policy (Conyngham and Guinan) or simply commercial horror fiction in the case of Alan Ryan's *Cast a Cold Eye*. As such, we must recognize that the Famine is being mobilized by these texts in support of their own agendas, and that unless we wish to be manipulated by these agendas, we must learn to be critical in our analysis of fictional representation. The need to bear witness thus stands opposed to the need for analytical criticism; remembering opposed to dismembering. And yet, both needs have deep and legitimate claims upon our attention which any attempt at coming to terms with the legacy of the Famine amongst the Irish diaspora ignores at its peril.

Notes

1. Patrick Sheehan, *Glenanaar*, Longmans, London, 1905; reprinted O'Brien, Dublin, 1989, pp. 198–9.
2. Cormac Ó Gráda,*The Great Irish Famine*, Gill and Macmillan, Dublin, 1989; Mokyr, Joel, *Why Ireland Starved: A Quantitative and Analytical History of the Irish Economy, 1800–1850*, George Allen and Unwin, London, 1983; revised edn., 1985.
3. It could be argued, of course that all forms of representation, even the most ostensibly scientific, rely upon metaphor, metonymy of synecdoche to some degree. By 'literary representation' in this case, however, I refer to those forms of writing which depend upon such tropes to an unusual extent, and which foreground that dependence, thus including forms of writing not usually considered 'literary', such as the nineteenth-century narrative history, or the polemical pamphlet.
4. Luke 10:30.
5. John De Jean Frazer, 'The Queen's Visit', *Irishman*, Vol. 1, No. 31, 4 August, 1849, p. 488; in Chris Morash (ed.), *The Hungry Voice: The Poetry of the Irish Famine*, Irish Academic Press, Dublin, 1989, p. 188.
6. Roland Barthes, 'De l'oeuvre au texte', *Revue d'esthétique*, 1971, p. 229; cited in Jonathan Culler, *The Pursuit of Signs: Semiotics, Literature, Deconstruction*, Routledge and Kegan Paul, London and Henley, 1981, p. 103.

7.   John Mitchel, *Jail Journal, Commenced on board the 'Shearwater' steamer, Dublin Bay, continued at Spike Island – on board the 'Scourge' war steamer – on board the 'Dromedary' hulk, Bermuda – on board the 'Neptune' convict ship – at Pernambuco – at the Cape of Good Hope (during the anti-convict rebellion) – at Van Dieman's land – at Greytown – and concluding at No. 3 Pier, North River, New York. With an introductory narrative of transactions in Ireland*. Irish Citizen Office, New York, 1854; reprinted University Press of Ireland, Shannon, 1982.

8.   David Lloyd, *Nationalism and Minor Literature: James Clarence Mangan and the Emergence of Irish Cultural Nationalism*, University of California Press, Berkeley, Los Angeles, London, 1987, pp. 49–50.

9.   Mitchel, *Jail Journal*, p. liv.

10. Mitchel, *Jail Journal*, p. 71.

11. Mitchel, *Jail Journal*, p. 134.

12. John Mitchel, *The Last Conquest of Ireland (Perhaps)*, 1861, reprinted Burns, Oates and Washbourne, London, n.d.; John Mitchel, *The History of Ireland from The Treaty of Limerick to the Present Time*, 2 vols, 1868; reprinted James Duffy, Dublin, n.d.

13. Patrick O'Farrell, 'Whose reality? the Irish Famine in history and literature', *Historical Studies*, Vol. 20, No. 78, April 1982, pp. 1–13.

14. Graham Davis, 'Making history: John Mitchel and the Great Famine', in Paul Hyland and Neil Sammells (eds), *Irish Writing: Exile and Subversion*, Macmillan, London, p. 101.

15. Mitchel, *Last Conquest*, p. 116.

16. Michel Foucault, *Madness and Civilization: A History of Insanity in the Age of Reason*, trans. Richard Howard, Tavistock, London, 1961, p. 63.

17. Mitchel, *Last Conquest*, p. 179.

18. Mitchel, *Last Conquest*, p. 218.

19. David Power Conyngham, *The O'Donnells of Glen Cottage: A Tale of the Famine Years in Ireland*, P.J. Kenedy and Sons, Excelsior Catholic Publishing House, New York, 1903, p. 275.

20. David Power Conyngham, *The History of Ireland, Ancient and Modern, Taken from the Authentic Records, and dedicated to the Irish Brigade. By the Abbé Mac-Geohegan. With a continuation from the Treaty of Limerick to the year 1882, by John Mitchel. Revised and continued to the present time by D.P. Conyngham, LL.D.* P.J. Kenedy and Sons, Excelsior Catholic Publishing House, n.d.

21. Mitchel, *Last Conquest*, p. 102.

22. Conyngham, *O'Donnells*, p. 440.

23. Joseph Guinan, *The Famine Years*, Catholic Truth Society, Dublin, 1908, pp. 9, 12; Mitchel, *Last Conquest*, p. 131; Mitchel, *History*, II, p. 417.

24. Guinan, pp. 16, 28.

25. James Joyce, *Ulysses*, 1922, ed. Hans Walter Gabler, Wolfhard Steppe, and Claus Melchior, Penguin, Harmondsworth, 1986, p. 270.

26. The reference to *The Times* and Turkish charity are direct paraphrases of Mitchel: Mitchel, *Last Conquest*, p. 92; Mitchel, *History*, II, p. 414. The mention of Rio de Janeiro has more distinctly Joycean twist. While Mitchel does not mention seeing Irish goods arrive in Brazil, a section of the *Jail Journal* was written in Brazil. It contains one of Mitchel's justifications of slavery, linking it thematically to the concern with racism which runs throughout the 'Cyclops' episode. One Joycean suggests that the mention of the 'lordly Shannon' earlier in the episode is also taken from Mitchel's *Jail Journal*, when Mitchel, looking at the River Shannon in Tasmania, 'dreams of its lordly namesake in Erin': Don Gifford, *'Ulysses' Annotated*, 2nd edition University of California Press, Berkeley, Los Angeles, London, 1988, 12.112 (p . 319).

27. Joyce, p. 331.
28. Mitchel, *Last Conquest*, p. 94.
29. Richard Ellmann, *James Joyce*, 1959, revised edn., Oxford University Press, London, New York, 1982, p. 96.
30. Louis J. Walsh, *John Mitchel*, Talbot Press, Dublin, 1934.
31. Louis J. Walsh, *The Next Time: A Story of 'Forty Eight*, M.H. Gill and Sons, Dublin, 1919, p. 165.
32. Mitchel, *Last Conquest*, p. 428.
33. Guinan, p. 28.
34. Guinan, p. 25.
35. Mitchel, *Last Conquest*, p. 101.
36. Liam O'Flaherty, *Famine*, 1937, reprinted Wolfhound, Dublin, 1984, p. 254.
37. O'Flaherty, p. 347.
38. Walsh, *Next Time*, pp. 155–6.
39. Guinan, p. 6.
40. Mathew cited in John O'Rourke, *History of the Great Irish Famine*, McGlashan and Gill, Dublin, 1875, p. 152. Sources such as Guinan indicate that O'Rourke's history of the Famine was still popular in the early twentieth century. However, the Mathew passage was often reprinted.
41. Mitchel, *Jail Journal*, p. xlix.
42. Sheehan, pp. 198–9.
43. John De Jean Frazer, 'The Three Angels', *Cork Magazine*, Vol. 1, No. 31, August, 1848, p. 602; in Morash, pp. 186–7.
44. John Keegan, 'The Dying Mother's Lament', *Legends and Poems*, Sealy, Byrne and Walker, Dublin, 1907; in Morash, p. 58.
45. *The Spectre: Stanzas with illustrations*, Thomas M'Lean, London, 1851; in Morash, p. 261.
46. James Clarence Mangan, 'The Funerals', *Irishman*, Vol. 1, No. 13, 31 March 1849; in Morash, pp. 133–4.
47. Guinan, p. 6.
48. 'Death by Starvation,' *United Irishman*, Vol. 1, No. 5, 11 March 1848, p. 46.
49. James Tighe, 'The Boreen Side', *Irishman*, Vol. 1, No. 39, 29 September 1849, p. 616; in Morash, p. 73.
50. 'Inquests,' *United Irishman*, Vol. 1, No. 14, 13 May 1848, p. 211.
51. Guinan, p. 15.
52. Edmund Spenser, *A View of the Present State of Ireland*, 1596; reprinted W.L. Renwick, Scholartis Press, London, 1934, p. 135.
53. Alan Ryan, *Cast a Cold Eye*, Tom Doherty Associates, New York, 1984, pp. 106–07.
54. Ryan, p. 29.
55. Ryan, pp. 73–4.
56. Ryan, p. 77.
57. Ryan, p. 88.
58. James J. Mangan, *Famine Diary: Journey to a New World*, Carraig Books, Quebec, 1982; reprinted Wolfhound, Dublin, 1991, p. 14.
59. Mangan, *Famine Diary*, p. 22.
60. Mangan, *Famine Diary*, p. 10.
61. Jim Jackson, 'Famine Diary – The Making of a Best Sellar', *Irish Review*, 11, Winter 1991/1992, p. 3.
62. Mangan, *Famine Diary*, p. 10.
63. Jackson, p. 6.

3 The Famine Irish in England and Wales

Frank Neal

The Famine Irish into Britain

Improvements in marine technology, and the subsequent introduction of steamships on the routes between Ireland and Britain from 1820 onwards, increased the number of Irish people travelling to mainland Britain.[1] By 1841, there were relatively large Irish communities in several British towns, principally Liverpool, London, Glasgow, Manchester and Salford. However, it was the increased level of immigration during and following the failures of the potato crops over the years 1845–49 which brought about a dramatic and significant increase in both the size and number of such communities. The magnitude of the Famine inflow, and the physical and economic condition of the majority of those making up the refugees posed major problems for the authorities in the recipient towns. The Great Hunger in Ireland coincided with increased population movements into British towns from the countryside and a number of reports revealed the severe problems accompanying rapid urban growth, in particular, poor housing, lack of sanitation and water supplies.[2] The large towns of northern England in particular were ill-equipped to receive a mass of destitute Irish, and for all concerned absorbing the Irish proved to be a far from painless process.

Table 3.1 Irish–born population of England, Wales and Scotland 1841–61

Area	Numbers of Irish-born residents (nearest 1,000)	Percentage of the population Irish-born
1841		
England & Wales	291,000	1.8
Scotland	126,000	4.8
1851		
England & Wales	520,000	2.9
Scotland	207,000	7.2
1861		
England & Wales	602,000	3.0
Scotland	204,000	6.6

Source: Census Reports, British Parliamentary Papers, 1841, 1851, 1861, 'Birthplaces of the People'

Table 3.2 Irish-born population of Wales, 1841 and 1851

County	1841			1851		
	Total pop.	Nos of Irish-born	Irish as % of total	Total pop.	Nos of Irish-born	Irish as % of total
Anglesey	50,891	137	0.23	43,443	338	0.78
Brecon	55,603	282	0.51	59,178	674	1.14
Cardigan	66,776	70	0.10	87,072	270	0.31
Carmarthen	106,321	163	0.15	94,672	514	0.54
Caernarvon	81,093	292	0.36	94,674	583	0.62
Denbigh	88,868	316	0.36	94,906	1,030	1.09
Flint	66,919	370	0.55	41,047	612	1.49
Glamorgan	171,188	3,174	1.85	240,095	9,737	4.06
Merioneth	39,332	52	0.13	39,927	77	0.19
Montgomery	69,219	95	0.14	77,133	205	0.03
Pembroke	88,044	292	0.33	84,472	703	0.83
Radnor	25,356	33	0.13	31,425	39	0.12
Totals	911,600	5,276	0.56	987,844	14,782	1.50

Source: Census Reports, British Parliamentary Papers: 1841 and 1851 'Birthplaces of the People'

Table 3.3 The increase in the Irish-born population of selected towns and cities over 1841–51

Town	1841	1851
Leeds (Borough)		
Population	152,054	172,270
Number of Irish-born	5,027	8,446
Irish as % of population	3.3	4.9
Birmingham (Borough)		
Population	182,922	232,841
Number of Irish-born	4,683	9,341
Irish as % of population	2.6	4.0
Bradford (Township & Borough)		
Population	34,560	103,778
Number of Irish-born	1,868	9,279
Irish as % of population	5.4	9.0
Bristol (City & County Hundred)		
Population	121,757	137,328
Number of Irish-born	4,039	4,645
Irish as % of population	3.3	3.4
Liverpool (Borough)		
Population	286,656	375,955
Number of Irish-born	49,639	83,813
Irish as % of population	17.3	22.3
Manchester/Salford (Town & Borough)		
Population	306,991	401,321
Number of Irish-born	33,490	52,504
Irish as % of population	11.06	13.1
London		
Population	1,873,676	2,362,236
Number of Irish-born	73,133	108,548
Irish as % of population	3.9	4.6
Sunderland (Town & Borough)		
Population	17,022	63,897
Number of Irish-born	695	3,601
Irish as % of population	4.1	5.6
Newcastle (Town & Borough)		
Population	33,238	87,784
Number of Irish-born	2,857	7,124
Irish as % of population	8.6	8.1
Macclesfield (Borough)		
Population	24,137	39,048
Number of Irish-born	900	2,358
Irish as % of population	3.7	6.0
Swansea (Borough)		
Population	16,787	31,461
Number of Irish-born	428	1,333
Irish as % of population	2.5	4.2
Hull (Town & Borough)		
Population	41628	84,690
No of Irish-born	1,044	2,983
Irish as % of population	2.5	3.5
Wigan (Borough & District)		
Population	25,519	77,539
Number of Irish-born	1,989	4,502
Irish as % of population	7.8	5.8
Carlisle (City)		
Population	24,016	26,310
Number of Irish-born	1,368	1,573
Irish as % of population	5.7	6.0

Source: Census Reports, British Parliamentary Papers, 1841 and 1851 'Birthplaces of the people'

Of the total *increase* of 229,000 Irish-born in England and Wales over the inter–censal period 1841–51, 65 per cent went to the northern counties, over 42 per cent going to Lancashire and Cheshire. Other areas in which the Irish congregated in relatively large numbers were the west of Scotland, the north-east of England, west Yorkshire, west Midlands, south Wales and London (see Table 3.3). These places had established Irish settlements before the Famine influx and all possessed a regional industrial base. At the level of individual towns, the degree of concentration was even more striking. The 1851 Census records 83,813 Irish-born residing in the borough of Liverpool, 22.3 per cent of the population; in Glasgow, the figure was 59,801 (18.1 per cent); Manchester and Salford, 52,504 (13.1 per cent) and London, 108,548 (4.6 per cent) An examination of the Census enumerators' sheets for smaller towns indicates even higher levels of density. For example, in the township of Prescot, near Liverpool, 1,607 or 25 per cent of the total population were Irish-born in 1851.[3]

The Irish-born population of Wales increased by 280 per cent from 5,276 in 1841 to 14,782 in 1851 (see Table 3.2). As in England, the concentration of Irish in specific areas is noticeable. In 1841, 60 per cent of all the Irish-born living in Wales were in Glamorgan. In 1851, the corresponding figure was 66 per cent.

In addition to the issue of concentration, two other factors need to be taken into account when assessing the impact of the Famine inflow into Britain. First, the large increase in the size of Irish communities resulting from the flight from Ireland took place over a relatively short period. The flood of refugees began to increase towards the end of 1846 following the disastrous return of the potato blight. Table 3.3 illustrates the scale of the inward migration into selected towns over the period which covers the period of the Famine crisis.

Liverpool is the town for which most data concerning Irish immigration exists and the scale of Liverpool's problem is shown in Table 3.4.

Table 3.4 Numbers of Irish landing at the Port of Liverpool in each of the years 1847–53

Year	Deck passengers, emigrants, jobbers & cabin passengers	Deck passengers (apparently paupers)	Total	Paupers as % of total
1847	180,231	116,000	296,231	39
1848	158,582	94,190	252,772	37
1849	160,437	80,468	240,925	33
1850	173,236	77,765	251,001	31
1851	215,369	68,134	283,503	24
1852	153,909	78,422	232,331	34
1853	162,299	71,353	233,652	31

Sources: The 1847 figures were quoted in the Head Constable's Report for 1848. The 1848 figures were estimated from newspaper reports of Irish landings at Liverpool. The 1849–53 figures were constructed from British Parliamentary Papers (HC), 1854 (300) LV, Return of the Number of Irish Poor Brought Over Monthly to Liverpool, p. 107

During 1847, 296,231 Irish landed at Liverpool and of this number 116,000 were officially described as paupers, i.e. having no visible means of support, and so likely to become a charge on the parish. Over the five years 1847 to 1851 inclusive, an estimated 436,788 paupers disembarked at the Clarence Dock, Liverpool; over the longer period, 1847 to 1853 inclusive, the corresponding figure was 586,563. Equally impressive, the size of Liverpool's Irish-born population increased by 34,174 between 1841 and 1851, a number exceeding the population of most Irish towns. Significantly, the Irish-born population of London increased by only 35,000. On a lesser scale the experience of enlarged Irish settlements was repeated throughout Britain. The main ports of entry were Liverpool, Glasgow, Cardiff, Swansea, Newport, Whitehaven, and to a lesser extent London and south coast ports. In addition to Liverpool, Newport in Monmouthshire was the only place to record the numbers of arrivals from Ireland, and then only during the tail end of the Famine crisis (see Table 3.5).[4]

Table 3.5 Arrivals at Newport from Ireland

Year	Numbers
1849	1702
1850	2140
1851	3739
1852	3052
1853	4812

Source: British Parliamentary Papers (HC), 1854 (300) LV, The number of Passengers landed at this Port from the Coast of Ireland, 1849–53

Unlike the authorities in Liverpool, the port officials at Newport did not distinguish between paupers and others. However, what is clear is that, when the inflow through Newport increased after 1849, the majority of Irish landing at the South Wales ports and Newport came principally via Cork.[5] By contrast, Edward Rushton, the very experienced stipendiary magistrate at Liverpool during the whole period of the Famine crisis, claimed that most Irish landing at Liverpool came from the far west of Ireland, particularly Mayo.[6] The second factor to be noted is that a large proportion of the Famine Irish arriving in Britain to stay were paupers, in a desperate physical condition from the effects of malnutrition and typhus, exacerbated by a gruelling journey to British ports on the overcrowded decks of cattle boats and colliers. During the winter and spring, many suffered from exposure on the waterlogged decks, some dying on the crossing, others dying soon after arrival in Liverpool, Newport and other ports.[7]

Arrival and survival

In judging the reaction of the indigenous population to the arrival of the Famine Irish, the relevance of their poor physical condition lay partly in the fact that local authorities had to finance an immediate increase in the level of poor relief and medical provision, paid for out of the poor rates. In addition, the Famine Irish immigrants were blamed by many for the typhus and cholera epidemics which raged through British towns in 1847 and 1849 respectively. In Liverpool and elsewhere, typhus was commonly referred to as the 'Irish fever' both in general conversation and official reports.[8] Compounding the effects of the immigration, the sudden influx of Irish into British towns occurred, significantly, at a time when a number of detailed investigations into the state of large towns had established a clear picture of the appalling conditions in which a large proportion of the English working-class population lived. These same reports also provide a picture of the pre-Famine Irish settlements in British towns and the new Irish immigrants added to the pressures in these already legendary impoverished areas.[9]

From December 1846 onwards the descriptions carried in the English press concerning events in Ireland shocked the middle-class reader. However, the reality of the condition of many Irish people was brought nearer to home by their absolute destitution and the fact that in their tens of thousands they wandered the streets of British towns. During 1847, all over Britain, the provincial press carried reports of the invasion. The following examples provide some idea of the flavour of the press coverage. The *Manchester Courier* of 16 January 1847 informed its readers:

> The stream of Irish mendicants which has for some weeks poured into this town, appears to increase and the wretched families met with at every street corner are painfully numerous. It is harrowing to the feelings to mark the suffering children, the almost infants who, without shoes or stockings and nothing but rags to cover them in this inclement weather, crowd after their parents, really and truly we believe, in the majority of instances, because their parents have no place to shelter them until they go out and beg the means of procuring the scantiest and coarsest food. The number who find their way to union offices increases in a fearful ratio, considerably more in proportion than the English.... .

The *Bristol Gazette* of 25 February 1847 reported the situation in Newport:

> The streets of our town present an alarming and lamentable appearance, being literally crowded with famishing and half–naked strangers from the most distressed parts of Ireland...hosts of squalid beings are induced to embark on board filthy hulks, totally unsuitable for a living freight, the miseries of whom, densely stowed upon damp ballast, suffering from famine and sickness during this tempestuous season, are almost beyond human expression cast as most of them have been, brutally on our shores, emaciated and in many instances diseased... .

One month later the *Newcastle Journal* reported that:

> The town of Sunderland is overrun with Irishmen who are in a miserable con-
> dition and herding twenty or thirty in a single room at the convenience of the
> town. The scenes of want and misery among them is indescribable but happily
> disease has not yet appeared among them. Every cellar and room that can be
> procured is filled in this way and they subsist in common on whatever they can
> get by begging or occasional work, but many of them are unable to find
> employment. The presence of such a number of lawless strangers among them
> occasions much alarm to the inhabitants of Sunderland.[10]

During the first six months of 1847 particularly, many Irish died in English
towns from the combined effects of malnutrition and disease although it is
not possible to establish the total number. The significance of these deaths
was two-fold. These deaths had a great impact on the newspaper–reading
middle classes throughout the country, helping to fuel the huge outpour-
ing of private charity for the relief of distress in Ireland. These tragic deaths
led to accusations of neglect against the relieving officers in the Union concerned. This increased pressure on the relieving officers, a group of local
authority workers already almost overwhelmed by the mass of Irish destitution. The problems posed for the Liverpool authorities eclipsed those in
all other towns. The following examples give some idea of the scale of destitution facing the Poor Law authorities throughout the country. In
November 1846, John Waters, his wife and eight children, left Mayo. On 30
December, his emaciated corpse was found in a filthy second floor room of
a house in Stockport. Waters was a 52-year-old labourer who had leased a
smallholding in Mayo. In the words of his wife, 'the want of potatoes, starvation and poverty obliged us to leave'. They had walked from Mayo to
Dublin, taking nine days; their total assets, £2, a blanket, two sheets and a
bolster. At Dublin, they paid ten shillings for their fare to Liverpool and on
landing in England, they set out to walk to Sheffield where John Waters
had a brother and at which place he hoped to find work. The family
walked through Prescot and Warrington, surviving by begging. At
Stockport, they stayed for two days at a run-down house rented by an
Irishman and here Waters died, almost naked, in a room devoid of fur-
nishings or cover of any kind, on a cold December morning. The coroner's
jury returned a verdict of 'death from apoplexy caused by the want of food
and warmth' and they also criticized the relieving officer.[11]

In Liverpool, the situation in January 1847 was causing extreme concern
to the Poor Law Commissioners because of the number of deaths, reported
in the press and elsewhere, of people from starvation.[12] One of these
deaths was that of Mary Brady, a 9-month-old Irish girl, whose family had
moved into a cellar in Lace Street, in the Vauxhall ward of Liverpool, a centre of Irish settlement. The whole family was totally destitute and the
mother had been too weak to help the child and only the intervention of
the parish officers saved the mother, father and remaining three children.[13]
The Curran family arrived in Liverpool on Christmas Eve 1846 from
Drogheda, and took a cellar in Ashby Street. Husband, wife and six
children were in a bad physical condition, having only eight shillings

when they arrived and the father did not apply to the parish for relief. On 7 January 1847, Dennis Curran, one of the children, died of starvation. The family's sole resource on that day was 3 lb of bread. The examining surgeon reported it was one of the worst cases he had ever seen.[14] On Tuesday 25 February, an Irishman named Dowling, his wife and five children arrived in Liverpool and reported immediately to the relieving officer in one of the districts. Mrs Dowling was carrying the dead body of one of the children. The child had died on arrival at Liverpool.[15] On 13 March 1847, the *Liverpool Journal* reported yet another horror under the heading 'A Skibbereen in Liverpool'. It was referring to Webster's court, off Oriel Street in Vauxhall. At house number 1, a family went down with typhus and received no help whatsoever. When Fr. Newsham, a priest from St. Anthony's visited the house, the mother had the corpse of a dead child in bed. There were 13 people in the house, some dying of fever, the only visitor being the Catholic priest. In another house, a family all had fever, and a child was burnt to death trying to make a hot drink. On Saturday, 8 May 1847, 8-year-old Luke Brothers died of starvation in a cellar in Liverpool. The inquest revealed no trace of any food in the stomach. The coroner was so shocked that he urged the local press to inform the public as soon as possible of the details of the case. All of the family of six went down with typhus on arrival from Ireland and were too ill to go to the parish office to claim relief. This was done by a neighbour who, it was believed, kept one shilling out of the three shillings allowance to the family. Yet again, the relieving officer was criticized but all the evidence indicates the man was overwhelmed by the sheer volume of cases he had to deal with. The coroner's jury was taken to visit the cellar and one juror told the press he could not believe such a place could exist in Liverpool. This comment highlights the social apartheid existing in British towns at the time. The *Liverpool Albion*, in its report on the case, commented caustically that the middle-class members of the Guardians had little idea of how the poor lived.[16]

Similar scenes of utter destitution and hopelessness characterizing many of the newly arrived Irish were repeated throughout the country though on a smaller scale. A correspondent of the *Cardiff and Merthyr Guardian* wrote:

A vessel named the *Wanderer* has just arrived here with nearly two hundred of the wretched, famished creatures, chiefly from Skibbereen, huddled together in a mass of wretchedness unparalleled. On examining the crowded vessel, it was found that between twenty and thirty starving men, women and children were lying on the ballast in the hold, in dying conditions. Their state was most deplorable and had it not been that surgical and charitable aid was rendered the moment the vessel came alongside the wharf, it is said that many would have been brought ashore dead... .[17]

The evidence of the appalling condition of many of the Irish coming to Britain at this time was not confined to the ports. In April 1847, a policeman doing his rounds in the village of Charlton near Cheltenham, heard groaning coming from a building subsequently described as a hovel. Inside, he found Jeremiah Sullivan, his wife and five children, one of which was already dead. The policeman organized parish relief for the family immediately, but three more of the children died, aged eleven, ten and five years. The verdict of the Coroner's jury was 'death from starvation'. The family had farmed a piece of land at Skibbereen, but the landlord turned them off the land early in 1847. Sullivan sold his horse and cow for £3 and this kept them going for a time, but as there was no improvement in their prospects, they went to Cork and took a vessel for Newport. After paying the fares, they had no money left at all. On landing at Newport, they started to walk to London, where Sullivan had an aunt who kept a shop. To survive, the family begged, but the results were inadequate. The mother's milk dried up and the 3-month-old baby was kept alive with water and sugar. On reaching Charlton, the baby died. Two more Sullivan children died soon after.[18] In Todmorden, on the Lancashire-Yorkshire border, an Irish father took his wife and four children to the house of the relieving officer where one of the children died on arrival. The inquest verdict was 'death from starvation'.[19] On 11 June 1847, James Crawley was found by a local man on the outskirts of Sunderland, in Co. Durham, in a distressed condition. He was taken to the Sunderland relieving officer by which time he was incoherent. He died during the night. The coroner's verdict was death from 'the want of the necessities of life'. Before he died, Crawley told the relieving officer he had never applied for relief: this was almost certainly because of a fear of removal to Ireland. An enquiry into the death by the Sunderland Union cleared the relieving officer of any responsibility for the death of Crawley.[20] Such cases were not a temporary phenomenon and this level of distress was not confined to 1847. For example, Ellen Kane and her five children, aged between nine months and ten years, arrived in Liverpool from Ireland, 22 January 1849. She had only a shilling on arrival but did not apply for poor relief because of her fear of removal back to Ireland by the Poor Law authorities. She and the children crossed to Birkenhead and moved into a room in an empty house in Oak Street where large numbers of Irish lived. There was no furniture in the house. On 24 January, she applied to the parish for medical relief to the overseer and obtained some money. She then applied to the Medical Officer of Health for some assistance and this was refused. On Sunday 28 January, Inspector McNeill of the Birkenhead police went to the room in Oak Street and found the dead bodies of Ellen Kane, aged 40 years, and her 9–month-old child. Four other children were in the room with the corpses. The subsequent inquest was told that the family had not eaten anything since Saturday morning. The verdict was that Ellen Kane and her baby died of starvation.[21] In April 1850, an inquest was held at the Griffin Inn, Bold, near St. Helens, in Lancashire on the body of Bridget Callaghan. The dead woman, with her four children, had landed at Liverpool from Dublin. She was accompanied by Rose Flood, her cousin and they were on their way to Dove Green in Yorkshire at which place the deceased had a sister. The sister had written to Bridget Callaghan inviting her over. On landing in Liverpool, the Irishwoman and four children started to walk to Yorkshire. On the first night they stayed in Knotty Ash and the following night they reached Bold. Here a local woman took pity on the family and gave them some porridge and coffee. They then slept under a hedge at the roadside. It rained heavily all night until about 5.00am. At this point, a woman in a nearby house heard children crying and went to investigate. The mother, Bridget Callaghan, was dead. The inquest verdict was death from exposure. [22]

The masters of the coal vessels bringing the Irish to Newport, Cardiff and Swansea faced increasing hostility from the local population, frightened of disease and resentful of increased parish expenditure. For the masters of such vessels, the Irish were a cheap form of ballast and so the motives for bringing them were often economic rather than humanitarian. To avoid incurring local wrath, some of the ships' masters resorted to the practice of landing the Irish along the coast before they reached Newport. The unfortunate Irish were told they were near to the town. Many, suffering from typhus and malnutrition, found it hard to struggle through the mud flats to reach the shore. Early in May 1849, the *Three Brothers* was observed crawling along the Welsh coast, landing Irish at different points. According to a report in the *Manchester Guardian* she carried 300 passengers 'in a state of filth worse than the beasts that perish, without food, without proper covering, without bed and without room to lie down.' One Irishman who died on board was buried in the mud flats and the corpse was washed ashore at Peterstone. Another Irishman who was landed clandestinely died almost immediately of starvation.[23] The Mayor of Cardiff was sufficiently worried by this practice of landing the Irish on the Welsh coast, that he wrote to the Secretary of State on the matter. The reply from the Home Office stated that the coastguards in the Swansea district had been instructed to look out for such vessels and, if observed, to check if they were breaking the law regarding numbers of passengers. [24]

Relief and removal

The immediate impact of the Famine influx was on those responsible for administering the Poor Law system. The legal and administrative frameworks within which the local authorities had to work when alleviating poverty were well established. England and Wales were divided into Poor Law districts, named Unions. Each Union consisted of a number of ecclesiastical parishes and the administration of poor relief within each Union was the responsibility of the Poor Law Guardians, elected annually by the ratepayers. Each Union had at least one Workhouse and so recipients of poor relief could either receive help by entering the workhouse (indoor relief) or receive payments of food, clothes or money, without entering the Workhouse (outdoor relief). The question of whether or not an individual was eligible for relief of either kind was determined in the context of laws regarding settlement and removal. To qualify for relief, an applicant had to establish that he or she had 'settlement' within the Union. That, in effect, meant they had been born in a certain parish, or by a set of other criteria, had acquired settlement in the parish. If a person did not have settlement, he or she could, if applying for relief, be physically removed to the parish where they did.[25] In 1846, the law regarding settlement had been changed so that anyone who could prove unbroken residence in a parish for five years acquired the legal status of residency and hence the right to relief. The Famine Irish clearly had no such claim in Britain, but disproving an Irish person's claim to five-year residency in a large town turned out to be almost impossible and posed a major administrative problem for Poor Law Guardians.[26] Ireland had its own Poor Law system from 1838 but the Irish Unions discouraged outdoor relief and were also underfunded.

Though the Poor Law Guardians in English towns had no legal obligation to provide permanent relief to the Famine Irish they did have a responsibility to prevent deaths from starvation in the short term. In general, most towns appear to have done their best at a time when the already outdated poor relief system was under pressure from a massive increase in applications from destitute English workers and their families. The reason for this was that the height of the Famine influx, 1846–51, coincided with widespread economic distress among the English, Welsh and Scots.[27] However, even by the standards of the English poor, the situation of the Irish immigrants was fearful. The official statistics regarding the amount of relief distributed, though an index of the burden on ratepayers, give an imperfect indication of the amount of Irish destitution in Britain resulting from the Famine immigration. The reason for this is that, in June 1847, a change in the law made the process of removal much easier. This was the culmination of a sustained two-pronged political campaign led by the Liverpool Poor Law Guardians, on the problem of Irish paupers in Britain. The first objective was to give the Irish a legal right to poor relief in Ireland in the hope this would stop the exodus from Ireland. The second aim was to make the removal of Irish paupers to Ireland a simpler administrative procedure so increasing the likelihood of removal for those not having resident status. These twin objectives were achieved with the passing in June 1847 of the Poor Relief (Ireland) Act and the Poor Removal Act (10 and 11 Vic. Cap. 33). The essential feature of the latter Act was that it made it unnecessary to obtain a summons before bringing an Irish claimant for relief before the magistrates. When viewing the removal laws as instruments of policy for dealing with Irish immigration, it is necessary to distinguish between their possible deterrent effect on immigration, and their effect on claims for relief on the part of the Irish in Britain. The Poor Relief (Ireland) Act, giving a legal right to relief in Ireland did not, however, stem the flight from Ireland as hoped. The Poor Removal Act did discourage some Irish paupers in Britain who did not have five years' residency, from applying for relief. This had the result that the published statistics understate the amount of Irish destitution. Rather than run the risk of removal, large numbers of Irish stopped claiming relief.

The question arises of how the destitute immigrants survived on arrival and *en route* for destinations away from the coast. It was known in Ireland that a well-established survival system was available in Britain to both destitute and those with funds. Initially, the Famine refugees would claim relief and then move on. Most Unions had a vagrancy ward or shed attached to the workhouse; these places offered accommodation of a very basic sort to people on the road. In Liverpool, vagrants using the shed had a bed with no blankets or mattress. Bread only was on offer for breakfast. In addition vagrants had to grind 30 lb of corn before receiving any food and grind 60 lb in total per day. Women vagrants admitted had to pick oakum.[28] Trampers moved from Union to Union on their journeys around the country. For people on the move the threat of removal was empty; by the time an order was made out, they had moved on. In addition to Union vagrancy wards, most towns had cheap lodging houses, often Irish owned. Such places, overcrowded and dirty, provided the cheapest accommodation available. Parochial relief could be also avoided, or supplemented, by begging.

Edward Rushton, the stipendiary magistrate at Liverpool during the whole of the Famine crisis, described the situation during the first quarter of 1847. On 27 April 1847, speaking of the Irish Famine immigrants, he stated:

> they lodge in cellars and in rooms of the lowest character, 15 or 16 to a room. There is no adequate provision for the offices of nature, no one convenience of civilised life. They are sleeping in the clothes they wear in the day, without beds, without utensils... .

He claimed that the Famine Irish arriving were generally not capable of work, 'they are broken down by suffering and it is distressing to see them.'[29] During 1847, the accommodation problem in Liverpool, in the worse sector of the housing market, was so bad that even the destitute began to move inland fairly quickly. Those who could not afford the train fare would start tramping from the dock area, heading due east, on their way to Manchester, Salford, the Lancashire mill towns, or the Midlands. For many, the first stopover was at Prescot, seven miles inland from the Mersey. In 1847, the population of Prescot town was approximately 5,000. During the first ten months of that year, between 8,000–9,000 Irish vagrants passed through the workhouse.[30] For the year ended 25 March 1848, 9,843 Irish vagrants were provided with overnight lodgings and food by the Prescot Guardians, at a cost of £214.[31] On leaving Prescot, many of the trampers would walk to Warrington or continue to Knutsford, where they would rest again. On 4 June 1847, the Poor Law Guardians of Knutsford wrote to the Poor Law Board in London, complaining of the influx of Irish poor into the town. They pointed out that Knutsford was on the main route between Liverpool and the south of England and had always been a 'great thoroughfare' for the Irish.

> Recently their numbers have increased greatly. Their practice has been to make Knutsford a stopping place for the night, and by their urgent solicitation of charity in the town and neighbourhood, to obtain money and food. As a natural consequence, a number of lodging houses of a very low description have been established, principally by Irish persons, who have permanently located themselves in Knutsford, and at those places, the inmates are crowded in such a way, and their habits so filthy, that disease is the frequent result, not seldom followed by death.[32]

Here again, the concern over the Irish spreading fever is evident. On 18 November 1848, J. Roscoe, one of the Knutsford Guardians, wrote to the Board, pointing out that the situation in Knutsford was as bad as ever. 'The increased influx of Irish poor is looked upon almost with alarm. The Irish will spread disease.'[33] Such fears were echoed as the Irish began to stream into the towns of the Midlands. The clerk to the Guardians at Burton-on-Trent told the Poor Law Board in February 1848 that the recently arrived Irish in the area had learned to 'take advantage of the system'. He claimed that the wives and children of able-bodied Irish labourers were wandering from Union to Union, claiming relief while the heads of the families concerned were working.[34] The clerk to the Wolverhampton Union complained to the Board that there had been a 'large influx' of destitute Irish into the Union and that, night after night, they were making the vagrant ward their home. He alleged that they possessed rudimentary kitchen utensils and at night cooked their food, which they had begged, such income being in addition to parochial relief.[35]

The secretary of the Oxford Anti–Mendicity Society wrote to Sir George Grey, the Home Secretary, on 27 May 1848. He complained of the number of Irish paupers flocking into Oxford in 'ever–increasing numbers' and gave statistics of the number of Irish paupers helped during the year; increasing from 119 in February to 787 during the first three weeks of May. A large proportion of those given assistance were women and children, unaccompanied by men. The secretary asked the Home Secretary 'who is paying their fares?' He also requested Grey to consider what measures could be taken to stop those landing at Newport without means of obtaining work, such as women and children, from proceeding inland.[36] As so often at this time, the request for action to stop Irish immigrants landing and moving around revealed an ignorance of the legal powers available to the authorities. The London Mendicity Society reported increased giving to Irish applicants. For the month of December 1847, the numbers assisted were 736 English and 14,943 Irish. For the same period in 1848, the corresponding numbers were 718 English and 21,578 Irish.[37]

Poor Law Guardians had discretion regarding the severity with which they applied the removal laws to the Famine refugees, the main restraint on their actions being the reaction of the ratepayers to their bills. The size of the ratepayers' burden was influenced not only by the immediate cost of removal but also by any subsequent litigation on the part of those recipient parishes which challenged removals. However, for those English and Welsh parishes away from the main ports of exit for Ireland, it was simply too expensive to remove the Irish. A parish officer of a London Union claimed:

> We try to get rid of them [the Irish poor] as much as we can, without taking out orders of removal. The removals are always attended with great expense. They cost us from £2 to £3 each. We avoid that. Sometimes by making them work in the stoneyard we get rid of them. After as many as half a dozen Irish families have been there awhile, a threat of taking them into the house [*sic* Workhouse] and removing them to Ireland, will make them all leave us. They probably go to another parish frequented by the Irish, and apply for relief there.[38]

Because of the lower cost of Irish removal for Lancashire Unions, the bulk of removals were from that county. For example, for the year ending 25 March 1853, of a total of 4,823 removal orders made for removing Irish people back to Ireland, 3,840 were made out by Lancashire Unions. In Liverpool, the parochial officers could remove a family to Ireland at a cost of ten shillings rather than relieve them for ten days or a fortnight at a cost of 10 shillings and sixpence. The same family in the London parish of St. Mary-le-Bone could not be removed for less than £6 or £7.[39] The pre-eminence of Liverpool parish *vis-a-vis* Manchester, in terms of removals, is illustrated in Table 3.6 .

Table 3.6 Numbers of Irish paupers removed from Liverpool and Manchester over the period 1846–53 inclusive

Year	Liverpool	Manchester	Total
1846	5,313	286	5,599
1847	15,008	553	15,561
1848	7,606	1,902	9,509
1849	9,409	617	10,026
1850	7,627	275	7,902
1851	7,808	400	8,208
1852	5,506	337	5,843
1853	4,503	362	4,865
Total	62,781	4,732	67,513

Sources: British Parliamentary Papers (HC), 1854, Vol. XVII, Report of the Select Committee on Poor Removal, Evidence of A. Campbell, q.5026 and J. Harrop, q.6230

The peak year for removals was 1847. It cannot be assumed that the much higher number of removals from Liverpool necessarily reflects a harsher policy than was the case in Manchester. The lower rate of removals from Manchester may have reflected a more relaxed attitude towards claimants for relief or a lower number of applicants for relief. The most plausible explanation for the difference in the numbers however is the fact that the large numbers of Irish passing through Liverpool gave rise to a greater volume of destitute Irish in need at any one time. To this must be added the number of Irish who made their way to Liverpool from other towns, claimed relief and obtained a free passage home. What is indisputable is that the threat of removal kept the financial burden on ratepayers in Liverpool and Manchester lower than what it would otherwise have been. There is strong evidence that this was the case. In his written evidence to the 1854 committee Robert Pashley, a distinguished lawyer and expert on the Poor Law system, stated with respect to the Manchester Clerk to the Union:

He [*sic*]. Harrop] certainly showed that the power of removal as exercised has the effect of removing to Ireland only a portion of those liable to such removal; but it seemed to me that this non–removal arose, not of any forbearance of the parish officers, but inasmuch as by their threat of removal, they were able to deter from receiving relief those who, if they had received such relief, would have been removed... The pauper, thus deterred from demanding relief for actual destitution, is either driven into another parish, and burdens the poor rate there, or becomes a vagrant or mendicant.[40]

There is ample newspaper evidence of the deterrent effect of the threat of removal on relief claims. Reference has already been made to the case of Ellen Kane and her four children at Birkenhead. It transpired that she had not applied for relief out of fear of removal. The inquest verdict was that she and the child had died of starvation. In May 1849 an inquest held in Liverpool on the body of Nancy McDermott recorded 'death from starvation'. She had been removed from Liverpool to Ireland twelve months previously and had returned to Liverpool. She did not apply for relief because of the threat of removal and had attempted to survive by begging.[41] Clearly, the power of the threat of removal at this time was derived from the fact that for many of the Irish immigrants the fear of conditions in famine stricken Ireland was greater than any worries over the hardships of surviving in Britain without poor relief. This was no temporary state of affairs. For example, during the financial year ending 25 March 1853 the Manchester Poor Law Guardians obtained 1,256 orders for removals, 363 against English families and 893 against Irish and Scottish. In fact only 190 Irish, 6 Scottish and 66 English families were removed. The *Manchester Guardian* congratulated the Manchester Poor Law Guardians on the success of their removals policy.[42]

Despite this punitive policy a long-term consequence of the Famine Irish immigration was a permanent increase in the number of Irish receiving poor relief in British towns and cities. As a deterrent to immigration the Removal Laws were a failure. It was simply too easy for those removed to return to Britain. In addition, the simple passing of time increased the numbers of Irish-born who could claim five years' residency and so receive poor relief.

The cost of the Famine immigration

Turning to the financial consequences of the famine crisis, the critical period that triggered off the greatly increased flow of immigrants into Britain was the winter of 1846–47, following the disastrous return of the potato blight. The impact of this inflow on the north of England in terms of numbers of Irish relieved is illustrated in Table 3.7.

Table 3.7 The comparative number of Irish relieved in several Unions in the March quarters of 1846 and 1847

	1846	1847		1846	1847
Lancashire			*Yorkshire (West Riding)*		
Ashton under Lyne	173	997	Leeds	756	3,120
Blackburn	12	65	Pateley Bridge	0	20
Bolton	209	1,815	Rotherham	265	611
Burnley	194	892	Selby	40	230
Bury	60	271	Sheffield	178	859
Chorlton	290	762	Skipton	0	899
Clitheroe	76	309	Thorne	5	194
The Fylde	39	309	Wakefield	73	463
Garstang	109	500			
Haslingden	18	229	*Yorkshire (East Riding)*		
Lancaster	46	70	Beverley	259	570
Leigh	25	153	Howden	11	56
Manchester	3,103	12,256	Patrington	2	3
Ormskirk	16	2,211	Sculcoates	13	167
Rochdale	37	648			
Salford	231	1,072	*Derbyshire*		
Warrington	28	310	Chapel-en-le-Frith	27	393
Wigan	460	1,657	Glossop	88	405
			Hayfield	21	446
Yorkshire (West Riding)					
Bradford	567	1,428	*Cheshire*		
Dewsbury	58	592	Congleton	690	1,617
Doncaster	145	505	Macclesfield	47	90
Halifax	194	2,066	Northwich	123	384
Huddersfield	136	544	Stockport	84	1,270
Keighley	1	247			

Source: British Parliamentary Papers 1847, [816] XXVIII, 13th Annual Report of the Poor Law Commissioners, Appendix A, Report by Alfred Austin, p.188

For the quarter ended 25 March 1846, the number of Irish–born persons receiving relief in the Manchester Union was 3,103. In the corresponding quarter for 1847, the figure was 12,256. It can be seen that in many of the less populous Unions, the effect of the Famine inflow was quite dramatic, for example, the cases of Ormskirk, Skipton and Congleton. The increased numbers of Irish receiving poor relief were reflected in increased expenditures by the Poor Law Unions. For the year ending 31 March 1845, Liverpool spent £3,140 on Irish poor relief. For the year ended 25 March 1848 it had rocketed to £25,926, a peak in the flow of expenditure on Irish poor relief. As can be seen from Table 3.8 both the absolute and the proportionate amount spent in Irish relief were permanently higher after

1846. The fall in expenditure on the Irish during the year ended 25 March 1849 does not mean the Famine crisis was over. It reflects the falling off in claims for relief on the part of the Famine Irish, frightened by the threat of removal. Of the expenditure of £12,674 on the Irish, about 85 per cent was on the Irish who had residency qualifications.

Table 3.8 Total annual expenditure on poor relief in the Liverpool Poor Law Union, 1845–54

Year Ending	Irish £	Non–Irish £	Total	Irish as % of total
25 March 1845	3,140	26,980	30,120	10.4
25 March 1846	2,916	28,367	31,283	9.3
25 March 1847	12,613	32,250	44,863	28.1
25 March 1848	25,926	39,364	65,290	40.0
25 March 1849	12,674	40,340	53,014	24.0
25 March 1850	14,049	39,068	53,117	26.4
25 March 1851	12,528	37,272	49,800	25.2
25 March 1852	13,479	38,699	52,178	25.8
25 March 1853	12,251	33,355	45,606	26.9
25 March 1854	14,433	36,602	51,035	28.3
Total	124,009	352,297	476,306	26.0

Source: British Parliamentary Paper (HC), 1854, Vol. XVII, Report Select Committee on Removal (1854), Minutes of Evidence, A. Campbell, Appendix No. 8

Note: These statistics do not cover costs of medical officers, salaries or other establishment charges. They refer essentially to food, clothing and other necessities of life distributed both indoor and outdoor.

In Manchester, the same financial year witnessed a peak spending of £21,179 on outdoor relief for the Irish, out of a total poor relief expenditure of £57,171. As in the case of Liverpool the subsequent reduced level of expenditure on the Irish was well above the pre-Famine levels and remained so. Unlike Liverpool, the majority of Irish in Manchester were long stay residents: hence the relatively high spending. For example, for the sixteen years 1830–46, the average expenditure on Irish outdoor relief in Manchester was 11.3 per cent of the total. As table 3.9 shows, the proportion increased significantly after the Famine.

It is beyond the scope of this chapter to assess the precise financial burden of the Famine Irish on local ratepayers because this involves fairly complex analysis and much of the relevant data does not exist. A preliminary exercise regarding Liverpool suggests that the cost of the Famine Irish to the Liverpool ratepayers during 1847 was sevenpence halfpenny in the pound. For a labourer renting a house at an annual rent of £10, this would have involved a poor rates bill of six shillings threepence and a halfpenny, a third of a weeks wage. In fact, 80 per cent of Liverpool's ratepayers were excused payment on the grounds of poverty and so the

Table 3. 9 Estimates of the amounts (£) paid in outdoor relief to English and Irish paupers in the Manchester Union, 1847–58

Year	English settled poor	English non-settled poor	Irish	Total	Irish as % of the total
Mar 1846–Mar 1847	5,331	14,428	4,651	24,410	19
Mar 1847–Mar 1848	20,824	15,168	21,179	57,171	37
Mar 1848–Mar 1849	17,114	10,237	14,994	42,345	35
Mar 1849–Mar 1850	13,447	5,930	10,428	29,805	35
Mar 1850–Mar 1851	11,980	4,953	9,263	26,196	35
Mar 1851–Mar 1852	11,808	5,357	10,712	27,877	38
Mar 1852–Mar 1853	8,766	4,344	7,185	20,295	35
Mar 1853–Mar 1854	7,843	4,525	7,494	19,862	38
Mar 1854–Mar 1855	9,928	6,689	12,748	29,365	43
Mar 1855–Mar 1856	10,198	7,603	12,859	30,660	42
Mar 1856–Mar 1857	5,583	7,592	8,372	21,547	39
Mar 1857–Mar 1858	8,339	8,887	14,032	31,258	45

Note: The data was obtained from the weekly returns of the Manchester Poor Law Union reported each week in the *Manchester Guardian*. They are estimates because a small number of weeks were missing. The figures for years ending March 1856 and 1857 are the official figures which were reported in the *Manchester Guardian*. Each year ends on Lady Day, 25 March.

burden was borne by the wealthier ratepayers, often employers of cheap unskilled labour.[43] With regard to the Welsh towns and the south-west of England, the data is less clear and none exists for 1847. For 1848, we have data but the terms are not clearly defined and so we do not know what categories of expenditure are referred to.

Table 3.10 The numbers of Irish who received poor relief in Bristol, Cardiff, Newport and Merthyr Tydfil, Newport and Bristol during the year ended 31 December 1848

Place	Numbers of individuals	Amount
Bristol	4,403	£243 0s 10¹/₂d
Cardiff St John & St Mary Parishes	2,063	£868 14s 7d
Newport Union	12,661	£184 15s 7d
Merthyr Tydfil Parish	1,346	£212 8s 0d

Source: British Parliamentary Papers (HC), Accounts and Papers, 1849, XLVII, The number of Irish Poor relieved during 1848 in the Parishes comprised in the Borough of Liverpool, City of Glasgow, City of Bristol, Borough of Cardiff, Borough of Newport, Borough of Merthyr Tydfil, Borough of Manchester, Borough of Salford, Borough of Preston, Borough of Bury, Borough of Leeds, Borough of Paisley and City of Glasgow respectively, and the money value of relief so expended.

It is clear on the basis of these data that the financial burden was much less than was the case in Liverpool, even allowing for differences in the rateable value of property. However, we do not know what proportion of the Irish receiving relief in the above named towns were long stay (five-year residents) and which were Famine refugees. Also we do not know which categories of relief are included.[44]

'Irish fever'

Whatever the concerns in Britain in 1847 over the cost of providing outdoor relief for Irish immigrants, they were overtaken by the fear of death from typhus or 'Irish fever'. In Liverpool, the typhus epidemic broke out first in the Irish areas and then began to spread to the English quarters of the town.[45] Essentially, typhus spreads easily in overcrowded, poverty stricken conditions and the agent of this process is an organism called Rickettsia Prowazeki: the Rickettsiae are transmitted from person to person by body lice. This was not known at the time of the Famine emergency. The typhus outbreak posed unprecedented problems for the municipal and Poor Law authorities, not least of which was the provision of hospital beds. In 1846, the Liverpool Workhouse had 84 beds reserved for fever patients, adequate under normal circumstances. By June 1847 an estimated 8,000 were ill with typhus and Dr Duncan, Liverpool's Medical Officer of Health, reported that over the year 60,000 had suffered from typhus and nearly 40,000 from diarrhoea and dysentery.[46] Temporary fever sheds were erected in the grounds of the Workhouse and in Great Howard Street. In addition, as a result of pressure on the government the Liverpool authorities were given the use of two vessels for use as lazarettos. The *Newcastle* was used as a hospital ship for the overflow from the fever sheds and the *Akbar* was used as a quarantine station for fever victims arriving on the Irish steamers.[47] There is absolutely no doubt that the majority of deaths from typhus and dysentery were Irish. Dr Duncan's statistics of deaths in the political wards indicate clearly that Scotland, Vauxhall, Exchange and Great George had the highest death rates, all areas of large Irish settlements.[48] Duncan himself recognized that the Irish suffered most. This is also borne out by pauper burials. The pauper churchyard in Cambridge Street received 1,655 bodies during 1846. The total number of pauper burials in 1847 was 7,509, mainly Catholic. Behind these statistics lie thousands of personal tragedies. The following Irish cases could be replicated many times. On the 13 May 1847, Roger Flynn, his wife and six children were taken into Liverpool's Workhouse fever shed suffering from typhus. On 15 May Bridget Flynn (16) died, followed by Roger (37) 26 May, Catherine (14) 11 June; Thomas (2) 24 June; Catherine (38) 12 July; John (4) 28 July; Mary (9) died on an unspecified date and the sole survivor Michael (7) was sent to the orphanage 9 August. On 20 May, Bridget, Mary, Margaret and John McIntyre all entered the fever shed at the Workhouse. The fact that there were no parents suggest they had already died. Margaret (10) died 4 June; John (7) 14 June; Bridget (19) 17 June and Mary

(12) 6 July.[49] The view that the appearance of typhus in an area was causally related to the arrival of Famine Irish was universal. The correspondence of Poor Law Guardians with the Poor Law Commissioners in London during Black '47 provides ample evidence for this claim. Unions throughout Britain sought permission from London to provide fever sheds and extra medical officers to deal with what was viewed as a crisis.

In his report on a visit to the Newport Union on 5 June 1847, John Lewis, assistant Poor Law Commissioner stated:

> The Guardians have acted with promptitude in providing for the exigency occasioned by the influx of Irish vagrants and the invasion of fever.[50]

The term 'invasion' is indicative of the perceptions of contemporary opinion concerning the nature of the problem in 1847 and it appears repeatedly in both official correspondence and press reports nationwide.

Throughout the country, fear of 'Irish fever' and increased poor rates spread as events in Liverpool were reported extensively in the metropolitan and provincial press. Such fears seemed to be confirmed as the destitute Irish began to stream into the towns of all the major industrial areas. For example, many of the Irish landing at Whitehaven made their way to Newcastle and County Durham. In April 1847, the *Newcastle Journal* reported that large numbers of Irishmen had arrived in the town, assuming wrongly that there was plenty of work available on railway construction projects going on in the area. The *Newcastle Journal* claimed that many of the arrivals had had their fares paid by parties in Ireland and commented sourly that the money had probably been sent from England to relieve Famine in Ireland.[51] On 12 June 1847, a meeting of magistrates was held in Newcastle to receive a memorial from Dr Riddell, the Catholic bishop of the northern district concerning 'Irish fever'. Riddell, while admitting that fever was spreading, claimed that it was not 'malignant' and was confined to the poor Irish. Five months after making this claim, Riddell died of typhus, caught while administering to the Irish in Newcastle. By September, Newcastle's fever hospital was full and stopped taking fever victims from Gateshead where typhus was spreading rapidly among the Irish in lodging houses.[52]

There were signs of panic as the flood of Famine refugees moved inland. In May 1847, D. Ball, a surgeon living at Burslem in Staffordshire, attended the police court at Tunstall to draw the attention of the magistrates to the large numbers of Irish immigrants attempting to settle in the town. Ball expressed the opinion that they would introduce fever into the town. However, it is not clear what he wanted the magistrates to do as they had no power to stop the Irish moving into the area, at least for short periods. Removal on a large scale was not practicable. They agreed to try and stop begging and ordered the police to move the Irish on.[53] The Burslem magistrates were addressed on the same issue by the Reverend G. Armstrong, who stated he was worried about the spread of fever. Early in 1847, the Rochdale Poor Law Guardians had set up a special committee to deal with the Irish because they had 'had so large an influx of Irish paupers.' The Vicar of Rochdale chaired a public meeting called because of local concern over 'Irish fever'. Though the Poor Law Guardians were responsible for the management of the Poor Law system in their Union, it was the relieving officers who bore the brunt of the pressure, particularly during 1847. Not surprisingly, mistakes were made. For example, the Duignan family from Leitrim arrived in Rochdale in 1847, where they all went down with fever. The father, mother and a child died, the remaining children Michael (12), Patrick (14) and Catherine (10), survived. On recovery they were taken from the fever hospital, put in an uncovered cart on a rainy day and taken to the railway station and sent to Liverpool. There, they were put on the overcrowded deck of the steamer *Duchess of Kent* supposedly in the care of two Irish women who were also being removed from Rochdale. Michael Duignan was lame and could not easily stand up. On the voyage to Dublin he died. The inquest verdict was that he died of exposure and the Dublin authorities were very critical of the Rochdale Guardians. Sir George Grey ordered an immediate enquiry into the affair, carried out by Alfred Austin. This revealed much confusion among the authorities regarding the precise legal requirements for removing paupers to Ireland. Austin concluded that Michael Duignan did not die of exposure but was trampled to death.[54]

The crisis arising from the Irish Famine refugees in many British towns revealed the same treasury attitudes that prevailed with respect to the emergency in Ireland. The requests of Liverpool, Glasgow and other places for financial assistance were unceremoniously turned down and the policy of throwing the whole relief operation onto ratepayers was invoked. Given the simultaneous rise in the level of pauperism among the indigenous population, the Famine influx could not have happened at a worse time. In these circumstances, the system for relieving destitution coped reasonably well, from the point of view of the local Boards of Guardians and ratepayers. The clearly observable rise in the level of expenditure on the Irish poor in British towns after the financial year 1847–48 reflects the impact of the Five Years' Residency Act rather than the cost of the Irish arriving 1846–51. The threat of removal did not stem the exodus from Ireland to Britain but it did deter many newly arrived Irish from claiming relief. The available evidence does not support the contemporary view that the Famine immigrants imposed a crippling burden on ratepayers. The success of the deterrent effect was at the cost of more destitution than would otherwise have been the case. Significantly, the threat of removal contributed to horrific overcrowding which in turn was a crucial factor in spreading typhus among the Irish during 1847. A reasonable estimate is that in 1847 a minimum of 6,000 Irish died in Liverpool alone of typhus and dysentery. [55] The Irish death rates, in many areas, were massively higher than the corresponding rate among the British working classes. However, many English, Scottish and Welsh sacrificed their lives helping the Irish Famine immigrants: policemen, doctors, nurses, relieving officers and most of all Catholic priests. Mistakes were made in the Poor Law Unions but there were few villains and many heroes.

The Famine immigration increased the size of existing Irish settlements in Victorian Britain and created new ones. Despite the fact that many did climb up the social and income ladders, it is flying in the face of all the evidence to deny that most remained in poor paid, unskilled jobs. The areas of British towns in which most Catholics lived were characteristically the poorest parts of the town. This was the case until the slum clearance programme of the 1960s. In many areas, local politics were coloured by the presence of large numbers of Catholics. For a generation after the Famine, tensions between British and Irish Catholics in Britain broke out intermittently in serious disturbances. In Liverpool and Glasgow they were endemic.[56]

Notes

1. For a detailed study of the conditions under which the Famine Irish were carried to Liverpool see F. Neal, 'Liverpool, the Irish Steamship Companies and the Famine Irish, '*Immigrants and Minorities*, Vol. 5, No. 1, March 1986, pp. 28–61. For a transport orientated study of the ferries between England and Ireland see H. S. Irvine, 'Some aspects of passenger transport between England and Ireland 1820–1850', *Journal of Transport History*, Vol. IV, 1959–60, pp. 225–41.
2. Essential reading for students of social conditions is E. Chadwick, *Report on the Sanitary Conditions of the Labouring Population of Great Britain*, PP (HC) XXVI (1842) and its successor, *Sanitary Enquiry: England. Local Reports on the Sanitary Conditions of the Labouring Population of England* PP (HL) XXVII, (referred to hereafter as Chadwick Local Reports). *First Report of the Commissioners for Enquiring into the State of Large Towns and Populous Districts*, PP XVII (1844). *Second Report of the Commissioners for Enquiring into the State of Large Towns and Populous Districts*, PP XVIII (1845). References to the Irish in Britain are found throughout all three reports. Excellent treatments of these social conditions are to be found in John Burnett, *A Social History of Housing 1815–70*, Methuen, London, 1978, parts 1 & 2; S.A.Wohl, *Endangered Lives*, Methuen, London, 1983.
3. Evelyn Neal, 'A statistical analysis of the enumerated population of the township of Prescot, 1841, 1851 and 1861', unpublished M.Phil. Thesis, Salford, 1994, Chapter 5, p. 113.
4. In 1847 The Home Office asked the authorities in various ports to record the numbers of Irish arriving. Only Liverpool produced comprehensive figures. Glasgow, Swansea and Cardiff produced no returns.
5. E. Evans, Chairman of the Board of Guardians of the Cardiff Union, *Select Committee on Poor Removal*, PP XVII (1854), referred to hereafter as S.C. (1854) Minutes of Evidence qq 6471–482; 6552, 6596.
6. E. Rushton, Stipendiary Magistrate of Liverpool, *Select Committee Settlement on Poor Removal*, PP XI (1847), referred to hereafter as S.C. (1847) Minutes of Evidence q. 4382.
7. See F. Neal, 'Liverpool, the Irish Steamship Companies and the Famine Irish', pp. 40–44
8 . W. H. Duncan, *Medical Officer's Report* for 1847, p. 16, *Liverpool Record Office*, H 352.4HEA. For a characteristic piece of newspaper reporting on 'Irish fever' see *The Cambrian*, 11 June 1847; *Newcastle Journal*, 5 June and 19 June 1847, *Bolton Chronicle*, 17 June 1847 and *Liverpool Chronicle* , 19 June 1847.

9.   For detailed descriptions of conditions in the large towns in Britain on the eve of the Irish Famine see *First Report of the Commissioners of Inquiry into the State of Large Towns and Populous districts*, PP XVII (HL) 1844. In particular Appendix: W. H. Duncan on 'The physical causes of the high mortality in Liverpool', pp. 29–30. Also Chadwick Local Reports, No. 19 Liverpool, No. 20, pp. 282–94; Manchester, pp. 284–336; No. 23, Leeds, pp. 348–409. See also J. P. Kay, *The Moral and Physical Conditions of the Working Classes Employed in The Cotton Manufacture in Manchester*, Ridgeway, London, 1832 (reprinted with a preface by W. H. Chaloner, Cass, London, 1970).

10. *Newcastle Journal*, 27 March 1847.

11. *Manchester Guardian*, 6 January 1847, *Bradford and Wakefield Observer*, 7 January 1847, *Stockport Advertiser*, 8 January 1847,

12. Unfortunately the correspondence between the Poor Law Commissioners and the Liverpool Select Vestry for the year 1847 has not survived. The problem of starvation deaths was not short term. The *Liverpool Mercury* of 17 March 1848 reported that the Select Vestry had received a letter from the Poor Law Commissioners concerning the number of deaths in Liverpool resulting from starvation.

13 . *Halifax Guardian*, 9 January 1847.

14 . *Halifax Guardian*, 9 January 1847.

15. *Liverpool Journal*, 27 February 1847.

16. *Liverpool Albion*, 10 May 1847, see also *Manchester Guardian*, 15 May 1847.

17. *Cardiff and Merthyr Guardian*, 12 February 1847. See also *Manchester Guardian*, 13 February 1847.

18. *Cheltenham Examiner*, 7 April 1847; *Sunderland Herald*, 16 April 1847, *Bristol Gazette*, 27 April 1847.

19. *Halifax Guardian*, 27 February 1847.

20. Public Record Office MH12/3270/Sunderland Union/17633/1847. Letter from Sunderland Union to Poor Law Commissioners.

21. *Liverpool Albion*, 29 January 1849; *Liverpool Mercury*, 30 January and 9 February 1849.

22. *Liverpool Mercury*, 16 April 1850.

23. *Manchester Guardian*, 19 May 1849. For evidence regarding the use of collier vessels to carry Irish immigrants see S.C. (1854), Minutes of Evidence, E. David, Chairman of the Cardiff Board of Guardians. Also evidence of J. Salter, Relieving Officer of the Newport Union. See also C. Lewis, 'The Irish in Cardiff in the Mid Nineteenth Century', *Cambria*, Vol. 7, No. 1, 1980, p. 16.

24. *The Times*, 2 July 1849.

25. There are a number of recent works explaining the English Poor Law system. See M.E. Rose (ed.), *The Poor and The City: The English Poor Law in its Urban Context 1834–1914*, Leicester University Press, Leicester, 1985. Also M.E. Rose, 'Settlement, Removal and the New Poor Law', in D. Fraser (ed.), *The New Poor Law in the Nineteenth Century*, Macmillan, London, 1976; M. E. Rose, *The Relief of Poverty*, Macmillan, London, 1972; P. Wood, *Poverty and the Workhouse in Victorian Britain*, Sutton, Stroud, 1991.

26. Edward Rushton (Liverpool Stipendiary Magistrate), S.C. (1847), Minutes of Evidence, qq. 4379–87, J. Beckwith (Leeds Union), qq. 4048–67, C. H. Richard (Vice-Chairman of the Manchester Board of Guardians) S.C. (1854); Minutes of Evidence, qq. 6314–16. T. E. Headley (Assistant Overseer Sunderland Union), qq. 2800–01.

27. It is certain that a detailed study of destitution among the English at this period would reveal much suffering both in scale and depth. See 'Death of an English woman from starvation', *Manchester Guardian*, 5 December 1849 and

'Death of five children from starvation', *Cardiff and Merthyr Guardian*, 5 April 1856.

28. George Carr, Liverpool Workhouse Master, S.C. (1854), Minutes of Evidence, qq.5592–5611.

29. S.C. (1847), Minutes of Evidence, E. Rushton, qq 4419–23.

30. PRO MH12/Prescot 6095/1847, Letter dated 11 November 1847 from John Heyes, Clerk to the Prescot Union to the Poor Law Commissioners.

31. PRO/MH12/Prescot 6095/1847, Letter dated 1 June 1848 from Prescot Guardians to Poor Law Commissioners.

32. PP (1850) Vol. XXVII, Second Report of the Poor Law Board, Appendix, p. 108.

33. PP (1850) Vol. XXVII, Second Report of the Poor Law Board, Appendix, p. 109.

34. PP (HC) 1847–48, Vol. LII, Reports and Communications on Vagrancy, p. 83.

35. PP (HC) 1847–48 Vol. LII, Reports and Communications on Vagrancy, p. 84.

36. PP (HC) 1847–48, Vol. LII, Reports and Communications on Vagrancy, p. 79.

37. PP (HC) 1847–48, Vol. LII, Reports and Communications on Vagrancy, p. 108.

38. S.C. (1854), Appendix No. 17, written Evidence of R. Pashley, pp. 664–5.

39. S.C. (1854) Appendix No. 17, R. Pashley, written evidence, p. 666.

40. S.C. (1854) Appendix No. 17, R. Pashley, written evidence, p. 665.

41 *Liverpool Standard*, 8 May 1849.

42. *Manchester Guardian*, 7 January 1854.

43. S.C. (1847) Evidence of M. D. Lowndes, Minutes of Evidence, q. 4618; E. Rushton, q. 4619.

44. For example, do they include cost of pauper coffins, hospital treatment, clothing, and soup, etc, or do they refer simply to the cash payments? The cost per head in Newport averages at $3\frac{1}{2}$d per head, indicating casual Irish-poor. In the case of Cardiff, the cost was 8 shillings and 5d per head, indicating more permanent Irish paupers.

45. Dr Duncan, *Medical Officer's Report*, 1847, p. 8.

46. Dr Duncan, *Medical Officer's Report*, 1847, pp. 18–19.

47. *The Times*, 8 May 1847. Sir George Grey told the House of Commons, on 7 March, that the Liverpool authorities could have use of the vessels.

48. Dr Duncan, *Medical Officer's Report*, 1847, Table IV, p. 14.

49. Liverpool Workhouses Admissions and Discharges Register, November 1846–February 1848, *Liverpool Record Office*, 358/Se1/19/3.

50. PRO/MH12/8089/Newport/1847, Report of John Lewis, Assistant Poor Law Commissioner, on his inspection of Newport Union on 5 June 1847.

51. *Newcastle Journal*, 17 April 1847.

52. PRO/MH12/3069/Gateshead/1847, Letter from Clerk to the Gateshead Union to the Poor Law Commissioners.

53. *Staffordshire Advertiser*, 15 May 1847.

54. The case of Michael Duignan caused a furore in Ireland and England and was covered widely by the press. It was the subject of an enquiry ordered by the Home Secretary. PRO/MH12/6176/Rochdale/1846–47, Secretary of State to Poor Law Commissioners, dated 6 October 1847. For extensive coverage of the enquiry held in Rochdale, see *Manchester Guardian*, 25 and 29 September; 2 October 1847.

55. I have completed a book on the experience of the Famine Irish in Britain during 1847, *Black '47: Britain and the Famine Irish* (forthcoming Macmillan, 1997). Using previously unused archive material the evidence concerning the overwhelming disparity in English and Irish death rates is strongly convincing. The study also includes the first attempt to cost the Famine refugee relief operation in major areas of Irish settlements.

56. For Manchester see S. Fielding, *Class and Ethnicity: Irish Catholics in England,*

1850–1939, Oxford University Press, Buckingham, 1993. For a detailed treatment of religious conflict in Liverpool see F. Neal, *Sectarian Violence: The Liverpool Experience 1815–1914*, Manchester University Press, Manchester, 1988. Also F. Neal, 'English–Irish conflict in the North West of England: economics, racism, anti–Catholicism or simple xenophobia?' *North West Labour History*, No. 16, 1991/92, pp. 14–35; F. Neal, 'English–Irish Conflict in the North–East of England', in J. Belchem and P. Buckland (eds), *The Irish in British Labour History*, Institute of Irish Studies, Liverpool, 1993, pp. 59–85.

4 The orphans of Grosse Île: Canada and the adoption of Irish Famine orphans, 1847–48

Marianna O'Gallagher

To Canada on the timber ships

The period known as 'the Great Migration' began in the years immediately after the Napoleonic Wars. The closure of war industries, and other post-war changes combined with the continuing timber trade from Canada across the Atlantic established a transportation network between Canada and the British Isles. The empty ships returning to Canada had, at the beginning of the nineteenth century, conveyed a small number of passengers, and certain quantities of manufactured goods to Canadian ports. But it was after the wars that the shipping companies realized that there were great profits in the 'immigrant trade', that is, in fitting their timber ships with a basic minimum of necessities, not to say comforts, and then taking on board a paying ballast – the displaced persons of England, Ireland, Scotland and Wales. It was sailing vessels like these that brought the earliest Irish thousands to Canada in the 30 years and more preceding the Great Famine.

When the Famine years arrived there was a mad rush to the ports to find safety overseas and avaricious ship owners put back into service many of the old tubs that had been abandoned after their use in the timber trade. It was these vessels that won the sobriquet 'coffin ships'.

The sad fleets of 1847 were often denied entry to the United States by the port authorities, under penalty of huge fines and head taxes: hence the great influx of 'Famine Irish' into Canada. Canada was a colony of Great Britain at the time and, therefore, could not refuse entrance to ships from the mother country. There were no restrictions on passengers disembarking from the British Isles and Ireland, like the sickly crowds who came from the Irish estates of the great English landowners such as Lord Palmerston of Sligo and Lord Darnley of Meath.[1] However, many individuals and families eventually made their way to the United States .

Though other cities on Canada's east coast received their share of immigrants, the story of the adoption of orphans more particularly belongs in the setting of Grosse Île and Quebec City. Quebec City, founded in 1608 by the French, stood at the height of deep water navigation, on the Saint Lawrence, at a place that the Indians named, 'Where-the-river-narrows'. In

1847 Quebec City was only beginning to lose pre-eminence to Montreal as the principal river port: most of the ocean traffic still stopped at Quebec. The city had become accustomed to hosting immigrants to the number of double its own population almost every year during the navigation season that usually lasted from May to November.

Quebec was connected by primitive roads, by steamship, and in mid-century by railroad to Montreal. Winter travel over frozen roads and indeed over frozen rivers was sometimes preferable to the joggling misery of stage coach over corduroy road in summer. However, it was in the summer-time that fleets of emigrant vessels filled the port. The roads and rivers formed the network over which the immigrants, and necessarily any orphaned children, would travel on their way to new homes.

Grosse Île: the quarantine station

In 1830 an epidemic of Asiatic cholera broke out in Europe, and Imperial British and local Canadian authorities sought some measures to confront an outbreak, and prevent the spread of disease into the colony. Money was voted in February 1832, for the establishment of a quarantine station. It was opened as soon as the ice left the river, in May, at Grosse Île – a small island about 50 kilometres downstream from Quebec City.[2] But cholera still travelled with the immigrant on the ships that by-passed the inadequacy of Grosse Île, and there were disastrous outbreaks in the cities of Canada. The same phenomenon was to occur 15 years later in 1847 when the island's hospital facilities were strained to overflowing and people – both evidently sick, and apparently well – carried the disease of typhus into the interior.

Even after the events of 1832 little had been done to improve facilities at Grosse Île. For example, a deep water pier was not finished until late in August of 1847 so all through the months of May, June and July of that year, the doctors and other inspectors had to board the ships from small boats and the passengers had to transfer in midstream from ships to the lighters which brought them ashore. Descriptions of this period abound: the scramble of sick, weakened, the old, the feeble, children, mothers with babes-in-arms, making their way down shaky structures, or ships' ladders, or being carried: corpses being winched out of the holds.

The army from the Quebec City garrison served as police. Later, civilians, drafted from among the immigrants, tried to keep order. The small island kept filling up – more than 20,000 by mid-June, some sick, some well.

Because Grosse Île was linked by steamship to Quebec City and to Montreal, and then by canal boats and by railway to other Canadian cities, and indeed to the United States, it was easy for people released from quarantine to travel inland. It was also easy for disease to be carried inland with the masses seeking to get away from Grosse Île. It is from this island that the orphans came in their hundreds.

Quebec City 1847

The first ship to arrive in the port of Quebec from overseas in 1847 was the *Albino* from Glasgow, which docked on 24 April. Although 24 April was early for the river to be clear of ice, cargo and a few passengers landed without incident. Usually the big sailing vessels did not come in until the end of the first week in May. By the end of April in 1847, however, 105 vessels had cleared quarantine and arrived in the port of Quebec, with cargo, and with cabin passengers. Incoming vessels reported, early in May, that there were hundreds of ships in the Gulf waiting for the ice to clear.

However, it was not until 14 May, that the alarm was sounded from Grosse Île concerning ships arriving with very large numbers of fever-ridden immigrants aboard. From the ports of Ireland and Liverpool, where many Irish families had fled in hope of quick passage to America, came the stream of ships that carried many confident people to as quick a grave as any in Ireland. The first vessel to fit the description of a coffin ship and bear the first bad news for a bad summer was the *Syria* from Liverpool, carrying 241 passengers, most of them sick.

Disturbing reports of the state of affairs on Grosse Île were made known very quickly in Quebec City in May. The priests from the seminary, serving as chaplains on the island, the military men, and the doctors spoke of what they saw, but the threadbare survivors who had been allowed to by-pass the quarantine as healthy carried a more powerful message. They were now dribbling onto the wharves of Quebec, ragged, and often barefoot, some – according to popular tradition in Quebec City – with their rosaries around their necks.

The numbers of children were noted by all concerned – especially by the priests writing from Grosse Île. By the end of May, Rev. Charles-Felix Cazeau, the secretary to the diocese of Quebec, began a correspondence that would continue to touch many lives through the next two or three years. In February the Archbishop of Quebec, Joseph Signay, had ordered a collection of money, for famine relief, throughout all the parishes of the diocese. Part of the money had already been sent to Ireland and Scotland. At the end of May, Cazeau wrote, in the name of the Archbishop, to the priests of the diocese:

> A great number of Irish emigrants have arrived here in complete destitution. Many among them who sought a better life here on this continent died during the crossing or at Grosse Île, and have left orphans who must not simply be abandoned. Given these circumstances, My Lord the Archbishop considers it proper to use in their favour the money originally destined for the poor in Ireland, money still in his hands, provided those who have given it have no objections. Consequently His Grace instructs me to write to you concerning this matter so that you may consult your parishioners who took part in the good work, and let me know as soon as possible their reply.[3]

Archbishop Joseph Signay was beginning to receive almost daily reports from his men at Grosse Île. In an attempt to stem the tide of people who vainly sought refuge in Canada, the Archbishop felt called upon to write to his fellow bishops in Ireland to warn them of the terrible conditions in Canada. His letter, dated 9 June, to the Irish bishops, was published in several Irish newspapers.

> Anchoring at Grosse-Île, about 30 miles below, where they are compelled to perform a quarantine, the transatlantic vessels were most commonly infected with sick and dying emigrants. Last week at that station were detained more than 2,000 patients, of whom scarcely more than a half could find a shelter on the hold of their respective vessels, in some cases abandoned by their own friends, spreading contagion among the other healthy passengers who were confined in the vessels, and exhibiting the heart-rending spectacle of a mortality three times greater than what prevailed ashore. Our provincial Government has undoubtedly manifested the greatest zeal and most parental anxiety in assisting the unhappy emigrants.... . Already more than a thousand human beings have been consigned to their eternal rest in the catholic cemetery, precursors of thousands of others who will rejoin them there, if the stream of emigration from Ireland continues to flow with the same abundance.... . One catholic clergyman alone in ordinary circumstances ministered to the spiritual wants of the Quarantine Station; but this year the services of even seven at a time have been indispensably required to afford to the dying emigrants the last rites and consolations of their cherished religion... . Amid the present confusion, we have had neither leisure nor opportunity to ascertain the number of orphans and families that are thrown for support on public charity.[4]

Meanwhile, in its role of quarantine – to prevent the spread of disease into the colony – the station authority required ships to anchor in the moorage between Grosse Île and Île Marguerite to the south, and await inspection by a medical officer. Sick passengers were obliged to disembark, go to the hospitals in the quarantine for treatment and recovery, while their questionably healthy relatives could wait for them in the part of the island assigned to them. The ships were then subjected to a cleansing, which consisted variously of washing down with disinfectants, or whitewashing, or simply hosing down of decks. Many of the ships carried cargo, and captains were anxious to continue upriver to Quebec to deliver the goods, and to land in the city whatever passengers had been given a clean bill of health and who wished to continue their journey inland.

The military ran the island. However, by the time Captain F. G. Scott, and Captain Reeve were on duty at Grosse Île in 1847, the medical superintendent directed operations: of inspection of ships, of landing passengers, of dismissing those who were considered well enough to travel up stream. Dr George Mellis Douglas, a Scot, had assumed the position of medical supervisor of the island in the late 1830s: at this point he would be tested in all his inventiveness, his patience and even his physical strength, for he, like many of those others working on the island, fell sick of typhus, but recovered before the end of the summer to resume his duties.

In an ideal situation, or in ordinary circumstances, this system should have worked. In 1847, however, as in 1832, the fleet of stinking vessels, and the flood of sick immigrants from them soon overwhelmed the facilities on the island. Early in the summer of 1847 the army had to send extra manpower to the island, and the crowds of sick continued to come. Both the

Catholic and Anglican chapels were soon being used as hospitals, and the soldiers who had been working as carpenters to build the sheds, were now called upon to pitch the tents supplied by the army.

The first recorded death in the parish register of St. Luke of Grosse Île for 1847 was that of a $4^1/2$ year old by the name of Ellen Kane, the daughter of the weaver John Kane and his wife, Bridget McNally of Kilmore in County Mayo. Father Bernard McGauran performed the sad office of requiem. However, he also had the joy, that same day 15 May , of baptizing Owen, the son of Henry Woods, sawyer, and Anne Duffy from Anamullen in County Monaghan, born on board ship on 21 April. The godparents were Patrick Coyle and Mary Smith. Four days later Father McGauran baptized Mary Ryan, born at sea on 5 May, daughter of Edward Ryan and Harriett Pole of Boker in Tipperary. Michael (H—illegible) and Johanna Croake were the godparents. However the registers of St. Luke carried a sadder burden for the rest of the summer. Daily records of death were kept by both the Catholic and Anglican priests, and by the hospital stewards. Due to the large numbers of burials it was impossible to offer individual graves. The trenches where the bodies lie are visible today on Grosse Île.

The orphans

Both letters previously cited – that of Secretary Cazeau dealing with money from the collections and Joseph Signay's appeal to the Bishops of Ireland – touched briefly on the presence of many orphans. Father Bernard McGauran, the first of the priests to go to the quarantine station in May, wrote on the 31st of that month: 'There are already a great number of orphans, and I recommend them to your Grace'.

On 3 June, Abbé Elzéar Alexandre Taschereau, who would later become Canada's first cardinal, wrote to the Bishop:

> The number of orphans is very large, and unfortunately we can do nothing more to date, than to confide them to a few mothers of families to whom we have been able to give a little money to help them buy food. Most will die like the others, happy not to continue in their misery here below! I saw a child playing with the hand of his mother who had just expired! I always thought that the presence of a corpse in the hold would elicit some sort of emotion, but I have had several pointed out to me with a sort of indifference as we passed by their beds where they lie until the coffins are ready: I regard this as a new mark of the degradation brought on by an excess of suffering and misfortune.[5]

From the requisitions submitted by Captain Scott in 1847 and 1848, it is evident that he provided space for the children on Grosse Île once they were freed from the hospitals. He hired a nurse to look after them.[6]

As a result of the appeals made by the Bishops of Quebec and Montreal to their parishioners urging them to accept the children into their families, a routine was established: a missionary released on furlough from Grosse Île, brought with him on his return to Quebec City by the steamboat, a crowd of little children whom he delivered to the Emigrant and Marine Hospital, or to the Charitable Ladies' orphanages, or to the General Hospital in Quebec. The priest then returned to his own parish, either in the city or in the countryside, explained the matter to his parishioners and then returned to Quebec, to fetch as many children as he could fit into a horse-drawn cart, and return to his parish. Many stories have been handed down in families concerning this dramatic interval in the lives of their great-grandparents.

Anglican records for the Diocese of Montreal recount that by 11 June 1847 a group of Protestant Irish children arrived in Montreal, and were received by Ann McCord at the orphanage there. The children varied greatly in ages: indeed, several young women were in their twenties, beyond the usual age for orphanage children. But Ann McCord reported that she could not turn these young women away for there was no care elsewhere for them. Several of these older girls were escorting younger brothers and sisters.

Documentation for the orphanages in Quebec City is much more detailed than for those of Montreal or Kingston, and the records reveal a number of patterns. For example, children in family groups under the care of an older sibling hardly out of his or her teens. Some children were orphaned by death on board ship or at the quarantine hospitals. Others were simply separated from their parents, and later were re-united. The term 'orphan' has been applied quite broadly. All the centres, Quebec, Montreal and Kingston reported at one time or another, and in one form or another, that parents came to find their children, or the children were forwarded to relatives, or that the children themselves left to find relatives.

The orphanages acted as hospitals or simply shelters, and became holding stations for parents and children who waited to find each other. One can imagine the running back and forth, the exchanges of information, the names of children being talked about in the city, the parents here, the children there; or children running away in despair. At such times the parish priests no doubt became central persons around whom would circulate much information, especially the Irish priest Father Patrick McMahon at St. Patrick's Church in Quebec City.

In Quebec City there were orphanages of long-standing, since the city was a seaport and a garrison town and had an unfortunate share of abandoned infants and children. But the care of the orphans also came into the hands of generous men and women in the cities of Quebec, Montreal, Ottawa, Kingston and Toronto. In most cases it was women who took charge, and in several instances it was newly formed religious communities of women, or new establishments of these women which came to the rescue of the destitute.

'Les Dames Compatissantes de Québec', usually translated as 'the Charitable Ladies of Quebec', was such an establishment: a group of ladies, English, and French, Protestant and Catholic, who had banded together in the 1830s to care for the children. In 1849 the Grey Nuns of Montreal took over their Quebec orphanage and preserved the documents of their predecessors' work – particularly an 1847–48 register of 600 children's names, parentage and origin, adoptive parents' names and where possible, home towns and the vessels they arrived on. With this kind of information carefully recorded, the document is among the most valuable and evocative of the reams of paper from that epoch.[7]

Additionally, the Anglican diocesan authorities of both Quebec and Montreal recorded names and sent reports to the Civil Secretary, as did the Sister Hospitallers of St. Joseph in Kingston, and the Sisters of Providence in Montreal. These reports are all valuable documents.

The first entry in the 1847–48 register was penned on 27 July: No. 1, John Jennings, thirteen year old son of Thad... No other information except that John died on 9 August. The second entry is for John Kane, on the same day: no background information. This John died on 13 August. Was he a brother of the Ellen Kane whose burial was the first recorded for the summer on Grosse Île? Other entries for Honorah and Timothy Kane are easily identifiable as Ellen's sister and brother, both of whom were adopted in Rimouski. The third and fourth entries are for July, with no specific day: Catherine (13), and Nancy (10, daughters of Thaddeus McGarrill and Mary Delary of Drumrily in Cavan, from the ship *Royalist*. Both girls were adopted in Lotbinière, near Quebec City, but Catherine eventually went to New York. The first sixty or so names have simply 'July 1847' as entry date.

Adoptions

The adoption procedure for these years also seems to have been a very informal affair. In those days in the Province of Quebec there were formalities concerning the care of children – especially children left to a widowed mother – in the form of a guardianship, duly signed before a notary, and usually exercised by a male relative over the children. But it is difficult to find instances of any such procedure being applied in the case of the Irish children.

Names

Many babies were taken in nameless and grew up knowing only that they were Irish. Some grew up using the name of their foster parents, but at the time of marriage reverted to the Irish name, if they knew it.

Within the lists themselves, one can see the difficulties faced by a French-speaking secretary, or for that matter, an English person not familiar with Irish names, or even Irish accents. There are very original and extraordinary names on the lists – sometimes the script is indecipherable. When the lists were typewritten in later years by one equally unfamiliar with Irish names, the errors were compounded. In other instances, only a vocalizing of the written word will help, because the writer at the time tried to render what he or she heard a child say: a case in point, is that of the Fitzpatrick family from Kilkenny. In 1847, they are registered as coming from DEROAR. They came from 'The Rower' in Kilkenny. On the 1848 list, another contingent of Fitzpatricks from the same place is listed as coming from 'Kowes', but this error is a result of poor interpretation of the writing.

Decipher if you will: Lardworty, Holaran, Holloran, Holaron, Linehan, Linen, Lennon, Goorivan, Ovans, McGauly, McGourty, Flamingham, Flammingan, Flinigan, Galcher, Goragons, Montyers, Flaveny, Mugafrom, McCoughan, McGousty, McFlousty, Jossangan.

Other information can be drawn from the lists. The limited number of Christian names, or given names, leads one to wonder if in these mid-century days the children still had old Gaelic names, but either used English ones, or had them imposed upon them by the list-takers. Anne, Brigid, Mary, Johanna, Catherine, Margaret, Peggy, Nancy, Jane, appear with great regularity; among the boys, James, John, Michael, Bernard, Patrick, Thomas, Edward, Dennis. Brigid is written as Bridget in Quebec, as Brigide in Montreal. Margaret is regularly written as Marguerite, Edward as Edouard. There are no Kevins, a rare Brendan, no Siobhan or even Patricia. Town and county names suffer too: Caree, probably for Kerry; Drone for Tyrone.

Orphanages and families

Before the Charitable Ladies' orphanages in St. Roch's and in the Upper Town of Quebec City began to receive children, many were taken in by families through the intercession of Fr. Patrick McMahon, other parish priests of the city, and priests of the rural parishes near Grosse Île. Saint Patrick's people had erected shelters for the orphans in the yard of their church on Ste. Hélène Street in the Upper Town, and families came directly there to take children into their homes. Thus there were many children whose names were never inscribed on any lists presented to the government when the Diocese later made an application for financial help. It is possible, however, that these families may have received some financial compensation for the extra food and clothing required for the care of the children since there is mention at the beginning of the summer of individual placements having been made.

In the Lower Town, closer to the docks, there was already a great deal of poverty. The city had been devastated by two huge fires; the most recent during the summer of 1846 destroyed 1,200 dwellings and killed ten people. Thus the churches of that part of the city do not generally feature in the adoption list kept by the Charitable Ladies. However, one individual in Diamond Harbour, the grocer Thomas Bogue is noteworthy: Bogue had been married barely two years, his establishment had burned in 1846, but he and his wife adopted 7-year-old Henry McDonald from Tyrone in the summer of 1848.

The Rev. Mr Beaubien, a French-Canadian priest attached to St. Patrick's parish, collected clothing and deposited it at the St. Roch parish convent of the Sisters of Notre Dame for distribution to the poor. One can imagine such efforts being duplicated around the city. And all the time there were more and more children either at Grosse Île or wandering in the streets.

There existed several orphanages in Quebec City: in the parish of St. Roch's in the Lower Town; on Richelieu Street in the Upper Town, near St. Patrick's Church. Besides putting up the shelters near the church, St. Patrick's parish rented a house, far out in the suburbs, on St. Louis Road, where children could be cared for and restored to health. The house was praised for its location far away from other dwellings, with plenty of fresh air and space to play. Contagion was still feared during that dreadful summer, and with good reason. There were unhappy results of placing children too early with families. *Le Canadien*, a Quebec City newspaper, reported on 16 July 1847 that a generous mother of eight children had taken in a small baby, had cared for it, and restored it to health. In doing that however, the mother had caught typhus and died. A similar, but numerically more horrible occurrence was reported by a Montreal paper ten days later: the Grey Nuns had brought some children from the sheds at Point St. Charles into their own orphanage, contagion spread and, in all, 117 children died, among them both residents and newcomers.

Individuals as well as parishes and the government came to the assistance of the children. James J. Nesbitt, the shipbuilder, gave over his house on Prince Edward Street, near the port, for the orphans in May.

Disease

During July the letters from the Archdiocese to the Governor General's office began to deal with the need for money to care for the many in distress. Bishop Signay wrote to Lord Elgin on 24 July:

> Your Excellency is no doubt well aware that here, as in Montreal, the sickness that has this year afflicted the emigrants from the moment of their departure from Ireland, has also deprived a great number of children of the support that their condition requires. Until now, public charity has come to the aid of these orphans; more than a hundred of them have been placed in respectable families where they have found care no less assiduous than what they would have received from their parents: and I have reason to believe that I could place an even larger number in the same fashion. But we are beginning to fear that these unfortunate children carry the germ of the sickness into the homes where they are gathered: already some of the newspapers have spread the alarm and it cannot be denied that a few facts do seem to support their contention. The result has been that the zeal that many of the people of my diocese showed at first to care for these abandoned children, now is almost entirely paralysed.
>
> Almost at the point of seeing these orphans without resource – and they will continue to arrive each week from Grosse Îsle and to continue to be discharged from the Marine Hospital; knowing above all that the Emigration Agent has no money on hand for their subsistence, I take the liberty of having recourse to Your Excellency to beg you to take the fate of these unfortunates into consideration....
>
> I submit with confidence to Your Excellency the predicament we find

ourselves in. I am certain that you will use the power that you have to assist us out of this difficulty.[8]

This letter was but one of many that would follow well into 1849, repeating the need for government assistance in paying for medical help, clothing, shelter, and the travel expenses required for the transport of the children to the country families that were willing to care for them.

There were sad effects in other ways too. Disease was carried into the country settlements despite efforts made to control its spread. The Reverend William King, Anglican priest of St. Sylvester, about 70 kilometres south of Quebec City, rode from his home parish to Quebec, and made his way to Grosse Île to minister to the sick. When he returned home, the state of his clothing transferred the sickness to his little son Frederick. The boy died. Later Mr King's service at Grosse Île was recognized by a grant of land in Northern Quebec offered to him by Queen Victoria.[9]

It was for reasons like these that the authorities preferred to build temporary shelters for the sick, or to keep the children in isolation in rented quarters until they were cleared of all disease. There was occasional panic, or refusal to take the children. Dominic Daly, the Provincial Secretary, issued a directive that children were not to be given up for adoption unless they were in good health. Evidence of this can be seen on the lists sent from the Emigration Agent – they included a column recording the child's health.

It was not only the parishes of the District of Quebec that gathered up the children. A letter from Father Thomas Cook, of Trois Rivières, addressed to the Archbishop on 18 July 1847, reads: 'Messrs Harper and O'Reilly [priests] went through here this morning, in great spirits. Charitable people everywhere are arguing over who is to have the orphans whom they have brought from Quebec'.[10]

The orphans: traditions in Quebec families

Léo Tye, French-speaking, 90-year old retired farmer of Ste. Croix de Lotbinière, in the province of Quebec, loved to repeat the story told him by his grandfather, Daniel Tighe of Roscommon. The family is French-speaking today, hence the phonetic spelling of the name. Léo Tye was eighty-three when he recounted this story:

> In 1847, Mary, widow of Bernard Tighe, left Ireland with her five children and her young brother. Because of the potato famine, she was obliged to leave her small lot of about two arpents [a French measure of land] of rented land in the parish of Lissinoufy, county Roscommon. Her ticket to Canada was paid for by the Queen of England. She embarked for Canada in Dublin, on the ship *Naomi*.
> The voyage was a long nightmare of eight weeks. Drinking water ran low and food was reduced to one meal a day. Comfort and hygiene were non-existent. Typhus broke out on board, and the ship was ordered to stop at Grosse Île. Of Mary Tighe's family only two children survived: Daniel, aged 12, and Catherine, 9 years old. When the children left the ship, they never saw the other family members again, nor did they have any word about them.

On 8 August 1847, Daniel and Catherine along with several other immigrants left Grosse Île on a sail boat which brought them to Quebec. On the high tide, the vessel entered the St. Charles River and brought the passengers to the General Hospital where they were very well treated.

Then one morning, the pastor of Lotbinière, Father Edouard Faucher [native of Bellechasse] came to get Daniel and Catherine and eleven other Irish children. He loaded them into his horse drawn 'express wagon with three benches'; himself, during the long trek, held one of the smaller children on his knees.

As had been agreed upon, he stopped at François Coulombe's farm on Rang St. Eustache, for all the children to have dinner, before going on the remaining few miles to his presbytery at Lotbinière.

Mr and Mrs Coulombe adopted Daniel and decided to keep Catherine for a few days while waiting for a house to welcome her. The children cried so hard at the idea of being separated that they were inconsolable. The Coulombes decided that they would adopt Catherine too.

The Coulombes proved to be good parents to these two orphans. Upon the parents' death, Daniel inherited their good farm, which since then, has been handed on from father to son. Today Richard Tye lives there.

In the cemetery of St. Louis de Lotbinière, Daniel raised a beautiful monument inscribed to his adoptive father and mother. All this I remember as if it were yesterday, for it was told to me by my grandfather, Daniel Tighe.[11]

There are other traditions in other families. A French-speaking boy by the name of Lynch from Montmagny, the town nearest Grosse Île, told this story about his ancestor:

My great-grandfather Lynch was only a boy, and he felt like a prisoner on the island, so he constructed a makeshift raft for himself, and half-swam, half floated the almost ten miles across the river from Grosse Île to the nearest town, Montmagny, where, after recovering with a kind family, he set off on a trek that took him to the United States. However, within a couple of years, he was back in Montmagny, to find the girl whom he had met so fleetingly in his bedraggled condition coming out of the water, out of a famine in Ireland and out of quarantine on Grosse Île. He married his girl.

The storyteller loves to remember this extraordinary Irish branch on his French-Canadian family tree.[12] Similarly, Patrick Kelly of Ste. Foy, Quebec, liked to recount to his children and grandchildren the story his grandmother, Catherine Leonard, had told him over the course of years.

We learn from history that many Irish died of typhus on their way to Canada in 1847. 'The bodies were thrown into the sea', we often hear it said. However, I am not going to go over the sad story of those years of famine and fever which killed millions of people.

I would prefer to tell you about my grandmother Catherine Leonard who was born in County Louth in Ireland. She emigrated at the age of 12, in 1847 with her brothers and sisters and her parents: Nicholas Leonard and Mary Carlin. When they reached the St. Lawrence, all the passengers who were still alive were dropped at Grosse Île, and put into quarantine. Doctors and nurses came down from Quebec to care for the sick. Some among them caught typhus and died.

My grandmother and one of her brothers were the only survivors in their family. My grandparents lived in our house when I was a boy. I often had visits with my grandmother and she talked to me about this sad part of her child-hood. I asked her how she was treated while she was sick on Grosse Île.

She told me how the government had had a hospital and several sheds built for the sick. Even these were not enough and they had also pitched canvas tents. In the tents there was straw for a mattress and a blanket for each person. Those in the tents had more fresh air than those in the hospitals, hence they got better faster than those in the hospitals. Medical science was not as advanced then as it is now.

Those who looked after the sick had to be careful not to catch the sickness themselves. Those who fed the sick did not go into the tents. To feed those within, they put food on a long-handled shovel and reached it in the door of the tent to avoid getting too close. The food consisted of porridge, milk and water. The sick were supposed to stay in the tents until they got strong enough to walk away under their own power. Despite this rigorous treatment, many did recover.

I can remember very well my grandmother telling me these things.[13]

We can find confirmation of this family story in the records. Catherine Leonard, born in Tullyallen in Louth, 1835, daughter of Nicolas and Mary Carlin, landed at Grosse Île in 1847 off the ship *Greenock*. According to the Charitable Ladies' record her older sister Anne and younger brother Michael were, like her, adopted in Frampton, Quebec: Catherine by Robert Duncan, the others by James and Patrick Farrell. A 9-year old sister Judith died in September of 1847, and a younger brother Nicholas, a 4-year old, 'disappeared' says the record. Catherine married John Kelly of Frampton and they had several children, some dying in youth as so often sadly happened in days gone by. Catherine outlived her husband by only a year and died in 1916. John and Catherine have numerous descendants: grandson Fr. Philip was a well-known priest who served in many parishes, both French and English, in the diocese of Quebec. His brothers John and Patrick (the storyteller) and their sister Emelia have many descendants.

There are many ways that the orphans of 1847 are remembered: Fathers Patrick and Thomas Quinn served in the Drummondville area of Quebec and have their stories recounted in the parish histories, and in the semi-naries where they studied.

Patrick was 6 years old in 1847 when he and his 12 year old brother Thomas came to Grosse Île. They were children of James Quinn and Peggy Lyons of Lisanuffy in County Roscommon. Deposited at Grosse Île off the ship *Naomi* at the end of June or beginning of July 1847, they were regis-tered in the orphanage in Quebec City on 9 July. They were befriended by Father Hugh Robson, who foreseeing his own death from typhus, put the boys into the care of a fellow priest, Father Luc Trahan who saw to it that they were adopted in Nicolet by George Bourke. Eventually both boys received their education at the classical college there, and both became priests in the diocese of Drummondville, Patrick in 1862, and Thomas in 1864.

There is also the story of Robert Walsh from the 1848 migration. He too became a priest in the same seminary, and was appointed professor at his ordination. In order to enhance education at the Séminaire de Nicolet,

Father Walsh travelled extensively in Europe and wrote of his return to Ireland. He is remembered also for a beautiful eulogy he wrote on the death of D'Arcy McGee, the Irish-born 'Father of Confederation', assassinated by Fenians in Ottawa in 1868 .

Children and families

Children who found their parents in Canada

There are many well documented examples of children who found their parents after the difficult summer was over, and some sort of peace came to the turbulent cities. As autumn and winter approached, fewer immigrants came, and those who found themselves in the cities could begin to put their lives together, find their children, or find their parents, and then take the next step of finding employment, with the hope of acquiring a piece of land upon which to farm or cut timber. The material that follows is drawn from the Register kept by Les Dames Compatissantes.[14]

Dennis Byrnes, for example, an 8-year old, son of Dennis and Biddy Byrne off the bark *Pandora*, spent almost a year with Francis Gallagher in Quebec, and then found his father in Montreal. Of Hugh Cawly, a 12-year old from Tipperary, son of Hugh and Peggy Cawly, off the *Sir Robert Peel*, adopted by Mr Wheeler in Frampton, it is noted that his mother is in hospital.

The same report is offered for the 14-year old, James Connors, son of James and Julia Reardon, of Kilfinane in Limerick, arrived on the *Jane Black*. Young as he was 'he went into service', says the orphanage register. His time in service did not last long for he soon returned for his 5-year old sister Mary, and they went to their brother in Boston.

There is a notation about Johanna Daly, a 6-year old who died in the month of September, that her father was living in the city, and the mother was in hospital. Another Daly child, John, aged 11, died while his father waited for him in the United States.

Children who came in sibling groups

The registers frequently offer other bits of information that lead us to believe that there were very many children sent out from Ireland in the charge of an older brother or sister, with the hope of reaching relatives already established here. In an effort to save the childen's lives, parents remained at home and paid the passage for the children. One report even went so far as to estimate that there may have been as many as 50 children for every adult on board some of the ships. It is easy to imagine parents making such a decision. Also, one can imagine, that on board ship, at the moment of a food shortage, many a mother gave up her ration in favour of her children, and thus risked her own life.

Such speculations are substantiated by, for example, an entry in the

Charitable Ladies' register: Patrick Donovan, 15 years of age, son of Patrick Donovan and Johanna McCarthy (of town of Caree? in County Cork), off the ship *Henriette Mary*. Patrick was taken in by Mr Donohue of Champlain Street. 'His mother is in Ireland', says the record. One can see a mother trusting her 15-year old to be able to look after himself.

Or look at the Fitzpatrick family from The Rower in Kilkenny: 18-year old Bridget shepherded her brothers (Edward 15, John 10), sisters (Anne 13, Ellen 8), and perhaps a 14-year old, Michael, who died on 23 August without his parents' names being registered. Of 8-year old Ellen it is noted that she was returned to her mother. On a research trip to The Rower in 1985, I learned that one of the Fitzpatrick boys had also returned to Ireland.

Children with relatives in the United States

As can be seen in the lists, some Irish families had relatives in the United States. During the summer of 1847, it was easier and cheaper to obtain passage in the old timber ships that had plied the ocean between Great Britain and Quebec, and which had been hastily refitted for the carriage of passengers eager to leave the desolation in Ireland. It was also less complicated, for many of the landlords were also ship owners with agents in Quebec, and they quite happily allowed their vessels to carry passengers to Quebec.

Perhaps the notation 'returned to father in New York', or elsewhere, indicates that the fathers, already working in North America, had sent for their children. Margaret Dowly, 10-year old daughter of John Dowly and Margaret Nellis, from Kellisha, off the ship *Superior*, died on 28 October. 'Mother is in the States', is added to the record. Mary (13), daughter of David and Mary Walsh, from Killaby in Mayo, from the ship *Anna*, returned to her mother in Ohio, after having been cared for by Mr Bowman in St. Roch's parish in Quebec.

Margaret Ryan (14), daughter of Michael Ryan and Catherine Hogan, from Nockevally in Tipperary, came on the ship *Avon*. She left on 14 November to live with uncle Hogan in Chateauguay, New York. Ann (15), Catherine (20), Ellen (12), Mary (19), Owen (14), Pat (10), children of James Sheridan and Mary Connor, from Lisanuffy in Roscommon, came on the *Naomi*, and left for Lockport, in the US, on 2 October 1847.

Jane McGuire (18), daughter of William McGuire and Jane Hays, from Drumlin in Cavan, off the ship *Jonah Elgin* was adopted by A. C. de Lachevrotière in Lotbinière, but married Gr. Commerford in Brooklyn, New York. Matthew Lynch (6), from Corte Hill in Cavan returned to his father in New York.

Follow the adventures of Mary Byrne (Byrnes): in August this 16-year old went to live in Frampton, Quebec, with Pat Wheeler (Whealan?), returned to the orphanage due to illness, but by December was well enough to go to Baltimore in the US to join her brother. In 1848 Mary Lally (5), daughter of John Lally and Mary, from Killadoon in Sligo, off the

Dromahair, was returned to her father in New York.

Many children's names showed up in more than one place, as monthly reports were filed. Others indeed were the subject of correspondence from one diocese to another. In the letterbook of Bishop Turgeon, Cazeau writes to the chief emigration agent, A. C. Buchanan in January of 1848 that Matthew Caroll, 7 years of age, arrived in June of 1847, his two uncles in Pittsburg having paid for his passage to Quebec. Father W. W. Moylan placed him with Mr MacFarlane. When the uncles did not respond to the news of his arrival in Quebec, the boy was taken by Father McMahon's command, and placed in the orphanage until the 'return of navigation' – that is until the ice went from the river. Moylan was evidently not to be foiled in getting the boy to his uncles. The simple notation on the orphan list, 'Sent to his uncle by the Bishop of Pittsburgh', shows a determined priest at work.

Children with families in Canada

These are some of the stories that can be deduced from reading the registers:

John Fitzgerald, from Kerry, the 10-year old son of Edward Fitzgerald and Catherine Leheay (Leahey) died on 7 October, while his brother languished for him in Montreal. Another mother, in desperation and poverty, gave her daughter away, says the register: Mary Hopkins, from Medor in Longford, was taken out of the hospital by her mother and given to the Grey Nuns.

Bridget Kennedy (17), daughter of Francis Kennedy and Mary Kenny, parish of Monaghan in Tipperary, from the ship *Albion*, returned to her parents in Quebec. The three Lennon children from Tipperary, Patrick (7), Steven (8), Anne (14), were returned to their father, Patrick, who was in hospital.

Mary (10), and Alice (14), daughters of Owen McCabe and Mary Prior, from Drumrily in Leitrim, off the ship *Superior*, left in November to find three brothers-in-law in Providence: Hugh, Michael and James Coley. Eliza McCull, (13), was with George McDonald and his family, grocer on St. Paul Street, until her mother Suzan Wafer, found her. The record does not say if the father, William McCull, from Ardamine in Wexford, off the ship *Royalist*, was still living.

Six-year old Catherine McDonnell went to stay with Jean Auger, while her 10-year old sister Mary Jane, went to Mrs Leblond, in St. Roch. Their mother, Anne Egan, whose husband Bernard had died, was still in the city. It is not stated whether the two Quebec families kept the children or not.

There is evidence of people getting employment on the spot because they were needed: Peter McGinnis, a 20-month old, was adopted by a family of Nicolas Boucher in Lotbinière, while the mother worked in the hospital in Quebec.

John and Ellen Mahon, from Riseisver, Leitrim, from the ship *Argo*, made their way to Toronto, where the children James (8), Margaret (14),

John (12), Terry (10), joined them having left Quebec on 28 October. The children brought with them the sad news that their little 5-year old brother, Thomas, had died.

Ellen Mulhern (13), Margaret (12), Mary (2), Pat (7), children of John Mulhern and Margaret McGauran of Fermanagh, off the ship *Henry* were sent to St. Jean Port Joli, but the mother is in hospital. Did the mother live? – there is no record.

Murdock Murphy (7), was returned to his father John, in Quebec – perhaps the mother Ellen Whelan was living and the family lived happily ever after.

Eliza and John Nolan (11 and 12), children of Peter Nolan and Mary Cassidy, of Strokestown, County Roscommon, off the ship *Blenheim* (Portsmouth to Cork), were returned to parents.

Eliza Nowlan (9), Andrew (12), Grace (7), children of Andrew Nowlan and Margaret Connors, from Capo White in Tipperary, off the brig *Ganges*, were taken in temporarily by different people, then given to their uncle John Connors on Champlain Street, a shoemaker.

Bridget Reilley (7), Helena Reilley (12), and Mary (5), the daughters of Thomas Reilly and Mary Barry from Roscommon, off the ship, *Avon* went to the Ladies of the General Hospital. Their parents found them there. Helena was educated by the Augustinians and eventually became a Sister at the General Hospital. She was the biographer of Bishop de St. Vallier of Quebec, the great benefactor of the General Hospital in its beginnings. Helena also wrote a history of the hospital. In 1860 Bridget married Michael Thomas Heuson (variously reported as Samson or Heuson) in Notre Dame des Anges chapel, at the hospital. Evidently this family stayed in Quebec.

Michael and Patrick Wall, 12 and 14-year old sons of James Wall and Mary Whalen from Abbeyleix in Queen's County (then so-called), from the ship *Wandsworth*, returned to their mother. By 1856 they had a confectionery business in Quebec City, and eventually all married Irish girls in the city. Their brother John joined with them in the family business. Perhaps he was an older brother who had preceded them?

The flowering of benevolence

One of the most striking phenomena of the nineteenth century was the establishment and the growth of the religious communities and benevolent associations in the cities. Besides the continued growth or the revival of the old congregations of nuns there were also new orders in Europe, especially in Ireland, which expanded to North America, as the nuns travelled with their fellow country people to the new world. New societies or religious orders were not the prerogative of the old world: North America witnessed the same zeal. The United States saw Elizabeth Seton and the establishment of the Sisters of Charity and the parochial school system; and Frances Cabrini and her order whose special interest was the care of immigrants.

In Canada, in the cities of Quebec and Montreal, there were many long-established communities of nuns who offered the usual care that a population required: education in boarding schools: care of the feeble-minded in institutions, of the sick in hospitals, of the abandoned in foundling homes and orphanages, and of elderly women in their convents. Early in the nineteenth century, however, both these cities were flooded with immigrants, mostly transient, but so numerous as to need care of a different kind, and to an unaccustomed degree.

The migration of 1832 had already brought the plight of sick immigrants, and the children they left behind, into sharp prominence, and groups of benevolent people, mostly women, began to gather together to attempt to minister to the poor unfortunates. In 1832 there had occurred the first outbreak of cholera in North America and in its aftermath there were many abandoned children needing care. All the cities experienced that epidemic and its consequences and dealt with them in different ways.

Lay foundations

Quebec City and Kingston, garrison towns as well as seaports, and Montreal, a port with a growing industrial base, experienced the inevitable results of a bustling city with many abandoned children, foundlings and orphans of all ages. There are institutions today in these cities that can trace their origins back to the generous men and women of all the social and ethnic communities who strove to better the lives of their fellows. Not many of these institutions took the time to write their own histories – hence many can be known in name only, mainly because their requests for money are preserved in government archives.

In Quebec City there were the Protestant Female Orphan Asylum, Elizabeth Taylor, secretary; the Male Orphan Asylum of Quebec, S. L. Ashworth Secretary; The Protestant Orphan Asylum of Quebec, Noah Freer, secretary; the Male Orphan Asylum at St. Roch; as well as the Catholic Orphan Asylum of Quebec, L. R. Chauveau, corresponding Secretary.

The great city of Montreal that would become an industrial and commercial capital had attracted many English merchants, and many Protestant churches had sprung up. In those days of mutual exclusion, it is not surprising to learn that the Protestants created their own care system.

However, for the general organization of emigrant care, adherents of the various faiths worked together. In Montreal, in 1818 the Society of the Relief of Emigrants was formed: the Curé of the Grand Séminaire, Rev. Monseigneur Lesaulnier, Rev. Mr Esson of old St. Gabriel Street Church and Rev. John Bethune of Christ Church were its officers. Mr Viger was the secretary. This brought together several of the strongest churchmen of the city of Montreal.

One story well documented among the stories of Protestant orphan care is that of the Montreal Ladies' Benevolent Society. It was founded in

December 1815, and was first called the Female Benevolent Society of Montreal: Mrs Gibb, Mrs Barrett and Mrs Aird were among its first officers. Their work led to the foundation of the Montreal General Hospital and the Protestant Orphan Asylum.

The society tried to look after the feeding and other care of each child. But in addition, the ladies were concerned about educating the children. The first house of the Benevolent Society was near the Quebec Gate, on Dalhousie Square near Place Viger and the Recollet suburb. There Miss Macfarlane, Ann Dade and Charlotte Seybold ran a school under the Lancastrian system. There was a house of recovery as well which received young people who had been released from prison. A soup kitchen, and a dispensary looked after widows and their children.[15]

The churches co-operated with collections and frequent charity sermons, such as the one that Bishop Mountain delivered on behalf of the work of the women. Most interesting of all their work was the establishment of a Register Office for domestic servants. During the summer of 1832, 10,744 destitute people were cared for by the society.

Other societies in Montreal were the Protestant Orphan Asylum, and the 'Montreal House of Refuge for Widows and Orphans from the Emigrant sheds' with Mesdames Smith and Fisher directing the operation.

Quebec

Conscious of the role that Quebec City was obliged to play in the care of emigrants, the city fathers had encouraged the building of a large Marine and Emigrant Hospital to care for sailors who fell sick, and for emigrants. Far away from the then city centre, the hospital cornerstone was laid in 1832, and the hospital opened in 1834.

In Quebec City, organizations existed similar to those founded in Montreal. Even the names are the same. La Société des Dames charitables de Québec was set up as early as 1831, but received civil incorporation by an Act of Parliament only in 1842. As in Montreal there were Irish women among the majority French Canadians who formed the groups. The women ran a school in which the bilingual Henrietta Chaffers and Ann McMahon were the teachers. Among the founders of the association was Marie Panet, wife of Jean-Thomas Taschereau. We have already met their son, Elzéar Alexandre Taschereau, Canada's first cardinal, but also one of the young priests who served an heroic chaplaincy on Grosse Île in the summer of 1847. Jean-Thomas Taschereau, father of the future cardinal, died in the cholera epidemic of 1832. Mrs Dennis Murray (Ellen Cannon), Mrs John James Nesbitt (Mary Cannon) and others formed part of this group.

Doctor Joseph Painchaud of Quebec had spent a year of study (1845) in Paris where he saw the work of Frederic Ozanam, and joined the local Society of St. Vincent de Paul. On his return he presented the idea to the Bishop of Quebec, and the first conference of the Society of St. Vincent de Paul was founded in Quebec City on 12 November 1846. Within a year, St.

Patrick's Parish had its particular council, and soon after its branches of St. Patrick, St. Anne, St. Stephen, St. Brigid and St. Louis. In an earlier period Painchaud had collaborated with Dr Edmund Bailey O'Callaghan in caring for emigrants in the port of Quebec.

In Quebec City, in 1847, besides the groups that had long before banded together to do something for the poor, individuals acted also: Dr Painchaud of the Society of St. Vincent de Paul, at his own expense had sheds put up in the courtyard of St. Jean-Baptiste Church. J.J. Nesbitt the shipbuilder offered his house as a stopping place for people waiting the release of their relatives from hospital. Before he knew it his dwelling on Prince Edward Street near the docks had become an orphanage.

The work of the religious congregations

Important in the story of orphan care in Montreal is the story of Emilie Tavernier Gamelin, the saintly foundress of the Sisters of Charity of Providence in Montreal, more popularly and simply known as the Sisters of Providence. In 1827, a lay group who called themselves the Ladies of Charity of Montreal (Les Dames de Charité de Montréal) was formed. Father Patrick Phelan, an Irish-born Sulpician priest of the Séminaire de Montréal, was one of the prime movers in the creation of the group. The very large city parish was divided by the women so that work would not be duplicated. It was not exclusively a French group within the large French parish of Montreal, for along with the pioneer members Mme Gabriel Cotté (aged 72 in 1827) and Mme Gamelin, were a Mary McCord, and Agathe Perrault Nowlan. Some Irish women around the city wards included: in Faubourg St. Antoine and St. Joseph, Emelie (Emily?) Munro; in Faubourg Ste. Anne, Miss Mary McCord, who eventually became a teacher at the orphanage; in Faubourg La Ville, Mrs Agathe Fleming. Later Catherine Pyke and Mme Alfred Fitzpatrick had their names added to the list.

These women worked in many different ways to alleviate the sufferings of the people of Montreal, both resident and emigrant, in those days of transient populations. In 1832, especially, they had experienced the misery caused by the cholera epidemic and were able to get funds from the Governor General, Lord Aylmer, to aid in their work. A sweep of the city at that time revealed that there were 172 widows and 520 orphans in the area around the Church of St. James. Madame Gamelin brought six orphans into her own home where she was already caring for four old ladies.

Incidentally, in 1832, alongside all the care being bestowed upon the miserable new arrivals, and the solicitude being voiced for them in the newspapers, there was a protest from within the Assembly: the great French-Canadian political leader, Louis Joseph Papineau railed against the British government for deliberately plotting the cholera epidemic and sending to the shores of Canada sick emigrants to swamp the French-Canadians with their disease and with their language. A closer look into the man's personal story shows that his sister Rosalie Papineau Dessaule had opened her home in St. Hyacinthe to care for cholera victims. Somehow she was able to prevent her own children from falling prey to the sinister disease. Unfortunately Rosalie and Louis Joseph Papineau's own mother died of cholera in Montreal.

It was to be expected that an orphanage should arise out of all these efforts and so the Montreal institution began, and, after several name changes, became known as L'Orphelinat Catholique de Montréal. On 13 August 1832, the charitable ladies were able to take over the abandoned Maison des Recollets at the corner of Ste. Hélène and Notre Dame streets for their orphanage. It soon housed a majority of Irish children.

Eventually Mme Gamelin felt drawn to the religious life. She gathered a group that intended to pursue the active and not the contemplative rule of religious life, 'the Sisters of Providence'. Religious life was attractive to Irish women as well as to the French, and so the order saw several young non-French women join their ranks. Catherine Brady for example, a novice in 1845, died at the age of 24, caring for the Irish in the sheds at Point St. Charles during the summer of 1847. Among her companions were Margaret Walsh, from Kilmore (Kylemore?) in Ireland, Elizabeth Morrison, from Queen's County (Laois) in Ireland, and Louise Henrietta Wilson from Richmond in England.[16]

At the same time as this congregation was in its infancy, another order in Montreal, the Sisters of Charity, or the Grey Nuns, had already established works of charity: the Hôpital Générale de Montréal, orphanages, and convent boarding schools for the education of girls.[17] Their work extended westward to the Red River in Manitoba. In the 1840s they had elected as their Mother Superior, Sister Elizabeth Forbes McMullen, and this community was to play a huge role in the succour of the victims at Point St. Charles.

Montreal

In the summer of 1847, just as the navigation season opened, the government ordered the building of thirteen sheds – the word 'shed' is always used without apology or explanation – near the waterfront at Point St. Charles. An old rope factory standing on the site was converted into a shelter intended for families. At one time in the summer the 100 ft long building had 200 families under its roof. Lean-tos were eventually built next to this to house the children who were sick with smallpox or measles.

The government had built the sheds but had not arranged for any staff to care for the new arrivals. When the Bishop, priests and religious of Montreal saw what was happening there they came to the rescue with an extraordinary effort of charity. The Grey Nuns, especially, came, the first to work amid scenes of desolation. By 13 June there were 23 nuns working in the sheds, caring for the people whom the newspaper *Mélanges Réligieux* described as 'of a thinness that made one shiver'.

Their clothes are falling in rags, they can hardly drag themselves along. In the shelters... one can see them bedded down on the straw pallets, two or three to a bed, prey to sickness, exposed to the dampness and to the extreme heat and cold that have succeeded each other these last few days.[18]

By 25 June it was realized that the Grey Nuns could not continue without relief to offer care in the sheds. The newly created Sisters of Providence were invited to take their place in rotation. The annalist of the Sisters of Providence wrote:

the Grey Nuns, luckier than we, were chosen first to go to the help of these unfortunates. It was only after the 25 of June when one could see that the Grey Nuns were almost worn out that our wishes were given in to, and our Superiors allowed twelve of us to go also to the service of these suffering members of Jesus Christ. Oh, what strength religion gives one! Mere observation of the hideous scenes could shake the courage of the most hardy, but in effect, it was almost as if a thirst like that for gold had overtaken the sisters, and compelled them to subject themselves to imminent danger.[19]

However, the Sisters of Providence were to go a step further in emulating the Grey Nuns. With the help of Bishop Bourget and many generous lay people of Montreal, a house was rented and given the name of Saint Jerome Emiliani House, so-named by the Bishop after an Italian saint who had given up his life looking after fever victims. The house was rented from the widow Perrault-Nowlan, the sister-in-law of Mother Gamelin, the founder of the Sisters of Providence.

The Annals of the Sisters of Providence continue, after describing scenes of filth and misery, particularly the emaciated state of the bodies of both living and dead, at the sheds:

But in the midst of these desolate scenes, there was nothing more touching than the spectacle of a multitude of little children, hardly knowing what it meant to be alive, and already so miserable, rolling around pell-mell helplessly on the paving, without even the failing hand of a mother to save them.

The dreadful misery of these innocents was painful to the eyes of Monseigneur Bourget... .

When the government agreed that a small allowance could be provided to the communities charged with the care of the Irish children, the Bishop hastened to come to their help as soon as possible... .

On July 11 our Sisters collected all the children from the sheds: the little girls were confided to the Good Shepherds, and the little boys were brought to the house which Monseigneur had just rented ... .[20]

One hundred and fifty children were collected. From another source one learns that the children were crying, some in Irish and some in English, for their lost mothers; some of the little girls cried because they would be separated from their brothers.

We hastened to get six carriages, in each of which rode two Sisters who held the smallest ones on their knees and in their arms. Some were only days or even hours old.

> Monseigneur Bourget preceded us in his carriage. Everyone hastened to see the touching cortege, which even the Protestants stopped to admire. Sister Sency and Sister Caron whom the Superior had charged with receiving the children at the new house had hastily prepared to welcome their new guests with twenty bales of hay spread on the floor to serve as beds where they put the hundred and fifty little ones transported from the sheds. The first night seven of the children died. Every day afterwards a few others quit this earth giving place for the numbers that kept coming. Our Sisters stayed at the sheds until October.

One of the first tasks that the Sisters had was to rid the children of the vermin that were devouring them.

> In order to give you an idea of the state of filth that the children were found in, let me tell you that when we cut off the hair that was full of lice, the lice were so numerous and so vigorous that they could walk away with the hair.[21]

During that autumn, the Sisters of Providence and the Grey Nuns placed children with families.

The Grey Nuns continued to be active in care, both at the sheds in Point St. Charles, and in their orphanages. Their Annals contain the same kind of graphic reports, children lifted from the arms of dying mothers, a baby trying to suckle a dead mother:

> Nothing could be sadder than to see these poor immigrants, trembling with weakness, with misery, and covered with vermin. They were lying two or three to a bed, others lay under them; some were half dead; some vomited on the floor. One could see nothing but dirt everywhere: you walked in filth – you had to watch where you put each foot.[22]

Appalling as it is to read such descriptions, it is heart-rending to read names of little girls and boys, of all ages, dying after a few days, or a few weeks, within reach of some kind of new life. Read this: 'Eight children arrived while this list was being made. From 11 July to 18 August we have received 221 children, of which 13 have been given to their parents or protectors; 103 have died; 105 remain.'[23] More hopeful were the stories of children reunited to parents or other relatives, or the success stories of later years.

In the long run what Father O'Rourke wrote in his *History of the Great Famine* was true: 'Much sympathy was shown in Canada for the poor emigrants, and their orphans were to a great extent adopted by charitable families.'[24]

The aftermath: 1848

The famine migration of 1847 has coloured Canadian history. Canadians generally tend to hold two mistaken impressions: they anchor the beginning of the Irish in Canada at that period and they have, therefore, caricatured all the Irish as poor and starving. Neither of these ideas is a reflection of the truth. When the poor unfortunates of 1847 were uprooted from their humble existences in all the corners of Ireland and driven away from the privacy and quiet of their individual or village lives a whole layer of a simple, hardy, but badly oppressed portion of a nation was poured out before the world. The Famine underlined the degradation imposed upon a people by a class system, by a powerful industrial neighbour, by a souless landlord system and by the general corrupting callousness of power and money.

In fact, in Canada, thousands of Irish had already established themselves during the 40 years preceding the famine. The provinces called British North America, along the Atlantic coast and in the valley of the St. Lawrence, had, amid Scots or French or English settlements, their villages entirely Irish in flavour, some Catholic, some Protestant, and some a happy mix of both. Irish men and women brought with them from Ireland their agricultural and organizational skills to create in freedom many a New Ireland in North America. The cities too had Irish among their working and professional classes – the lawyers, notaries, doctors, teachers, priests, nuns, as well as the soldiers and policemen, craftsmen, workmen, entrepreneurs and founders of unions; how many St. Patrick's Churches and St. Patrick's Schools there must be from Newfoundland to Lake Superior, including at least seven in the French province of Quebec.

These early settled Irish came to the assistance of their fellow countrymen in the Famine times. But even though the image of the Famine has been etched into the psyche of Quebec and Canada, the immigrants of 1847 were in search of a haven in 'America', that is, the United States: at least 15,000 crossed the border into the United States from St. Jean-sur-Richelieu in 1847.[25] Others were moved westward to settle in the province of Canada West, urged on and assisted by the Emigration agents.

Though this chapter has striven to give examples, it is in reality quite difficult to find in Quebec direct lines of descent from the Famine survivors. In some cases there may have been a deliberate blotting out of traumatic memory. The daily cares of living can also absorb all interest, and distresses of the past can be forgotten without deliberate intent. The search for the descendants is not an easy one. Even the marriage registers of the villages in Quebec, where many orphans were adopted, have few traces of their presence. In many cases children's names were not known. In other instances the young people moved to the United States as soon as they achieved some autonomy.

The authorities of the orphanages, and the secretaries of the dioceses were not shy or slow to apply to the government for help. There are bills for clothing in general; there are bills for coats especially as the winter approached. There are bills also for the transport of the children to the rural parishes. Miss Ann McCord of Montreal requested money for stoves for the Protestant orphanage. From Montreal, Mesdames Smith and Fisher, of the 'House of Refuge for Widows and Orphans from the Emigrant Sheds', requested aid in February of 1848. On 1 October 1847 the civil secretary agreed that the government would pay for clothing and transport, and an amount of 387 louis was sent to Bishop Signay of Quebec.[26]

In reply to your letter of September 30 asking if the government is ready to pay for or to reimburse the expenses of travel of the orphaned emigrant children under the care of His Lordship the Archbishop of Quebec, into the different parishes of the Diocese where the children have been placed, I have the honour of informing you that it has pleased His Excellency to order that the cost of transport in question be paid from the public purse, His Excellency having received the assurance that these expenses were as moderate as the circumstances would permit.[27]

That the government was pleased with settling the children into willing families, is clear in the following:

At the same time I pray you to tell me, for the information of His Excellency, what prospect does His Grace the Archbishop of Quebec hold for the immediate or very near placement of the orphans who are in the country parishes, so that in those cases where a placement cannot be promptly made, the Government can advise on the means to take, in order to ease the Province of those expenses that the present arrangement causes.[28]

Records show that a government cheque for £100 was sent to an institution in Toronto, in February 1848. In May of 1848 another amount of 275 louis (about $1,720) was received by the diocese of Quebec.[29] These are but fragmentary notes. A small idea of the enormity of 1847 can be arrived at in comparing three years' expenditures for Grosse Île: 1846, £2,380; 1847, £16,000; 1848, £2,938.[30]

Correspondence was to continue for a long time. Cazeau wrote a long letter in January of 1848, stressing the differences between the cities of Quebec and Montreal:

May His Excellency kindly note:

1. that here in Quebec, unlike Montreal, we do not have uncloistered religious to whom the orphans could be given and who would care for them gratuitously. We were obliged to put them in the care of persons who had to be paid in proportion to the danger that they ran in exercising that ministry. And the danger was such that five among them caught the fever and two died, and we could not hire anyone else unless we agreed that sick or well, their wages would continue to be paid;

2. that we were obliged to pay a considerable indemnity to the four families who occupied the house at the St. Louis Cemetery when they were obliged to find lodging elsewhere, and to make numerous repairs on the house so that it could serve its purpose;

3. that, since the house is a mile distance from the centre of the city, it was necessary to rent a horse and cart for part of each day; 1, so that the priest could go to the asylum each morning, and often in the afternoon, to register the names of the children who arrived each day from Grosse Île or from the Marine Hospital, or from the sheds, and to put the children into the hands of those who wanted to adopt them; 2, for the person in charge of supplies for the establishment; 3, to bring to the asylum the people who came from the country to get the orphans; 4, to carry sick children to the Marine Hospital and to bring back those released in good health.

The account for this would be much higher were it to include all the expenses put out for the orphans before July 25, the moment that the Government took charge. But collections taken up at the time, and the remainder of the collection made in the country on orders of the Archbishop for the unfortunate of Ireland having been used for the care of the orphans, we did not find it necessary to ask for the extra.

His Excellency will take into consideration, I do not doubt, that of the more than 500 children admitted to the asylum before and since July 25, more than 350 have been placed with respectable families or sent to their relatives through the care of the priests charged by the Archbishop with that work, and who thus relieved the Government of seeing to their future.

His Excellency will learn, no doubt with satisfaction, that in placing the children care was taken, as much as possible, not to separate children of the same family, and in nearly all cases, we succeeded at least in placing them in the same parish. We desired that in their misfortune these poor children could at least meet often and console each other for the loss of their parents.[31]

In October of 1848 the Diocese of Quebec was still requesting money for assistance in keeping the orphans of 1847.[32] Again as late as 1849, Father McMahon of St. Patrick's Church in Quebec City requested the government pay for orphans as they had in the past: he had just received word of a family of six Catholic children whose parents had died at sea.[33]

The Civil Secretary's office attempted further to cut down on the expense of child care by defining 'orphan' as narrowly as possible:

Henceforward we will receive at the asylum, according to the decision taken by the Government, only the children of those parents who die at the Marine Hospital.

But a difficulty now presents itself, that is to know should the parents be admitted sick to the Marine Hospital, if we can from now on receive the abandoned children as we did before. It is important that we know the Government's opinion on this subject for surely even before the navigation season a case of this nature will present itself.[34]

There was an immediate outcry. Where were the children to stay while their parents were in hospital? What of the sick or disabled children already in the orphanages whom no one wished to adopt? In the Quebec City register of those very days of December to February, there are notices of the entry of one child after another, or several at a time during the winter months. Where had they been in the meantime? Certainly some had been cared for at the Emigrant and Marine Hospital. It is evident that many stayed at Grosse Île long into the autumn. During the summer not all the children were brought immediately to Quebec: as we have seen, Captain F. G. Scott, commandant of Grosse Île, in July of 1847 had requested that a nurse be engaged to look after the children who were living in the healthy part of the island. A letter from Cazeau to Buchanan acknowledged that Father McMahon, at St. Patrick's Church in Quebec City, as well as the chaplain of the Marine Hospital, had been authorized to dispatch children to the various orphanages. The ordinary people in close contact with the children continued to provide for them as best they could in all circumstances, whether there was money coming in from the government to help, or strict regulations being made to hinder.

Montreal orphans

In Montreal in February of 1848 there were still 150 boys at the Jerome Emiliani House, and 90 still at the sheds at Point St. Charles. On 8 March , Bishop Bourget made a direct appeal to the classical colleges, the religious communities and families to take in the children. Now that the danger of infection was over, it was safe for families to welcome them. To that end there was an open house held at the Jerome Emiliani Home on 13 March, and the people came. The Sulpicians took 12 boys, promising to educate them. The Christian Brothers took six, for whom only five names could be found, with interesting spelling: Michael Bonns (14), John Neekton (13), John Maguire (15), Philip Riely (15), William Kane (17). 12 boys are listed for the Collège de Montréal: Hugh Kane (15), Patt Lowry (15), John Donohy (14), Mark McGuirk (13), John Delasey (3), Patt McCoy (12), Patt Manah (12), Patt Condon (12), Patt Lavery (11), Laurence Linen (10), James Doyle (10) and Thomas Cosgrove.

The Sisters of the Congregation de Notre Dame and those of the Bon Pasteur took six girls and promised to educate them. The Congregation of Notre Dame distributed their girls to their boarding schools around Montreal: Brigide Driscoll (13) went to the Notre Dame boarding school in Montreal itself, while Brigide Foley (8) went to Ste. Claire; Anne Barney (13) went to St. Denis: Anne Shortel (12) went to St. Hyacinth; Anne Riley (12) and Brigide Carte (8) went to Stanstead Convent near the American border.

The girls who went to the Good Shepherds were: Catherine Hear (14), Catherine Lalor (10), Brigide Donoho (8), Brigide Cox (11), Brigide Murphy (8), Johann Ratchford (15), Margaret Mahoney (9), Ellen Hogan (11), Margaret Berney (12), Margaret Crihan (12), Eliza Allen (10), Rose Berns (13). The spelling of the names is that in the original records.

One woman came with the intention of adopting a little girl but went home with a girl and her brother. There are probably many other examples of that kind of warmth. The Grey Nuns and the Sisters of Providence took in all the children that were still sick. An association of lay people formed itself around them to raise money to help the Sisters in their care. The Mayor of Montreal, Edouard Raymond Fabre put £25 for the care of the children into the hands of Father O'Dowd and the Rev. Mr Bethune for distribution to the care givers. (Mayor Fabre's predecessor, John Mills, had died of typhus contracted when he worked with the sick in the sheds in the summer of 1847.) By evening there were but 17 children left in the orphanage: seven girls, aged 9 to 16, and ten boys. It was easy to house and care for these at the Emiliani House.

As late as 6 May 1848, there were many children still being adopted out of the orphanage. Some were late arrivals from the 1847 migration. Another sad contingent would begin drifting in from the emigration season of 1848.

After the typhus epidemic, the Jerome Emiliani House, says the annalist of the Sisters of Providence:

continued to exist and we kept there, the little orphans who had not been placed in homes, and other abandoned children, especially those who had been released from prison. The chapel and the house were big enough that the Priests of the seminary offered the public offices of the Church there for the Irish who lived in the Quebec suburb. Rev. Mr. Lagasse took a few rooms to receive the deaf children and he taught them there. In 1852 a hospital was established for the sick Irish. This hospital was confided to the care of Sisters Wilson, Catherine Stanislas and Marguerite, with a lay committee to support them. It opened January 2. This establishment received the sick of different origins and religions. The number received there was about 300.

This state of affairs lasted until the 8 of July when a terrible fire consumed half of the city of Montreal. The Jerome Emilian House was completely destroyed. We brought 70 sick children to the Hotel Dieu. The Sisters came back to the Motherhouse.[35]

Quebec City

In Quebec City, in addition to the actual day-to-day care and attention to the children, there were continual collections going on. The Minute Book of the Committee of Management of St. Patrick's Church, under date of 14 February 1848, noted:

The treasurer was authorized to pay to his Grace the Archbishop the sum of £200 for the orphans of the Emigration of last season, the same being part of the collection taken up for them in St. Patrick's Church last summer.[36]

The orphanages, one in Lower Town and one in Upper Town near St. Patrick's Church, both run by the Charitable Ladies, received constant attention from the people of St. Patrick's under the leadership of Father Patrick McMahon. Occasionally children were taken from the foster homes and placed back in the orphanage. Both Father McMahon and Father Cazeau, despite the latter's onerous tasks as Secretary of the diocese, and later as Vicar General, followed as well as they could the lives of their protegés. Thus one finds notes about marriages and ordinations in the Register kept in Quebec.

The Upper Town Orphanage could hold 250 children. Because there were always Irish orphans around the city, the place provided a school using the Lancaster System and offering classes in English. Ann McMahon and Marguerite Byrne were teachers there. The school had achieved an excellent reputation, was recognized and hence subsidized, by the government.

One story from that orphanage is told in the Annals of the Grey Nuns, who took over from the Charitable Ladies in 1849:

In the orphanage the boys and girls lived in different quarters. One very small girl could not be shaken out of a state of bewilderment and loss; she complained all the time and seemed always in search of something. The Sisters allowed her to wander anywhere, she was so distraught. In her wanderings she came into the kitchen just as a line of little boys filed in for their meal. Suddenly the little girl began to laugh as she recognized her brother among the boys. Gone were loss and bewilderment. The tears of joy were not only among the children in that kitchen.

A less charming story forms the background to the following notice that appeared in a Quebec newspaper – evidently there were opportunist criminals ready to prey on the charitable:

> Patrick McMahon, Bernard McGauran, H. McGuirk and M. Kenyon, priests, warn the Irish Catholics of Quebec that 'Macarias' from the United States has no authority from ecclesiastical or other authorities to collect money in Quebec. Gazette please copy.[37]

Remembering

There are monuments in several spots on Grosse Île, and in the cities, to commemorate the tragic passage of the Irish. Kingston has a beautiful stone angel over what is left of its cemetery. In Quebec City the monument that honours Canada's first Cardinal also honours his presence among the Irish as a young priest at Grosse Île. On the island itself the doctors, the priests, the unnamed thousands are venerated in stone, none more suitably than the victims of Black '47 in the 40 ft Celtic Cross that stands on the highest point of the island.[38] However, there are many other ways of remembering, and in this, the Irish share with the French the motto of Quebec, 'Je me souviens' – 'I remember'.

Many families gather at Grosse Île recalling the words of a grandparent who experienced a sojourn there or who heard a tale or two. The Kelly, Fitzmaurice, Conway, McKenna, and McConomy families as well as Avril, Roy, and Michaud are a few among them.

There are gatherings in Montreal, also: there is the annual commemorative 'walk to the Stone'. In 1858 and 1859 when Irish navvies, working on the Montreal harbour front, excavated for the approaches to the planned Victoria Bridge, they found themselves on the site of the 1847 sheds. To their consternation they unearthed the cemetery that had received the bones of the unfortunate hundreds who had died there. Within a short time, with the collaboration of their employers, Peto, Brassey and Betts, the navvies put in place a huge stone dug up from the very riverbed. It was dedicated in an impressive ceremony. To this day the Irish of Montreal 'walk to the Stone' in May and hear speeches to remind them to hold very close this part of their history.

In 1989 a greater than usual gathering was held to commemorate the 80th anniversary of the unveiling of the Celtic Cross on Grosse Île. The highlight of that 19 August was a Mass concelebrated by the Archbishop of Quebec, Maurice Cardinal Vachon, Bishop Gaumond of St. Anne de la Pocatière, and Bishop Leonard Crowley of Montreal, in the presence of Bishop Allen Goodings, Anglican Bishop of Quebec. The celebrant spoke of the role of the French clergy of Quebec, Bishop Goodings of his predecessor Bishop Mountain, and Bishop Crowley of the role of the priests and people of Montreal in the rescue of the unfortunate.

After the homilies, the most evocative point of the Mass was the offertory procession. One by one representative people tendered items or objects that elicited a memory or a recognition of history. An 1847 Famine cross from Ireland was on loan for the event. Nothing, however, was more touching than the juxtaposition of a man and a woman carrying the basics of life between them: Rose Masson Dompierre, granddaughter of the baker of Grosse Île, presented a loaf of bread which she had baked in her own kitchen; Léo Tye carried a basket of potatoes from his own farm in St. Croix de Lotbinière, the farm that had been deeded by François Coulombe to his adopted Irish child Daniel Tighe, grandfather of Léo. Léo's son now operates the farmland. The pathos and irony were not lost on the crowd of both French-speaking and English-speaking pilgrims who knew the story of the coming of the Irish.

The guest of honour on that August day in 1989 was the Irish Ambassador to Canada, the Honourable Edward G. Brennan. His attendance brought into focus the relative positions of both Canada and Ireland in 1847 as colonized by Britain; even in 1909, at the original unveiling of the Celtic Cross, amid the hundreds of Irish-born participants, and North American-born children of Irish emigrants, there was no official state of Ireland representative. In 1989 the Ambassador of the Republic of Ireland to Canada attested by his very presence the changed status of both nations, and offered these touching words in both French and English in his speech at the dinner following the Mass:

> To all of those people known and unknown of humble station or high estate, layman and cleric, who aided and succoured the destitute Irish emigrants of 1847 on this island and off it, is owed an immense debt of gratitude. On behalf of the government and people of Ireland I should like to pay tribute to their memory. They will never be forgotten by a grateful Irish nation.[39]

Notes

1. Donald MacKay, *Flight from Famine: The Coming of the Irish to Canada*, McClelland & Stewart, Toronto, 1990, pp. 286–7, pp.189–90.
2. For a fuller history of Grosse Île see Marianna O'Gallagher, *Grosse Île: Gateway to Canada, 1832–1938*, Carraig Books, Quebec, 1984, MacKay, *Flight from Famine*, Chapters 8 and 15.
3. Rev. C.F. Cazeau, Secretary, Archdiocese of Quebec, to the Pastors of the parishes: Archives of the Archdiocese of Quebec/*Mandements de l'Evêque de Québec* [hereafter AAQ], Vol. III (1806–1850), p. 509, translated from the French.
4. Bishop Joseph Signay of Quebec: Circular letter to the Catholic archbishops and bishops of Ireland, AAQ, Vol. III (1806–1850). The original is in English.
5. Abbé Elzéar Alexandre Taschereau to the Bishop of Quebec: Archives of the Diocese of St. Anne-de-la-Pocatière [hereafter APOC], LM– 47, Nos. 19 and 20, translated from the French.
6. RC 1 E1 State Book H (C114), p. 655; also RG 4, C, 1, Provincial Secretary's Office, Vol. 231.
7. O'Gallagher, *Grosse Île: Gateway to Canada*, pp. 117–43. The list is reproduced in the book.

8. AAQ, 210 A, RL, Vol. 20, pp. 38–9, translated from the French.
9. Julien Bilodeau et al. *St. Sylvestre se Raconte, 1828–1978,* Comité des recherches historiques, St.-Sylvestre, 1978.
10. Father Thomas Cook to the Bishop of Quebec, AAQ, 1 CB, Vicaires Généraux, Vol. XII: 40, translated from the French.
11. Léo Tye recounted this story to me in August 1989 on the occasion of his first visit to Grosse Île.
12. The young man by the name of Lynch recounted this tradition to me on the occasion of a trip to Grosse Île, when the boy in question was serving as a deck hand on the ferry.
13. Patrick Kelly told his story for the newsletter *La Traversée,* Vol. 1, No. 1, published in Montmagny, in June 1987.
14. Detailed information on the orphans is taken from the Register from the orphanage of 'Les Dames Compatissantes de Québec', preserved in the Archives of the Grey Nuns of Quebec. This Register is reprinted in O'Gallagher, *Grosse Île: Gateway to Canada.*
15. N. C. Pearce, *History of the Montreal Ladies Benevolent Society 1815–1920,* Montreal, no date.
16. Denise Robillard, *Emilie Tavernier Gamelin,* Les Editions du Méridien, Montréal, 1988.
17. The Grey Nuns, or Sisters of Charity of Quebec, had been founded, in the eighteenth century in Montreal, by Marguerite d'Youville.
18. *Mélanges Réligieux,* 18 June 1847.
19. 'Annales', Annals of the Sisters of Providence, Montreal, manuscript (translation from the French).
20. Annals of the Sisters of Providence, Montreal.
21. Annals of the Sisters of Providence, Montreal.
22. Annals of the Grey Nuns of Montreal, Archdiocesan Archives of Montreal: manuscript translated from the French.
23. Report of the Ladies of the Good Pastor, August 1847 RG4 C1 3660. The usual English term is 'Sisters of the Good Shepherd', but the translator, unfamiliar with ordinary English usage in Quebec, writes 'Ladies of the Good Pastor'.
24. John O'Rourke, *The History of the Great Irish Famine of 1847 with Notices of Earlier Irish Famines,* Duffy & Co., Dublin, 1902.
25. *British Parliamentary Papers,* Canada, 1847–1848, Vol. 17, pp. 457–67
26. The term 'louis' was frequently used interchangeably with 'pound'. Some have calculated the 387 louis as less than $2,500.
27. Dominic Daly, Provincial Secretary to Rev. C. F. Cazeau, priest secretary of the diocese, AAQ, 60 CN G, Vol. VIII: 26, translated from the French.
28. Dominic Daly to Cazeau, AAQ, 60 CN G, Vol. VIII: 29, translated from the French.
29. AAQ, G, Vol. VIII: 38, 3 May 1848.
30. Parliamentary Paper, 1852, XXXIII (1474), 39, cited in Helen I. Cowan, *British Emigration to British North America,* University of Toronto Press, Toronto, revised 1961, p. 295
31. AAQ, 210 A, RL, Vol. 22, p. 202–05
32. RG 4, C, 1, Provincial Secretary's Office, Vol. 236 Reg. Vol. 2859
33. AAQ, 559 – Father McMahon to James Leslie Provincial Secretary, 12 June 1849. The record book of the Committee of Management of St. Patrick's Church also records that the collections made in the parish on St. Patrick's Day and during the Bishop's campaign were applied to the relief of orphans.
34. AAQ, 210 A, RL, Vol. 22, pp. 219–20, translated from the French.
35. Annals of the Sisters of Charity of Providence of Montreal, Archives of

    Providence.
36. Minute Book Committee of Management, St. Patrick's Church, 14 February 1848.
37. *Quebec Mercury*, 14 December 1847
38. O'Gallagher, *Grosse Île: Gateway to Canada.*
39. Edward G. Brennan, speaking in the the Radharc documentary film, *Grosse Île: The Gateway and the Graveyard*, Dublin, 1990.

5 The Deer Island graves, Boston: the Irish Famine and Irish-American tradition

Francis Costello

Recent accounts of the fate which befell many Irish men, women, and children on Canada's Grosse Île while seeking to flee Ireland's Great Famine have made it clear that arrival in British North America was no guarantee of escape from disease or death.[1] This chapter looks at the harsh reality that awaited other Famine refugees, in Boston in the United States, and stresses that many of the Irish who sought refuge in that city from famine-ravaged Ireland faced further travails on the far side of the Atlantic. While the Massachusetts capital and many neighbouring communities were among the earliest and most generous in providing relief from the horrors of the 'Great Hunger', considerable misery still awaited many Famine refugees in Boston.

To understand the response of the pre-Famine Irish community in Boston we need to be aware, as were the Irish in Boston, that mass death from famine was not new to Ireland. As many as 300,000 men, women, and children may have perished from famine in 1740–41. Michael Drake's 1968 essay on that crisis was, says E. Margaret Crawford, 'the one notable exception' to Irish historiography's concentration on the Great Famine of 1845–50.[2] The famine of 1740–41 was not the result of damage caused by potato blight but by a long and particularly severe winter frost, which affected all crops, but which seems to have been especially destructive of the potato.[3] Owing to the paucity of records, the full extent of the loss of human life that occurred during the famine of 1740–41 is unclear. But Drake found instructive data from such sources as Workhouse admissions in Dublin City: for example he listed admissions of young children as foundlings and those who subsequently died in that facility. By way of comparison, at the end of December 1737 there were 176 foundlings in the Dublin Workhouse. Six years later the number had risen to almost 700. A total of 3,892 foundlings entered the workhouse between those years, of whom 2,754 died. The appearance of starvation and the ailments related to malnutrition characterized most of the children when they entered.[4] Michael Drake notes:

> For seventy years or so after the crisis of 1740–41, the Irish enjoyed an abundance of potatoes. Eaten in large quantities, as they seem to have been, potatoes

provided a more than adequate diet. Whether the crop was deficient, as it must have been from time to time, we can assume that it was the cottar's pig, not the cottar and his family, that went short.[5]

This suggestion, the famous 'gap in famines', has been much criticized of late.[6] Certainly by the beginning of the nineteenth century there was an awareness of the vulnerability of 'the cottar and his family' to a failure of the potato. Data, such as William Wilde's 'Table of Irish Famines' suggest that failure of the potato caused 'distress', near famine conditions or famine among the poor in at least some parts of Ireland in 1801, 1821, 1822, 1825, 1831, 1833, 1835, 1836, and 1839.[7] 'The final victory of the potato as the exclusive diet of the labourer and small farmer had been achieved (outside of Ulster and parts of Leinster) by 1800… The narrowing of the diet had of course the effect of removing the safety-net of a second subsistence crop… '[8]

Of course, the Great Famine of the 1840s produced a level of horror so incomprehensible that it easily erased the famine of 1740–41, and later periods of starvation and distress, from the popular memory. Word that a potato blight had struck Ireland in a manner far more disastrous than those earlier famines came to Boston with the arrival of the *Britannia* – a Royal Mail steamship – on 20 November 1845. Soon after the *Boston Post* reported that a third of the potato crop had been destroyed, accompanying the report with the warning that 'famine, gaunt, horrible, destroying famine, seems impending… '[9]

The Irish in Boston

At this time, the Irish of Boston numbered some 25,000 out of a total population of 165,000. The number of Irish in Boston would grow exponentially during the next five years, due to the calamity in Ireland. It is clear that the news of the potato crop's condition filled at least some of the Irish who lived in Boston with a sense of foreboding. They knew far better than anyone how dependent were the family members and friends they left behind on the potato for their very existence. They knew the exploitative system of land tenure that the Irish native population endured. They knew that this system forced reliance on multiple potato yields from small plots, while other crops and produce, including oats, barley, and butter, along with cattle and pigs, were marked for export, as the landlords' rents.

One man in the Boston area who threw himself whole-heartedly into the early efforts at famine relief was Fr. J. Flaherty of St. Mary's Church in Salem. Fr. Flaherty called a conference in Boston on 2 December 1845 which lead to the creation of the Irish Charitable Fund. This initiative marked the first evidence of an American response to the mounting human crisis in Ireland. It also marked the beginning of the first ever effort, from within the United States, to direct humanitarian aid abroad. Within the span of a few short weeks, Fr. Flaherty had collected over $2,000, largely from people of quite limited means, and most of them of Irish origin.[10]

His earnest efforts were minimized, however, by a debate that broke out within the Boston Irish community, a debate that had its origins in Dublin. Heated division occurred within the ranks of the Boston branch of the Repeal Association over whether large-scale famine relief from the United States was in fact necessary. From his vantage point in Dublin, Thomas D'Arcy McGee, a former Editor of *The Boston Pilot* – the Catholic journal of that city – argued that all fundraising efforts should be directed towards gaining repeal of the Act of Union, which bound Ireland within the United Kingdom. Claiming to base his views on the opinion of 'leading public men in Ireland', McGee argued that Boston's efforts at famine relief were 'under the circumstances rather hasty and ill advised... .'[11] His comments helped to cripple the work of Fr. Flaherty and others in Boston. That McGee, then only 20 years old, was acting solely on his own accord, did not become apparent until some time later.[12]

By the late spring of 1846 the blight in the potato crop appeared to sub-side. But this was to prove only a temporary reprieve by nature. Within a period of a few days at the end of July, the potato crop throughout Ireland was affected in a most horrific fashion. By then those who were now engulfed by the devastation of hunger in Ireland had lost a devoted friend. Fr. Flaherty was dead in Boston.

While there was generosity in personal terms from many individual Britons, the largest humanitarian response came from the United States. Of the $1 million raised by the Central Relief Committee established in Dublin in November 1846 by the Society of Friends (the Quakers), almost two thirds came from the United States. Slowly, the British government acted, but instead of the outright provisions of food, it offered a public works programme which would itself be abandoned the following year when the Tory Administration under Lord Russell came to power. Between 1845 and 1850, £7 million , including Workhouse relief, was spent by the British government to alleviate the famine. Yet, by comparison, £20 million had been raised by the British Treasury during the 1830s to reim-burse the slave owners of the West Indies for emancipation, while some £70 million was spent on the Crimean War disaster of 1854–56.[13]

One of the most stirring appeals for aid in Boston was delivered from the pulpit of Boston's Cathedral of the Holy Cross by Bishop John Fitzpatrick in February 1846. 'A voice comes to us from across the ocean...', Ireland, he said, 'no longer laments her lost abilities... nor com-plains of her galling fetter that still bind her, but she bewails her sons and her daughters and her little children, suffering, starving, and dead.' The worshippers listened intently, many weeping openly, as their bishop brought his sermon to a dramatic crescendo. 'It is vain and idle... to dis-cuss the causes to which such calamities may be traced. It is vain and idle to discuss of the duties of Parliament and of landlords, and debate whether it is the will or the power that is wanting in them to afford relief. In the meantime, men that are our brethren all like specters, crawl over the ground like worms, and die because they have no food...'[14]

Indeed Bishop Fitzpatrick's reference, to the futility of casting political blame, was given obvious validity in Ireland by the degree in which the separatist nationalism, advocated by Thomas Davis and the Young Ireland Movement, had become irrelevant in a country ravished by famine. As Seamus Deane has astutely noted: 'If Irish cultural identity was to be preserved or created by an initial repudiation of British industrialism and utilitarianism, then the kind of state intervention needed to meet the requirement of the Irish people during the famine was, in theory at least, not to be welcomed.'[15] The fact was that Ireland required massive amounts of public and private relief. In the event, the amount of public relief was inadequate. Could private charity fill the gap?

The voyage of the *Jamestown*

Private charity in Massachusetts tried to help. We have the examples of those who went to Ireland to expedite the delivery of humanitarian assistance, in addition to those who donated for famine relief. Captain Robert Bennet Forbes, the scion of a wealthy Massachusetts shipping family, was among the first in the United States to attempt to bring aid to Ireland directly. And, through his efforts, Forbes played a key role in launching the first instance of US government involvement with humanitarian assistance abroad, a policy development whose long-term consequences are still with us today.

In February 1847, the US Congress considered the question of whether to appropriate $500,000 in famine aid for Ireland and Scotland, a measure proposed by Senator J. J. Crittenden of Kentucky. Due to Constitutional concerns, the proposals languished in the House and Senate for months. President James Knox Polk – himself a product of 'Scotch-Irish' roots – remarked in an entry in his diary that had the measure reached his desk he would have felt compelled to veto it: 'I have all the sympathy for the oppressed Irish and Scotch which any citizen can have… but my solemn conviction is that Congress possesses no power to use public money for such purpose.'[16]

An amendment was suggested, altering the call for outright commitment of US Government funds to a proposal seeking approval for the use of US naval vessels to transport food to Ireland and other countries. This too was rejected. But in that amendment lay the basis for a proposal by Captain Robert Forbes' brother, John Murray Forbes, that Congress should be petitioned for a single warship. Captain Robert Forbes acted on the idea, with a petition to Congress requesting the loan of the US naval sloop, *Jamestown*. Robert Forbes offered to lead a relief voyage to Ireland with the vessel – then anchored at Charlestown, Massachusetts. Congressman Robert Winthrop of Boston was joined by several others in moving the Boston proposal in the House, attaching to it a similar petition from New York.

On 3 March 1847 a joint resolution was approved, authorizing the use of the *Jamestown* by Captain Robert Forbes, and the use of a second vessel, the USS *Macedonian* by Captain George DeKay of New Jersey. Two days later, President Polk called a Cabinet meeting when it was agreed that the vessels should be made available to Forbes and DeKay – marking the first time in US history that a matter involving Ireland had been discussed at that level. Almost immediately, Captain Robert Forbes set to work on his mission, backed by the resources of his family, and in particular by his brother, John Murray Forbes. Together the brothers were able to expedite the voyage: for example, they enlisted the support of their network of shipping contracts in London to gain permission for the *Jamestown*'s cargo to be placed in the British government's warehouses in Cork, and to have any port charges waived for the return voyage.

In preparation for the Forbes' voyage, the former Mayor of Liverpool, William Rathbone set up offices in Cork. Robert Bennet Forbes readied the ship with supplies and the necessary outfitting. George Hilliard, a Boston historian of the time, commented that the 'whole thing is too beautiful to think of – the sympathy, the quickness to give relief, the warm benevolence running like an electric shock through the whole land, in aid of a distressed foreign country are truly exhilarating.'[17] Robert Forbes selected a total of four officers for the voyage. Each officer was an experienced captain in his own right. For the crew, Forbes placed notices in local newspapers and actively sought out experienced able-bodied seamen in Cape Anne, New Bedford, Cape Cod and South Dennis, in addition to Boston. In the event, many of these towns paid the wages of those who went on the voyage.

On 28 March 1847, the *Jamestown* set out for County Cork. A vessel built for war was now embarked on a mission of mercy. Its provisions included 400 barrels of pork, 100 tierces of ham, 655 barrels of corn meal, 7,375 barrels of bread, 353 barrels of beans, and 83 barrels of peas. Three weeks later, the *Jamestown* caught its first glimpse of the Irish coast. Thousands lined the streets of Cove (Cobh – later, in August 1849, to be renamed 'Queenstown' in honour of Queen Victoria's visit) where the vessel dropped anchor. In Cork City, the bells of Shandon were rung throughout the day.

In the end, 800 tons of relief provided by Captain Robert Forbes and his Boston Committee were divided over some 160 localities in allotments of 5 tons each. Twenty tons went to Cork City, 100 tons to Bantry, 80 tons to Glandore, 60 tons to Clonakilty, while other parts of the cargo were dispatched by British naval steamers to other selected Irish ports. The arrival of the *Jamestown*, and soon after, the *Macedonian*, marked an end to the British requirement that ships carrying such humanitarian foodstuffs had to be transferred to British owned bottoms before the cargoes could be unloaded. Relief vessels could now go directly to Irish ports. The two ships showed the way for more than 100 other vessels from the United States which would carry some 20,000 tons of provisions, to a total value of £280,000. (Today that would represent a value of approximately $30 million, or £15 million.)[18]

The authorities marked Boston's generosity with a reception given in the visitors' honour by the citizens of Cove, and another reception in Cork City itself given by the Temperance Institute, which the organization's founder, Father Theobald Mathew, attended. Captain Robert Forbes, however, elected to remain in Cork to oversee the distribution of food, declining invitations to enjoy the Crown's hospitality in Dublin and London. Forbes provided his own first hand account of what he witnessed in Cork City, where he had to avoid being crushed to death by a throng of desperate people seeking his assistance.

> I went with Father Mathew, only a few steps out of one of the principle streets … into the Valley of the shadow of death?… It was the valley of death and pestilence itself. I would gladly forget it if I could the scenes I witnessed. In two hours walk I saw more actual distress and poverty than I ever saw in my whole life, not excepting during a residence of years in China…[19]

Ironically, the recollections of the visitor from Boston were not too far removed from an account by the English Member of Parliament and journalist William Cobbet of a hamlet in the nearby town of Middleton some 13 years earlier: Cobbet described in graphic detail the grim poverty of its residents in the decade before the Famine. The residents lived in a cluster of some 40 to 50 hovels, all of which were constructed of mud walls, covered with rafters and straw. The houses were 21ft long and 9ft wide. Cobbet observed:

> The floor the bare ground. No fireplace, no chimney, the fire (made of potato haulm) made one side against the wall, and the smoke going out of a hole on the roof. No table. One chair. There was one window, 9 inches by 5 and the glass broken half out. There was a mud wall about four feet high to separate off the end of the shed for a family to sleep, lest the hog should kill and eat the little children when the father and mother were both out … . And it happened some time ago that a poor mother, being ill on her straw, unable to move and having her baby dead beside her, had its head eaten off before her own eyes![20]

Throughout April and May of 1847, other shipments of food reached Ireland from the Boston Committee which Forbes had established. Thus, on 7 April, a ship named the *Tartar* left Boston's India Wharf with $29,753 worth of supplies. The Boston Committee also acted to enable relief from New York to reach Ireland on board the other US Naval ship, the *Macedonian*. This ship had languished in New York for months, without supplies or food, owing to various factional disputes in that city over how the vessel should be used and who should captain it. In mid-June of 1847, the *Macedonian* finally left New York for Ireland with 4,000 barrels of corn meal, rice, peas, and beans.

Deer Island

For those able to leave Ireland, emigration, by any vessel available, had become, by 1847, in the vast majority of cases, a necessity for survival rather than simply one option among many. For those who sought a new life in Boston the wretched journey, which averaged from six to nine weeks, on the 'coffin ships' that left from the ports of Derry, Galway, Cove, and Liverpool, was often perilous for even the strongest who undertook the voyage. Many who climbed the gangway of those vessels were already plagued by sickness or infirm through old age. Others would contract cholera, typhus, and other diseases aboard ship. The misery which abounded on these vessels has been well chronicled elsewhere. In the end, the average span of life left to those who survived the Famine was only six years. The quickened pace of mortality was undoubtedly due to the effects of hardship, malnutrition and exposure – in Ireland and America, and on the long journey between – on those who survived the Famine.

The Famine indeed led to a mass exodus from Ireland. The threat of starvation combined with the evictions of the holders of small farms, the destruction of entire villages under the Irish Poor Law of 1847, paved the way for a new class of landowners under the Encumbered Estates Act of 1850 and combined to make emigration a necessity for many between 1846 and 1850. But not all who left Ireland during these years were destitute. While the first wave of Famine-affected emigrants included many who were driven out by the fear of starvation, among the number of these Famine 'escapees' were some better-off farmers and artisans, and urban dwellers. One such emigrant was Thomas Fitzgerald, who clung to his farm until 1848 when the situation became completely hopeless. His great-great grandson, John Fitzgerald Kennedy, would become the first Catholic President of the United States.[21] Patrick Kennedy, President Kennedy's paternal great-grandfather had left Ireland for Boston somewhat earlier, but he appears to have been led forth by a search for opportunity, rather than driven by a fear of starvation. Indeed, as Cormac Ó Gráda notes, while the Famine may have encouraged, or forced, emigration from groups who had not greatly featured in previous migrations, 'nevertheless a poverty trap may well have prevented some of the very poorest from leaving.'[22]

The vast majority of the 25,000 immigrants who arrived in Boston during 1847 were from Ireland. At first the ill and dying arriving at Boston's Long Wharf were taken to a temporary facility from which they were later dispatched to local hospitals. By May of that year, however, the City of Boston officially established a quarantine hospital and 'Alms House' on Deer Island. The facility was opened by City of Boston officials 'as a precautionary measure to ward off a pestilence that would have been ruinous to the public health and business of the City.'[23]

However, the decision to open the quarantine hospital and alms house on a small island in Boston harbour appears to have been motivated not by health considerations alone. A petition signed by several hundred residents of Boston following a rally at Fanueil Hall in 1847 demanded that the city fathers 'take all appropriate steps to cause all paupers in our Alms houses to be sent or conveyed to the places beyond the seas or otherwise, to which they may belong.' That these sentiments were taken to heart by the municipal government is evidenced by an order passed by the City Council and signed by Major Josiah Quincy on 21 June 1847. The order called upon the City's health commissioners to 'adopt stringent measures as may be in their power to prevent further transportation by land or seas of foreign paupers.' It is at least implicit from official records that not all who were quarantined on Deer Island were in fact ill at the time of their arrival. For example, we see the quarantining of entire families. Furthermore the location of an alms house for the poor within the same structure as a quarantine facility for infectious diseases stresses the low value attached by Boston's city fathers to the lives of the indigent Irish immigrants.[24] The establishment of the quarantine facility at Deer Island during a period of unprecedented Irish immigration to Boston, due to the Famine, serves to underscore the point made by a Thomas O'Connor on the difficulties faced by the Irish immigrant to Boston for much of the nineteenth century:

> If there has existed in the nineteenth century a computer able to digest all the appropriate data, it would have reported one city in the entire world where an Irish Catholic, under any circumstances, should never, ever, set foot. That city was Boston, Massachusetts. It was an American city with an intensely homogeneous Anglo-Saxon character, an inbred hostility toward people who were Irish, a fierce and violent revulsion against all things Roman Catholic, and an economic system that precluded most forms of unskilled labour. Boston was a city that rejected the Irish from the very start and saw no way in which people of that ethnic background could ever be fully assimilated into the prevailing American culture ... Yankee Boston was unique in the depth and intensity of its convictions.[25]

From its opening in May 1847, to the end of 1850, a total of 4,816 men, women, and children were admitted to the quarantine hospital and alms house at Deer Island. According to the official records, some 4,069 of the total admitted to Deer Island during those years were ill upon arrival. More died on Deer Island than were buried there – so that it is likely that at least some of the dead were claimed for burial by family or friends. During the four-year period cited, 852 Irish Famine refugees were buried on the island. Almost one in five of those sent to Deer Island died.

Today, the mass grave, containing the remains of the 852 Irish immigrants who died on Deer Island, is atop a hill on the north-east portion of the island facing the outer reaches of Boston Harbour, the gateway to the Atlantic that brought them. To the rear is the skyline of the city they came so close to living in. But the Irish on Deer Island are not alone. Scattered throughout the island are the remains of some 500 native Americans who had been left there to starve to death by the colonial governors of Boston, 150 years before the Irish Famine. The involuntary resting place for the two peoples produces an image at odds with the Pilgrim father John Winthrop's vision of Boston as a 'shining city on a hill'.

The first entry into the death ledger at the quarantine facility was made days after it opened on 29 May 1847. The first victim was 6-year old Mary Nelson, who succumbed to typhus. She was followed to the grave shortly afterwards by 1-year old Mary Connelly and 21 year old Mary Flaherty, also dead from typhus.

A review of the death records shows that typhus was by far the greatest cause of death for the Irish on Deer Island. This very infectious disease caused severe prostration and was accompanied by nervous symptoms and an eruption of red spots on the victim's body. The disease was transmitted by lice and fleas. Dysentery, equally painful and horrific, because of the prolonged agony it caused the sufferer, came next among the causes of death. Ironically, the same disease would claim the life of James Knox Polk after he left the Presidency of the United States in 1849.

Steadily, over the course of months, disease claimed more and more Irish refugees from the Famine. The life that they had tried to rescue from Ireland was finally seized from them on an island in Boston Harbour. Death on Deer Island affected a wide age range. To give some examples: on 2 October 1847, 8-year old Patrick Fanning, 30 -year old Rosanna Egan, and 48-year old Timothy Curtain perished there from disease. What went through the minds, we might ask, of such older victims as Rose McFarland and Bridget Reynolds, aged 65 and 75 respectively. Did they, at their advanced age, regret that they had not died in Ireland after all, rather than enduring a journey of several weeks on a crowded upper desk, only to die not quite a mile from their destination?

The grim drama continued into the last days of 1849 and well into the first days of 1850, as disease on Deer Island continued to claim the young and the old. Three-month old Alice Leahy and 10-year old Patrick Hourahan both succumbed to typhus on Christmas Eve.

More tragedy follows

The awful decade of the 1840s, however, refused to end without imposing still more tragedy on those Irish seeking a refuge in Boston from the Famine. On the night of 6 October 1849, a ship named the *St. John*, bound for Boston from Galway with just over 100 passengers, was struck by a severe storm at the outer reaches of Boston Harbour. The ship's hull was knocked about repeatedly by the lashing winds. Moving southward at 4 am on the following day, the ship's captain tried to avoid the rocks off Marblehead and reach the wider expanses of Massachusetts Bay. But the storm grew in intensity. Off Grampus Ledge, near the village of Cohasset, the *St. John* was driven onto the large granite rocks, but not before a whaling vessel, passing to one side, ignored the pleas of those on board the struggling ship.

In all, 92 of the Irish immigrants on board were drowned. Only the captain, a few crew members, and a small number of passengers were able to launch the boat's longboat for a safe landfall. A total of only 15 passengers survived the wreck. Four of them later returned to their native village of Leitir-Meallain (Lettermullen) off the coast of County Galway. Virtually all of the *St. John*'s passengers had come from the same community.

But, as one commentator has noted, the story of the *St. John* cannot serve as an example of British heartlessness, for the *St. John* was 'Irish built, Irish owned, and Irish manned.'[26] The ill-fated 20-year old vessel had been built in only one week in Galway City. The ship's name came from its maiden voyage to New Brunswick in the mid-1820s. When it set sail for Boston on that fateful day in August 1849, the ship's hull was rotten. Off the coast of Cohasset, on the same day that the *St. John* went down, a ship named the *Kathleen* weathered the storm and made it safely to port with another full load of Irish refugees.

A young Massachusetts girl watched the tragedy of the *St. John* unfold. Along with other spectators on the shore she saw the ship's hull split:

> Soon the multitudes with which the beach was thronged began to wave their hats and halloo, and I understand afterwards that then they observed people on the wreck, it was as a motion for a whale boat to come alongside, which paid no heed to the demand, which was one of many inhuman actions of the day.... . The waving of hats led me to infer there were human beings onboard the wreck forthwith I began to put things in readiness, to heat the room with blankets, make beds [since our house] was the nearest house the sufferers would all be brought to for relief. I had enough to do with an occasional glance out the window. At last I perceived some miserable looking creatures that reminded me of drowned rats... they could scarcely walk and were led by men on either side of them... Such a shuddering, shivering, my ears never heard before and such a set of half drowned, half naked, half frightened creatures my eyes never beheld.[27]

The fate of the *St. John* was also chronicled by the acclaimed American writer Henry David Thoreau, who bore witness to the grim spectacle off Cohasset. Thoreau saw the bodies pile higher as each wave washed ashore more contorted corpses, many wrapped in sea weed, their skin turned pale like ivory, their battered bodies drained of blood. He looked at the wreck, and noted from direct contact that some of the ship's timbers 'were so rotten that I could almost thrust my umbrella through them.'[28] Over the course of several days spent there viewing the aftermath of the tragedy, Thoreau observed the affects it had on the residents of the community.

> They would watch there many days and nights for the sea to give up its dead, and their imaginations and sympathies would supply the place of mourners far away, who as yet knew not of the wreck. Many days after this something white was seen floating on the water... It was approached in a boat, and found to be a woman, which had risen in an upright position, whose white cap was blown back with the wind. I saw that the beauty of the shore itself was wrecked for many a lonely walker there, until he could perceive, at last how its beauty was enhanced by wrecks like this.[29]

Thoreau also offered this epitaph to the memory of those who perished:

> If the *St. John* did not make her port here, she has been telegraphed there. The strongest wind cannot stagger a Spirit; it is a Spirit's breath. A just man's purpose cannot be split on any Grampus or material rock, but itself will split rocks till it succeeded.[30]

Conclusion

Over time, among the survivors in Boston of the Irish Famine, there would develop a sense of outrage about the Famine that transcended any initial view that its grim workings were simply the will of God. Indeed, the same *Times* of London that at one stage during the Famine famously expressed satisfaction at the flight of the Irish from Ireland, on more sober reflection recognized that Britain's limited official response could well reap a whirlwind against the British Empire in America:

> If this goes on as it is likely to go on... the United States will become very Irish.... So an Ireland there will still be, but on a colossal scale, and in a new world. We shall only have pushed the Celt westwards. Then, no longer cooped between the Liffey and the Shannon, he will spread from New York to San Francisco, and keep up the ancient feud at an unforeseen advantage... We must gird our loins to encounter the nemesis of seven centuries' misgovernment. To the end of time a hundred million spread over the largest habitable area in the world, and, confronting us everywhere by sea and land, will remember that their forefathers paid tithe to the Protestant clergy, rent to the absentee landlords, and a forced obedience to the laws which these had made. [31]

The Times concern for the impact that those teeming masses of Irish immigrants would have on the social and political fabric of the United States and subsequently on British rule in Ireland was well founded. Whether using America as a launch pad for groups like the Fenians in one generation, or providing material support for the Irish Revolution in the next century, a new species called Irish-Americans, spurred on by the hatred which the Famine had fuelled within them, became increasingly more dangerous to Britain as they climbed the ladders of success in American society.

Most of those claiming Irish heritage in the United States today owe their ancestry not to the waves of Irish immigration in the twentieth century but to those who fled the Famine. To many Irish in America the British response to the Famine, or indeed lack of response, provoked a visceral reaction. British inaction in Ireland laid bare what was to them a glaring double standard and one which fuelled agitation in the United States for an end to Ireland's union with Britain. If Ireland was indeed a part of Britain, the argument went, then why during the height of the Famine, was it treated as an outcast state with its citizens, 'British subjects', allowed to die in great numbers? It was pointed out that many of the fatalities occurred in areas still accessible to various means of transportation for the distribution of food.

Like Isaac Butt in Ireland, the Irish able to settle in America were forced by the Famine to ask questions about the connections between political union with Britain and Ireland's economic collapse.[32] In the crisis the United Kingdom parliament had simply abdicated its responsibilities. Was the Famine then the logical outcome of a whole range of catastrophes stemming from that political union? The list of catastrophes included the collapse of the Irish agricultural prices after 1815, Ireland's integration into the British 'common market' in 1824, and the creation of a land tenure system which forced the bulk of the native population to depend on a single crop for their existence and which would thereby make the results of the potato blight far more severe than in Scotland, within the British Empire, or in Poland, on the continent.

These questions, raised among the Irish in Boston and in other American cities, helped foment rebellion in Ireland for generations to come. They became the stuff which helped build an Irish nation in exile. The combined weight of the bitterness the Famine engendered on a personal basis would have a lingering effect, on those who were forced to flee their homeland and who lived to see their families destroyed in Ireland or destroyed *en route* to America, And, as it had shown in the Famine relief effort, Boston would be among the most prominent centres in America to provide a home to Irish separatist causes in the decades that followed.

At the core of the Irish-American enterprise was something far greater than sentimentality. It was a belief that is still felt today in Boston, against the grim historical backdrop of the wreck of a vessel filled with starving Irish refugees on the approaches of Boston Harbour and the mass grave of Irish Famine victims a few miles away, on Deer Island. Certain truths have not been silenced here by efforts elsewhere to present the Great Famine as something banal. The totality of the suffering – the suffering endured in Ireland and the agony which continued to plague many of the Irish in America – informed the view that the forced migration of a million people and the death of a million more would simply not have happened had Ireland been able to govern itself.

During 1998 the dead on Deer Island will at long last be given a proper burial. A single headstone will list their names, erected by those who came after them. There will be a park at hand where visitors can go to reflect – the result of a co-operative venture with a Massachusetts state agency, the Massachusetts Water Resources Authority, which now has jurisdiction over the island.

It is hoped that, long after the conferences are over and the new volumes that conferences produce have found their places on the bookshelves, the living here will be reminded – whether Irish or not – of the frailty of their humanity. And perhaps they will understand that it would be the greatest insult of all to the memory of those buried on Deer Island to allow the callousness that provoked their consignment there to be replicated in the hearts of their survivors towards other immigrants to Boston in the present.

Notes

1. Donald MacKay, *Flight from Famine: the Coming of the Irish to Canada*, McClelland & Stewart, Toronto, 1990, Chapters 8, 14, 15.
2. Editor's 'Preface', p. v, in E. Margaret Crawford (ed.), *Famine: The Irish Experience, 900—1900*, John Donald, Edinburgh, 1989; speaking of Michael Drake, 'The Irish demographic crisis of 1740–41', in T. W. Moody (ed.), *Historical Studies VI, (papers read before the Irish Conference of Historians)*, Routledge & Kegan Paul, London, 1968.

3. Drake, 'Crisis of 1740–41', p. 109.
4. Drake, 'Crisis of 1740–41', p. 120.
5. Drake, 'Crisis of 1740–41', p. 123.
6. K. H. Connell, *The Population of Ireland, 1740–1845*, Greenwood Press, Westport, 1975 (reprint of 1950, Clarendon Press, Oxford), p. 144, broadly accepts the theory that a 'gap in famines' caused population-increase. David Dickson, 'The gap in famines: a useful myth?', in Crawford (ed.), *Famine: The Irish Experience*, is more critical.
7. 'William Wilde's Table of Irish Famines, 900–1850', edited by E. Margaret Crawford, in Crawford (ed.), *Famine: The Irish Experience*. Wilde's Table has been criticized, because it is a retrospective study, 'deeply influenced' by the Great Famine: see Cormac Ó Gráda, 'Poverty, population, and agriculture, 1801–45', in W. E. Vaughan (ed.), *Ireland Under the Union*, Volume V of *A New History of Ireland*, Clarendon Press, Oxford, 1989, p. 111. However, Ó Gráda accepts that there was in this period a strong 'psycho-social perception of famine': see Ó Gráda, *Ireland: A New Economic History, 1780–1939*, Clarendon Press, Oxford, 1994, p. 12. My point is that the speed of the initial response by the Irish community in Boston shows an awareness of the *vulnerability* of the poor in Ireland to potato crop failure.
8. Dickson, 'The gap in famines', p. 108.
9. *The Boston Post*, 21 November 1845.
10. H.A. Forbes and Henry Lee, *Massachusetts Help to Ireland During the Great Famine*, Metcalf, Boston, 1967, pp. 2–3.
11. Forbes and Lee, *Massachusetts Help to Ireland*.
12. In the Ireland of the 1840s, Thomas D'Arcy McGee was also a propagandist for the pro-separatist Young Ireland movement. His views on Irish national aspirations evolved, however, to the point of open and virulent opposition to the Fenian movement, with its origins in the United States. McGee emigrated to Canada where he rapidly attained high office. He was principal author of the North American Federation Act of 1867 which lead to the creation of Canada's self government within the British Empire. McGee's antipathy to the Fenian movement led to his assassination in 1868 by elements in that American-based secret society. See, Nicholas Flood Davin, *The Irishman in Canada*, Irish University Press, Shannon, 1969 (reprint of first edition, Maclear, Toronto, 1877), p. 648, p. 658.
13. Kevin Whelan, 'Bitter harvest', *Boston College Magazine*, Vol. 55, No. 1, Winter 1996, p. 23; Joel Mokyr, *Why Ireland Starved: A Quantitative and Analytical History of the Irish Economy, 1800–1850*, George Allen & Unwin, London, 1983, p. 292; Christine Kinealy, *This Great Calamity: The Irish Famine, 1845–52*, Gill & MacMillan, Dublin, p. 351; Cormac Ó Gráda, *Ireland: A New Economic History*, Clarendon Press, Oxford, 1994, p. 191.
14. Forbes and Lee, *Massachusetts Help to Ireland*, p. 13.
15. Seamus Deane, 'The Famine and Young Ireland', in *The Field Day Anthology of Irish Writing*, Norton & Co., New York, 1992, Vol. II, p. 117.
16. Forbes and Lee, *Massachusetts Help to Ireland*, p. 27. My attention has been drawn to a helpful article about these debates, Timothy J. Sarbaugh, '"Charity begins at home": the United States Government and Irish Famine relief, 1845–1849', *History Ireland*, Vol. 4, No. 2, Summer 1996.
17. Forbes and Lee, *Massachusetts Help to Ireland*, pp. 31–32.
18. Thomas Gallagher, *Paddy's Lament*, Harcourt, Brace, Jovanovich, New York, 1982, p. 79, citing *Transactions of the Central Relief Committee of the Society of Friends during the Famine in Ireland in 1846 and 1847*, Hodges and Smith, Dublin, 1852.

19. Robert Bennet Forbes, *Jamestown* Copybook I, Diary entry of 14 April 1847: Robert Bennet Forbes Collection, Robert Bennet Forbes Museum, Milton, Massachusetts.
20. Molly Townshend, *Not by Bullets and Bayonets: Cobbetts' Writing on the Irish Question: 1795–1835*, Sheed & Ward, London, 1983, pp. 80–81.
21. Doris Kearns Goodwin, *The Fitzgeralds and the Kennedys*, Simon & Shuster, New York, 1987, pp. 11–12.
22. Cormac Ó Gráda, *Ireland: A New Economic History,1780–1939*, Clarendon Press, Oxford, 1994, p. 177.
23. Massachusetts Senate document of 1847, cited in a memorandum, 'Deer Island Deaths and Burials, 1847–1850', by Edward W. Quill, City Archivist for Boston, City of Boston Archives, 16 May 1990.
24. Quill, 'Deer Island Deaths and Burials', p. 17 .
25. Thomas O'Connor, *The Boston Irish*, Northeastern University Press, Boston, 1995, pp xv–xvi.
26. Paddy Mulkerrins, *The Irish Echo*, 14 April 1984.
27. From the Diary of Elizabeth Lothrop, Cohasset Historical Society, Cohasset, Massachusetts.
28. Henry David Thoreau, *Cape Cod*, Penguin, New York, 1987 (original edition 1865), p. 13.
29. Thoreau, *Cape Cod*, p. 13.
30. Thoreau, *Cape Cod*, p. 15.
31. *The Times* of London, as quoted in *The Nation*, May 1860.
32. David Thornley, *Isaac Butt and Home Rule*, MacGibbon & Kee, London, 1964, p. 18.

6 Lost in transit: Australian reaction to the Irish and Scots Famines, 1845–50

Patrick O'Farrell

The Great Irish Famine has long possessed a dual character – giant fact and giant myth. Its catastrophic dimensions were evident, if erratically comprehended, at the time; its mythologizing came later, from the 1860s, first through the work of John Mitchel, political activist writing as historian. He '"invented" the Great Irish Famine of 1845–49, that is, gave it initially the place it has come to occupy in commonly perceived historical and imaginative understanding. '[1] Mitchel's construction had the benefit (in addition to literary genius) of a decade's perspective and of deliberate historical intent – the Famine arranged and presented as work of pondered historical art.

As contemporary historical insight, the story of the Australian reaction[2] takes interpretation in the opposite direction – away from the imposition of order and attribution of blame – into the operation of the immediate realities of confusion, powerlessness, and self-interest and manipulation of very different stimulus and origin. Of course the scale is tiny: the Irish-born total for all Australian colonies at this time was barely 70,000. But for reasons of distance, circumstance, and social and political context, the Australian reaction magnifies, to a degree which makes startlingly clear (bizarre, even), those elements in the Famine situation which were inchoate, mysterious, obscure, contradictory, fragmented, divisive and paralysing – and resistant to effective confrontation; resistant also to any process of making Irish common cause. The Mitchel interpretation imposes a subsequent structure and plan on chaos, hammering disparate and random facts into a monstrous deliberate plot to exterminate, convicting on the charge that a million and half Irish were 'prudently, and peacefully slain by the English government.' The Australian encounter is contemporary – it is lived through rather than thought through – but its geography is such that it exaggerates to their maximum the factors of time and distance operative on all those not immediately involved. Here is the Famine perceived belatedly, spasmodically, and in the midst of a jumble of other information and polemic of widely varying worth and relevance. And it is the Famine seen, not in itself or the context of Ireland – the concentrated focus natural to the picture the historian is able to contrive – but it is the Famine as filtered through local preconceptions and interests, the

Famine as an external incident or process that has to be absorbed into the structures and demands of another, very different, scene.

As history, the Great Irish Famine now seems clear-cut, singular and scorching as a war, the subject of books and chapter headings, branded into the historical consciousness of a people, unmistakable as both phase and turning point in Irish history. Even those revisionist historians who seek to stress continuities, and to minimize its revolutionary impact on society and economics, drape their arguments around the orthodox structure. The Famine has come to be seen as the theatre of all Ireland in which various political, personal and social dramas, of lesser importance, were staged 1845–50. That was not the way things seemed to contemporaries, particularly those whose encounter with Ireland was through the press – or even those centrally involved: Mitchel's first book (*Jail Journal*, 1854) was highly political, with little on the Famine. Indeed, although the basic elements of his later argument (developed in *The Last Conquest of Ireland (Perhaps)*, 1861) are sketched in the introduction to the *Jail Journal*, the weight of his contention was that Ireland was in a constant state of famine, which merely varied in intensity. The commonplace nature of Irish famine – always somewhere, to some degree – was something accepted, in the sense of known, by contemporaries: the statistician William Wilde compiled in 1851 a table of famines, 900–1850.[3] Its bias was towards the recent past – 1800–45 – a situation suggesting that in 1845 the appearance of famine would have had a certain 'normalcy': who was to know, at its beginning, or even earlier stages, that here was cataclysm? So, particularly the outside or distant contemporary observer turned from harrowing tales of famine, with whatever degree of sameness and familiarity may have weakened their impact, to the rest of what was happening in Ireland – which was new and dramatic. The Australian reader was treated to the continued agitation for Repeal; to the rise of the new men of Young Ireland; to the struggles of the great O'Connell and his extraordinary journey towards death in 1847; and to the movement towards revolution in 1848, that being treated by the newspapers first as most serious sedition, than as farce. Then followed the state trials and transportation to Tasmania. These were the headlines of the day, more than famine.

For the Australian Irish, if anything heralded the death of the old Irish world it was not the Famine, but the passing of O'Connell, the Liberator, giant in their British colonial, effectively emancipated world. Their obsessive affinity with O'Connell lay, not only in his Kingship of Ireland, but in his role in their other orbit of interest and loyalty, in their colonial persona, in the British Parliament: O'Connell had taken beneficent interest in Australian affairs. O'Connell's doings, then the question of who would fill his place, dominated the Australian Irish mind.[4] Nor did that mind, unlike the American, have constant, inescapable physical reminders of the Famine in the form of massive numbers of those fleeing from it in desperation and terror, in the face of death. The Irish immigration to Australia for the Famine years was small: MacDonagh says 14,000 over the period.[5] Few of these were direct victims, rather those who feared they might become so. It was possible, for Irish Australia, while knowing of and responding to the fact of Famine, to yet continue its stereotyped cultural business as usual – whimsical stories, nostalgic tourism, doggerel – as if famine did not exist. It was possible to care, even deeply, yet have in mind above all, the concerns and demands of the local scene.

Governing the entire character of the Australian reaction was the delay in the receipt of news from the British Isles, a time lapse so great as to render events virtually historical: they were lost in time for the participants long before Australians first heard of them. Or at least such was the usual course: who was to know this Famine would stretch to be radically different? The news delay – the dictate of vast distance, and of the pace and vagaries of early sail at sea – was paralysing: the norm in the 1840s was five months and a response would take hardly under a year. 'Overseas intelligence', as the local newspapers labelled their deliveries of home publications, was more in the nature of historical documentation, its impact unreal, confusing: it both involved the reader in the personal novelty of its messages, and reminded him of his irrelevance to what had long passed.

The first American news of the Irish potato blight was received by the *Boston Pilot* in November 1845: the first American relief meeting was held later that month.[6] Similar information first appeared in the Sydney *Morning Chronicle* the only Irish-owned paper in Australia, on 25 February 1846. It was five months old, culled from the *Northern Star* of 18 October 1845, which had itself delayed 'alluding to the subject' in the 'hope that these statements were exaggerated'. Initially viewed as a popular panic, famine awaited the corroboration of 'gentlemen of skill and experience' before the *Northern Star* would take it seriously.[7] Some areas were convinced that the blight would not reach them. The London *Times* conveyed an initial impression of a famine general to Europe and England, and in wheat and corn – the potato also, undoubtedly, but seen in terms of a 'panic which has so mysteriously risen and fallen'.[8] Fallen. Mere panic. And the rural picture one of a peasantry disheartened, apathetic, careless, inactive and indifferent to advice.[9] Such were the early reports emanating from Ireland, accepted by Irish nationalists in Ireland itself to the extent of their intervening in America to stop relief collections. They argued that the blight might be temporary; the 1846 crop would obviate the problem. But the main Irish motivation was national pride: relief campaigns made the Irish look like paupers.[10] Both these considerations – the image of the Irish, and convenient reliance on the assumed health of next year's crop – were central to the Australian reaction.

Given the initial press (and these inhibiting factors) it is hardly surprising that the Australian Irish hastened very slowly to respond in what would now seem obvious ways – criticism of British government inaction and establishment of a relief fund. That criticism was to be a very muted Australian theme, nor surfacing until July 1846 and then narrowly focused on the Prime Minister Sir Robert Peel personally. The first of a series of relief fund meetings took place in Melbourne in August, quickly followed by Sydney and a few country centres.[11]

The proceedings of these meetings soon revealed why there had been no rush to hold them. The initial Melbourne meeting was criticized by the powerful *Argus* as aggressively sectarian, convened by a Roman Catholic clergyman in a Catholic schoolroom, and prompted the editor's claim that he had not attended because Irishmen had vowed to kill him.[12] In fact, this meeting, and all the relief meetings, were at pains – and considerable public success – to make non-sectarian declarations and to pursue ecumenical aims, the funds raised being directed jointly to both Anglican and Catholic Archbishops of Dublin. But, beneath the surface, sectarian and national tensions could be easily glimpsed. The *Argus* argued the Famine as a reason why O'Connell should cease his Repeal of the Union Fund.[13] John O'Shanassy, then a Melbourne councillor, later Premier of Victoria, sneered at the Melbourne mayor's separate relief meeting as 'the imparial': it was attended by only 12 Empire lovers, and not the mayor, and raised £20 in comparison with the £800 raised at the 'Catholic' meeting.[14] Possession of local control of meetings and authority over collecting was a point of tension. In Bathurst the parish priest, Dean O'Reilly, rose to attack the local meeting as a hole in the corner affair got up by those opposed to him: he ensured it be reconvened under his chairmanship.[15]

But the deepest divisions were not sectarian, but among the Irish themselves. That meetings had been so long delayed was obviously a consequence of prior contention. The counter arguments were dealt with explicitly at the meetings themselves. All Australia could raise would be 'a mere drop in the bucket', and in any case given the distance and time involved, it would arrive far too late: the point was brutally put – 'sufferers are either killed or cured ere this".[16] But it was also revealed that 'many persons', some even feigning interest, 'have underhandedly used every exertion to counteract it' – that is, the Melbourne relief meeting.

Why? The explanation lay in the first resolution proposed to that meeting, by O'Shanassy: 'That this meeting repudiated the term *eleemosynary* [alms-giving], as applicable to our exertions in contributing to the objects of this meeting'. He went on to insist that Ireland had her pride, more than paid her way, with revenue from Woods and Forests. O'Connell had suggested this be applied to relief but the government had refused. Evidently many Irish in Australia were not prepared to see their own country cast in the pauper's role, or contribute themselves to a fund which implied it. The efforts of the relief fund organisers to avoid the stigma of alms-giving were vehement but ultimately futile – self-defeating: it *was* alms-giving and most Irish – even those who gave – had no liking for it.

So O'Shanassy argued that to give was a duty; for their countrymen to receive was their right. If, said another, 'there be an Irishman so debased as to not join heart and soul, in compassing the relief of his fellow countrymen, let … "Barbarian" be written on his unsanctified forehead'![17] If shame would not do it, perhaps new pride in Australia might. A generous subscription 'will show to Ireland, Europe, and the whole world, that there is such a place as Australia …';[18] it indicated colonial wealth, the prosperity and social eminence achieved by the colonial Irish, and would attract immigration – these were common claims by speakers at relief meetings, often with self-absorbed, self-congratulatory or defensive dimensions focused on their local achievements.[19] Indeed some meetings swiftly drifted away from Famine concerns into 'racy anecdotes and extemporaneous wit', which 'caused many an aching side'.[20] Audiences craved entertainment and were easily amused. At a meeting of female friends of Ireland, Mr James Wallace said, 'Surely I am not flattering the fair sex, when I assimilate them to angels; (laughter) only they have got no wings (Roars of laughter, in which the ladies heartily joined)'.[21] There is no record of the reception accorded the then *Port Phillip Herald's* singularly inapposite quotation, in the Famine context, of the 'noble bard' Lord Byron:

> There is something so warm and sublime in the core
> of an Irishman's heart that I envied him dead.[22]

Who was to blame for the Famine? Speakers at relief meetings faced this question within the context of their own requirements. It could not be the Irish themselves, a people without guilt (reportage of violence was later to weaken that conviction.) It could not be the British government: Australia it self was a contented British colony. Unanimously speakers discerned 'an act of God', 'one of those inscrutable and mysterious dispensations of God, with which he sometimes for good and wise purposes visited the sons of men'.[23] A few went on to indicate what they believed Providence had in mind – to encourage the Irish to grow grain, to put an end to the Corn Laws, above all to draw attention to Ireland's general plight in a dramatic and inescapable way: surely now Ireland's basic problems of poverty, landlordism and government neglect must now be addressed. Only one source saw Providence as dispensing punishment, and that to Britain. The fundamentalist Protestant *Sentinel* believed that Britain had long been indulging Popery in Ireland (establishing Maynooth, not enforcing Penal Laws) instead of preaching the glorious gospel of Christ; 'The sin of the ruler involves the whole nation in guilt, and the righteous suffer with the wicked'.[24]

Towards the end of 1846, two significant amounts were transmitted to Archbishops Whately and Murray in Dublin – £1,362 from Melbourne,[25] £3,271 from Sydney.[26] It was ecumenically given and collected – Church of England clergymen were active particularly in the NSW fund – and given for impartial aid distribution. There was virtually no public sectarian abrasion. Nor was that to be the problem which divided and crippled the next phase of Famine aid.

On 17 December 1846 the *Sydney Morning Herald* printed a letter which argued that Irish Famine Relief money should have been used to buy colonial wheat or flour or salted beef: 'Why should we send hard cash out of the colony, to our own injury… as our money will doubtless be expended in American or other foreign provisions…' This tapped a deep vein of colonial hard-headedness, and drew also on a degree of impatience among the Australian Irish with Ireland's situation – or at least what was being made of it by the London *Times* via the reprints in the *Sydney Morning Herald*. It was no pleasure for those who had contributed to relief funds to read of bitter divisions between Ireland's leaders – particularly O'Connell and Smith O'Brien – to be told 'Alas, for Ireland had she no friends but Irishmen, her state was poor indeed'; to learn of violence and murder being rife; and particularly to be informed that 'The peasantry have turned famine into a gain and from its proceeds purchase firearms'.[27] And while Australian Irish could have had little respect or trust for either the *The Times* or the *Sydney Morning Herald*, such reportage was disturbing, corrosive: lies and slander might be discounted, but the facts of famine, the evident collapse of dignity and moral values under the pressure of hunger, tried local Irish patience. The Irish-owned *Sydney Chronicle* lamented: 'Self, self, seems to have taken possession of the breast of almost all these poor creatures …'.[28] These were not the deserving poor, but the perpetrators of crime and outrage, so that the *Sydney Chronicle* could adjust its passive Providential interpretation to one which implied elements of active blame – of the Irish – which merited retribution: 'We can only pray that the arm of the Lord be not shortened, but that in the midst of judgment he will remember mercy'.[29] It was the first emergence in Australian-Irish history of a frequent theme – to the embarrassment and anger of the local Irish, the Irish in Ireland were seen to be behaving as a liability, undermining the reputation of the locals in their pursuit of acceptance.

But help was at hand from a most unusual quarter – Queen Victoria. The Queen's speech to the opening of the British Parliament had been given on 19 January 1847. Copies arrived in NSW in early May. The *Sydney Chronicle* fell on it with gratitude, as it solved several of its local problems. For the first time the state of Ireland occupied the most prominent position in a speech from the throne, and for the first time Royalty had expressed a wish and determination for a permanent solution. Now, it seemed, the Irish had the full attention they deserved and the terminology they merited: not putting down crime or galvanizing apathy, but – it was a Queenly phrase – 'raising the mass of the people in comfort'. This allowed the *Sydney Chronicle* to make a fulsome affirmation of loyalty which put the aspirations of Irish colonials at their most extravagantly ambitious: 'Sentiments such as these expressed by our gracious Sovereign are full of hope for Ireland. They cannot fail to rivet deeper in the hearts of her warm hearted children those feelings of loyalty, for which they have ever been distinguished'.[30] Such words, for all that they court denial or scepticism, run closer to the actualities of the time than presumptions of rebel intent: the disposition of such successful Irish as the *Sydney Chronicle* represented was ambivalent (they were passionately O'Connellite); it was Irish, but Irish within the context of an idealized, liberal, generous Empire.

Furthermore, the Queen's speech did more to remove from the colonial Irish the burden of being – or at least feeling – socially suspect and apart. It led on the formation in Britain of a relief fund for Irish and Scottish distress, an initiative immediately taken up – in May 1847 – in New South Wales (reports of Scottish distress had been circulating since early in the year) thus broadening and defusing the whole destitution issue and moderating the atmosphere of blame it generated; and also generalizing the area of potential community support. Or so it was thought. In fact, the outcome was to subdue collecting, divide the community on a range of issues, and gradually introduce, indirectly, the racial and religious prejudice latent in colonial life.

From the beginning of the Famine relief movement in August 1846, its organizers vehemently repudiated 'eleemosynary' intentions, although essentially alms-giving was what they were about. The new 'Irish and Scottish' phase of famine relief saw this attitude come immediately to the fore, and take firm practical form. From Sydney to Hobart organizers and press were agreed that, as the *Sydney Chronicle* put it: 'The only means which in our opinion, can give effectual relief to Ireland is EMIGRA-TION'.[31] This would permanently solve the problem for the destitute and provide Australia with desperately needed labour. It would settle disputes over the character of such labour: 'Were our local legislators, instead of wasting their time, in attempts to introduce here a race of godless heathens, and effeminate Coolies, strongly to recommend'[32] that the Imperial government send the Irish, good would flow in all directions. This course was particularly attractive as it supposed that the imperial government would bear most of the cost. It might, for instance, provide unemployed men-of-war to solve any major transport problem for the immigrant influx.

Both organizers and their press support had miscalculated or, at least, not thought through what they proposed. The broader Irish-Scots appeal base produced smaller meetings and donations, not larger; concentration on emigration as the solution produced not only division of opinion, but fragmentation – and a degree of obsessive self interest in which the purpose of the exercise – to aid famine victims – was soon lost to sight.

The first protest was from those who objected to the initial intention to spend all moneys collected on bringing out migrants – 'monstrously selfish' a correspondent to the *Sydney Chronicle* called it.[33] It took the *Free Presbyterian Messenger for Australia Felix*[34] to do the obvious humanitarian sums: emigration would benefit the few – £3,000 would bring 240 people to Australia; £1,000 would relieve a thousand families and perhaps save lives. Besides, in emigration, who would have first claim – the starving or those best for the colony? And further Presbyterian sense: separate Scots and Irish Relief funds would prevent dissention – and raise more money.

Under pressure from those who wanted their donations to be sent to the United Kingdom for immediate and direct aid, both Sydney and Melbourne funds agreed to provide that option. Their problems were just beginning. Some thought subscriptions should be sent 'home' in wheat, or other kind: this would diminish surplus and remit what could be spared (it would also place money in the hands of producers). Some producers would give produce but not money: should this be sold locally (if it could) or sent (at great expense) to the United Kingdom?

However, it was the migration plans that generated most difficulty. Relief meetings swiftly degenerated into immigration debates. Indeed some were obviously intended as a forum on that issue. In Parramatta, Hannibal Macarthur launched a tirade against imperial immigration policy, bemoaned the paralysing effects on squatters like himself of the NSW labour shortage, and introduced a petition to the House of Commons addressing that grievance, not the Irish or Scots Famine.[35] In September a Melbourne meeting of 80 squatters took a similar course, petitioning the Governor, with the variation that their demand was for labour for the Port Phillip district exclusively;[36] their agitation was to trickle on into October in the form of claims of neglect and exploitation of their district.

The take-over by self-interested and wealthy squatters of the Famine relief movement led to protest; but that movement was already in a state of contradiction. The *Port Phillip Herald* denounced the initial Melbourne meeting as being held to promote able-bodied immigration, whereas the paper held that the purpose of the whole relief exercise was to enable destitute immigration, the bringing to Australia of Famine's direct victims.[37] This view was probably the basis for the circulation of the rumour that the dimension of the fund which was to be used for immigration 'was to be appropriated in the introduction of the lame, the blind, and other disabled persons, from Ireland and Scotland...' An outraged Fund chairman declared 'the funds were not going to be wasted in such manner ... it could never be intended to flood this place with a stream of disabled paupers'. A Fund meeting denied the 'purpose of bringing out persons of no use to the colony'. It sought to have the best of ideal worlds, bring out 'only able-bodied labourers and their families, these being brought from the districts in Ireland and Scotland where greatest destitution prevails'.[38]

But did it so prevail? Throughout 1847 reports from Ireland were conflicting, horror stories alternating with constant rumours that things were getting better. And perhaps enough was being done already. Some accounts had the British government doing nothing: next would appear a detailed account of some impressive government activity. The Irish-owned *Sydney Chronicle* appears to have preferred the latter possibility; if its verse be a guide:

'Poor Erin! thy sister [England] with fond love has flown
To dry up thy tears, and to hush thy deep moan;
And with her sweet mercy and warm hearted train
With bright feet have crowded across the dark main,
So thy children shall smile ...[39]

And if the balance of its editorials be heeded. Because there can be no doubt that the Australian-Irish wanted only good news from Ireland, or at least such bad news as would allow them to live in some harmony with their two allegiances, imperial and Irish. So, in March 1847, the *Sydney Chronicle* pronounced 'the depth of gloom has been passed and brighter days begin to dawn. The supply of provisions which has been poured in, and the employment that has been found, have very sensibly relieved the disastrous calamities'.[40] Having opted for such a position, it was not easy to vacate – in a British colony, in terms of consistency, and in terms of the information available. Besides, information was available – in abundance from the British press – on Irish conduct for which their Australian countrymen had little patience. It was easy for those not directly experiencing famine situations to have a different, wider, view of Irish reality. Even in

Ireland itself there were constant calls for perspective, frequently, of course from self-interested English sources, for an end to political factionalism and agitation, and particularly to crime, bloodshed and lawlessness, in the face of the common enemy of death.[41] In Australia where O'Connell was the great Irish hero, and constitutionalism the accepted mode of Irish action, Irish political division and particularly the constant reportage of violence, in the context of Famine, presented the Irish with major difficulty. A local versifier reached the humane conclusion, but not before putting it to the test:

> Speak not of their crimes, for their source was despair;
> Oh, smite not the wounded – in mercy forbear!
> Have they erred? they are punished: then hasten to save,
> Ere famine and pestilence sweep to the grave.[42]

It was not only the fact of such activity that gave Australian-Irish pause; it was the question of what it might imply. If Ireland's great leaders could continue to devote themselves to endless squabbling and to political and personal point scoring – even to a pathetic and unsuccessful revolution in 1848 – and all in the midst of allegedly the greatest human disaster in Irish history, surely something was most seriously wrong. Either those leaders were grievously unworthy or the Famine crisis much exaggerated. Most likely the latter, for surely Ireland's own leaders would not continue with personal plans and stratagems – and ego trips and feuds – if the very nation was at risk of really major calamity?

By 1847, the sensible conclusion to reach at Australia's remove appeared to be that, while there certainly was a famine situation in Ireland, it seemed to be fluctuating and within some limits of control or tolerance within Ireland itself. From Australia's distance there was little that could be done given the obscurity of the situation, reluctance and division over doing anything, and the enormous practical problems that beset every initiative.

So, what of the Irish and Scots Famine funds launched in May–June? By November they were stationary and had been so for four months.[43] They were finalized early in 1848. The Melbourne fund, divided into the options of money given to finance immigration, and that given for direct aid, realized £733 towards immigration and a tiny £168 towards direct aid. The aid was sent to a British relief organization.

The immigration fund was not used. The *Argus* reported on 26 December 1848 that 'many of our wealthiest and most intelligent men', had kept this money for a year and then divided it up again among the donors – and this just when news had arrived that the potato had failed again.

Sheer selfishness and stupidity should not be discounted as contributing to this situation. Bureaucratic difficulties and government policy made the situation in the United Kingdom highly resistant to Australian immigration. Assisted immigration to NSW was suspended in 1846 and 1847. That there was a trickle of such immigration from 1847, and that mainly re-united the families of ex-convicts, was mainly due to the efforts in London, of Caroline Chisholm. But the major Australian obstacles to Irish Famine immigration were matters of preference. From the 1830s the Australian colonies had set themselves vigorously against any British policy of 'Shovelling out Paupers': the whole idea of receiving immigrants generated by famine circumstances could hardly have been more frontally repellant to such sentiments. The wonder is that the relief funds of 1847 contained an immigration dimension, not that it was not implemented. Even those supporting Famine immigration spoke the language of pauperization. Thus the *Port Phillip Herald* of 29 June 1848 urged as the only solution to Irelands problems:

> an extensive and judicious system of emigration: not to America where the poor wretches die in hundreds the moment they land, but to Australia when instead of becoming 'paupers' as the Noble Premier would have it, they can find plenty of employment, at the threefold advantage of benefiting themselves, the colony, and the mother country.

What the Victorian Premier foresaw as happening was the general view, but the *Herald's* advocacy was of the cause of 'poor wretches' and the context that of American horror stories of mass deaths at their destination: it was phraseology and imagery which strengthened every Australian fear.

What had happened on and after the passage to America was well known in Australia. So were such stories as that of the servant girl who had toiled to send home $100 to bring all her family to join her. They brought also the famine pestilence. All died.[44] In the face of the threat of typhus and other diseases – remote, impossible though it might be – self sacrifice and generosity were simply ill-judged, misplaced.

Then there was Catholicism. These useless, disease-haunted paupers would be Irish Catholics, a religious group tirelessly attacked by the Presbyterian minister J. D. Lang, most famously in his 1841 pamphlet *The Question of Questions! Is this colony to be transformed into a Province of the Popedom?* – to which the general answer was emphatically no. When at last some Famine casualties – 4,175 orphan girls between 1848 and 50 – were sent to Australia, there was uproar, first in Ireland (the *Nation* dubbed it one of the most diabolical British schemes since Cromwell's day), then in Australia. By 1850 colonial criticism had become so intense as to force the termination of the scheme.[45] Although the Australian Irish community vigorously defended the orphan girls, it was a defence forced upon it, rather than any energetic campaign to expand the intake of Famine victims. The noises emanating from Ireland itself had been hostile, not only in terms of Cromwellian purges, but in regard to Australia as a destination: there, pure Irish girls were being shipped out to serve the lusts of depraved 'bushmen and savages'. Australia had a long way to go before it was to lose its Irish reputation of being the domain of barbarians and criminals. But a variant of the reverse applied. The Australian Irish, whatever their origins, had no wish to see their bid for respectability and community acceptance pulled back by an influx of starving indigents, the dregs of a degraded, primitive and violent Irish society. And they had no interest in preserving the memory of, or even sustaining the idea of, 'the potato Famine' as an overwhelming Irish national disaster: the very notion that this could be so was in itself demeaning. It would be much better if the cause of Ireland's calamities could be viewed as political and the humble potato seen – or better, forgotten – as symptom, not cause.

Such was the Australian-Irish mind on these matters, but this was merely one side of the coin, an analogy that goes direct to the heart – and again the imagery is apposite – of the other dimension of the Australian-Irish reaction. From September 1846 – over £1,000 had already been collected at the point – the *Sydney Morning Herald* began printing subscription lists for the Irish Relief Fund. It did the same for the Irish and Scotch Relief Fund of 1847–48. These detailed lists, appearing in long columns every few days, convey the practical realities of the Irish Famine response. Few large donations, many small. The city was canvassed door to door: country stations organized by owner or managers. Clergymen collected in church, workplaces were visited, tradesmen gave in groups, the gasworks, miners, foundrymen, police, soldiers, even prisons, yielded their lists, most named – a veritable census of the proud Irishry. And of course the inevitable 'Widow's mite' and 'A Poor Irishman'. The outcome? £4,633 from Sydney and Melbourne to the first fund; £1,000 from Adelaide, these just the known amounts. The final published Sydney list for the Irish and Scotch Fund brought it to a total of £3,708: unlike the Melbourne Fund this had a very small 'immigration' component. Presuming this to have been sent, as the aid segment of the Melbourne Fund was, the total remitted for famine aid in 1847–48 was over £8,500. But this takes no account of smaller centres – Hobart, for instance – that sent money direct to Ireland, or the remittances of private individuals: it was evident from the proceedings of relief meetings that many intending donors wished to deal directly with their own families or districts. Any estimate of a total would be guesswork, but given the known public figure, it could hardly be less than £10,000 – and that is in a context of an Australian total of around 70,000 persons Irish-born, the overwhelming majority of whom had little financial resource.

The lesson is clear. However unclear in their minds they might be about the problems raised by news of famine, and however they might doubt the wisdom of importing the destitute, their generosity to give to those in want was unclouded. Or rather, it survived, save in Melbourne, the efforts of self-interested immigration enthusiasts to exploit famine for their own gain. From 12,000 miles away there was little the tiny Australian-Irish community could do other than give its money. And that it did.

When a new Irish newspaper was founded in Sydney in June 1850 (to have a continuous existence, after amalgamation, to the present) this antipodean *Freeman's Journal* was sparse in its references to famine; indeed its terminology preferred 'potato blight'. And it had its causative priorities firm and clear:

All reflecting Irishmen, who feel for the woes of their country, are convinced that its present deplorable state cannot be owing to the successive failures of the potato crop. for if something else were not radically wrong in the state, the partial failure of one article of human food could not produce that deep and wide-spread ruin ...'[46].

As American interest, experience and circumstance – and John Mitchel – inflated the Famine to be the measure of all things Irish, Australian interest, circumstance and experience – at vast remove – minimized it: on any standard 'the partial failure of one article of human food' was a grossly inadequate description of what had happened in Ireland. And so, as the Famine swirled America closer to the mental orbit of Ireland and its involvement in its affairs through the sheer linkage of numbers but no less importantly in the visions of the mind's green eye, that distant potato blight spun the Australian Irish further away, out of real Irish concern and comprehension, into paths of their own choosing.

Notes

1. P. O'Farrell 'Whose reality? the Irish Famine in history and literature', *Historical Studies* (University of Melbourne), Vol. 20, No. 78, April 1982. This article, highlighting the role of Mitchel's oratorical genius and blazing partisanry in the artistic formulation of the Famine, and arguing that this is 'a consummate example of style making history', has itself a significant history. First given in May 1981 to a Canberra symposium on 'Peasants in History and Literature', its general purpose was to argue that the common understanding of many historical events was determined not by professional historical criteria but by their most powerful and coherent artistic depiction, particularly if that served political purposes or tapped strong human emotion. The article was submitted to an American journal where it was at first accepted by the executive editor, then rejected: patently the journal's higher authorities saw it as out of step with received American orthodoxy on the Famine – which was, and is, straight Mitchel. *Historical Studies* in which it was then published, is readily available in Irish university libraries, but at a session on the Famine at the Irish Social and Economic History Conference in Dublin in September 1990 it was evident that speakers – which included some authors of standard recent works on the Famine – were not aware of the article, even though it had been used by British scholars (M. J. Winstanley, *Ireland and the Land Question 1800–1922*, Methuen, London, 1984, p.44). This British attention to the Mitchel factor has been developed beyond my own treatment by Graham Davis, 'Making history: John Mitchel and the Great Famine', in P. Hyland and N. Sammell (eds), *Irish Writing: Exile and Subversion*, Macmillan, London, 1991, pp. 98–115, and Graham Davis, *The Irish in Britain*, Gill and Macmillan, Dublin, 1991, pp. 21–31.
    The point at issue here seems to me neither trivial nor personal. If the Mitchel interpretation is a rhetorical contrivance for political purposes, the traditional orthodox stance of American and Irish accounts stands in serious question, particularly as they sustain in part currently active attitudes of hostility and misunderstanding relevant to Northern Ireland.
2. In locating material for this chapter, I acknowledge the support of the

Australian Research Council and the assistance of Karen Hutchings and Damien McCoy of the University of New South Wales.

3.   This is reprinted in a recent book whose very title emphasises the frequency of famine in Irish history: E. Margaret Crawford (ed.), *Famine: The Irish Experience, 900–1900: Subsistence Crises and Famines in Ireland*, John Donald, Edinburgh, 1989.

4.   See P. O'Farrell, 'The Image of O'Connell in Australia', in Donal McCartney (ed.), *The World of Daniel O'Connell*, Mercier (for the Cultural Relations Committee of Ireland), Dublin, 1980.

5.   O. MacDonagh 'Irish emigration to the United States of America and the British colonies during the Famine', in R.D. Edwards, and T.D. Williams (eds.), *The Great Famine: Studies in Irish History 1845–52*, Browne and Nolan, Dublin, 1956, p.359.

6.   T. J. Sarbaugh, 'A Moral spectacle: American relief and the Famine, 1845–1849', *Eire-Ireland*, Vol. 15, No. 4, Winter 1980, pp. 6–7.

7.   Quoted in *Morning Chronicle* (Sydney) 25 February 1846. Beginning as the *Australasian Chronicle* this paper changed its name to the *Sydney Chronicle* later in 1846.

8.   *Morning Chronicle*, 7 March 1846.

9.   *Morning Chronicle*, 4 April 1846.

10.   Sarbaugh, p. 8.

11.   *Morning Chronicle*, 1 July 1846. This present article, and its source coverage, concentrate on the two main areas of the then Australian settlement, the Sydney and Melbourne districts. Very occasional references in these sources indicate that famine relief activity was also taking place in the other Australian colonies. For instance the *Sydney Morning Herald*, 24 April 1848, reported back from a London source that £1,000 had been received from South Australia.

12.   *Argus* (Melbourne), 14 August 1846.

13.   *Argus*, 18 August 1846.

14.   *Argus*, 8 September 1846.

15.   *Sydney Morning Herald*, 28 September 1846.

16.   *Port Phillip Herald* (Melbourne), 15 September 1846.

17.   *Port Phillip Patriot*, quoted in *Sydney Chronicle*, 22 August 1846.

18.   *Port Phillip Herald*, 27 August 1846.

19.   *Port Phillip Herald*, 18, 27 August 1846; *Sydney Chronicle*, 14 November 1846.

20.   *Port Phillip Herald*, 25 August 1846.

21.   *Port Phillip Herald*, 1 September 1846.

22.   *Port Phillip Herald*, 18 August 1846.

23.   *Sydney Chronicle*, 23 August, 2 September 1846.

24.   *Sentinel* (Sydney), 31 December 1846.

25.   *Argus*, 10 October 1846.

26.   *Sydney Chronicle*, 9 December 1846.

27.   *Sydney Morning Herald*, 27 January, 29 May 1848, reprinting, *The Times*, London.

28.   *Sydney Chronicle*, 15 May 1847.

29.   Ibid.

30.   Ibid.

31.   *Sydney Chronicle*, 7 July 1847.

32.   *Sydney Chronicle*, 17 July 1847.

33.   *Sydney Chronicle*, 28 August 1847.

34.   *Sydney Chronicle*, 16 July 1847.

35.   *Sydney Chronicle*, 4 August 1847.

36. *Argus*, 21 September 1847.
37. *Port Phillip Herald*, 5 August 1847.
38. *Port Phillip Herald*, 13 August 1847.
39. *Sydney Chronicle*, 20 March 1847.
40. *Sydney Chronicle*, 20 March 1847.
41. E.g. see *Sun*, 19 October 1846 quoted in *Sydney Chronicle*, 24 March 1847; also 14 April 1847.
42. Mrs Carey 'Help, or they perish!' *Sydney Chronicle*, 13 February 1847.
43. *Port Phillip Herald*, 18 November 1847.
44. *Port Phillip Herald*, 29 June 1848.
45. For a general coverage of Irish immigration to Australia see P. O'Farrell, *The Irish in Australia*, New South Wales University Press, Sydney, 1986, 2nd edition, 1993.
46. *Freeman's Journal* (Sydney), 13 February 1851.

7 Potatoes, providence and philanthropy: the role of private charity during the Irish Famine

Christine Kinealy

The sources of relief that were made available during the Great Irish Famine were diverse. Historians have tended to focus upon the role of the government in responding to the great need that was created by the successive years of loss of the potato crop. Yet, the role of private charity was of major significance in alleviating the hardships caused by food shortages in Ireland. This chapter examines the role of private charity in responding to the challenges posed by the Famine, and explores those factors that shaped the size and nature of this response.

The Irish Famine was the first national disaster to attract large-scale international sympathy and support, beyond even the reaches of Britain's far-flung Empire. Donations, in fact, were received from all five continents. Yet the people who contributed towards the Famine relief often had little in common, ranging from heads of state to London policemen and to convicts in prison hulks. They were, however, united in their desire to help to alleviate the suffering in Ireland, regardless of geographical distance and differences in culture, religion and nationality. The role played by private philanthropy was short-lived: most of the donations ceased following the harvest of 1847 when the British government declared the Famine to be officially 'over'. Overall, however, private charity to Ireland was significant and it provided a substantial amount of relief, in money, food, clothing and seeds, at a crucial period during the Famine.

Private donations to Famine relief were numerous and diverse in their origin. The British Relief Association alone recorded over 15,000 individual subscriptions. It is not possible to look at each contribution in detail. However, this chapter will examine the donations of a number of key individuals and organizations. Queen Victoria and Pope Pius IX, for example, both of whom exerted influence on large numbers of people throughout the world, were contributors to relief, and were key leaders of public opinion. However, in regard to Ireland, public opinion could be fickle and it changed over time.

A number of philanthropic organizations became involved in the provision of relief, most notably the Society of Friends (the 'Quakers') and the specially constituted British Relief Association. These organizations were important not only for the amount of donations they raised, but also for their practical involvement in the provision of relief within Ireland. Subscriptions also came from the poorest groups in society, such as ex-slaves and criminals; demonstrating that the suffering of the Irish poor aroused the sympathy of even those people who themselves had few resources to spare.

Financing the Famine

While the public contribution to Famine relief was relatively easy to quantify, private contributions were far more diverse and less easy to identify. However, throughout the Famine years, private charity was an important supplement to official – and often inadequate – relief. Furthermore, while public relief was often deprecated and given only reluctantly, private relief was for the most part praised and encouraged by government. This attitude highlights the ideological conflicts that underpinned the response of the government during a period of Famine, and reveals attitudes towards poverty and the giving of relief, under any circumstances.

During the critical Famine years of 1845–51, the British government provided just over £10,000,000 on relief, mostly in the form of loans. Over half of this money was spent in the 12-month period which followed the second appearance of potato blight in 1846. For example, almost £5,000,000 was expended on the ineffective public works scheme in the winter of 1846–47 which failed so markedly to save lives: instead, mortality, disease and emigration increased sharply.[1] After the harvest of 1847, the British government decided that relief expenditure should be financed from within Ireland through the mechanism of local Poor Law taxation. Thus, in 1848 and 1849, the British government subscribed only £156,000 and £114,000 respectively towards Famine relief. Moreover, after 1847, entitlement to relief was subject to more stringent conditions than had previously been the case, most notably through the notorious Quarter Acre Clause.[2] The consequences of the changeover to this new system of providing relief was both understood and accepted by leading members of the government. Charles Wood, the Chancellor of the Exchequer, justified it on the grounds that 'except through a purgatory of misery and starvation, I do not see how Ireland is to emerge into a state of anything approaching peace or prosperity'.[3] After the autumn of 1847, not only the government, but middle class opinion in Britain was opposed to providing any further financial assistance from the central government to Ireland. The influential newspaper *The Times* repeatedly made a comparison between the 'deserving' English poor, and the 'undeserving' Irish poor, and it posed the question 'Why should the United Kingdom pay for the extravagance of Ireland?'[4] At the beginning of 1849, in response to the persistence of high levels of mortality, the government proposed to give a final, and relatively small, grant of £50,000 for Irish relief.[5] *The Times* again marshalled a vitriolic campaign against further assistance to Ireland, pointing out to its readers, the 'total absence' of gratitude shown by the Irish people and adding that this money had 'broken the back of English benevolence'.[6]

Approximately half of the money spent by the British government was provided as an interest bearing loan. It represented less than half a per cent of the British Gross National Product during the Famine years.[7] The contribution from the British Treasury was also smaller than the £13,000,000 raised from Irish taxes for Famine relief. Also, it was far less than the £20,000,000 given by the British government in 1833 to plantation owners in the West Indies as compensation for the ending of slavery.[8] It was also a fraction of the £69,000,000 spent during the Crimean War of 1854–56.[9] The comparison between Famine expenditure and the payment given to slave-owners was drawn by Archbishop McHale in 1846 when he warned the Prime Minister that if the government persisted with a policy of non-intervention 'you might as well at once issue an edict of starvation'.[10] Ultimately, the most revealing evidence of the inadequacy of public relief was the fact that during the Famine, Ireland lost 25 per cent of her population, making the Irish Famine the most demographically lethal famine of modern history.[11]

The ideological background

The intellectual and moral forces that informed and shaped policy formation after 1845 were dominated by a mixture of classical economic thought, a desire to modernize and regenerate Ireland, and an evangelical faith in the machinations of God both in the affairs of man and in the market place. Throughout the course of the Famine, some of the most influential formulators of relief policy were themselves influenced by the twin doctrines of political economy and providentialism. The belief that the Famine was a 'visitation of God' was widely accepted among clergy of all denominations. It was also an interpretation favoured by a number of leading politicians, notably, Sir James Graham (Home Secretary under Sir Robert Peel), Charles Wood (Chancellor of the Exchequer under Lord John Russell), Sir George Grey (Home Secretary under Russell) and Charles Trevelyan (Permanent Secretary at the Treasury during both Peel and Russell's governments). These men were bound by their moralist vision of the Famine as a judgement of God from which only suffering and atonement could bring salvation. This meant that a disaster, even one on the scale of the Famine, could be regarded in a positive light as a sign of 'divine encouragement to reformation and redemption before it was too late'.[12] Moreover, it was widely assumed that such oblique tactics had succeeded in bringing benefits to Ireland or, as Trevelyan stated 'Supreme wisdom has educed permanent good out of a transient evil'.[13]

Throughout the course of the Famine, a clear distinction was made by the government between official and private relief, although both were to be given with due regard to public probity, economy and frugality. Government relief, however, was never to be provided gratuitously but instead pre-conditions and 'tests' of destitution were built into the relief giving process. The philosophy which underpinned this approach was particularly evident in the debate leading up to the introduction of a Poor

Law to Ireland in 1838.[14] During the Famine, this philosophy was applied even more rigorously, the government insisting that 'Relief should be made so unattractive as to furnish no motive to ask for it, except in the absence of every other means of subsistence.[15] An exception to this policy occurred in the summer of 1847 when, for a few months only, the government successfully provided free food in the form of soup and bread. This scheme, however, was from the outset only intended to be an interim measure to bridge a gap between the failed public works scheme and the introduction of an amended and extended Poor Law.[16]

In 1848, the Poor Law Commissioners provided practical guidelines for the implementation of the new Poor Law legislation. One of their stipulations was that every recipient of relief was to be forced to undertake some task of work which 'should be as repulsive as possible consistent with humanity'.[17] These restrictions reflected a perception that Irish people were only too willing to depend on the government for a livelihood.[18] However, finding a balance between avoiding starvation and providing minimal relief was also difficult. Avoiding criticism from various factions concerned that either too much or not enough was being done for the Irish people was a further consideration. The dilemmas brought about by the Famine were evident. In a letter to John Russell, the Prime Minister, Lord Clarendon, the Lord Lieutenant in Ireland, complained:

> Esquimaux (sic) and New Zealanders are more thrifty and industrious than these people who deserve to be left to their fate instead of the hard working people of England being taxed for their support, but can we do so? ... we shall equally be blamed for keeping them alive or letting them die, and have only to select between the censure of the Economists or the Philanthropists. Which do you prefer?[19]

The role of private charity

The inadequacy of public finance, and the parsimonious way in which aid was distributed made the provision of private charity a valuable resource for the starving Irish. Furthermore, private relief avoided the administrative overheads and bureaucratic delays that were part of government relief, and also had the advantage of distributing assistance directly to those who required it. Most of the private relief was provided through the medium of well-known and highly regarded relief associations, the most prominent being the Society of Friends, the Catholic Church and the Protestant Churches, and the British Relief Association – which was formed at the beginning of 1847 by financiers in London, included the well-respected philanthropist, Lionel de Rothschild.

For a short while, raising subscriptions for the starving Irish became a fashionable way of combining philanthropy with pleasure, fund-raising with fun. Many of the larger donations were given in a way which was highly visible – the major newspapers carrying lists of subscribers to Irish distress and other worthy causes.[20] As private relief was a matter of public interest, this may have exerted pressure on people in the public eye to maintain an image by donating some money, regardless of their private feelings. Also, having a royal patron or receiving a donation from Queen Victoria gave additional prestige to a charitable organization.

The spread of information regarding the Irish Famine was impressively efficient. News of the suffering in Ireland was carried in a variety of ways: in the newspapers, through the fund-raising activities of the main relief associations, at the pulpits of the churches, through the mechanism of the British Army (a large portion of whom were Irish-born) and by word of mouth, not least of all by Irish emigrants who had personally witnessed the scenes of distress. Ireland's Catholicism also linked Ireland with an international network of co-religionists. The activities of Daniel O'Connell had heightened awareness of Ireland throughout Europe. O'Connell's death in 1847, at the height of the Famine, probably increased sympathy for the Irish poor.[21] Finally, perhaps ironically, Ireland's new role as part of the United Kingdom ensured the spread of philanthropic activities to the rest of the British Empire, which resulted in donations being received from places as far apart as the West Indies (the Caribbean) and India. In fact, the first recorded private donation to Ireland was raised in Calcutta at the end of 1845, and led to the formation of the 'Indian Relief Fund'.[22]

The role of private charity has also been the subject of controversy and debate. This is due largely to the association, especially in folk tradition, of private charity with proselytism: the belief that the hunger of the Irish people was used to convert them to the Protestant faith. Those who allegedly took the food or 'soup' were known as 'jumpers' or 'soupers'. Although such activity was less widespread and less successful than was popularly believed, and was condemned by the majority of Quaker, Protestant and Presbyterian clergy, the fact that it did exist at all left a legacy of distrust and bitterness against Famine relief. Also, as far as contemporary ideological and political doctrines were concerned, many of the economic ills of Ireland were identified with the Catholicism of the majority of the people. It was, therefore, regarded as desirable to make Ireland a more Protestant country as a first step in the much desired aim of economic regeneration.[23]

The greatest part of the money raised was distributed via the Society of Friends (over £200,000) and the British Relief Association (almost £450,000). The smaller relief organizations and the churches also contributed significant amounts of money. For example, it has been estimated that donations from the international Catholic Church were in the region of £400,000, much of which was channelled through the Catholic Archbishop in Dublin.[24]

Relief was also often sent in kind, most frequently food, but donations of clothes, blankets and seeds were also made. Moreover, after 1847, private remittances from emigrants became increasingly important, especially as a means of financing the next generation of emigrants. This money became particularly significant beyond the end of 1847 when international donations reduced dramatically.

Although a precise figure cannot be put on the amount of monetary relief contributed privately, it was certainly in excess of one million pounds and possibly far higher. What is certain is that without this additional private relief, many more people would have died during the Famine years. The variety of sources of Famine relief raised for Ireland, especially in 1846 and 1847, displayed for the time, a perhaps unprecedented ability to reach the attention and stimulate the response of a mix of places throughout the world, across racial and cultural groups, touching all classes of society. The most enduring source of assistance came from the Irish emigrant community. Their remittances to those left at home, not only in the desperate Famine years but beyond, helped to shape the development of Irish society in the late nineteenth century. Furthermore, the emergence of an Irish diaspora, many of whom had their roots in the Famine years, placed Irish affairs very clearly on an international stage in the decades following the Famine.

Leading by example: the role of royalty, the Pope and the sultan of Turkey

At the time of the first appearance of blight in Ireland, Queen Victoria was aged 26. She had come to the throne in 1837 and three years later married her cousin, Prince Albert Saxe-Coburg who, in her own words, 'completely won my heart'.[25] During Victoria's long lifetime, she visited Ireland only three times. Her first visit had been planned for 1846, but the appearance of the blight, together with Victoria's own reluctance to visit Ireland, resulted in a postponement.[26] The rescheduled visit took place finally in August 1849. Victoria, Albert, and their young children visited Cork, Dublin and Belfast. When Victoria first landed in Cobh, it was renamed Queenstown in her honour. The royal visit was brief, carefully stage-managed, and confined to the east of the country. Also, apart from a brief visit to the model estate of the Duke of Leinster, Victoria travelled by yacht and not overland.

Victoria's visit was intended to provide proof that the Famine was finally over, and to attract capital and investment into the restructured Irish economy. These aspirations proved to be illusory. In 1849, the workhouses were still providing relief to over one million people and, in some areas, mortality in 1849 was higher than it had been in Black '47.[27] Nor did the much desired British capital flow into Ireland in the wake of the visit. Victoria did note the poverty of the Irish people, especially the rags worn by the women, leading her to comment, 'they never mend anything'.[28] Overall though, Victoria appeared to be delighted with her visit to Ireland and wrote from Dublin: 'the women are really handsome – quite in the lowest class – as well Cork as here; such beautiful black eyes and hair, and such fine colours and teeth'.[29] To a large extent, Victoria's enthusiasm for her Irish subjects was reciprocated. However, a note of discord was apparent. A group of Young Irelanders planned to kidnap Victoria during her visit, but were frustrated by the security arrangements.[30]

Victoria's contribution to Famine relief was protracted, varied and ambiguous. Like many of her contemporaries, her attitude to Ireland was ambivalent: she was sympathetic to the starving Irish poor and described their suffering as 'really too terrible to think about', and she believed that Irish landlords were irresponsible and not providing sufficient Famine relief.[31] Yet, when she heard of the murder of an Irish landlord at the end of 1847 she commented 'Really, they are a terrible people'.[32] Victoria's donation of £2,000 was the largest single donation to Famine relief, yet the epithet 'Famine Queen' has proved to be both enduring and controversial.[33] A common tradition was that Queen Victoria simultaneously donated £5 to Irish Famine relief and a far larger sum to a London dogs home. The reality was far more complex.

The role of the British monarchy and the royal family as fund-raisers, patrons and philanthropists was long established. George III (1738–1820) was probably the most generous of all British monarchs, giving away approximately £15,000 a year, that is, 25 per cent of his privy purse income. Queen Victoria donated in the region of £12,000 each year, or 10 per cent of her Civil List allowance. Little of this money was given to Ireland, apart from during the Famine years.[34]

At the beginning of 1847, a committee known as the 'British Association for the Relief of Distress in Ireland and the Highlands and Islands of Scotland' was formed in London. The Committee decided that, in recognition of the food shortages that were also apparent in the north of Scotland, one-sixth of the money which they raised should be used for Scottish distress. The influential members of the Association asked for contributions for Ireland and Scotland to be channelled through their office in London. One of the first people to respond to this appeal was Queen Victoria, although it is difficult to ascertain whether this was a personal intervention by the Queen or was undertaken on her behalf by her government ministers.

The British Relief Association recorded in their Minutes in January 1847 that the Queen, through the intermediary of the Prime Minister, John Russell, had responded immediately to their appeal with a donation of £2,000 and a promise to provide further sums 'as the exigency might demand'.[35] This official entry, however, disguises the real amount provided by Queen Victoria. Initially, Victoria sent £1,000 to the British Relief Association, and without any accompanying promise to send any further money. Stephen Spring Rice, the Secretary of the Association, to whom this money had been sent, responded swiftly and unequivocally. He wrote a terse note on the back of the original donation saying: 'Receiving this, I refused to place or abstained from placing the subscription on the list and went to G. Grey, Secretary of State, to say that it wasn't enough. It was increased to £2,000'.[36] Apart from her donation to the British Relief Association, Victoria also subscribed £500 to the Ladies Clothing Fund.[37]

Other members of the royal family followed Victoria's lead and contributed as follows:

H.R.H. Prince Albert	£500
H.M. the Queen Dowager	£1,000
H.M. the King of Hanover, as Duke of Cumberland and Chancellor of the University of Dublin	£1,000

H.R.H. the Duchess of Kent	£300
H.R.H. the Duke of Cambridge	£500
H.R.H. the Duchess of Gloucester	£200
H.R.H. the Duchess of Cambridge	£100
H.R.H. Princess Sophia	£100[38]

In addition to making a direct donation to Irish and Scottish Famine relief, Queen Victoria played an important role in encouraging other British people to donate to relief organizations. On 13 January 1847, a Queen's Letter was issued which was sent to the Archbishop of Canterbury, with a copy to the Archbishop of York. It requested that an appeal should be read in each church announcing that a collection for Famine relief would be made over the following few weeks. The money raised would then be lodged in the Bank of England for distribution within Ireland and Scotland. A copy of this letter was published in *The Times* newspaper a few days later. The complete text of this letter was:

QUEEN'S LETTER TO HIS GRACE THE ARCHBISHOP OF CANTERBURY FOR A COLLECTION IN AID OF THE SUBSCRIPTIONS ENTERED INTO FOR THE RELIEF OF A LARGE PORTION OF THE POPULATION OF IRELAND AND IN SOME DISTRICTS IN SCOTLAND.

Victoria Regina,

Most Reverend Father in God, our right trusty and right entirely beloved councillor, we greet you well. Whereas a large portion of the population in Ireland, and in some districts of Scotland, is suffering severe distress, owing to the failure of the ordinary supplies of food; and whereas many of our subjects have entered into voluntary subscriptions for their relief, and have at the same time humbly prayed to us to issue our Royal Letters, directed to the Lord Archbishop of Canterbury and the Lord Archbishop of York, authorising them to promote contributions within their respective provinces for the same benevolent purpose.

We, taking the premises into our Royal consideration, and being always ready to give the best encouragement and countenance to such humane and charitable undertakings, are graciously pleased to condescend to their request; and we do hereby direct that these letters be by you communicated to the several Suffragen Bishops within your province, expressly requiring them to take care that publication be made hereof on such Sunday in the present or ensuing month, and in such places within the respective dioceses, as the said Bishops shall appoint; and that upon this occasion the ministers in each parish do effectually excite their parishioners to a liberal contribution, which shall be collected the week following at their respective dwellings by the churchwardens or overseers of the poor in each parish; and the ministers of the several parishes are to cause the sums so collected to be paid immediately into the hands of the Bank of England, to be accounted for by them, and applied to the carrying on and promoting the above mentioned good designs.

And so we bid you very heartily farewell. Given at the Court at St James, the 13 day of January 1847, in the tenth year of our reign'.[39]

Following this, a Proclamation announced that 24 March 1847 would be appointed as a day for a 'General Fast and Humiliation before Almighty

God'. Its purpose was to raise money 'on behalf of ourselves and our brethren, who in many parts of this United Kingdom are suffering extreme famine and sickness'. It also served to reinforce the idea that the Famine was a judgement of God, and that atonement was the necessary antidote. Overall, this fund-raising venture was very successful. Within a few weeks, £171,533 was raised by the Queen's Letter and the Fast; this sum was given to the British Relief Association for distribution in Ireland and, to a lesser extent, in Scotland.[40]

In a private capacity, Victoria also showed her concern for the victims of the Famine in Ireland when, as an economy measure, she prohibited the use of 'first flour' (high-quality flour) in her households, and restricted all residents in the palace to one pound of bread daily.[41] Victoria did this at a time when over three million people within Ireland were dependent on a daily ration of soup and bread from the government's 'soup kitchens'.[42] Sympathy for the Irish was also shown by Queen Victoria's servants; they raised £247 12s 0d for Famine relief, almost one-eighth of the amount donated by their employer.[43]

In October 1847, Victoria issued a second Queen's Letter. It was timed to coincide with a day of national thanksgiving for an excellent harvest in England. In Ireland, although there had been little evidence of potato blight, the crop was far smaller than usual. The response to the second Queen's Letter demonstrated that, even within the space of ten months, attitudes to Irish relief had changed, and little cash was raised by the appeal. At this stage also, *The Times* newspaper was aggressively promoting a policy of non-intervention in the financial affairs of Ireland and they criticized Victoria for the publication of 'her ill-advised letter'. *The Times* printed many letters which were overwhelmingly opposed to giving further monetary assistance – either public or private – to Ireland. Repeatedly, the Famine was interpreted as a divine intervention and judgement on the people of Ireland. Furthermore, as England was itself undergoing a commercial and economic crisis in 1847, *The Times* urged that any money collected should remain within England, and be used to help unemployed English workers. A typical letter to *The Times* warned that:

> to misdirect all such generous outgoings to the bottomless pit of Irish wretchedness, crime and perdition, is in effect to dam up the tide of British sympathy, and to make the national thanksgiving a lamentable failure.[44]

Another letter, which again viewed the Famine as a judgement of God, argued that further financial assistance would only confirm the Irish people in their bad habits, and stated:

> A wise Providence has put a check upon the brute creation to prevent an excessive increase, but man has been left to be guided by reason. These Irish, however, seem to have none, nothing but a mere brute instinct and appetite totally unguided by reason or foresight. What commiseration can we have for these people, and why should we be called on to support them? To do so is, in effect, a premium for recklessness and improvidence.[45]

Overall, the attempt by Queen Victoria to raise a second subscription for Ireland elicited more criticism than cash, and the Queen's second letter collected only £30,167 14s 4d. This response indicated that much good will and charitable spirit towards Ireland was exhausted. This also marked an end to Victoria's involvement in Famine relief. However, in addition to Victoria's personal contribution, her position as head of the United Kingdom, of the Church of England and of the British Empire, had helped to raise additional funds for the Irish poor. Ultimately, though, not even the intervention of the Queen of England could overcome the growing antagonism towards any further financial subventions to Ireland.

Another person who wielded considerable international influence and who became involved in Famine relief was the Italian Pope, Pius IX. Pius, a liberal (in contrast to his predecessor) was elected Pope in 1846, at the age of 57.[46] Pius was thought to be sympathetic to the desire for Italian unification and to other national movements. Daniel O'Connell, the Irish nationalist leader, was *en route* to the Papal States when he died in Genoa in May 1847.[47]

When Pius became Pope, the Papacy and the Papal States wielded considerable political as well as spiritual power. Pius had a dual role as both Pope and Italian Prince. However, during Pius' long reign (he died in 1878) the Papacy lost much of its temporal power. In 1848, the year of revolutions in Europe, Pius lost support in Italy for refusing to declare war on Austria, and he was forced to flee from Rome.[48] Following this, Pius' political power began to decline. He also abandoned many of his earlier liberal attitudes and became increasingly conservative.[49]

Pius, like Queen Victoria, contributed to Famine relief both directly and indirectly. In January 1847, a committee was established in Rome. It was chaired by a Mr Pakenham who arranged for all donations for Ireland to be channelled through the English banks in Rome. The Pope was one of the first people to contribute to the committee, giving 1,000 Roman crowns from his privy purse.[50] The committee also received a donation from the staff and students in the Irish College in Rome, who missed a meal to raise money for Ireland.[51]

In addition to financial assistance, Pius also provided spiritual support. On 25 March 1847, he took the unusual step of issuing an encyclical to the international Catholic community appealing for assistance for victims of the Famine. Catholic Bishops throughout the world were asked to set aside three days in which to pray for the people of 'the Irish Kingdom … oppressed by the most terrible and awful distress from the lack of food'. Pius explained that the Irish people were particularly deserving of such prayers for their long-standing devotion to the 'Apostolic See'. Pius also offered spiritual rewards to those who prayed for Ireland; three days of prayer for the Irish poor would attract a seven-year indulgence, while three days of prayer combined with receiving communion and going to confession, would gain a highly valued plenary indulgence.[52]

The international dimension of Pius' appeal was emphasized by the fact that the three days of prayer in Rome were in Italian, English and French respectively; led by Padre Ventura, advisor to the Pope, who led the prayers on the first day; Dr Paul Cullen, the rector of the Irish College in Rome, who led the prayers on the second day; and the Bishop of Montreal, on the third day.[53] Pius' request received much support, especially within Europe. In a number of areas, collections for Ireland were already underway, but Pius' intervention added weight and gravitas to their efforts. Many Bishops reprinted the appeal in their own diocesan newsletters, and some set aside the Lenten collections for this purpose. Catholic newspapers such as *Le Correspondant* in France and *The Tablet* in England also undertook collections on behalf of Ireland. The Vincent de Paul Society, whose headquarters were in France, had already raised £5,633 for relief, and they were able to collect a further £5,000 after the Pope's encyclical. This money was sent directly to the Irish branch of the Society which included as members John O'Connell, heir to Daniel O'Connell, and Charles Gavan Duffy, the Young Irelander.[54]

By the summer of 1847, money was pouring into the Catholic Church, led by a donation of 23,365 francs (almost £1,000) from the diocese of Strasbourg. In Denmark, the local parish priests raised £504. Subscriptions came from much further afield. Most of it was sent to Archbishop Murray in Dublin. The donations included £177 from Fathers Scanlan and O'Callaghan in Caracas in Venezuela, over £600 from Father Fahy in Argentina, £70 from Grahamstown in South Africa, and £1,500 from Sydney in New South Wales.[55]

In addition to donating money personally and encouraging other members of the Catholic Church to give both spiritual and financial assistance to Ireland, Pius also gave support to more worldly ways of raising money for Ireland. In May 1847, Pius was asked by some English fund-raisers if he would provide his autograph to be auctioned at one of the numerous bazaars being held in England for Ireland. Pius not only agreed to contribute his autograph, but he also wrote a letter 'scritta di sua mono' for the same purpose. In addition, he provided a set of rosary beads made out of agates, and a carnelian medallion, engraved with the head of Christ. All of these items were to be auctioned and the proceeds to be sent to Ireland.[56] At the beginning of 1848, Europe was thrown into turmoil following the February revolution in France. This uprising had repercussions throughout the rest of Europe, including Italy and Ireland. For the Catholic Church in general this posed a dilemma whether to condemn or condone the revolutionaries. For the Pope, the consequences of the uprisings in Europe were immediate as the Italian nationalists sought to unite their country in the face of determined opposition by Austria. Pius was caught in the middle of this power struggle and political concerns took priority over spiritual ones. Although individual priests and Catholics continued to send money to Ireland, Pius was increasingly absorbed in a power struggle within the Papal States. Overall, the Pope's brief involvement in Famine relief, although successful, was ultimately overshadowed by Pius' concern for his own political and personal survival.

Another significant benefactor to Ireland was the Sultan of Turkey. When Abdulmecid became Sultan in 1839 he was only 16 years old. He inherited a recently defeated army and navy, and a bankrupt Treasury.

Although the Ottoman Empire had once been powerful and extensive, in the early nineteenth century its weaknesses had encouraged Russian expansion southwards and expansion northwards by its nominal vassal, Egypt.[57] From the beginning of his reign, Abdulmecid was under the influence of a number of 'westernized' government ministers who encouraged closer relationships with the rest of Europe, especially England and France. The governments in London and Paris welcomed this rapprochement as they wanted a strong Sultan who would act as a buffer against the expansionist aspirations of Russia.[58] The conflict between these powers was to come to a head in 1854 when England and France supported Turkey against Russia in the Crimean War.[59]

When the potato blight appeared in Ireland, the Sultan of Turkey was only 23 years of age. Despite his Treasury being virtually bankrupt, Abdulmecid had acquired a reputation for personal generosity. His awareness of the suffering in Ireland is generally thought to be due to the fact that his personal medical advisor, Dr M'Carthy, was Irish, although it may also have resulted from eagerness to foster closer diplomatic relationships with London. Abdulmecid contributed £1,000 to Irish Famine relief which he gave via the British Relief Association.[60] According to a popular tradition, which dates back to 1853, the Sultan initially offered a far higher donation than this – possibly as much as £10,000. However, he was dissuaded from giving this amount as it was considered to be distasteful for the Sultan of Turkey to give more money than the Ruler of the British Empire.[61]

The donation from the Sultan was delivered to the British Embassy in Constantinople (Istanbul). In response, the British Ambassador and staff of the Embassy visited the 'Bab-i Ali' (Turkish government departments) to extend their thanks and gratitude to the Sultan. This was followed by a letter from the Ambassador in Constantinople which conveyed 'the thanks and feelings of gratitude expressed by Her Majesty the Queen, as well as the British Empire for the benevolent act of the Sultan in order to alleviate the sufferings of the Irish people'.[62] The action of the Sultan was widely reported in the British press, and it was agreed that the Sultan's generosity did him 'great credit'.[63]

The Queen of England, the Italian Pope and the Sultan of Turkey made strange bedfellows, as they were divided by nationality, culture, religion, and personal and public aspirations. They were united, however, by the fact that they each gave large contributions towards Ireland and, more importantly, by doing so, they encouraged other people to make subscriptions towards Famine relief. To some extent, therefore, it was less the size of their donation that was important, but what it represented to the public. Although Queen Victoria made the largest individual donation, tradition has judged her contribution to be miserly and parsimonious. However, as the unhappy outcome of the Queen's second letter demonstrated, public opinion was a potent force in determining attitudes and contributions to Irish relief.

The role of philanthropic organizations

Philanthropic organizations were an important vehicle for providing relief during the Famine. The two most important agencies were the British Relief Association and the Society of Friends, but a number of other associations also raised funds on behalf of Ireland. Within Ireland itself, large donations were raised for Famine relief ranging from £200 from the Royal Irish Art Union, to £1,000 donated by the Irish Benchers, and a subscription of £429 given by the Irish Coast Guard.[64] A large number of Irish landlords also contributed either directly or indirectly to Famine relief. Examples of these included a subsidy from Lord and Lady Waterford to finance relief in the local soup kitchen, the provision of free seed to their tenants by Maria Edgeworth in Edgeworthstown and Lord Lansdowne in Kenmare, a 50 per cent rebate by Daniel O'Connell on his estates in Kerry, and regular 'and generous' donations by Lord Lurgan in County Armagh.[65] A change in relief funding after the 1847 harvest shifted most of the burden for financing relief on to the local landlords. The consequence of this was that even benign landlords became more parsimonious towards their tenants, while a large number of landlords used the new legislation as an opportunity to commence a wholesale eviction of their tenants.[66]

Within Ireland, the two most important fund-raising organizations were the Irish Relief Association and the General Central Relief Committee, both of which had headquarters in Dublin. These agencies raised £42,000 and £63,000 respectively, although the activities of the Irish Relief Association were marred by accusations of proselytism.[67] A number of private relief organizations or their agents were also active within Belfast, including the Belfast Relief Fund, the Society of Friends, the National Club (from London), the Durham Relief Association, the Indian Relief Fund, the Belfast Ladies Association and the Belfast Ladies Industrial Association for Connaught (the latter two alone raising over £7,000 between them).[68]

The work of the Society of Friends, or Quakers, during the Irish Famine is probably the best known example of private philanthropy. Before the Famine, apart from their involvement in charitable activities, the Society of Friends were well known for their campaigning on behalf of disadvantaged groups, such as slaves, the aborigines and prisoners. Their involvement in the Irish Famine, both as fund-raisers and distributors of relief, extended their role in charitable activities on an unprecedented scale.

The Quakers became publicly involved in Famine relief following the second disastrous appearance of potato blight in 1846. In November 1846, at the suggestion of Joseph Bewley, a Central Relief Committee was established in Dublin. Shortly afterwards they obtained an office in William Street. In the following month, a similar committee was established in London. Even before the latter committee was formed, £5,600 had been raised by Quakers in England for Irish distress. The Irish Quakers also made contact with Friends in America, which was to become the largest contributor to the aid efforts. The Quakers were fully aware of the limits to the help which they could provide, and acknowledged that for every 100 people they did help, there would be 900 that they would not be able to assist. In the words of Joseph Bewley, however, the Quakers were to act as 'a suitable channel' for receiving and distributing subscriptions for Ireland.[69]

One of the first actions of the Dublin and London committees was to raise funds by asking other members of the Society to make 'a liberal contribution' to Irish relief. In England, however, it was emphasized that local relief work was to have priority over Irish distress. Also, mirroring the philosophy of the government, the Friends stated that their activities should not interfere with the normal workings of trade. Hence, when the Quakers subsequently brought food into the country, they chose rise and peas which were not usually available within Ireland.[70]

To obtain accurate information regarding the extent of distress in Ireland and the best way of responding to it, a number of English and Irish Quakers travelled to the west of Ireland. Once there, they were appalled by the scenes of devastation and famine that confronted them, and they were openly critical of both absentee landlords and the relief schemes introduced by the British government.[71] The reports made by the Quakers working in the field were invaluable as they provided first hand personal accounts of the extent of the Famine from sources who were regarded as impartial and reliable. In England and America, these reports were particularly useful in countering the unsympathetic accounts which were appearing in *The Times*, *Punch* and other newspaper reports.

Donations to the Society of Friends flowed in quickly. By May 1847, £4,800 had been raised by Friends in Ireland, £35,500 in England, and £15,000 in America. An additional £4,000 had also been received by non-Quakers in England.[72] The amounts donated by individual Quakers varied, although many of the wealthier members made an initial contribution of £500. Smaller amounts were also given. The Friends in Liverpool collected £1,750, a portion of which came from Quakers in Birkenhead 'very few of whom are in affluent circumstances'.[73] In Ireland, the Quakers received almost all of their money from Friends, although the brewer Arthur Guinness gave them two separate donations of £60 and £100.[74]

The most significant amount of Quaker assistance came from America. This was provided in the form of cash, food, seed and clothing. The main agency for co-ordinating this relief was the Irish Relief Committee in New York. Throughout 1847, 91 ships from the United States brought 9,911 tons of food to Ireland. The transport of food was more difficult than the transport of cash. At the beginning of 1847, when the impact of the Famine was most severe, the export of food was delayed by bad weather and a shortage of ships. The cost of transporting bulky goods was also expensive, but this was eased when the railway companies in America provided the free carriage of goods, while the British government agreed to pay the duties and other costs incurred in the transport of goods from the States. Some of the relief provided in America presented the Quakers with a moral dilemma as they received a donation from the 'slave cities' of Baltimore and Charleston. After much public debate, they decided to accept this money.[75]

The type of relief provided by the Quakers varied, ranging from soup kitchens to the provision of seed and fishing tackle. The first soup kitchens were opening in the south of Ireland in November 1846, the period when the public works were demonstrating their inability to cope with such widespread distress. The provision of free soup was felt to be less ideologically objectionable than other forms of relief as it had little resale value. The provision of food also had the advantage of confronting the problem of hunger directly, unlike the public works. In January 1847 a 'soup shop' was opening near Ormond Quay in Dublin which decided to sell soup to the poor of Dublin. This soup kitchen was also to act as a model for the establishment of similar ventures elsewhere.[76] In fact, the Quakers' soup kitchens provided a model for the government soup kitchens established in the summer of 1847, which was possibly the most successful of the various government relief schemes. The Quakers also played an important role in this scheme as they provided many of the soup boilers which were necessary for the provision of cooked food on such a large scale. Moreover, in the hiatus between the closing of the public works and the opening of the government soup kitchens, the relief provided by the Quakers was frequently the only assistance available to a large number of people.[77]

Assistance was also provided by the Society of Friends in the form of clothes. This was felt to be particularly necessary as reports from the Quakers in Ireland described people dressed in rags, even those who were employed on the public works in the bitterly cold winter of 1846–47.[78] The initiative for providing clothes came from female Quakers in London, and they appealed to other women to send clothes to the Central Relief Committee in Dublin. The response to this appeal was very successful. In 1847, 210 packages of clothing had been sent from England to various parts of Ireland. The transport of the clothes was provided free by the railway companies in England and by the Irish steam ship companies. As a consequence of the success of this scheme, a separate women's committee had to be established in Dublin, which rented a warehouse in Upper Bridge Street and hired staff to operate it.[79] By July 1847, as the new harvest approached, the clothing crisis was thought to be over, and in the following month, the Ladies committee in London wound down its activities. During the seven months of its existence, apart from the distribution of clothing, the Ladies Committee had given over £1,800 to Irish distress.[80]

Following the harvest of 1847, the Quakers decided that instead of providing direct relief in Ireland, they should channel their energies into helping to bring long-term improvements in Ireland. This was to be achieved through the provision of capital equipment such as seeds, farming implements and fishing tackle. They also pointed out that many of their members were exhausted from having worked so closely in the distribution of relief. The British government initially welcomed this change and used the Quakers' intervention in the supplying of seed to small farmers to withdraw from this activity themselves. However, as famine continued to rage in Ireland in 1849 and mortality soared, Trevelyan, acting on behalf of Lord John Russell, secretly approached the Society of Friends and offered them one hundred pounds if they would again provide direct relief in the west of Ireland. Jonathan Pim, responding on behalf of the Quakers, declined to accept this offer, on the grounds that the situation was 'beyond the reach of private exertion'. He went on to explain 'the only machinery which it was practicable to employ was that under the control of the public author- ities' and that consequently the 'government alone could raise the funds, or carry out the measures necessary in many districts to save the lives of the people'.[81]

The involvement of the Quakers in the provision of relief was brief but successful. They not only gave money and other necessities to the people of Ireland; a large number of Quakers gave of their time generously to oversee the fair distribution of relief.[82] As Table 7.1 demonstrates, although the Quakers were primarily active in the south and west of the country, their involvement was spread throughout the whole of Ireland. The integrity of the Society of Friends gave a credibility to their appeals for funds and their reports of the distress that few other organizations pos- sessed. Within Ireland, the Quakers were respected for their refusal to use the Famine as an opportunity to win religious converts. As a consequence, the contribution of the Quakers during the Famine not only saved many lives but won a lasting gratitude from many Irish people.

Table 7.1 Distribution of Quaker relief in Ireland, by province.

Province	Food (tons)	Boilers	Money (£)	Seeds (pounds)	Clothing grants
Ulster	1,078	35	3,431	20,225	296
Leinster	459	37	1,889	9,158	353
Connaught	2,382	65	5,284	106,174	358
Munster	5,357	157	10,087	33,924	275
Total	9,276	294	20,691	169,481	1,282

Source: Appendices, Translations of the…Society of Friends

The British Relief Association was even more successful than the Quakers in raising subscriptions for Ireland. It was established in response to the suffering evident following the second appearance of the potato blight in 1846 and it was disbanded in 1849 when its funds became exhausted. The Association became a mechanism through which the sympathy already evident for Ireland and the money already raised could be more effectively harnessed and channelled. The declared purpose of the Association was to provide relief to 'those very numerous class of sufferers … who are beyond the reach of the government'. The Association believed that the most efficient way of doing this was through the distribution of direct relief in food, fuel or clothing, but not in money.[83]

The British Association was formed on 1 January 1847 by a number of wealthy businessmen in London. The most influential figure was Lionel de Rothschild, a banker, a Jew and a noted philanthropist. In 1847, he was elected as a Whig member of Parliament, but as a Jew he was unable to take the parliamentary oath and, therefore, could not take his seat.[84] Rothschild was assisted by many other successful businessmen such as Thomas Baring, member of the banking family. Stephen Spring Rice, son of Lord Monteagle, was the secretary of the committee. A number of leading Quakers were also involved with the Association including Jonathan Pim, the Dublin Quaker, and Samuel Guerney, the English Quaker. This demonstrated the close working relationship between the Society of Friends and the Association. Unlike the Quakers though, the British Relief Association employed a full-time official to oversee the distribution of their relief. In January 1847, they appointed Edward de Strzelecki, a Polish nobleman and noted explorer as their agent in Ireland. The Association also decided to work through the relief committees and machinery already established by the British government.[85] As a consequence, the British Association was sometimes viewed as being an organ of and controlled by the British government.

Strzelecki travelled immediately to Westport where he was appalled by the scenes of suffering and starvation which confronted him. He wrote a full account of what he witnessed to Charles Trevelyan, the influential Secretary at the Treasury. Throughout the remainder of the Famine, Strzelecki remained in contact with many of the leading figures involved in the provision of Famine relief and he provided them with an impartial account of the situation in the west of Ireland.[86] His advice, however, was often ignored, and he became increasingly critical of the role of the government in Famine relief.

The fund-raising activities of the British Relief Association were highly effective and by the time they closed their operations, they had raised almost £500,000. However, at the beginning of 1847 when the Association commenced its public appeal, there were some indications of a reluctance to give any further assistance to Ireland. *The Times* newspaper was critical of the fund raising appeals which were being made and Trevelyan warned the committee that 'Feeling in London is so strong against the Irish that I doubt if much progress will be made in subscription until further horrifying accounts are received'.[87] At a public meeting held at the London Tavern in March, a speaker warned that money being sent to Ireland was being used to purchase firearms.[88]

Although the Association received large sums of money from abroad, it was most successful in raising money within England, largely helped by the intervention of Queen Victoria. The subscriptions to the Association were provided by a diverse range of social groups. Among the first contributors were the rich merchant bankers of London, following the lead of Rothschild. Thus, the companies of Jones, Loyd and Co., Baring Brothers and Co., Truman, Hanbury and Co., Smith, Payne and Smiths, and Overend, Guerney and Co., all contributed £1,000 to Famine relief. This was increased by £50 from the clerks and £8 from the workmen, employed in the Truman company, while cashiers employed in the Bank of England gave £3 8s 6d.[89]

Many leading members of the government also made donations ranging from £50 to £200 to the British Relief Association. They included Lord

John Russell, the Whig Prime Minister. Sir Robert Peel, the former Prime Minister, Charles Wood, the Chancellor of the Exchequer, George Grey, the Home Secretary, and the Earl of Clarendon, Lord Lieutenant of Ireland after 1847. Charles Trevelyan, the influential Secretary at the Treasury, also contributed the sum of £50.[90] Throughout England and Wales relief committees were established which held public meetings to raise funds. This resulted in many subscriptions being received. The largest donations were from Manchester and Salford (£7,785), Newcastle and Gateshead (£3,902), Hull (£3,800), Birmingham (£800), Leeds (£2,500), Huddersfield (£2,103), Wolverhampton (£1,838) and York (£1,700). Significant amounts of money were also raised in Cambridge, Chester, Birkenhead, Liverpool, Cardiff, Neath, Rugby, Scarborough, Gloucester, Bristol and Glasgow, among others.[91] The Channel Islands also made collections, £32 being raised in Guernsey and £342 in Jersey.[92]

Numerous other donations were given to the Association from unexpected and diverse sources. For example, the London Metropolitan Police, collected £161, and the Chief Constable in Burslem raised £250, with a promise of further assistance. The President and scholars of Magdalen College, Oxford contributed £200. A collection of Chinese artefacts was displayed at Hyde Park in London on behalf of Ireland and workmen in the Dowlas Iron Works raised £171 17s 10d. A special performance was held in Drury Lane on behalf of Ireland: the disappointing turnout was attributed to the bad weather.[93]

Members of both the British army and the British press, neither of which was traditionally regarded as a friend of the Irish people, made donations. The sums given by the press included £24 from *The Record*, £10 from the editor of *The Tablet*, a Catholic newspaper, £37 from the *Daily News*, £50 from the *Observer*, £100 each from the *Morning Herald* and the *Daily News*. The most surprising contribution was £50 from the journalists on *Punch* magazine, which had been a vociferous critic of Ireland.[94]

The British army and navy, even in the furthest flung parts of the Empire, raised money for Ireland. Most of the donations were from the rank and file, although some officers also made a contribution. For example, £3,000 was raised by the soldiers in Regent's Park Barracks in London. The Officers of the First Battalion Rifle Brigade gave £22. Officers in the Dublin Garrison Amateur Theatre Company donated £15, the proceeds of one night's performance.[95] The officers and crew on board the *Hibernia* raised £167 for Ireland and the officers and men of the East India Company Depot at Worsley Barracks donated £51.[96]

Collections were also made by various religious groups. The Wesleyan Methodists collected £5,000 for Irish relief. The Anglican Church in Amsterdam collected £561. In Cambridge, the Baptist Chapel in St. Andrew Street raised £500. A sum of £2,211 was sent for Ireland from the Vicar Apostolic in Mauritius. The congregation of the Octagon Chapel in Norwich gave £87 and members of the Unitarian church donated £100. In Neath in South Wales, the Somerfield Independent Chapel collected £7 on behalf of the British Asociation.[97]

In 1848, the funds of the British Association had almost dried up and

Strzelecki started to wind up their activities. They decided that their balance of £12,000 should be given to the Poor Law Commissioners. Thousands of people in the west of Ireland had received relief from the Association, and it had been particularly successful in introducing a scheme to feed schoolchildren, despite the opposition of the government.[98] When the British Association finally closed its operations, Ireland was about to enter its fourth year of distress, and it was left to Irish taxation to finance it alone.

The international response

A unique feature of the Irish Famine was the way in which fund-raising was carried out in almost all parts of the world. For the most part, subscriptions to Ireland were made in the nine months which followed the more widespread failure of the potato crop in 1846 and, with the exception of donations to the Catholic Church and private remittances from Irish people abroad, they dried up following the harvest of 1847.[99] Most of the money was channelled through the British Relief Association, the Society of Friends, the Catholic Church, and some of the smaller relief organizations such as the Irish Relief Association or the Belfast Ladies Industrial Association for Connaught. Throughout the course of the Famine, these philanthropic bodies acted independently which resulted in some duplication of effort.

The first recorded international subscription for Ireland was raised in Calcutta, following the first appearance of potato blight in 1845. This resulted in the formation of the Indian Relief Fund in January 1846, which appealed to other British people living in India to initiate similar collections. Much of the money raised was donated by members of the British Army serving in the East Indies. Within the space of a few months, the Committee of the Indian Relief Fund had collected almost £14,000 (including donations from England and elsewhere).[100] The funds placed at the disposal of the Committee are shown in Table 7.2

Table 7.2 Donations to the Indian Relief Fund

Bengal	£8,200
Bombay	£2,976
Madras	£1,150
Ceylon	£718
Hong Kong	£82
Mobile (USA)	£192
Toronto	£300
England	£302

Source: Charles Trevelyan, *Irish Crisis*, pp. 84–5

The Indian Relief Committee appointed a committee of Trustees in Dublin to oversee the distribution of this money. The Dublin Committee included the Duke of Leinster and Archbishops Whately and Murray, the Anglican and the Catholic Archbishops of Dublin. The Committee received over 2,000 applications for a grant and by December 1846, the funds of the Committee were exhausted.[101]

Apart from the money given to the Indian Relief Fund, other collections were made in India on behalf of Ireland. At the beginning of 1847, when Famine mortality was rising sharply, in the space of just one week, £3,000 was raised in Bombay.[102] An even larger donation was provided by the Freemasons of India, who promised to raise £5,000 for Famine relief. In addition to this sum 'the wealthy Hindoos (*sic*) of High Castes who have latterly been admitted into the order by the authority of the Grand Lodge of England' promised to raise a separate subscription for Ireland.[103]

The most important contributions to Famine relief came from the United States. Until 1776, America had been part of the British Empire, but even after this date strong links had been maintained with America as a result of trade and emigration. Improvements in steam shipping in the 1820s had further improved the passage of goods and people to America. At the beginning of 1847 a large public meeting was held in Washington to discuss the condition of Ireland. The meeting resolved that:

> The enlightened and improved spirit of the age, the dictates of humanity, and the authority of our holy religion all suggest to the people of the United States that such exampled calamity and suffering ought to overcome in their regard all considerations of distance, foreign birth and residence, and difference in national character, and that it is enough that they are men, women and children, and as such belong to our own intellectual human nature.[104]

It also recommended that committees should be established throughout the country to organize contributions and collections. The proceeds were then to be forwarded to the two general committees in New Orleans and New York. Cash donations were used to purchase flour, Indian corn, meal or any other provisions deemed to be expedient, and this was then transported to Ireland.[105]

Following the Washington meeting, similar ones were held throughout the States. In Philadelphia, a local newspaper commented that the philanthropic bug appeared to have bitten the local inhabitants especially the Irish domestic servants as 'Their only desire at present appears to be to give every farthing they possess'.[106] The newspaper also wryly noted that Americans were in a good position to give as they had enjoyed a bumper harvest in 1846, and admitted 'of course, the misery of Ireland is our prosperity, and the prices obtained by producers are far beyond anything ever dreamed of'.[107]

One of the most publicized acts of charity from the United States was the sending of the ship of war, the *Jamestown* to Ireland, laden with food. The ship was manned by volunteers and no freight charges were made. The *Jamestown* sailed from Boston to Cork in only 13 days. The progress of the ship was closely followed in both England and Ireland. When the *Jamestown* arrived in Cork, William Rathbone, the Liverpool philanthropist, was one of the people who met it, in order to help assist in 'an impartial distribution to the necessitous in Ireland'.[108] For the cargo on board the *Jamestown* see Table 7.3.

Table 7.3 The cargo of the *Jamestown*

	cwt	qtrs	bshl
Wheat		4	0
Barley		3	4
Oats		2	4
Rye		9	2
Peas		30	0
Beans		279	3
Indian corn (maize)		339	2
Wheatmeal	96	1	0
Barley	19	2	16
Indian corn meal	4,220	3	0
Rice	154	1	4
Bread & biscuit	1,048	3	21
Potatoes	61	1	1
Apples, dried			6
Pork	707	0	16
Hams	291	3	4
Fish	4	0	0
Clothing	10 cases, 18 barrels		

Source: Charles Trevelyan, *Irish Crisis*, pp. 90–91.

Much of the money and goods raised in the States were channelled through the Society of Friends and the Catholic Church, or the British Relief Association.[109] By the spring of 1847, cash and provisions were pouring into Ireland from America, which led the Prime Minister, Lord John Russell, to praise publicly the generosity of the American people.[110] The government also agreed that it would pay the freight and other charges on goods imported from America. In 1847 alone, this amounted to over £50,000 in duties etc.[111] The arrival of this relief, however, came too late for the many thousands of people who had died in the winter of 1846–47.

Large donations were also received from Canada, an estimated £20,000 being collected in the first few months of 1847.[112] In addition separate subscriptions were raised in Nova Scotia, which contributed £1,000; New Brunswick, £1,640; and Newfoundland, £850. Smaller amounts were also raised in Miramichi, Guelph, Prince Edward's Island, Three Rivers, Bathurst and Halifax.[113] For many Irish emigrants, Canada was a popular and affordable destination, but in a two-month period in 1847, 4,572 Irish immigrants died at the quarantine station at Grosse Île near Quebec. While this evidence of the impact of the Famine may have aroused sympathy for the Irish in both the United States and Canada, impoverished and disease-ridden Irish emigrants were often regarded as unwelcome arrivals.[114]

Donations were received from other parts of the world. For example, British residents in Mexico raised £652, even though Mexico was then at war with the United States.[115] In Florence, a Relief Committee was formed of English residents and it raised £500. A Society Ball was also held, hosted by the Prince de Demidoff. It raised £891 17s 2d. Moreover, the servants who looked after the English aristocracy in Florence, made their own subscription of £9 13s 9d.[116] In Madras, £2,150 was raised for the Irish destitute, £6 came from Belgium, £134 from Paris and £100 from Corfu. Donations came from even further afield. A sum of £2,644 was contributed from St. Petersburg, and £620 from Constantinople. The islands of Malta and Gozo sent £720, and Gibralter, £100. Mauritius donated £3,020, which included £111 and £16 from the poor native inhabitants of the Seychelles and Rodrigues respectively.[117]

Overall, following the second blight of 1846 the poor in Ireland became the recipients of international sympathy on a scale previously unknown. This sympathy was translated into practical action resulting in balls, bazaars, auctions, knitting circles, art exhibitions and various other fundraising activities taking place on behalf of the starving people in Ireland. These actions went beyond the traditional philanthropy and paternalism exercised by the upper classes as money and food were contributed by all groups within society. During the early months of 1847, the poor in Ireland became an international 'cause celebre' which evoked a response that went beyond the parameters of religion or nationality. By the end of 1847 most of this sympathy disappeared almost as suddenly as it had appeared, coinciding with the official withdrawal of the British government from financial involvement in the Famine. To a large extent, therefore, after 1847, Ireland was left largely to its own devices.

Poverty supporting poverty: the contribution of convicts, Native Americans and ex-slaves

One of the smallest yet most impressive donations to Irish Famine relief was provided by a group of convicts in England, who were on board a prison hulk in Woolwich, the *Warrior*.[118] This donation was all the more remarkable in view of the conditions in which the prisoners were themselves living. Prison ships had initially been used only for prisoners of war, but they were increasingly used for convicts as land prisons became overcrowded.[119] Although Botany Bay was established as a penal colony after 1787, floating prisons or hulks continued to be used in Britain, Bermuda and Gibralter as a solution to the ever-growing numbers of convicted criminals.[120]

In 1788, hulks were established in Woolwich, primarily for the purpose of making more dockyard labour available to the Admiralty. The convicts on board the hulks had to perform hard labour, which generally had to do with the improvement of the river ways. They worked in gangs of 10–20 and wore a distinctive uniform. Punishment, even for petty misdemeanours, was by whipping.[121] The mortality on board the hulks was extremely high; at the beginning of the nineteenth century, approximately one in five prisoners died while in captivity. Although there were many calls for an ending to the use of hulks, convict labour continued to be needed on the docks. By 1845, 70 per cent of home-based convicts were still kept on board prison ships.[122]

The prison ships in Woolwich were regarded as being among the worst and most harshly administered in England. In January 1847, the MP for Finsbury made a statement in the House of Commons condemning the ill-treatment of convicts in Woolwich and demanding that a Select Committee be appointed to enquire further into this matter. The Select Committee confirmed the atrocious conditions, the poor diet, the ill-health (especially from scurvy) and the general ill-treatment of prisoners in Woolwich.[123] Regardless of such public condemnation, the use of hulks continued for a few more years. The hulks at Woolwich were among the last in England to be closed, in 1856. Elsewhere within the British Empire, they were phased out over the next 20 years. The last hulk in Gibralter was closed in 1875.[124]

At the beginning of 1847, there were 311 prisoners on board the *Warrior* prison ship in Woolwich, although five years earlier, there had been 671 convicts on board.[125] Information regarding the Famine in Ireland came to the attention of the convicts when they noticed boxes of food etc. in various parts of the dockyards for shipment to Ireland, and to a lesser extent Scotland. When they were given the reason for this transport of food, the convicts asked if they might be permitted to make their own contribution for Ireland. The prison authorities agreed on the condition that 'the donation must be perfectly voluntary on the part of every convict'. In total, the amount collected in Woolwich totalled 17 shillings, all of it being paid in pennies and half-pennies. This money was then forwarded to the Society of Friends for distribution within Ireland.[126]

Donations from other impoverished groups were also sent to Ireland from further afield than England. These donations demonstrated that sympathy for Ireland cut across cultural, religious and national differences. The way in which the donations were noted, however, often demonstrated the acceptance of racial and cultural stereotyping. The money raised for Ireland included contributions from Native Americans in America and Canada. The Governor of British Canada, referring to these donations in one of his official dispatches, estimated that Canadian subscriptions were in the region of £20,000. He added that:

> The habitants of all creeds and origins have liberally contributed. It will be gratifying to Your Lordship to hear that several of the Indian tribes have expressed a desire to share in relieving the wants of their suffering White Brethren. The sum described by them already exceeds £175.[127]

Another group which provided a subscription to Ireland despite their own poverty and degradation was the Choctaw Nation. The Choctaw people were themselves familiar with suffering, starvation and mortality. In 1831,

Andrew Jackson's government had confiscated their ancestral lands in the Mississippi and then forcibly removed them to Oklahoma, a distant and alien territory. Approximately 21,000 Choctaw people began the walk, but an estimated 50 per cent of them died *en route*. In Choctaw tradition, this journey is known as 'The Trail of Tears'.[128]

The Choctaw Nation were told of the suffering in Ireland by members of the Society of Friends. A meeting was held at the Choctaw Agency in Oklahoma at which a letter was read out appealing for donations. Money was given by the missionaries, the traders and the Indians, the latter providing the largest portion of the fund. The amount raised was $170. The simple, humanitarian gesture of the Choctaw Nation, however, was viewed in terms of the success of Christian teaching on a heathen people. The Society of Friends in New York, for example, recorded that:

> Among the contributions last received is a sum of $170 of which the largest part was contributed by the children of the forest ... these distant men have felt the force of Christian sympathy and benevolence and have given their cheerful aid in this good cause, though they are separated from you by miles of land and an ocean's breadth.[129]

A local newspaper also noted the generous contribution of the Choctaw Nation, commenting that:

> What an agreeable reflection it must give to the Christian and philanthropist, to witness this evidence of civilisation and Christian spirit existing among our red neighbours. They are repaying the Christian world a consideration for bringing them from out of benighted ignorance and heathen barbarism. Not only by contributing a few dollars, but by affording evidence that the labours of the Christian Missionary have not been in vain.[130]

Donations to Ireland also came from a number of other groups who were themselves impoverished. This included money raised in the British West Indies by black labourers who only ten years earlier had still been slaves.[131] The British involvement in the Caribbean islands was longstanding. In the seventeenth century, the islands had provided a convenient receptacle for convicts and religious non-conformists, although white workers were always a minority within the labour force. In the eighteenth century, the economy of the islands was dominated by two valuable commodities, slaves and sugar. During that century, European colonial powers were engaged in vicious warfare to maintain dominance of the West Indies. As a consequence, the Caribbean islands constantly changed hands. However, by the nineteenth century, the West Indies were declining in both political and economic importance. The ending of slavery in the British colonies in 1833, following years of anti-slavery agitation, occurred at a time when many of the economies of the islands were in decline.[132]

The black workers in the West Indies were no strangers to starvation and death. Between 1780 and 1787, 15,000 slaves had died in Jamaica from starvation, and 100 in Antigua in 1788.[133] News of the Irish Famine reached the Caribbean islands through the medium of various missionary groups active on the islands, especially the Baptists and the Society of Friends. Also the Governors of the islands, in accordance with a request by the Colonial Secretary, Earl Grey, issued a proclamation and held a public meeting in order to raise money for both Ireland and Scotland. Table 7.4 shows the sums raised for this purpose, which were contributed in the first half of 1847.

Table 7.4 Money subscribed in the British West Indies

Bermuda	£500 0s 0d
Jamaica	£575 0s 0d
Barbados	£2,000 0s 0d
Bahamas	£2,000 0s 0d
Trinidad	£1,350 0s 0d
Grenada	£565 1s 3d
Tobago	£310 3s 5d
St. Lucia	£604 0s 11d
Antigua	£645 2s 3d
St. Christopher	£500 0s 0d
British Guiana	£3170 5s 8d

Source: Despatches from Governors in West Indies to Colonial Office

The donations received from these islands were made by both the labouring population and their colonial masters. The government of Barbados, for example, sent £2,000 in recognition of money they had received from Ireland 65 years earlier, when some of the islands had been devastated by a hurricane.[134] Donations were also provided by many of the poorest groups in the West Indies – the black labourers. An example of this is 'the negroes of Antigua… from their own scanty resources' who raised £144.[135] The governor of the island in his official despatch commented that 'it was gratifying to observe that many of the emancipated race readily united with the other classes of the community in contributing to this charitable object'.[136] This pattern was repeated in the other Caribbean islands. In Tobago, the Governor informed the Colonial Secretary 'Your Lordship will learn with pleasure that the negro population of Tobago have come forward on this occasion with much liberality and good feeling'.[137] In British Guiana, which raised one of the largest amounts towards the relief of Famine distress, the Governor noted 'that among the subscriptions from the rural districts, those of many coolies are to be ranked, who have contributed a day's wage cheerfully'.[138]

The compassion of the Native Americans, the convicts in England and the ex-slaves in the Caribbean, demonstrated that poverty did not deter people from wanting to help the starving Irish. In absolute terms, their contribution to Famine relief may have been small, but in relation to their own incomes, it represented a real sacrifice. Of all of the donations raised throughout the world for the Irish Famine, these acts of generosity, done for neither political nor personal gain, are probably the most remarkable.

Conclusion

The response of private individuals and organizations to the Irish Famine was generous and compassionate. It also demonstrated an international knowledge of and practical sympathy for a severe, yet localized, catastrophe. In this sense, the way in which the suffering in Ireland became the concern of a diverse and geographically distant number of people was without precedent.

A critical factor in this international response was one of communication and awareness. Information was spread through newspapers, letters, religious sermons, word-of-mouth, government despatches, and the publication of subscription lists. As much of this information was second-hand and could not easily be verified, it had to be taken on trust. In this context, contacts which were established throughout the British Empire, especially within the army, through the medium of the Catholic Church and other religious organizations, through the public profile of Daniel O'Connell, and through the network of the Irish diaspora, all provided important access to a global and informed community of potential donors.

Apart from geographic diversity, those who gave to Irish relief were also socially diverse. The motivation of these groups is not easy to identify. The donations provided by Queen Victoria, the Pope, the Sultan and various government ministers may have combined political with personal concerns. The Irish Famine is remarkable, however, for the impact it made on groups who had no prior connection with Ireland and no reason, other than humanitarian, for providing relief.

An important factor in determining the response was the way in which the potato failures were perceived and interpreted by the British Government. To a large extent, the Famine was defined in terms of political, economic, and providential concepts rather than in terms of humanitarian ones. This was most evident after 1847 when the Famine was declared to be over. Although the British government continued to receive reports of suffering and mortality in Ireland far beyond this date, official interest in the Irish affairs was reduced, and the Famine was marginalized as an issue both within Westminster and within the British press. It is no coincidence that after the autumn of 1847, donations to Ireland fell drastically. Famine or compassion fatigue alone, however, cannot explain the sudden falling off in private donations at the end of 1847. The Queen's second letter though, and the poor response which it elicited, suggest that a number of factors shaped both the public and the private response to the Famine.

Increasingly, the role of British public opinion, expressed through middle-class newspapers and journals such as *The Times, Punch,* the *Economist* and the *Edinburgh Review* was an important factor in shaping perceptions of the Irish Famine and in portraying an image of a people who were becoming ever more dependent on external assistance. As Ireland entered its third consecutive year of shortages, which was followed by a feeble uprising in 1848, fears regarding Ireland's dependency and ingratitude were confirmed. Furthermore, this coincided with a financial and commercial crisis within Britain in 1847–48, which affected the industrial middle classes most severely. The 1847 General Election had affirmed the ascendancy of these groups within Westminster, and their cries for retrenchment were welcomed within the British Treasury. John Russell, the Prime Minister, was aware of this when he said:

> The great difficulty this year respecting Ireland is one which does not spring from Trevelyan and Charles Wood but lies deep in the breasts of the British people. It is this – we have granted, lent, subscribed, worked, visited, clothed the Irish; millions of pounds worth of money, years of debate etc – the only return is calumny and rebellion – let us not grant, clothe etc. any more and see what they will do.[139]

Although organizations such as the Society of Friends, the British Relief Association and the Catholic Church continued to provide assistance to Ireland beyond 1847, there is no doubt that the great wave of public philanthropy had subsided. In March 1849, the British Relief Association made its final grant to Ireland and three months later, the Quakers withdrew from Irish relief. Following this, the British government again became the main recourse of the distressed Irish people.

Yet, for a short period, the suffering of the Irish people produced a response that was hitherto unparalleled in its magnitude, geographic extent, social diversity, and motivation. The involvement of private charity in Famine relief provided an important life-line for many Irish people at a time when official relief was limited, late in arriving, and distributed with parsimony and reluctance. The provision of private relief was vital to the survival of many.

The sense of human value and dignity that lay behind the donations provided a glimmer of humanitarian light against the dark bureaucratic frugality of the official response.

Acknowledgements

I would like to thank Don Mullan of *Concern Worldwide* and Gary White Deer of the Choctaw Nation for encouraging me to write this chapter. I am also grateful, for suggestions and support, to Eileen Black, Séan Egan, Geoffrey Keating, Arthur Luke, Gerard MacAtasney, Josie McCann, Val Smith, Tony Walker and Chris Yates.

Notes

1. For more on the failure of the public works see Christine Kinealy, *This Great Calamity: The Irish Famine 1845–52*, Gill and Macmillan, Dublin, 1994, Chapter 3.
2. The Quarter Acre, or Gregory Clause, introduced in 1847, decreed that any person who occupied more than a quarter of an acre of land was not entitled to receive relief: see Kinealy, *This Great Calamity*, p. 219 onwards.
3. Charles Wood to Clarendon, Hickleton Papers, 23 July 1848. The originals of these papers are in the Borthwick Historical Institute, Yorkshire – microfilm copies are widely available.
4. *The Times*, 5 October 1847, 6 October 1847.
5. Christine Kinealy. 'The poor law during the Famine: an administration in crisis', in E.M. Crawford (ed.), *Famine: The Irish Experience 900–1900*, John Donald, Edinburgh, 1989.
6. *The Times*, 1 February 1849, 12 February 1849.
7. Joel Mokyr, *Why Ireland Starved: A Quantitative and Analytical History of the Irish Economy 1800–1850*, George Allen & Unwin, London, 1983, pp. 292–3.
8. Eric Williams, *From Columbus to Castro: The History of the Caribbean 1492–1969*, André Deutsch, London, 1970, p. 332.
9. Mokyr, *Why Ireland Starved*, p. 292.
10. Quoted in the *Freeman's Journal*, 5 August 1846.
11. Mortality during the Irish Famine was relatively higher than in even recent famines such as in Bangladesh, Somalia and Biafra. For more on this see, Cormac Ó Gráda, 'The Great Famine and today's Famines', in Cathal Póirtéir (ed.), *The Great Irish Famine*, Mercier Press, Dublin, 1995. p. 250.
12. Boyd Hilton, *The Age of Atonement: The Influence of Evangelicalism on Social and Economic Thought 1785–1865*, Clarendon Press, Oxford, 1988, p. 11.
13. Charles Trevelyan, *The Irish Crisis*, Macmillan & Co., London, 1880, p. 1.
14. Kinealy, *This Great Calamity*, pp. 18–26.
15. Trevelyan, *Irish Crisis*, p.138.
16. In July 1847, over three million people daily were receiving free rations of food from the soup kitchens. For more see Kinealy, *This Great Calamity*, pp. 136–54.
17. Edward Twistleton, Poor Law Commissioner, to Charles Trevelyan, Public Record Office London, T.64.370 C/4, 27 February 1848.
18. Trevelyan, *Irish Crisis*, pp. 138–40.
19. Lord Clarendon to Lord John Russell, 10 August 1847, Clarendon Papers, Bodleian Library, Oxford.
20. For example, on 22 January 1847, one page of *The Times* carried subscription lists for 'The British Relief Association', 'The Committee of the Irish Society', 'The National Philanthropic Organisation for the Relief of Metropolitan Destitution' and 'The Church Education Society for Ireland'.
21. T. D. Williams, 'O'Connell's Impact on Europe', in K. B. Nowlan and M. R. O'Connell (eds), *Daniel O'Connell: Portrait of a Radical*, Appletree, Belfast, 1984.
22. Trevelyan, *Irish Crisis*, pp. 85–6.
23. Irene Whelan, 'The stigma of Souperism', in Póirtéir, *Great Famine*, pp. 135–6.
24. Donal A. Kerr, *'A Nation of Beggars'?: Priests, People, and Politics in Famine Ireland 1846–52*, Clarendon Press, Oxford, 1994, p. 59.
25. Quoted in Asa Briggs, *The Age of Improvement*, Longmans, London, 1959, p. 255.
26. Queen Victoria to Lord John Russell, 3 August 1846: see Arthur Christopher Benson and Viscount Esher (eds), *Letters of Queen Victoria: A Selection from Her Correspondence between the years 1837 and 1861*, Volume 2, 1844–53, John

Murray, London, 1907, p. 111.

27. See Kinealy, *This Great Calamity*, Chapter 6, passim.

28. Queen Victoria, 'Journal', 8 August 1849, quoted in Elizabeth Longford, *Victoria R.I.*, Weidenfeld & Nicolson, London, 1964, p. 191.

29. Queen Victoria to Leopold, King of the Belgians, 9 August 1849, *Letters of Victoria*, p. 268.

30. A ballad sung on the streets during Victoria's visit goes:
    Arise ye dead of Skibbereen
    And come to Cork to see the Queen.
    For more on this see, Thomas P. O'Neill, 'The Queen and the Famine', in *Threshold*, Vol. 1, No. 2, Summer 1957, pp. 60–63.

31. Queen Victoria, 'Journal', 28 September 1846, cited in Longford, *Victoria R.I.*, p. 190.

32. Queen Victoria 'Journal', 5 November 1847, cited in Longford, *Victoria R.I.*, p. 191. This comment probably refers to the murder of Major Mahon of Strokestown, who was assassinated near his home on 2 November 1847. The incident was widely reported in the British newspapers.

33. This legacy of bitterness was evident during the opening of an exhibition at University College Cork to commemorate the Famine's 150th anniversary in 1995. The decision to display a statue of Queen Victoria which had been buried in the College grounds in the 1930s, but which had been exhumed for inclusion in the exhibition, provoked national criticism. See, for example, *Cork Examiner*, 14 June 1995.

34. Frank Prochaska, *The Sunday Times*, 23 July 1995.

35. Minutes of British Relief Association, National Library of Ireland, January 1847 (MS 2022).

36. I am grateful to Thomas P. O'Neill for giving me copies of this correspondence. The original letters are in the Monteagle Papers, National Library of Ireland.

37. Trevelyan, *Irish Crisis*, pp. 142–4

38. *The Times*, 22 January 1847

39. *The Times*, 22 January 1847

40. Trevelyan, *Irish Crisis* p. 86.

41. *Roscommon and Leitrim Gazette*, 29 May 1847.

42. *Fourth Report of the Relief Commissioners constituted under the Act Vic. cap. 7 with appendices*, 1847 [859] xvii.

43. Eighth Subscription List of the British Relief Association, February 1847.

44. *The Times*, 19 October 1847.

45. *The Times*, 19 October 1847.

46. E. E. Y. Hales, *Pio Nono: a Study in European Politics and Religion*, Eyre and Spottiswoode, London, 1954, pp. 17–102.

47. Kerr, *'Nation of Beggars'?*, p. 69.

48. Harry Hearder, *Italy in the Age of the Risorgimento, 1790–1870*, Longman, London, 1983, passim.

49. Hales, *Pio Nono*, passim.

50. *The Times*, 30 January 1847

51. Kerr, *'Nation of Beggars'?*, p. 53.

52. Pius IX, *Pontificus Maximi Acta*, January 1847, Vatican Archives Rome. I am grateful to the Vatican for allowing me to see a copy of this document.

53. Kerr *'Nation of Beggars'?*, p. 53.

54. The Society of St. Vincent had been founded in 1833 and was active in France, Italy and Ireland. See also, Kerr, *'Nation of Beggars'?*, pp. 53–5.

55. *Report of the British Relief Association*, Richard Clay, London, 1849; Kerr , *'Nation*

of Beggars'?, p. 58.

56. *The Times*, 20 May 1847.
57. For more information on this see Alan Palmer, *The Decline and Fall of the Ottoman Empire*, Murray, London, 1992.
58. Palmer, *Ottoman Empire*, pp. 104–7.
59. J. L. Herkless 'Stratford, the cabinet and the Crimean War', in *History Journal*, Vol. 18, No. 3, 1975.
60. *Report of the British Relief Association*, p. 181.
61. O'Neill, 'The Queen and the Famine', p. 62.
62. Letter from the Ministry of Foreign Affairs to the Sultan, Ottoman Archives, 27 May 1847. The original is in the Ottoman Archives – a copy is now in the National Library of Ireland, donated by the Turkish Ambassador to Ireland.
63. Report from *The Globe* carried in *The Times*, 17 April 1847.
64. Trevelyan, *Irish Crisis*, p. 90; *The Globe*, 15 January 1847.
65. *The Globe*, 9 January 1847, 8 May 1847; Gerard MacAtasney, 'The Famine in Lurgan, 1845–47', unpublished M.A. thesis, Queen's University, 1995.
66. James S. Donnelly Jr., 'Mass Eviction and the Great Famine' in Póirtéir (ed.), *The Great Irish Famine*, pp. 155–73.
67. Cecil Woodham-Smith, *The Great Hunger: Ireland, 1845–49*, Hamish Hamilton, London, 1962, p. 156.
68. MacAtasney, 'Famine in Lurgan', p. 40.
69. Rob Goodbody, *A Suitable Channel: Quaker Relief in the Great Famine*, Pale Publishing, Bray, 1995, pp. 10–16.
70. Goodbody, *A Suitable Channel*, p. 8.
71. James H. Tuke, *Report of the Society of Friends on Distress in Ireland, 1847–48*, National Library of Ireland, Ir 9410859: hereafter Tuke, *Distress in Ireland*.
72. Appendix VII, *Transactions of the Central Relief Committee of the Society of Friends during the Famine in Ireland in 1846 and 1847*, Hodges and Smith, Dublin, 1852 (hereafter *Transactions of... the Society of Friends*).
73. *The Globe*, 3 January 1847.
74. *Report of the British Relief Association*.
75. Goodbody, *A Suitable Channel*, p. 24.
76. Goodbody, *A Suitable Channel*, pp. 28–31.
77. Kinealy, *This Great Calamity*, pp. 140–48.
78. Tuke, *Distress in Ireland*, passim.
79. Goodbody, *A Suitable Channel*, pp. 40–41.
80. Goodbody, *A Suitable Channel*, p. 43.
81. Charles Trevelyan to J. Pim, Public Record Office, London, T.64.367. B/2, 24 August 1848; Charles Trevelyan to Jonathan Pim, 2 June 1849, Pim to Trevelyan, 5 June 1849, *Transactions of the... Society of Friends*, Appendix XXIV, pp. 452–4. During the course of the Famine almost 20 Quakers died from exhaustion or fever.
82. *Transactions of the... Society of Friends*, Appendices.
83. Minutes of the British Relief Association, 1 January 1847.
84. *Dictionary of National Biography*, pp. 304–05.
85. Minutes of the British Relief Association, 1–30 January 1847.
86. Strzelecki to Trevelyan, 10 February 1847, Public Record Office, London, T.64. 369. B 3; Strzelecki to Lord Clarendon, 26 August 1848, Clarendon Letter Books, Bodleian Library, Oxford.
87. *The Times*, 5 January 1847; Trevelyan quoted in Woodham–Smith, *The Great Hunger*, p. 169.
88. *The Times*, 12 March 1847.
89. Trevelyan, *Irish Crisis*, p. 87.

90. *Report of the British Relief Association.*
91. Trevelyan, *Irish Crisis*, pp. 87–8; *Report of the British Relief Association.* Parts of Scotland were undergoing their own famine at the time, which may have accounted for the small sums donated there.
92. *Freeman's Journal*, 2 July 1847.
93. Trevelyan, *Irish Crisis*, p. 88; *The Times*, 21 March 1847; *The Globe*, 9 February 1847.
94. Trevelyan, *Irish Crisis*, p. 90; *Report of the British Relief Association.*
95. *Report of the British Relief Association; Freeman's Journal*, 2 July 1847.
96. Trevelyan, *Irish Crisis*, p. 89.
97. Trevelyan, *Irish Crisis*, pp. 87–8.
98. See Kinealy, *This Great Calamity*, pp. 207–8.
99. For more on Catholic donations, see Archbishop Murray's Papers, Dublin Diocesan Archives.
100. Trevelyan, *Irish Crisis*, p. 85
101. Trevelyan, *Irish Crisis*, pp. 84–5.
102. *Roscommon and Leitrim Gazette*, 1 May 1847.
103. *The Globe*, 11 January 1847.
104. *The Times*, 24 March 1847.
105. *The Times*, 24 March 1847.
106. Letter from Philadelphia reprinted in *Northern Whig*, 23 March 1847.
107. *Northern Whig*, 23 March 1847
108. *Liverpool Mercury*, 12 April 1847.
109. Trevelyan, *Irish Crisis*, p. 93.
110. *Roscommon and Leitrim Gazette*, 27 March 1847.
111. Trevelyan, *Irish Crisis*, p. 90.
112. Earl of Elgin, Government House, Montreal to Earl Grey, *Copies of Despatches to the Secretary of State for the Governors of Her Majesty's Colonial Possessions*, BPP 1847 (853) LIII, 28 May 1847.
113. *Freeman's Journal*, 2 July 1847.
114. Kinealy, *This Great Calamity*, pp. 302–04.
115. *Report of British Relief Association.*
116. Trevelyan, *Irish Crisis*, p. 87; *Report of British Relief Association.*
117. Trevelyan, *Irish Crisis*, p. 88. The small size of the donation from Belgium may have been due to the fact that Belgium had suffered a widespread failure of the potato crop in 1845, and consequent food shortages.
118. *The Times*, 24 April 1847.
119. Sean McConville, *A History of English Prison Administration, Volume 1 1750–1877*, Routledge & Kegan Paul, London, 1981, pp. 106–07.
120. Portia Robinson, *The Hatch and Brood of Time: A Study of the First Generation of Native-Born White Australians*, Oxford University Press, Oxford, 1985.
121. McConville, *English Prison Administration*, p. 109.
122. McConville, *English Prison Administration*, p. 197.
123. *Report of an Inquiry into the General Treatment and Condition of the Convicts in the Hulks at Woolwich*, BPP 1847 (18) XXIX.
124. A. G. L. Shaw, *Convicts and the Colonies: A Study of Penal Transportation from Great Britain and Ireland to Australia and Other Parts of the British Empire*, Faber and Faber, London, 1966, p. 349.
125. McConville, *English Prison Administration*, p. 198.
126. *The Times*, 24 April 1847.
127. Earl of Elgin, Montreal, to Lord Grey, *Copies of Despatches to the Secretary of State from the Governors of Her Majesty's Colonial Possessions*, BPP 1847 (853) LIII.
128. I am grateful to Gary White Deer of the Choctaw Nation for his assistance in

the writing of this section of the chapter. The special relationship between the Choctaw and the Irish people has proved to be enduring, and in 1992 the Irish President, Mary Robinson, was made an honorary chief of the Choctaw Nation.

129. Minute of M. Van Schaick, Chairman of Irish Relief Committee, New York, May 1847. I am grateful to Don Mullan of *Concern Worldwide* for providing me with a copy of this Minute.
130. *Arkansas Intelligence*, 3 April 1847.
131. Slavery within the British possessions ended in 1833 but the plantation owners were allowed a seven-year transition period to free their slaves.
132. Williams, *From Columbus to Castro*, passim.
133. Williams, *From Columbus to Castro*, p. 226.
134. *Roscommon and Leitrim Gazette*, 17 April 1847.
135. *Northern Whig*, 8 May 1847.
136. Governor Higginson to Earl Grey, *Copies of Despatches*, 11 May 1847, p. 16.
137. Lieutenant Governor Graeme to Earl Grey, *Copies of Despatches*, 4 May 1847, p. 15.
138. Governor Light to Earl Grey, *Copies of Despatches*, 19 March 1847, p. 17.
139. John Russell to Lord Clarendon, 24 February 1849, quoted in Peter Mandler, *Aristocratic Government in the Age of Reform: Whigs and Liberals, 1830–1852*, Clarendon Press, Oxford, 1990, p. 252.

8 'Where the poor man is not crushed down to exalt the aristocrat ': Vere Foster's programmes of assisted emigration in the aftermath of the Irish Famine

Ruth-Ann M. Harris

Twenty-three thousand or more women[1] migrated to America because an Anglo-Irish diplomat's son, whose first glimpse of Ireland was during the worst year of the Great Famine, committed his fortune and his life's effort to assist those he perceived to be most in need of the opportunities America offered. Vere Henry Lewis Foster (1819–1900) was certainly not the first person to become enamoured with the problems of Ireland. Foster was, however, no Tom Broadbent, George Bernard Shaw's character in 'John Bull's Other Island', the English civil engineer who with his virtues of money, iron and coal sought to bring improvement to Ireland.[2] Indeed Vere Foster was not a romantic, as Shaw portrayed Broadbent, but an altogether practical individual.

Vere Foster 's first visit to Ireland was in 1847 to carry out his father's wish to assist one of their tenants in emigrating to America from the family property in Co. Louth. Prior to that time Foster appears to have been vaguely interested in following his father into a diplomatic career. A tour of Cork and Kerry two years later, when those regions were still prostrate from hunger and disease, left him resolved to:

> take a farm in the West of Ireland... in the hope of making myself useful by falling in with any practicable scheme for giving increased employment to the people, and for providing against a recurrence of similar destitution in the future.[3]

Vere Foster was of the Protestant Ascendancy, a class that had consolidated authority and wealth for itself centuries earlier. Their comfort and security began to be undermined 19 years before his birth when the Act of Union and later Catholic Emancipation spelled an end to their monopoly of privilege. But while many yearned for a past which could not be recovered, some like Foster sought innovative roles in the emerging new order. Foster became in the words of one scholar, a kind of benevolent buccaneer who fought social evils wherever he found them.[4]

Vere Foster was very much product of his age, that of the post-Enlightenment with its emphasis on scientific principles. Individuals such as Foster saw themselves as inheritors of a tradition asserting not the immutability of the human condition, but transformation through social engineering. As a Protestant he inherited a set of beliefs that emphasized the role of individual responsibility in bringing about change. His awareness of the two streams of his inheritance – religion and science – must have been intensified when his father, tormented by his inability to reconcile an orthodox view of the Bible with emerging scientific thought, committed suicide in 1848.

After having found the purpose to which he could direct his life, Foster enrolled in a course at the Glasnevin Model Farm in Dublin, with the intent of reforming Ireland's backward agriculture. Working in the fields at Glasnevin with young men from all over Ireland, he learned at first hand not only of the tragedy of the Famine but of the vitality and courage of Irish country people. Gradually his plan emerged: the long-term remedy for Ireland must be reform of the land system, while the immediate remedy must be to assist the ambitious poor to emigrate to a land of greater opportunity.[5] Despite the losses of the Famine, the country remained over-populated. People needed to emigrate in order to utilize their talents, skills of energy, drive, and perhaps most important of all, a faith in their future. He stated his aim as:

> [To raise] the condition of the poorest families in the poorest districts of Ireland, by assisting the emigration to North America of one able-bodied member of each family (in most cases a woman), specially selected on account of her poverty, good character, and industrious habits, with the expectation that she will herself take the remaining members of her family out of poverty.[6]

Seeking to gain first-hand knowledge of the travel conditions, Vere Foster went to America at least once every year and sometimes twice between 1850 and 1857. His testimony to parliamentary committees resulted in reforming legislation.[7] In October 1850 Foster took steerage passage on an American ship, the *Washington*. Considered the best of the emigrant ships, it was new, strong and dry, and carried a crew of 31 when it departed from Liverpool for New York with 934 passengers. Observing the sadistic treatment of the steerage passengers by the crew, he remonstrated with the mate, who responded with curses. When, five days into the journey, no food had been served to passengers despite their tickets stating that they would be fed every day, Foster wrote a letter of complaint to the captain. Again the response was abuse, but this time the first mate knocked Foster unconscious, accused him of being a pirate and threatened him with a diet of bread and water. Vere Foster was the wrong person to insult. He immediately wrote a long account of the conditions on board the ship, endorsed by 128 passengers. (His papers contain the original of 66 of these and it is significant that 27 of these were marksmen – that is, unable to sign their own name.)[8] The experience taught Foster the power of public exposure. Within the next two years he made two more such trips and became the scourge of those who would abuse emigrants. He also collected systematic information on conditions in North America by soliciting information through periodicals such as *The Freeman's Journal* and wrote a guidebook for would-be emigrants, giving away 250,000 copies before being compelled to charge one penny apiece for them.

Despite the fact that in the years following the Famine it seemed as if every family in the west of Ireland had one or more of its members leaking toward America, emigration as the solution to the problem of persistent underemployment in Ireland was not universally welcomed, and efforts to sponsor emigration schemes often met with considerable opposition. Foster received a vicious letter, invoking the image of the notorious Captain Rock, accusing him of seeking to ruin the virtue of innocent young Irish women by sending them to America.[9] A report from Foster's Irish Female Emigration Fund noted the opposition to emigration schemes in general, as well as his response:

> Assisted Emigration and its advocates have been repeatedly denounced in the bitterest terms by portions of the Irish Press and by the Irish Land League as a 'curse' to Ireland or to any other country; ... The history of Emigration is coeval with the history of the world. Assisted Emigration is the only practical suggestion, for there is at present a desire, amounting almost to a mania, among the juvenile portion of the population in the West of Ireland to emigrate to America, but they are without the means of gratifying their desires, while the demand for female domestic servants and for laborers and mechanics in America is practically illimitable.[10]

Throughout his life Vere Foster was faithful to the principle of keeping any influence of religion or religious bias from influencing his efforts, and thus opposed proselytizing in any form. An example of this was his response to the wife of a neighbouring landlord seeking assistance for a young woman who had been converted to Protestantism. Foster's response was characteristic:

> If Eliza Adams was in the same position as those other girls I would gladly send her along with them at my own expense entirely, but she has no one depending upon her for help, and she is said to have many friends among the ladies and gentlemen of the neighbourhood, who I trust will take as much interest in the welfare of her body as they have exhibited in that of her soul... The expenses from my own purse for the emigration of the persons from this neighborhood who will sail the week after next exceed £300. I think it is but little to expect from the ladies and gentlemen above alluded to that they will subscribe amongst them £5.10 and clothes for this poor girl who has lost sympathy among many of her former co-religionists by becoming a Protestant and who is said to be a good girl.[11]

Foster's files are replete with petitions from parish priests seeking sponsorship for indigent young women, which contrasts sharply with the attitude of the hierarchy of the Church. The following illustrates the attitude of the hierarchy:

> How happy, in comparison, and how blessed would have been the lot of an Irish girl, the poor betrayed victim of hellish agencies of vice, had she remained

at home and passed her days in the poverty, aye and wretchedness, of a mud wall cabin – a wife and mother, mayhap – her path in life smoothened by the blessed influences of religion and domestic peace until it ended at a green old age in the calm, peaceful repose of God's just.[12]

Foster was careful to ensure that emigrants had realistic expectations of what awaited them. Utilizing his extensive network of social contacts, he sought informants to advise him on the most suitable placements for emigrants. He had a slight preference for the United States, 'owing to the advantages of home government, the United States are likely to progress much more rapidly than colonies whose government is at a great distance; consequently, both public and private employment are likely to increase in a superior and ever-accumulating ratio.'[13] On his 1850 trip he travelled more than 10,000 miles throughout North America in an effort to ascertain the position of the working classes and the prospects for emigrants, accompanied by the ladies of an immigration society:

We took cooked meat and fruit and bread with us, and telegraphed ahead morning and evening to wayside stations for hot coffee or tea and milk to be ready in pailfuls. We took all our meals for two days in the train, the length of the journey being about a thousand miles. On one of these journeys I placed 30 girls at Decatur, 30 at Springfield, and 40 at Jacksonville, all in the State of Illinois, and could have obtained situations for at least twenty thousand in the same State alone, if we had had sufficient funds.[14]

In Springfield, Illinois, he placed one of his girls with the then distinguished Springfield lawyer, Abraham Lincoln. Some years later he recounted the story of this visit:

Among the families at Springfield who had volunteered to provide for any of the girls whom we would recommend was that of Abraham Lincoln, then a distinguished lawyer and afterwards President of the United States. Mr and Mrs Lincoln had most kindly offered to give a home certain for a month, and to treat as one of the family, any one whom we should bring to their house, so I placed one of the girls with them, and, calling a few days afterwards to see how she was doing, a bed was made up for me on the floor of the drawing-room, and I stayed all night. Mr Lincoln was most agreeable and entertaining, full of humour, and overflowing with the milk of human kindness. He had pursued numerous avocations as railsplitter, raftsman, farmer, tavernkeeper, attorney, etc., and his memory was well stored with incidents of travel. Numerous are the anecdotes attributed to him.[15]

Upon returning home to Ardee, Co. Louth, he told the following story:

After much traveling in Canada and the States, I returned home, the whole of the personal expenses of my journey for ten months, from the time I left Liverpool till I embarked from New York, having been less than £50; for I traveled in the least expensive manner in some parts of the country, and was treated as a dead head [*sic*] in others, on account of my supposed occupation as an emigration agent bringing traffic to the roads. I frequented the cheapest hotels, or, as was more often the case, enjoyed free quarters at the houses of my emigrants, or of their employers, and neither drank, smoked, nor chewed; the money saved in these various ways being available for prosecution of objects in which I was interested. I reached Ardee after dark, and having hired a room with large windows on the ground floor in the main street, I covered the windows with photographs of the emigrants, and watched the effect next morning. For some time occasional passers-by looked idly at the likenesses, children gathered till at length a cry was raised, 'Maggie', 'Biddy', 'Arrah! see here's Peggy Malone, I declare', and 'Here's Biddy Cassidy that lived in our land,' and so on, till numbers of the portraits were recognised, and mothers and all the town came in to inquire the news of the Ardee girls, and to receive the numerous messages that I had brought home.[16]

Despite the originality of his approach, Vere Foster never became a well-meaning crank, and his papers show him always retaining a personal touch. He carried messages for immigrants whom he had assisted. In one instance, when he carried a flowerpot of Irish clay and a shamrock for a nostalgic Irish girl, the young women, to whom he had entrusted it for safekeeping, forgot and left it in the immigrant depot. The superintendent found it, and, knowing the connection with Foster, preserved it, although it had almost completely withered before it was finally claimed. Foster told the story to the editor of the *Irish American* who immediately took charge of the withered shamrock and delivered it to its destined owner in Boston.

Foster's emigrant guide drew on the regular reports such as the following from Horace Greeley, the prominent and respected editor of the *New York Tribune*, who wrote to Vere Foster as a personal friend. While Greeley is remembered for having advised young men to seek their fortunes in the western parts of the United States, this was not the advice he gave in 1852:

> The State of Virginia, though first colonized of any, is today the best ground for the immigrant. It is now constructing heavy Public Works, beside profiting largely by those of Maryland. Land is very cheap there: the climate advisable; water power abundant; minerals unsurpassed; and the western half is little cursed by slavery. Emigrants who come over in bodies can buy land cheaper and will find the climate more agreeable in Western Virginia than in cold Upper Canada, Wisconsin, etc.[17]

Greeley cautioned Foster against encouraging persons to expect American wages immediately:

> I think European mechanics who can get a $1 and board for working in the country may consider themselves well paid; $1.1/4 without board may be a fair average. European laborers, being uneducated, and not so generously fed as our people are less vigorous and efficient, consequently their labor will not command the best prices of American labor. We mow, reap, chop, etc. a far larger area in a day than Europeans do. Digging is about the only vocation wherein they can hold their own with us. They are very awkward in handling our tools and conforming to our ways when they first come here. I think, therefore, that an Irishman just landed who can find some really *good* American farmer who would give him $60 to $80+ and board for a year's fruitful labor, and promise to instruct him in our ways, ought to accept it at once. Those who find work in the cities *receive* more but *save* less; and it is a common remark that

the Irish are more difficult to satisfy in the matter of wages than any other people. Pray urge them not to stickle for high wages but look more to the chance of
learning during their first year how to earn high wages thereafter... those who
come later than the 1st of October must expect a hard winter. Work is very
scarce here during the winter months and not much better anywhere but in the
lumbering regions where Europeans are worth very little, a Yankee will
outchop half a dozen of them.

Thomas Bouchier, from Scariff, Co. Clare, had farmed in Illinois for two
years with his wife and four children when Vere Foster visited him in 1851.
A letter from Foster to the editor of the *Irish Farmer's Gazette* described
Bouchier as an example of a successful emigrant:

> Indeed it is difficult to find an Irishman who is not perfectly satisfied with hav-
> ing emigrated to this country. Mr Bouchier has forty acres of land under culti-
> vation, which is partly on Congress land, which he will cultivate until it shall
> possess an owner; and partly on a farm of forty acres, which he bought of its
> former occupant with buildings and fences on it, for five dollars per acre... Mr
> B[ouchier] strongly dissuades any emigrant from taking a farm of uncleared
> land, as the process of clearing land, for a livelihood to an emigrant, wholly
> inexperienced, as he is, to the use of the axe in such an occupation is enough to
> drive him crazy. There is always plenty of cleared land to be bought from native
> Americans, who are seldom unready to sell – and that at very reasonable prices
> – to newcomers, and to proceed further west, to clear new land, at which they
> are expert, and to enjoy their favourite sport of hunting deer, turkeys, squirrels,
> and other game.[18]

A year later Bouchier responded to Foster's circulated query about conditions in America. Since Foster's visit in 1851, Bouchier had brought out his
father from Ireland.

> I beg to thank you Sincerely for thinking of me so long, and must say it affords
> me much pleasure in giving you the Requested Information to the best of my
> knowledge and Experience. [to Foster's query regarding employment] We can-
> not afford to Employ female Servants in the backwood farms, nor can we afford
> to Employ labourers now, tho threw Summer Months for which the pay [is] $10
> per month, half in cash, the other half in Cattle or produce, but as the Central
> Railroad which was in Contemplation when you visited this part of the Country
> is now in [operation?]. Steady labourers can get $25 per month and board. This
> work will not be completed before three years.[19]

Another respondent to his query, William Chambers, co-founder of
Chamber's Journal, concerned himself with the development of the railways
in the United States and Canada, strongly recommending that Foster
direct persons not to buy land on arrival but to work for wages so as to
save money while learning the ways of the country: 'You should strongly
counsel emigrants against buying land *at first*. Recommend all to wait a
while, and take employment at wages, so as not only to save money but
learn the ways of the country.'[20]

P. Kennedy, apparently a recent immigrant, writing from Virginia, reinforced the claim that America was a good poor man's country. Women, he

believed, fared badly in a land where there was little compassion for the poor. Thousands of newspaper advertisements placed in search of missing husbands, fathers and brothers confirm Kennedy's observation that it was not uncommon for women to be abandoned.[21] He also referred to nativist sentiment, exacerbated he believed by evangelical crusaders from England, Scotland and the north of Ireland. As was true of many other Irish immigrants, he reserved special scorn for Yankees, particularly Yankee Abolitionists:

Good sensible Labourers will do well if he keeps from whiskey. I have seen many a labouring man who left Ireland with perhaps £1 in his pocket is worth now perhaps $30,000, but still there is a heap of misery. Many is the poor woman I have seen on bended knees and uplifted hands called the curse of God on Irish Landlords and the British Government who have driven them from their homes to be risked in a foreign land where there is but little compassion for the poor...

Servant Girls can do well in this Country. They get from $6 to 7 and sometimes $8 per month. They thus get easily $6 or 7 per month. Houses are very high in this country. You cannot get any kind of a house less than $6 and sometimes $10 per month. Clothing is very high, cannot get a good suit of clothes less $20, but a person can buy very cheap cloths in Jews stores that would do nice. Fuel or Firewood is very high in Citys. In fact every thing is high for a poor man... [Irish] Merchants has no chance of getting Employment in Citys as the American will not work with them and at present it is worse than ever. Milliners are numerous so are Tailoresses and are poorly paid, shoemakers can do nothing here for sometime as they have to learn to work quick for here a bootmaker will make 3 Pair of Boots per day – and you can b[u]y Boots cheaper here than you can in Europe. The best thing a Foreigner can do when he comes to this country is to try to get a Farm of Land. He can get that any day if he only has money – land is cheap every where, and when he lands in New York he will get any information he wants from the Irish Immigrant Society, no matter what country he comes from. They have agreements made with the Western RRs and Steamboats to carry Emmigrants to the Western Country cheap. They can get their ticket in the office and they will be protected from Land Sharks who infest New York. The Northern and Southern states are not favourable to immigrants but if they have friends before them, so much the better for then they can go at once to them no matter whether in the North or South or West...

There is as much difference between a Northerner or Yankee and a Southern slave holder as there is between a robber and an honest man. A Yankee will do nothing except he will make money by it, and he is into any speculation that he can make money, while the Southern man is independent and will not stoop to a mean act. This is a fact and the moment a Yankee lands on English soil he ought to be spurned out of society, no matter what shape or garb he comes in whether a preacher or not, for they will enslave the poor emigrant, burn his house of worship, and do everything in their power to injure him, in order to forward their business, so it is in its respect to slavery, if they can make money by it, they are into it, not for the sake of the slave, but for the sake of lining their pockets. If the hatred against foreigners continues, and now it is on the increase, emigrants will have to remain at home, and not come to this country as persecuted they will be here. A man that wants to purchase land in this country should come himself first, or send a friend, so that he could look, and buy his farm, and have it ready for his family to go into it. It will cost about $20 to go to the West from New York, perhaps cheaper, if they take a deck passage, it will not cost half so much.

I am afraid some of the above may be disagreeable to you. You may be an English Gentleman by birth, or perhaps an Irish Landlord; one thing, I believe you are an honest gentleman who is trying to assist poor emigrants, no matter what country they are from, and that you have nothing to gain by your trouble, except the prayers of some Irish woman, or man, for an Irishman never forgets a good act done for him. May God in his mercy reward you and your family for the trouble you have taken on behalf of the poor stranger who is looking for a home in this ungrateful country, is the prayer of a poor ejected tenant of Ireland from the land of my birth...

P.S. The *Boston Pilot*... is the organ of the Irish in this country, and has a circulation of 80,000 a week to all parts of the Union and has always letters from every state giving the price of land and the best localities to buy and everything wanted by the Emigrant. It is owned and edited by P[atrick] Donaghue, and price to Europe is only $3 per year. It is published in the city of Boston.[22]

James MacNamara, also living in Virginia, saw generally good prospects for immigrants. MacNamara's familiarity with Foster suggests that he may be the 'marksman'[23] of that name who signed the petition attesting to ill-treatment toward passengers on the *Washington*: 'The prospects of emigrants are rapidly increasing each day, that is as much as I know about them at present. I have sent home to my wife about six weeks ago, £7 British [sterling] I want her to come out to me.'[24]

Alexander Sullivan of West Derby, Liverpool, wrote as a concerned citizen with a deep interest in the welfare of Irish emigrants, and an acquaintance of Horace Greeley. He had visited the Castle Garden Immigrant depot in New York where he observed passengers from two emigrant ships disembarking. He proposed to Foster the need for an immigrant hostel in Liverpool such as he had seen in Bremerhaven for German emigrants. His remarks are useful inasmuch as they provide a disinterested person's description of the conditions under which emigrants departed and immigrants arrived:

To you I need enter into no longer argument to show the necessity there exists for some such institution in Liverpool – from which part the amount of emigration is far beyond that of Bremerhaven. To you I need not point out the moral depravation of the emigrant wrought under the present system. You have already shewn how well you understand all this, and given practical proof of how deeply you feel it, but I do turn to you for at least your opinion as to whether something may not be done – whether some effort might not be made to set on foot a movement towards establishing in Liverpool an institution similar to the Emigrant House of Bremerhaven. I know and have estimated all the difficulties to be encountered; some of these peculiar to this case. Bremerhaven is in Germany – Liverpool is not in Ireland; yet perhaps we shall [ ] with pleasure the 'Merchant Princes of Liverpool' supposed to act not the less warmly because that the Irish emigrant does not stand towards them in every respect in the relation of the German emigrant to the men who in Bremerhaven have stepped forward for his protection.

Might I ask you to give[?] this project your consideration and in case you are of opinion that an effort ought to be made, to enlist for it the support of men able to make it a success. The New York Commission of Emigration will– officially and otherwise – give all their influence in aid and cooperation.[25]

By the middle 1850s Vere Foster began to receive many letters from persons whom he had assisted. Patrick Kelly, originally from Feakle, Co. Clare, arrived in the first contingent of emigrants. Writing from Davenport, Iowa, his letter is a good example of the appreciation many expressed to Vere Foster, and his paean to America, which he calls the home of the exile, shows literary skill. Some comments suggest that not everyone shared Kelly's enthusiasm for the place of their adoption. 'No Matter what folks may say of America, I love it as my Adopted Country':

The Western Country I think deserves admiration. Look for a moment on its vast Prairies. Can any place outdo them for Cultivation. Look at its produce and its Growing population, its grand navigable rivers, its railroads and every thing to make a country rich and prosperous. Look even out here at the energy which seems to enkindle the hearts of the western Pioneer and still Look at the vast field for Speculation that lays open to every Man that has a spark of energy. Although I have Different work now to what I had in Washington, still I admire the west. No Matter what folks may say of America, I love it as my Adopted Country. I love it for its noble and liberal Institutions. In fact I look on its Construction and the basis in which it is founded as being nothing short of an Almighty and Providential Scheme. No wonder it should be called the home of the Exile. I have taken the necessary steps so far to become one of her adopted sons and am glad that you had become an Instrument in the hands of Providence to emancipate me from that Country of Oppression to this Grand republic where a man knows he is a man, where equal rights is guaranteed to every man, where the poor man is not crushed down to exalt the aristocrat and where a love of liberty inflames every heart and as a proof of what I say (regarding a love of Liberty) Just let the stars and stripes be unfurled even here on these western Praires, blow a trumpet and Chant a tune of Yankee Doodle or Hail Columbia and see how many will be in a few moments under arms rallying beneath the banner of Liberty, not like John Bull that must show his horns to drive them to it, or use some scheme. Cheat them to it or Pass an act to force them to it, no Man will step up and ask how much Bounty [i.e. payment]. But like Brothers one mans matter is every Mans, no Question asked, but where is the enemy. No Matter What our Partisan Quarrels May, no matter what Commenting the London Times may use, this Country if tested will be E pluribus Unum...

Dear Mr Foster, I could not but admire your generous Disposition and untired labors in seeking redress for my Countrymen. All I have to say, may Heaven enable you and May reward you with a long and happy healthy Quiet Passage through life and eternal happiness in the Next and as a proof of my thanks to you I would Gladly Contribute a little towards your Charitable funds. I bought a lot in East Davenport and paid $300 for it, or at least mean to within the 1st of next Nov. – I paid $100 on hand and notes for the rest. Sister told me you promised to bring some flannel when you come to the U. States again and if you do if you would not be Overburthened I would request of you to bring me some. Home made Irish frieze as much as would make an overcoat to show those Yankee Women we can do something in Ireland. I would send the Money now but there is nothing steady about our Westren Banks, yet any expenses on them I am willing to pay – the Weather is not to say very Cold, on and about the Midle of November was very cold. Mercury stood the morning of the 16th at 6 and varied on up to the 26th to 12 deg. below zero. Since it has not been so Cold, very little snow. I have no more or rather no more room to say, but take my respects again and present my Love to sister and family and May God Bless you is the earnest Prayer of your Hon[ora]ble Serv't.[26]

Michael Maginn's letter, written in 1858, illustrates how opportunity released the energies of immigrants. He may have been another passenger on the *Washington* because there is a person with his name as one of the signatories. He had been in America less than a decade, yet his accumulated assets had enabled him to bring out five more persons to America, and he had immediate plans to bring out three more. In addition to acquiring income property and owning a fine house in Charlestown, Massachusetts, he had sent home to family and friends a total of $325:

> Believing as I do that there is nothing would give you more pleasure than to hear of the success of those whom you were instrumental in raising from poverty to a state of independence, I have to inform you that since you put your helping hand to me I have been very successful which success I owe to you...
> I have one request to ask of you, namely if ever you come to this country that you will call to see me and have the pleasure of seeing my add to your list as I only consider myself paying a debt of Gratitude, which Gratitude has expressed into admiration – our family which you were instrumental in making happy for I flatter myself when you see how I am situated you will consider yourself amply paid, for besides having a splendid residence I have three thousand dollars per year coming to me from the remainder of my property for the last nine years. I have sent my father and other friends three hundred and twenty five dollars and have brought five other persons out to this country, four of whom are doing well and i have made other arrangements to bring three more out this fall... [27]

Of all the letters sent to Foster advising him of prospects for Irish persons in America, 68 spoke directly to the need for female labour. From this Vere Foster concluded that the demand for females in America was everywhere even greater than the demand for males.

Not surprisingly, many of the letters which Foster received in Ireland were from persons wishing assistance to emigrate, either for themselves or for their families. One writer was John Boyle O'Reilly, later known and greatly respected as an Abolitionist, the beloved promoter of liberal causes in the United States, and proprietor of the well-known *Boston Pilot* newspaper. At a time when his health and his prospects appear to have been very low, O'Reilly wrote the following letter to Foster, requesting assistance in helping his sisters to emigrate:

> You perhaps have not forgotten me. When I saw you in Boston you were kind enough to speak of my family. I meant then [to] try and get them out here. Since then I have been in bad health and I am disappointed somewhat. My sisters are very poor and very industrious. They could do nothing in New England but sew or go as house servants. They might as well remain at home. I wish that they could get to Canada. I am really ashamed to trouble you, a stranger, but I know you have helped so many you will as least advise these poor girls. There is an emigration scheme for Canada now being put into practice in Ireland. A letter from you to the agent, for my sisters, will ensure their protection. I will pay a part of their passage money: I did mean to pay it all, but my money is nearly gone, and they cannot well wait. I am sure they would do well in

Canada. I hate New York and Boston, which are all corruption and misery for poor girls. If you can help me in this, dear sir, you will make me very happy and very grateful.[28]

There is no indication of Foster's reply to O'Reilly's letter, nor of the outcome of the request. Despite his friendship with Foster, O'Reilly was a man of principle, so that after becoming editor of the *Boston Pilot* he strenuously opposed emigration, even to the point of refusing to assist Foster in an appeal for funds in 1883.

The first phase of Vere Foster's emigration scheme drew to an end by the late 1850s when the numbers of persons leaving Ireland diminished. From 1849 to 1857 Vere Foster defrayed the entire expenses of 1,250 female emigrants from Ireland to America, plus similar expenses for a smaller number of men and boys.[29] For a decade and a half following this he turned his attention to improving the condition of schools and textbooks within Ireland.[30] By the 1870s Foster's attention would turn again to emigration as a panacea for Ireland's problems. Agricultural depression caused by severe weather in 1869, in addition to competition from the impact on agricultural prices of North American wheat flooding European markets, threatened another crisis period. It is believed that between 1874 and 1880 more than 10,000 families were turned out of their homes by eviction.[31] Foster's files bulge with letters such as the following from John McCarthy of Dromdaleague, near Skibbereen, Co. Cork, reflecting the conditions created by this agricultural depression and showing how swiftly an already poor person's situation could turn catastrophic:

Having seen in the public papers your kind and very generous offer of granting a sum of £15,000 to assist intending emigrants to America I am induced to lay my case before you being confident that is one of the most urgent to claim your sympathy and kind assistance. It is simply this – Sometime ago I engaged to raise a sum of money for a distressed friend which I expected he would be able to pay when 'the times would get better' as he said, but unfortunately the times have got worse, not better since, and the result was that he being unable to pay this debt I had to lie to the loss, which in additions to a few other demands on me rendered me quite unable to meet, so that the end was that my farm of land was sold by auction to pay these debts and here I am now with a wife, 3 Sons, 1 daughter and 1 grand daughter without any means whatever. The ages of the children are about the following –

1 son	26 years
1 "	24 "
1 "	19 "

The daughter, 21 [years] and the grand daughter 19 [months?]

So you see from this that all my family would be able to make out a living for themselves if I could only make up as much money as would take them to some country where they would have an open[ing] for working for themselves.

I have been advised by some friends to try to get them to Kanses as a very good place. I would feel very grateful if you gave me your advice as to the best place to go.[32]

In once again starting to collect funds to help Irish persons to emigrate, this time Vere Foster sought the assistance of Charles Stewart Parnell, who was at the time in America collecting funds for relief of distress in the west of Ireland. In an open letter to the *New York Herald*, Foster appealed to influential persons for practical solutions to the distress in Ireland:

> I desire to invite your attention to assisted emigration, as the most practicable and certain mode of not only temporarily but permanently, relieving the present poverty and ever-recurring distress in the West of Ireland... If you shall think [it] proper to embark in [*sic*] such a project, I feel sure that you will receive the hearty co-operation in money and work of the American people... In proof of my sincerity, I hereby express my willingness to subscribe towards the proposed emigration fund at the rate of £2 for each young man or woman between eighteen and thirty-five years of age, in the proportion of one of the former to two of the latter, because as men earn higher wages than women, they are usually better able to provide for themselves.[33]

Parnell ridiculed his suggestion, preferring the path of political agitation. Following this challenge Foster received a flood of letters of application from clergymen, school teachers and individuals seeking aid for people in the most distressed areas of Ireland – Connacht, Clare, Kerry and Donegal.

Patrick McGroarty, from the parish of Inver, Co. Donegal, sought assistance to emigrate for himself and a new wife around the same time. McGroarty's letter shows how well informed and knowledgeable even poor farming persons could be.

> I perceive from your letter to Mr Parnell that you are largely bent on favouring emigration from this country to the United States and Canada. I see you are of the opinion that a fund should be got up by Mr Parnell or some leading men in this country, and that you offer to subscribe as high as £15,000 to such a fund. Now it is my humble opinion that there won't be a general wave of emigration this time, at any rate such as succeeded the famine years of '46 and '47; and supposing there would, there is no appearance of such a fund being got up in time to send out emigrants to America this spring and any longer postponement will be useless in alleviating the burthen which has fallen upon the country. Pardon one therefore, if I suggest to you that you can be of most service, and promote your charitable ends best, by attending to the cases you see most fitting as they are liable to arise. I do not consider that in doing so a greater call will be made on your generosity than the sum you offer to subscribe and by taking the matter in hand yourself at once, it would look like practical business and be in the nick of time.
> I am a young man lately got married; myself and wife both being within the prescribed limits of age mentioned in your letter, we are both well used to farm work, industrious and steady and would expect to do well beyond the sea. We have not the means at present to enable us to get out to America, and I would make bold therefore to ask you for aid to get us out – our passages in whole if you can think it possible – or otherwise assistance in part.
> We can produce any evidence you require that we are both about the most suitable type of person likely to benefit themselves and their adopted country by emigration, and in enabling us to go out your beneficent wishes for the welfare of the Irish race would in no wise be put to false account.[34]

Anthoney Hamrough, of Brownstown, townland of Hollymount, Co. Mayo, sought money to enable the emigration of his eldest son, a young man of 20, who would in turn then bring out the rest of the family.

> I am the Father of Eleven in familly, the oldest boy is 20 years of age. I have 11 acres of inferior land. I am Verry much redused by the bad times, seeing no hopes for the future welfare of myself and weak familly but emigration as he (the son) D.V. would help in bringing the others.
>
> If you would kindly assist me with a few pounds I would by the aid of a nother kind friend send him to America which is the only coars opened to me and weak familly. I shall as in duty bound forever pray [for you].[35]

The prospective emigrant of the post-1870 period faced a far different situation than had earlier emigrants. Transportation had improved dramatically. Ships expressly designed for the emigrant trade were now plying a schedule of regular routes to North America, and most persons from the west of Ireland could expect to have their way eased and often their fare paid by a family member already living abroad. Foster no longer felt the need to lead 'swarms,' as he called them, of young women to America. Thus the schemes he established now took account of the fact that would-be migrants often needed relatively small amounts of money to facilitate their journey. This enabled him to send many times the number of persons of the previous period. Each prospective emigrant required a sponsor – usually the parish priest or the schoolmaster.

Foster received more than 228 letters of appeal in 1880 alone. The following sequence of letters illustrates the general situation at that time. In the letter which immediately follows we learn of a young woman who had a trans-Atlantic ticket, but the ticket was due to expire one year from the date of issue and she could not afford the cost of transport from Co. Mayo to the emigrant ship.

> I enclose a list of names soliciting your kind assistance. All have friends in America but are so poor that they cannot pay the necessary expenses to Liverpool.
>
> You could scarcely undertake a nobler work of charity than assisting the poor people to join their friends in America, and I hope you will not refuse to send them some little means to pay their passages as they would be well provided for if they reached America.
>
> I will give you an instance of the anxiety of the people to go to America.
>
> On[ly] yesterday a poor man and his daughter came to me to send a notice of the daughter's intention to sail for America. Her passage being paid on the 6th March 1879 would oblige her sail before twelve months after its issue or forfeit the ticket (as it is distinctly stated on all passages that it will not be accepted afterwards)
>
> Her Father did not know what to do as he could not supply her with the necessary amount in time to enable her to reach Liverpool before the 6th March next (on which date her passage would expire) he stated he could not get the money even to Borrow and I believe him as he is a poor man having lost his wife within the last 12 months, which was the means of depriving his daughter to join her sisters before this. I told him I would try to get the time extended (and I hope to succeed) to enable him to get the money which would be about £1.10s.0d or over... [36]

D. M. O'Donnell, of the Templedouglas National School in Letterkenny, Co. Donegal, wrote to Foster, suggesting that he reconsider his decision against sponsoring male emigration. The young women of his area did not need to emigrate because they could always find employment in knitting, but because of small farms and a lack of public works to provide employment young men were the more needy.[37]

The following letter of sponsorship from a Castletown Bere, Co. Cork schoolteacher, contained an interesting note regarding the way in which the prospect of emigrating was transforming clothing fashions in the west of Ireland.

> The young men and women of this remote and distressed peninsula are getting themselves ready in scores to go to America in a fortnight's time. At the last fair held in Castletown Bere on the 9th inst. male and female apparel, newly made to American fashion, was everywhere conspicuous. In almost every instance, the passage have been prepaid by friends in America, as, I need scarcely observe, very few can go if they were dependent on what their parents, or friends, or themselves can put together this bad year. I am sure a great many more, both boys and girls, would emigrate if they only had the means of doing so, a loss which is very much to be deplored, considering the present distressed state of Ireland.[38]

Clothing was again an issue in the townland of Ballyhaunis, parish of Bekan, Co. Mayo, with an acreage of 15,363 and an 1841 population of 5,505 persons.[39] One hundred young people from that district were anxious to emigrate but lacked sufficient clothing for the journey.

> I know over one hundred Boys and girls here who would be very glad to go to America if they had cash to pay their passages, and I also know a number of girls whos passages are paid the last six month but could not b[u]y a stick of cloths to take them anywhere. Now if you wish, I will Lend you a list of the names of the Boys and girls who are anxious to go and then you may if you will, give or pay yourself the £2 in part payment of this passages. Plase write to me as soon as you can and let me know what I will say to those people. I would not like to tell them go to their parish priest and tell him advance £2.0.0 in part payment of their passages untill such time as you otherise[authorize] me to do so. Until then I would request you to write to the parish priest here and tell him [what] you told me to do. So hoping you will excuse me for trespassing so much on your time.[40]

A year later a report came back to Foster that the reports from the young women of this townland who had gone to America were 'cheering', and that others had not written but were said to be doing fairly well. Note that the writer's opinion was that the people of this impoverished parish were unlikely to profit from the provisions of the Land Acts which were then being proposed:[41]

> I am happy to inform you that I have received very cheering reports from the girls who left this parish by means of the aid given by you. There are a few from whom I have not heard directly. I have however got some information about

them from other parties, and was glad to learn that they too are doing *fairly* –

I don't think many *families* will be found in this part of the west of Ireland disposed to avail themselves of the provisions of the emigration clauses of the Land Act. I dont think that money lent by any company to families for the purpose of Emigration would ever be repaid – principal or interest. There are a few girls still to be found here anxious to join those who left last year, but would not leave till spring.[42]

'The blackest spot on the map of Irish distress' was what Hubert Walsh, teacher of the National School of Maam Cross, Co. Galway, called his district. In his letter he expressed regret that Parnell refused to back Vere Foster's efforts in sponsoring emigration:

In no part of Ireland is emigration so necessary as in this large parish of Rosmuck which has been admitted as the blackest spot on the map of Irish distress. It is a life-long loss, yes, and to future generations that your princely offer towards Irish emigration was not accepted, and supplemented by the labours of those who profess to lead the Irish people to contentment and prosperity.

Knowing that you are willing to afford assisted passages to female adults, I beg to recommend to your favour the following who are healthy, strong, able and accustomed to farm work, and also to indoor business, and able to read and write, and if assisted will manage to provide the remainder themselves. Inserted here are the names of the young women.[43]

In the following letter a National School teacher wrote in lieu of the parish priest who was opposed to emigration:

Knowing your desire to assist the poor and improve their condition long before I ever saw any advertisement from you, I have no hesitation in complying with the request of a young woman named Margaret Brew of this parish, who has asked me to write to you for the assistance you have so kindly offered to enable her to emigrate. She is the daughter of a labouring man who has twelve in family, and she could not possibly spare from her wages as much as would pay her passage to America, as the needs of the family constantly required her wages before it was earned. She will contrive to borrow or beg what will enable her to emigrate in addition to what your philanthropy has prompted you to offer. I desired that she would make her application through the P.P. but she says that he does not wish to be encouraging emigration at all. Diversities of opinion will always exist on the usefulness of emigration, but I certainly concur with your views, that where the population is too dense, it is the most speedy and the most humane way of relief that could be offered to the poor. In the course of time when the Land Act will stimulate the people to honourable exertion, and when the farmers have capital and intelligence to improve their farms and make the most of them, it may not be so necessary to send away the labouring classes; but under existing circumstances when the farmers are steeped in debt and when they are ignorant of the proper modes of farming, I do not know that any money could be more usefully expended than in removing the surplus population to a place where their labour is much wanted and where it is sure to meet with a ready market.[44]

The following letter of sponsorship also attests to the success of Foster's efforts when this teacher told of emigrants who had already sent remittances home to their poor families.

> I am proud to tell you Maria Cody has paid her father, mother, and brother's passages and sent five pounds for equipment. Annie and Bridget Duggan have got good situations and expressed their thanks to you in their first and last letter to their friends here. Ellen Gleeson has sent another two pounds to her sister.[45]

J. Downes, emigration agent for Co. Sligo, applied for assistance for several females, requesting that they be permitted to select the ship on which they will sail. His comments attest to the concern shown by parents who wished their daughters to sail only on the best regulated steamship lines:

> I beg to enclose a list of young girls of a most exemplary character who are anxious to emigrate in order to assist their parents and other members of this family at home and eventually take others out from this Country. Most of these are at service this last year and could not avail themselves of the late assistance which you so generously gave to those who emigrated before 17th inst. as their terms of Service were not completed.
>
> I need not say how particular the Irish are in respect to sending their daughters on the best regulated steamships, and I have known people unwilling to send their children on any except the ship that other members of the family sailed in. When favourably reported, Miss O'Brien's expositions have made people more cautious...
>
> I know that the 'National' and the 'Allan' lines would be glad to receive your vouchers and if you kindly consent to assist those poor girls, and to issue your vouchers – even at a reduced amount – on the above named lines it would confer a lasting benefit on Eight poor families and eventually lead to most of them being enabled to emigrate from this poor locality after some time...
>
> I have kept up a correspondence and enquiry after the welfare of every girl that left here last year under your generous assistance, and have to report to you most favourably of every one of these except one girl who got delicate in health, but who is now recruiting.[46] All the rest have sent large sums of money to their parents.
>
> I also beg to assure you that it is not for Commercial advantage alone I am acting as Emigration Agent, but as a kind of safe guard to my poor neighbours. And in order to make myself thoroughly acquainted with the details I visited Derry, Galway, Liverpool, and Queenstown last August and sailed in some of the Emigrant S.S. to and from these ports.[47]

A letter from Rev. P. J. McHugh, C.C., of Kilglass, Co. Sligo, recommended 12 young women for emigration. His comment about the girls spending some time in Ballina is unclear, but they may have been working there either as maids or harvest workers for part of the year.

> God is helping you. May you long remain to assist poor Emigrants. I am very much obliged to you for your Kindness and I'll continue as in the past to pray for you. I never knew a worse year. In my little collection I am £10 worse than last. I got to £5 last year and I won't come near it this year.
>
> I have been asked again to give or get through your kindness assistance for some of those in Ballina. I have refused but I promised to write to you. Many there are from this parish and surrounding. They are birds of passage and except that for the quarter they are in Ballina no one has an interest or control

over them. I put the case then before you and you can decide. I am sure however that I won't trouble you more than last year altho' there is a greater [need?].

[The names of the young women were listed.]

I won't trespass too much but there is a general exodus. For my part I'd
sooner they'd go to the States than anywhere else. If I can I wont trouble you
again for some time but I can't promise. If there be no chance of marriage then
many shall cross the pond. Wishing you many happy years of usefulness and
thanking you again and again.[48]

Vere Foster sought information on the conditions of those who had been
assisted through his schemes. Reports which appear in the following section suggest reasons why some persons succeeded in America, while others did not. An earlier letter from the Rev. Patrick Grealy, parish priest of
Carna, spoke of the probability of another poor harvest that year.
Connemara was so poor that even if the inhabitants had to pay no rent
whatsoever, they still would be steeped in poverty, a story which is consistent with Cormac Ó Gráda's findings that large areas of this region
remained mired in pre-Famine conditions well into the late nineteenth
century.[49] In his second letter Rev. Grealy wrote:

I am glad to inform you that most of the girls assisted by you to Emigrate as far
as I could ascertain have been fairly successful in America. On the other hand,
not a few have turned out badly. And others have not ever been heard of since
they entered the Emigrant ship.
    Very many of the Carna [parish of Moyrus] girls want of success is attribut-
able to their ignorance of the English language and of household work. No
doubt a great number of others would Emigrate if they could get larger aid than
you have hitherto given. A Society for their Protection on landing would be a
great boon and blessing to those poor girls who have never been 10 miles from
home.[50]

The Rev. Thomas Heany, the Incumbent of Calry, Co. Sligo, whose letter
follows, had recently met with some of the emigrants from his parish
while travelling in Canada. His report of them was overwhelmingly positive. Sir John A. McDonald, with whom he met while in Canada, was at
the time the prime minister of Canada.

In all cases that I have met, with one exception, the girls are happy and would
not come back on any condition. The wages they are receiving varies from £15
to £30 per annum, about three times as much as that they had at home. They are
all unanimous about the food they receive, in fact 'no complaints' might be
accepted is the testimony of all. The want of female help is one of the greatest
now in the Dominion [of Canada]. In all Ontario the cry of the people I mixed
with was send us as many girls as you can. I mentioned your liberality to all
from Sir John A. McDonald down to the lowest official and I am bound to con-
fess they express their admiration and gratitude. I have received Commissions
to send out 250 girls but I am straitened as to means.[51]

A fragment of a letter sent to Vere Foster (the writer is unnamed but noted as 'one of my emigrants' by Foster at the top of the page) shows the writer to have been a member of the unpopular Irish Constabulary before emigrating.[52] The letter is rich in information and opinions seldom communicated by the Irish in America such as that Catholics were converting to Protestantism and the behaviour of the Irish in America.

> I must explain to you the cause of my leaving N. Carolina and coming to this part of the Country. Lonergan [his employer] had the most inveterate dislike to the Peelers [police] and frequently said in my presence, that he would not entrust with a cent anyone who ever served a day in them.
>
> I was therefore obliged to have recourse to various stratagems in order to conceal from him the appalling fact that I was actually for more than 4 years a member of that wicked and diabolical corps, as if he knew it, I am confident he would as soon harbour a rattlesnake, and would not only discharge me *instanter*, but do all he could to injure me, so dreadful was his hatred of the jacket – I found out a clew to at least a part of this violent animosity. An uncle of his, who resided recently in the State of Arkansas, was obliged to fly from Ireland in consequence of various acts of *Ribbonmen*[53] – I have frequently been thoroughly disgusted at hearing him relate the exploits of this ruffian, and his various encounters with the Police, act for which if he got he deserts, he would have ended his days in quiet seclusion in Van Diemen's Land or Spike Island, instead of being a Citizen of the United States.… .
>
> I am sorry to say that Religion and Morality are at a very low ebb in this country and this is particularly the case with the children and descendants of Irishmen who generally speaking either join the creed of the Majority or become Infidels.
>
> There are a great many Irish both in N. Carolina and Baltimore, and tho' there are many respectable men amongst them, I am sorry to say that the generality are a set of low degraded, drunken wretches who disgrace their country by their conduct, so that the name of Irishman is often associated in the minds of Americans with every thing vile and worthless…
>
> You will perhaps consider it strange, but it is a positive fact, that such an animal as a man or a woman does not exist in this country, and the numerous cargoes of this species which we are daily receiving from Europe, become immediately transformed into Gentlemen and Ladies; to call them by any other name would be an unpardonable vulgarity, and this feeling extends to the most ignorant and unenlightened clodhopper I have met with…[end of ms][54]

The next letter writer sought a wife. Having been happily married to one Irish woman, he now sought another through Vere Foster's assistance:

> Having Been in your country a few years ago and married one of your country women I am sory to say that Death has taken her from me and now I will join hands with any young irish lady of protestant Birth Between the age of twenty and twenty five who will volinteer to come to this Country and bee my bride. The same to bee of good habits, of good form and virtuous. If you find one I will pay the extray expence from ireland to america and pay all expences from new york to MacKinaw City. The Best of referince Given. I am a Carpenter and demand two and a half a day and have a farm of sixty five acres of land.
>
> Let the lady write to me if she can write and express herself to me. I am twenty five years old and weigh 150 pounds.[55]

Regrettably, there is no indication of Vere Foster's response.

Vere Foster kept six letters written by a Mary Harlon who arrived with the first group he sent to America.[56] It is not possible to know much more about her than what can be gleaned from her letters, and we do not know what happened to her after her last letter in 1865. It appears likely that she was a Mary H[ ] the rest of whose surname was obscured on a list of persons recommended for funding.[57] If she is the same person, she was 23 years old and unemployed – 'Not at Work' was the phrase – when she left Ireland, she had at least two brothers who were only partially occupied earning fivepence a day, and was an orphan, which was not uncommon among persons who migrated to America.

The very ordinariness of Mary Harlon's letters tell a story of what life might have been like for a young Irish woman working as a domestic. They show her to have been excessively deferential to male authority – to her brothers, to her priest, and to Foster. This was hardly surprising, however, because she came from an authoritarian society in which power filtered down from the top: first from the colonial legislature in London, then from the hierarchy of the Catholic bishops through the local priesthood, and from them through the male figures of authority in the Irish family.

If Mary Harlon's behaviour was at all typical of most Irish domestics in America it is hardly surprising that the Irish Bridget was not only valued but that her name became stereotypical so that the Bridgets of America became standard features of American domestic life. Nevertheless, despite the excessive deference expressed in her letter to Foster, she did not lack independence. When one employer refused her request for a raise she left and found another job immediately through the newspaper.

In her first letter, written from New York City, Mary Harlon spoke of having had a number of situations following what was probably her first. She described various employment perils which she had survived before finding one which she now considered satisfactory. Happy in her present post, she now had a bank account with $80 saved, and was putting aside money for a new silk dress.[58] Two years later her second letter shows that she was still employed by the Taylor family of Varick Place in New York City, indicating that her brothers had denied her permission to go to California (she may have had an opportunity to work there, or in her devotion to Vere Foster, she may have sought to follow him when she heard that he went there on a visit). In either case she was probably, like so many immigrants, unaware of the distance to the west coast.[59] A month later she wrote to Foster once again requesting him to inform her priest of her well-being in the following words:

> I Pray for you the same as I do for my Brothers because you are the only Friend I have and I may say the only True Friend. Mr Foster, if you Plase, when you see Father Smyth, tell him I am as free and as happy as whe[n] I last seen him. Tell him I go to here Mass every Sunday and to Holy Communion as often as I can. Ask him to Pray for you and me. I do not wish to tire you with a long letter for I know your eyes is tender yet.[60]

Writing five months later, she showed that once again she had asserted her independence by leaving an unsatisfactory position:

> After I come from the Country I ast the lady for to rise my wages and she would not, so there was a advertisement in the paper for a girl to go out south with a lady for six months and do the ginerl housework of a small Family at 12 Dol. a month. I tuck the place and when I come I got so sick that nothing would agree with me so now I am well, thank God, and I am all alone out here. I have no person but a Colard man that dos house work around the place and I read to him when I have time and he is very glad to here me read to him. He wants me to let him have my Books so I lend thim to him.[61]

A fore-lock tugging humility was expected behaviour from the Mary Harlons of Ireland when they addressed the gentry – not because she was Irish, but because the poor were expected to be meek and express gratitude toward their betters. And while Mary's letters show she knew what was expected of her, nevertheless this young woman who obeyed her brothers and her priest, had learned the lesson of many others who immigrated – that in America you didn't have to remain where your efforts were not appreciated. Employers could be abandoned because the newspapers carried advertisements for new opportunities, and suitors who did not please could be refused.

Vere Foster deserves a special place in the history of nineteenth-century Ireland. The young man who was appalled by the suffering of the Irish people which the Famine brought to light, harnessed his immense talents and his creative instincts in devising schemes to improve their social condition. While other sons of the Ascendancy such as Robert Emmet, Thomas Davis, John Mitchel and Charles Stewart Parnell sought political deliverance, Vere Foster aligned himself with causes serving the national need for social and economic change. He spent his last years in Belfast, dying there, still unmarried, on 21 December 1900, having exhausted his personal fortune, entirely devoted to the national need.

Notes

1. A report submitted by Foster in November 1889 stated that as of that date 22,615 women had been assisted since 1847 and he planned to send thousands more: Vere Foster Papers, NIPRO, D3618/D/10/14.
2. George Bernard Shaw, *John Bull's Other Island*, Penguin Books, Harmondsworth, 1984 (first performed 1904, first published 1907).
3. NIPRO, D3618/D/6/14, 'Incidents of Travel in America', a lecture delivered by Vere Foster in the Rosemary Street Lecture Hall, Belfast, 27 January, 1879.
4. Private communication with D. H. Akenson.
5. See Mary McNeill, *Vere Foster, 1819–1900, An Irish Benefactor*, David & Charles, Newton Abbot: for the Institute of Irish Studies of Queen's University, Belfast, 1971, for the only book-length study of Foster. The author does not appear to have had access to the full range of his papers, which have since publication of the book been fully catalogued and are available for consultation in the Public Record Office, Belfast: Vere Foster Papers, NIPRO, D3618.

6. Statement of Purpose which appears on subscription lists and reports among the Vere Foster papers, NIPRO, D3618/D/10/4.

7. Vere Foster was not the first of his class to seek this experience. In 1847 Stephen de Vere, Lord Monteagle's nephew, made the journey to Quebec as a steerage passenger, taking with him a party of emigrants. For graphic description of the conditions he encountered, see Henry Stanley Hyland, *Curiosities from Parliament*, Wingate, London, 1968, as quoted in McNeil, p. 58.

8. NIPRO, D3618/D/4/8. Original list of 66 of 128 signatures collected by Foster from passengers on board the *Washington*, 2 December 1850.

9. NIPRO, D3618/D/13/3. Copy of 'Assisted Emigration' circular issued in September 1880 by Foster and returned to him by 'Captain Rock' with a threatening letter. Captain Rock was the signature of one of many anonymous individuals who led secret societies in nineteenth-century Ireland. Rough justice was meted out by them to anyone who betrayed the code of secrecy under which they operated. Their principal weapons were murder, assault, shooting into houses and other forms of intimidation, cattle-maiming and crop-burning.

10. *Mr. Vere Foster's Second Irish Female Emigration Fund Report*, NIPRO, D3618/D/10/7.

11. Vere Foster to Mrs Filgate, 23 April 1856, NIPRO, D3618/D/10/6. Eliza's story furnishes evidence of allegations of proselytizing. Foster offered to help her as far as Liverpool but must have regretted it when in Drogheda her pockets were searched and found to contain hundreds of gospel tracts. See McNeill, pp. 89–92.

12. Joseph Guinan, *Scenes and Sketches in an Irish Parish or Priest and People in Doon*, Gill, Dublin, 1903; sixth edition, 1925 as quoted in J. J. Lee, 'Women and the church since the Famine,' in *Women in Irish Society*, Margaret MacCurtain and Donncha O'Corrain, (eds), Arlen House Ltd, Dublin 1978, p.43.

13. NIPRO, D3618/D/9/6. A copy of a letter addressed by Mr Vere Foster to the directors of the American Emigrants' Friend Society of Philadelphia, No date, c.1850.

14. NIPRO, D3618/D/6/14, Vere Foster 'Incidents of Travel in America,'.

15. 'Incidents,' p. 10

16. 'Incidents,' pp. 14–15.

17. Horace Greeley, New York, to Vere Foster, 4 June, 1852: NIPRO, D3618/D/8/5.

18. NIPRO, D3618/D/9/2 Reprinted from the *Irish Farmer's Gazette*, 8 June, 1851, in the *Morning Chronicle*, London, 29 August 1851.

19. Thomas Bouchier, Drury Creek, (Jackson Co., Illinois) to Vere Foster, 24 October, 1852, NIPRO, D3618/D/8/6.

20. W. Chambers, Edinburgh (Scotland), to Vere Foster, 25 February 1854, NIPRO, D3618/D/8/7.

21. For more on this finding, see the analytic introduction to *The Search for Missing Friends: Irish Immigrant Advertisements in the Boston Pilot, 1854–56*. Ruth-Ann M Harris, co-edited with B. Emer O'Keeffe, Assistant Editor, Bridget Knightly. The New England Historic Genealogical Association, Boston, 1993, Volume III of projected 16 volumes.

22. P. Kennedy, Strasbourg, Virginia, to Vere Foster, 19 March 1855, NIPRO, D3618/D/8/9.

23. See Note 7.

24. James Macnamara, Mechum's River, Albemarle Co., Virginia, to Vere Foster, c.1852–54, NIPRO, D3618/D/8/11.

25. Alexander M. Sullivan, West Derby, Liverpool, to Vere Foster, 5 August 1857, NIPRO, D3618/D/8/10.

26. Patrick Kelly, Davenport, Iowa, to Vere Foster, 12 January 1858, NIPRO, D3618/D/25/3.
27. Michael Maginn, Charlestown, Massachusetts, to Vere Foster, 4 April 1860, NIPRO, D3618/D/25/6.
28. John Boyle O'Reilly, Boston, Massachusetts, to Vere Foster, 24 May 1874, NIPRO, D3618/D/25/15.
29. 'Incidents', p. 15.
30. For an excellent account of Foster's accomplishments in this area, see McNeil, pp. 101–88.
31. Quoted in McNeil from Edmund Curtis, *A History of Ireland*, Methuen, London, p.379, 1936 edition.
32. John McCarthy, Dromdaleague, to Vere Foster, 31 January 1880, NIPRO, D3619/D/14/7.
33. This extract from the *New York Herald*, 6 January 1880, appears on the reverse side of Foster's letter to Parnell. NIPRO, D3618/D/13/1.
34. Patrick McGroarty, Keeloges, parish of Inver, Co. Donegal, to Vere Foster, 17 February 1885, NIPRO, D3618/D/14/69.
35. Anthoney Hambrough, Brownstown(?), Hollymount, parish of Kilcommon, Co. Mayo, to Vere Foster, 20 June 1880, NIPRO, D3618/D/14/212.
36. John M'Henry, Charlestown(?), Co. Mayo, to Vere Foster, 19 February 1880, NIPRO, D3618/D/14/80.
37. D. M. O'Donnell, Templedouglas, Letterkenny, Co. Donegal, to Vere Foster, 21 February 1880, NIPRO, D3618/D/14/104. This was his second letter to Foster. See NIPRO, D3618/14/17.
38. Denis McCarthy, Eyeries, Castletown Bere, Co. Cork, to Vere Foster, 12 April 1880, NIPRO, D3618/D/14/190.
39. *Census of Ireland*, 1841, p.396.
40. Patrick Flynn, Ballyhaunis, parish of Bekan, Co. Mayo, to Vere Foster, 24 February, 1880, NIPRO, D3618/D/14/136.
41. The Land Act was the 1881 Land Law (Ireland) Act which was drawn up at the height of the Land War, of which the first phase lasted from 1879 to 1882. This second of a series of Land Acts established the principle of dual owner-ship by landlord and tenant, gave legal status to the Ulster Custom through-out the country, providing for compensation for improvements and distur-bances and established a Land Commission and a Land Court. The acts were intended not to destroy the landlord system but to make it workable. The First Land Act had few immediate benefits because it failed to cover the predica-ment of nearly 280,000 tenants who were either leaseholders or in arrears with their rent, and also because the situation on the land was deteriorating rapidly with evictions and starvation common throughout the west of Ireland. It was followed up late in 1882 by an Amending Act which cancelled arrears for those tenants who had fallen less than £30 behind in their rents, thus provid-ing a cushion for the very poorest tenants.
42. Peter Geraghty, Ballyhaunis, parish of Bekan, Co. Mayo, to Vere Foster, 24 September 1881, NIPRO, D3618/D/15/29.
43. Hubert Walsh, Rosmuck, Maam Cross, parish of Kilcummin, Co. Galway to Vere Foster, 26 May 1880, NIPRO, D3618/D/14/207.
44. Cornelius McDermott, Cooraclare, parish of Kilmacduane, Co. Clare, to Vere Foster, 10 March 1882, NIPRO, D3618/D/16/7.
45. M. A. Kelly, Belvoir, Sixmilebridge, parish of Kilfinaghta, Co. Clare, to Vere Foster, 23 May 1882, NIPRO, D3618/D/16/19.
46. 'recruiting' in the sense of a new supply of health; renewal or restoration of health.

47. J. Downes, Riverstown, parish of Kilshalvy, Co. Sligo, to Vere Foster, 20 March 1882, NIPRO, D3618/D/16/10.

48. P. J. McHugh, C.C., Eniscrone, parish of Kilglass, Co. Sligo, to Vere Foster, 12 February 1889, NIPRO, D3618/D/19/4.

49. Cormac Ó Gráda, 'Seasonal migration and post-Famine adjustment in the West of Ireland, 1850-1880,' in *Post-Famine Adjustment: Essays in 19th Century Irish Economic History* (unpublished Ph.D. thesis, Columbia University, 1973).

50. Patrick Grealy, P.P., Clifden, parish of Omey, Co. Galway, to Vere Foster, 26 September 1881, NIPRO, D3618/D/15/35.

51. The Rev. Thomas Heaney to Vere Foster, Calry Glebe, Co. Sligo, 27 October 1881, NIPRO, D3618/D/15/88.

52. There were various attempts to provide an efficient police force in Ireland where resorting to military forces consistently alienated the civilian population. In 1814 Sir Robert Peel attempted to establish a force called the Peace Preservation Force, whose members were popularly known as 'Peelers'. Later, when this force proved inadequate: the County Constabulary was established in 1822, so that until the two were consolidated in 1836 there were two police forces in the country. After the consolidation, the new body was known as the Irish Constabulary. (They did not become the Royal Irish Constabulary until 1867.) By 1840 there were 8,500 constables stationed throughout the country. Members of the force, who were mainly Catholic, were recruited from among the tenant-farmer class.

53. The Ribbonmen were local groups of vigilantes, part of an underground of agrarian secret societies, sometimes known as 'Ribbon Societies'. In the eighteenth century they were known as 'Whiteboys' because of the white clothes which they wore at night to distinguish themselves. Their purpose was to prevent exploitation of tenant-farmers and protest the payment of tithes to support the Anglican Church. Their methods included intimidation by threat and by actual violence such as maiming cattle, burning crops, and murder. Counties in which their activities were strongest were Queen's (Leix), Kilkenny, Monaghan, Tipperary and Limerick, where there was also the most competition for land between farmers and agricultural labourers. As a rule the Ribbonmen were most active during the winter months.

54. Name unknown, Woodbury, Queen Anne County, Maryland, to Vere Foster, August 1853, NIPRO, D3618/D/25/1.

55. B. F. Psaulturne, Mackinaw City, Michigan, to Vere Foster, 17 December 1882, NIPRO, D3618/D/25/14.

56. In a diary notation made during a trip to America in 1864, Vere Foster indicated that he replied to one of her letters on 20 June 1864. 'Diary of Vere Foster's Trip to America, 1864,' NIPRO, D 3618/6/10.

57. D3618/21/24.

58. Mary Harlon, New York, to Vere Foster, 9 May 1862, NIPRO, D3618/D/25/7.

59. Mary Harlon, New York, to Vere Foster, 28 June 1864, NIPRO, D3618/D/25/8.

60. Mary Harlon, New York, to Vere Foster, 27 July 1864, NIPRO, D3618/D/25/9.

61. Mary Harlon, Key West, Florida, to Vere Foster, 20 December 1864, NIPRO, D3618/D/25/10.

9 The Famine world wide: the Irish Famine and the development of famine policy and famine theory

Patrick O'Sullivan and Richard Lucking[1]

Mention Ireland

It is very rare to come across a book on famine policy or a book of modern famine theory that does not mention Ireland. But, by the same token, it is rare to come across a book that does more than mention Ireland, a book that draws substantially on the Irish experience and on Irish Famine historiography, or a book that interacts substantially with Irish material. Yes, Ireland will be mentioned – but only mentioned. Sometimes indeed a book will mention Ireland, but 'Ireland' will not be listed in the Index – an indication that, to the indexer at least, Ireland is not central to the book's argument.

Some examples will show the pattern to these mentions of Ireland. The examples have been chosen as indications of key themes in the later development of this chapter.

Stephen Devereux's important book, *Theories of Famine*, does mention and index 'Irish famines'. But that one mention turns out to be a quotation from Amartya Sen, listing examples of the apparent anomaly that food often leaves famine areas: 'such food "counter-movement" has been observed in famines as diverse as the Irish famines of the 1840s, the Ethiopian famine in Wollo of 1973 and the Bangladesh famine of 1974.'[2] Sen's source, in turn, is Cecil Woodham-Smith, *The Great Hunger*.[3]

John W. Warnock's *The Politics of Hunger* does index Ireland's Famine, and has four pages, in an intriguing context – the writer's own family history is one starting point for a developing interest in famine theory. In his Preface Warnock points out that he has dedicated the book to the memory of his great-great-grandfather, 'John Wilson Warnock, who, with his family, fled Ireland during the Great Famine in the spring of 1846. They had little to lose. They were tenant farmers at Dunfanaghy, County Donegal, on land owned by A.J. Stewart of Ards, growing flax.'[4] The next four pages of the Preface summarize explanations of the Irish Famine and lead to a brief account of changing approaches to 'political economy, commonly identified as interdisciplinary social science.'[5] Warnock's Preface is not referenced, and his assumption is that knowledge about the Irish Famine is common knowledge. His source is Cecil Woodham-Smith, *The Great Hunger*.[6]

Michelle Burge McAlpin, in her study of famine in India, *Subject to Famine*, lists the possible causes of famine, and observes that 'A plant disease may begin the deadly pattern, as the potato blight did the great Irish famine of the 1840s.'[7] 'Ireland' and 'Irish' are not in her Index. Her source is Cecil Woodham-Smith, *The Great Hunger*.

Jean Drèze and Amartya Sen, in *Hunger and Public Action*, demonstrate that 'quite a few famines have taken place without much violation of law and order. Even in the disastrous Irish famines of the 1840s (in which about an eighth of the population died, and which led to the emigration of a comparable number to North America), the law and order situation was, in many respects, apparently "excellent".'[8] Later in the same book Drèze and Sen, like Devereux, comment on the movement of food out of famine areas.[9] Their source for Ireland, in both cases, is Woodham-Smith.

The same point, about the movement of food out of the famine area, is made by Megan Vaughan in her excellent study, *The Story of an African Famine: Gender and Famine in Twentieth-Century Malawi*. Her source too is Woodham-Smith.[10]

Irish specialists, noting the recurring reference to Woodham-Smith, will at once remark that – never mind more recent work – there was another, more academic book about the Irish Famine that might have been cited by our famine theorists, the still useful multi-authored volume *The Great Famine*, edited by Edwards and Williams.[11] It is possible to find references to Edwards and Williams in older famine material.[12] But generally, Woodham-Smith dominates, and it is Woodham-Smith's best seller which allows famine theorists to speak of knowledge of the Irish Famine as if it were common knowledge, almost in passing, to support a more general point.

But, at the same time, our famine theorists are already forcing us to interrogate Woodham-Smith and 'common knowledge' about the Irish Famine. Thus aspects of the Irish Famine which are often cited as peculiarly horrible or uniquely horrifying turn out, while remaining horrible and horrifying, not to be peculiar or unique. A number of commentators note the fact that often there is food in a famine area but that this food is somehow not available to starving people. A number of commentators note the fact that very often food is exported from a famine area – citing Woodham-Smith on Ireland as but one example among many. This perception seems not available to Woodham-Smith herself.[13]

The pattern of citation is changing, and two further examples might indicate the direction of change:

1. Accounts of famines are full of horrifying and sad accounts of the breakdown of family, kinship and neighbourhood ties. But, to anticipate our discussion later, these accounts themselves often seem to connect with beliefs about the nature of human nature, and justify certain approaches to famine relief. A practical famine theorist, interested in the planning of famine relief, and the maintaining of family ties, needs a better understanding of the processes involved. Drèze and Sen suggest that there is evidence, from studies of a great number of famines,

that the mortality rate of infants and young children is not as great as might be expected. The suggestion is, of course, that in a food crisis a family first makes efforts to save the children: adults eat less, and give what there is to the children. One of the studies Drèze and Sen cite is a study of the Irish Famine, by Cormac Ó Gráda.[14] This can be adduced as evidence that the efforts by Ó Gráda, from his base within Ireland and within Irish economic history, to make links with development theory and famine theory are paying dividends.

2. The link between famine and emigration, which is such a feature of the Irish experience, is not so great within famine literature generally – more on this later. But certain connections can be made, particularly by scholars of peasant consciousness and politics. Christopher V. Hill, writing on India, has drawn attention to Anand A. Yang's characterization of peasant reaction to oppression: 'the cultivator had three choices: rebellion, submission, or desertion'. And Yang, in turn, drew on Albert O. Hirschman's thesis concerning 'exit, voice and loyalty.'[15] To make the connection between India and Ireland, where 'exit' or 'desertion' were also peasant options, Hill cites Kerby A. Miller, *Emigrants and Exiles*.[16]

Through these recurring but not always essential references to the Irish Famine, today's famine theorists are, perhaps, making an anti-racist point. The Irish Famine was not Europe's last famine: Ó Gráda makes comparisons with the famine in Finland in 1867–68.[17] We should add the famines in Russia, 1891–92, in the Ukraine, 1932–33, and various war-induced subsistence crises.[18] But the Irish Famine was a famine in Europe, at the heart of the nineteenth-century British Empire: it is the famine that most English-speakers, and English-readers, will have heard of. Bringing in the Irish Famine broadens the discussion, of famine as a 'Third World' issue, and makes general points about the patterns of famine and humankind's vulnerability.

A chapter like this must 'paint with a broad brush', and deal only briefly with many specialist research areas, not doing justice to subtleties of argument and evidence. We apologize for infelicities, and hope that the importance of our subject matter will encourage specialists to amplify and explain where we have been able only to outline and suggest. Some specialists will already have noted the appearance of key names and themes from specific areas. Scholars of Irish economic history will have noted the name of Cormac Ó Gráda; scholars of Irish migration will have noted the name of Kerby Miller: two scholars who, as the citations listed here testify, have tried to make connections.

Scholars of economic theory will already be nodding sagely, noting the names of Amartya Sen and Albert Hirschman, who are, above all, associated with the re-thinking of our heritage of economic 'utilitarianism'.[19] Perry Anderson has said of Sen that his 'writing more than that of any other member of his generation has renewed the classical connexion of philosophy and economics.'[20] It is of particular relevance to Ireland that Sen's personal intellectual odyssey has taken him through a critique of our utilitarian heritage to a central role in the development of late twentieth century thinking about poverty, development, famine and food 'entitlement'.

This chapter looks mainly at the place of the Irish Famine in the development of nineteenth-and twentieth-century famine theory, while offering some pointers for further research. We can only touch briefly on important questions. In what ways was the Irish Famine like or unlike other famines? Are there ways in which the Irish Famine was unique? This introductory section ends with two further citations which map out the further course of the chapter.

1. Jean Drèze's own study of famine in India does not, as ever, list 'Ireland' in the Index and lists no Irish material in its bibliography. But Drèze does mention Ireland, and in a context that is one of the starting points for this chapter.

   Under the rule of the East India Company, famines were frequent and severe – sometimes extremely severe, as with the calamitous famine of 1770 in Bengal. Relief efforts were, moreover, at best half-hearted, and in any case lacking in effectiveness. The laconic remarks of the Famine Commission of 1880 on this subject are revealing enough:

   'the earlier despatches of the Bengal Government, while breathing a tone of sincere compassion for the sufferings occasioned by famine, are busied rather with its fiscal results, as affecting the responsibility of the Company towards its shareholders, than with schemes, which would have seemed wholly visionary, for counteracting the inevitable loss of life.' [21]

   And Drèze continues:

   How did the 'breath of sincere compassion' gradually turn into a serious preoccupation with the prevention of famines after the British administration took over in 1858? In other words, why were the British rulers so concerned to avert famines in India? Oddly enough, the answers that have been proposed to this question have remained extremely fragmented and speculative. The report of the Famine Commission of 1880 repeatedly invokes the 'duty of the State' in this context. But what this rhetoric actually masked is rather hard to say... It is unlikely that this issue could be satisfactorily resolved without also considering British policy in Ireland and even in Africa, where very similar situations and debates were encountered. This, however, would take us far beyond the scope of this chapter and can only be proposed here as a theme for further research.[22]

2. An important chapter by Lance Brennan looks at the politics, and the personalities, behind this British change of policy and the creation of the Famine Commission of 1880. He wonders if there were not some connections with the debates leading up to the creation of the English New Poor Law of 1834, and the further debates and controversies after its implementation:

   Relief of the poor was a hotly debated matter in Victorian England, and the issues debated there included a number of the same issues that were involved in famine relief in India, viz. should people needing support have to work for it in workhouses or on special public works; how could administrators identify those who needed relief using self-administered and deterrent tests of labour for basic subsistence, separation (in England), and distance (in India); and whose responsibility was it to fund and control provisions for the poor or the famished?[23]

But Brennan adds that the last thing that the British administrators in India wished to consider was an Indian equivalent of the New Poor Law. And he goes on:

> There remains another possible source of influence on policy related to a colonial rather than a metropolitan situation and concerned with famine rather than endemic poverty, viz. British experience with the Irish famine of 1846–49. This is a question which would almost certainly repay closer enquiry, but while on the surface there are a number of points of similarity, such as the absence of any impediments to the export of food from either country during the famines, and the common concern to secure labour for relief, the Irish situation was not drawn upon as an example in the Indian correspondence on policy making during the later 1870s.[24]

We will return to this point. Irish specialists will know that discussion of the Irish Famine, and discussion of British famine relief policy in Ireland, are interwoven with discussion of the New Poor Law of 1834, and the extension of its policies to Ireland with the Irish Poor Law of 1838. This point has been made most cogently by Christine Kinealy:

> The Irish Poor Law was modelled to a large extent on the 'new' English Poor Law of 1834, but there were a number of significant differences that indicated that pauperism in Ireland was to be treated more harshly than in England... Overall, both in principle and in underlying ethos, the Irish Poor Law was intended to be more stringent than its English counterpart. Its provisions illustrated an approach to policy that underpinned the government's response to the onset of famine in Ireland only seven years later.[25]

We should also note that the English Poor Laws, the 'Old' Poor Laws, can themselves be seen as a response to famine, and as a long-term, and highly successful, famine prevention scheme. The rulers of England in the sixteenth and seventeenth centuries were anxious that harvest failure should not lead to famine, unrest, population movement and epidemic disease. British elites in the eighteenth and nineteenth centuries knew this history, but somehow lost sight of it or assumed that the times of famine were past.[26] And, in the observations by Brennan and by Kinealy, we seem to have, within the collective British imperial mind in the first part of the nineteenth century, a kind of hierarchy: the English poor will be allowed a harsh Poor Law, the Irish poor will be given an even harsher Poor Law, and the Indian poor will not be allowed any Poor Law at all.

And lastly in this introductory section we should deal with a point that has come up in informal discussion of this chapter: we know that some readers will be perturbed at the very thought of something seemingly so detached as 'famine theory' – it seems somehow inhuman to theorize about human catastrophe. Stephen Devereux writes: 'If famine is to be prevented, it must first be understood... effective policy depends on good theory, and the theory of famine is confused.' Famines have occurred in our own times, he points out, despite the best efforts of those afflicted, their governments and donor agencies, to prevent them. 'In these cases, it is arguable that deficient *theory* was partly to blame. Problems were misdiagnosed or not foreseen, leading to inappropriate or late intervention. Many people died, often unnecessarily.'[27] Famine policy has a history, famine theory has a history, and this chapter is an exploration of those histories. As we will see, when we explore the history of famine in British India, gathering information about human catastrophes, and theorizing, are first steps towards prevention.

Imagine India

Drèze, we have seen, mentions famines under East India Company rule in India. Indeed it has been suggested that the frequency of famines in India actually increased under British rule. Commentators make a distinction between the different phases of British and East India Company rule. Osmani notes that, in its early years 'the operation of the East India Company consisted of purchasing exportable commodities from India, financed mostly by import of bullion from England.' This trade would then have been broadly in balance.

After the battle of Plassey in 1757 the East India Company moved into a position where it owned taxes and revenues: 'Their appropriation of land revenue in Bengal now provided the necessary "investment fund". In other words they could now obtain the export commodities practically free, and their exporting business amounted to an unrequited transfer of Bengal's surplus to England. Faced with this happy prospect of being able to do business with other people's money, the Company set out to maximize its gain by extracting as much revenue as possible from the Bengal peasants.'[28] Thereafter the East India Company, through further conquests, itself became, in effect, the ultimate landowner and ruling monarch, subjugating and sometimes displacing Indian elites.

Warnock has a substantial section, citing a wide variety of sources, explaining why East India Company rule and later British 'direct rule' should have increased the likelihood of famine. Explanations for the increase include the destruction of industries, making more people dependent on agriculture; disruption by changes in land tenure systems and land revenue collection or taxation; and straightforward exploitation through taxation. After 1860 Indian exports were primarily agricultural products. The price of food increased, while wages for employment outside agriculture stagnated. 'Poverty and vulnerability to famine increased substantially among three sections of the rural population: agricultural labourers, tenant farmers, and weavers.'[29] Thus a greater proportion of the population had been made vulnerable in any agricultural crisis. Such crises in India are usually, but not always, caused by drought – the failure of the seasonal rains.

The reader will realize at once that this suggestion, that the number of famines increased under British rule, sits uneasily with the rhetoric of empire. The classic imperialist adventure always involves a rescue, and the rhetoric of imperialism demands that the imposition of empire be associated with 'progress'. Thus, in tropes that will be familiar to scholars of Irish history, the British historians of British India had to see the imperialist adventure as rescuing the people of India from stagnation and from corrupt, despotic and cruel government. James Mill's *History of British India*, completed in 1817, is the 'hegemonic textbook', but the subsequent century saw the production of numerous – we are tempted to say 'countless' – similar works.[30]

The trope has even more complex consequences. The situation in the conquered country immediately before conquest is fixed in the imperialist mind as 'traditional' culture: timeless, unchanging, stagnant. In fact, the culture of the conquered will already have been disrupted, in the short term or the long term, by crises before the invasion, the movement of armies, population movement and general disruption, and by ad hoc solutions to these crises. The situation that the invaders meet is unlikely to be 'traditional' in any real sense, and progressive or dynamic elements within that 'traditional' culture will be invisible to, or ignored by, the invaders.[31]

As Indian scholars, especially nationalist scholars before and after independence, tried to seize their own history they became uneasily aware that they must work through British sources and British redactions of non-British material. Indeed it is only comparatively recently that scholars of India, Indian and non-Indian, have established how much their understanding of India's history had been distorted by specifically British understandings of India's culture and history.

> Until the 1960s, it remained possible to conceive the coming of British rule as representing 'the beginnings of modernisation' and to write Indian history in terms of an 'heroic' struggle to fulfil the civilising mission: 'heroic', in the British sense, because it largely failed... In the 1960s, however, some historians began to wonder whether the West's invitation had been seriously or honestly offered; and whether India's failure to modernise was not the result of colonial intent... During the 1970s, the questioning started to take a new direction. Now, while it was agreed that many of the cultural and societal relations of colonial India did not conform to ideal types of the modern(-ising) or the western(-ising), it began to be doubted that they conformed either to the social relations which had actually existed before the colonial conquest... [32]

The key text within this discussion is Ronald Inden's *Imagining India*. Inden argues that all the characteristics which are seen as distinctively 'Indian' are artefacts of British rule or British historiography and ethnography. Examples are 'castes' as things, with rigid boundaries; the 'village community' as the centre of most economic activity; and a people dominated by imagination rather than reason.[33] Inden has his critics, but really his book is but one example of a cumulative reappraisal of their unwieldy inheritance by scholars of India. Scholars within European and North American traditions will at once realize that this reappraisal must, in turn, force a rethink of a variety of materials within a variety of disciplines which ultimately draw on this British historiography and ethnography of India: Max Weber or Barrington Moore, Jr., and the notion of the 'passive peasant', Karl Marx and 'the Asiatic mode of production' are obvious examples.

India: an East India Company famine policy

Did the East India Company have a famine policy? Traditional British histories of the Company see the Company's servants gallantly striving to alleviate human suffering, Indian histories differ.[34] But Ambirajan thinks that, broadly, in the latter part of the eighteenth century, the East India Company carried on the interventionist famine policies of the Indian states it had replaced. Warren Hastings felt that 'a well regulated state' would not suffer from famine – in 1800 he offered advice to his home country, based on his own experiences in Bengal, on dealing with the near-famine conditions in England at that time.[35]

But the summing up of the East India Company's policy by another British source, the Famine Commission of 1880, has already been cited:

> the earlier despatches of the Bengal Government, while breathing a tone of sincere compassion for the sufferings occasioned by famine, are busied rather with its fiscal results, as affecting the responsibility of the Company towards its shareholders, than with schemes, which would have seemed wholly visionary, for counteracting the inevitable loss of life. [36]

Ambirajan quotes, as many a commentator has quoted, the response of Elphinstone, Governor of Bombay, when the wisdom of the 'classical' policy of non-interference in famine was questioned by his civil servants, J. F. Thomas and John Sullivan. Elphinstone wrote: 'The remarks of Adam Smith appear to me to bear with such force upon this argument that I shall make no apology for introducing them.'[37] And Sen comments: 'Adam Smith's long shadow has fallen over many famines in the British Empire over the last two hundred years, with Smith being cited in favour of inaction and letting things be.'[38]

Adam Smith and 'Adam Smith'

References to Adam Smith can be found throughout the Company's records and histories, and throughout the Famine Commission's enquiries into earlier famine policies:

> Following the faith of the British in the doctrine of laissez-faire in India, Smith was made compulsory study for the students of the East India Company's East India College at Haileybury, for the future administrators of India. Also after

the Crown's takeover the Wealth of Nations was prescribed as the first text in political economy for the elitist Indian Civil Service Examination...'[39]

Certainly, it would seem, the concept of the free market is seductive. But it has to be stressed that the theorists of the free market had themselves no experience of the realities of a free market economy. They lived in protected economies. Throughout most of Adam Smith's own life Britain was at war, or about to go to war, and protectionist. And there are (at least) two distinctly odd things about the way that the British policy makers of the East India Company and the British Empire cite Adam Smith, the apostle of market forces and free trade.

1. There was no more jealous guardian of monopoly and privilege than the East India Company. Adam Smith himself disapproved of the East India Company.[40] And there are tensions, to say the least, between the demands of free trade and the demands of empire and monopoly. The nineteenth-century biographer of James Mill conscientiously acknowledges these tensions, which became starkly visible during the debates and negotiations, in 1830–33, about the renewal of the East India Company's charter:

   > It may seem a little strange that Mill, whose views on Trade were of the most advanced school, should be exerting himself heart and soul to counter-argue the demands of the trading community on this occasion. The reason can easily be gathered from the perusal of his evidence. The mercantile interest could not see, in the light of an official, the very stagnant condition of the native population in India; and seemed to believe that, but for the obstruction of the Company's Government, there would be a great and sudden development of industry – exports and imports – to the benefit of the home producers.[41]

   The writing is clumsy, the writer is embarrassed. But here we can see that 'an official' – in this case Mill, the historian of the British in India – can be asserted to have special knowledge which cancels out the demands of free trade. And that knowledge is knowledge of Indian 'stagnation'.

2. If the thought of 'Adam Smith' is genuinely brought to bear on questions of famine policy and famine theory it is by no means certain that 'Adam Smith' would counsel inaction. What follows here expands on key pages by Sen but there are links with material elsewhere in this chapter.[42] Sen points out that Adam Smith does mention famine a number of times in *The Wealth of Nations*. Thus, in one section, Smith can foresee a situation when the wages of the poor would be driven down and 'want, famine and mortality would immediately prevail in that class... .' Smith then specifically cites subsistence crises in Bengal as an example:

   > The difference between the genius of the British constitution which protects and governs North America, and that of the mercantile company which oppresses and domineers in the East Indies, cannot perhaps be better illustrated than by the different state of those countries.[43]

In another section, the much-cited 'Digression Concerning the Corn Trade and Corn Laws', Smith defends the right of corn traders to raise prices in a time of scarcity, and adds:

> Whoever examines with attention the history of the dearths and famines which have afflicted Europe... will find, I believe, that a dearth never has arisen from any combination among the inland dealers in corn, nor from any other cause but a real scarcity, occasioned... in by far the greatest number of cases by the fault in the seasons; and that a famine has never arisen from any other cause but by the violence of government attempting, by improper means, to remedy the inconveniences of a dearth.

And later Smith suggests world-wide free trade as 'not only the best palliative of a dearth, but the most effectual preventative of a famine...' [44]

Obviously these key quotations from Smith can be read in different ways. They should be read in context, as a 'Digression on... the Corn Laws' in a chapter on 'Bounties'. In our own time Smith can be read as an invitation to develop famine theory: 'Whoever examines with attention the history...' Sen suggests, that, in these various comments on famine, Smith is distinguishing between two distinct elements: the 'pull' of a person wanting food, and the supplier's 'response'. If a person has no means of buying food then that is a failure on the 'pull' side. If manipulative traders corner the market and there is an absence of supply, then there is a failure on the 'response' side.

> Smith's point that response failure would not arise from collusive action of traders has a direct bearing on the appropriate form of famine relief. If his point is correct, then relief could just as easily be provided by giving the deprived additional income and leaving it to the traders to respond to the new pull through moving food to the cash recipients. It is arguable that Smith did underestimate the extent to which traders can and do, in fact, manipulate markets, but at the same time the merits of cash relief do need serious examination in the context of assessing policy options. [45]

In other words – and Sen cites some examples – getting cash to the famine-stricken can get the markets on the side of famine relief, and is certainly a useful part of the famine-relief repertoire: 'the real Smithian issue in a situation of famine is not "intervention versus non-intervention", but "cash relief versus direct food relief".' [46]

So, if the standard response of East India Company and British administrators in India, when asked for famine policy, was to cite 'Adam Smith', what is going on? We suggest that the words 'Adam Smith' constitute a sort of code, linking, within the minds of the ruling elite, elements of the thought of three men: Adam Smith, Jeremy Bentham and Thomas Malthus. We cannot here do justice to the complexity, or the utility, of the works of these three men. [47] Their works have attracted a massive amount of secondary literature, which it would take many lifetimes to absorb. We are here considering not so much the thought of Adam Smith, Bentham or Malthus, but that thought as shaped into a famine policy by key figures within the East India Company structures in England – notably, in the first place, James Mill, his son John Stuart Mill, and Thomas Malthus himself, teaching at the East India College at Haileybury – and that policy when sometimes put into practice by administrators in India. What we demonstrate is the creation of a famine policy within a specific cast of mind, and within a specific caste – the British elite in India.

Cumulatively this is what Ambirajan calls 'a classical famine policy', since it ostensibly derives from the thought of the 'classical economists' – Adam Smith and his followers: 'every time there was a famine and an appeal was made to introduce measures such as price control and so on, the principles of political economy were cited to justify a policy of non-interference.'[48]

It is easiest to imagine the process as beginning in Haileybury – the college, near Hertford, England, opened in 1806, for the education and training of young men before they entered the East India Company's service in India.[49] The influence of Haileybury is acknowledged in every history of British India, and every history of the British Empire: generations of rulers were 'indoctrinated at Haileybury College, before they ever went to India, with the idea of British superiority, moral and cultural as well as military.'[50] Haileybury sought to inculcate into its young men sound first principles, before untidy empirical reality could cloud their judgement.

'Adam Smith' is, as we have seen, the first 'first principle': market forces, laissez faire, the invisible hand, about which enough has been said already, except to note 'the predisposition established by Adam Smith to equate the behaviour of the total economy with the conduct of the individual or the single firm...'[51]

Jeremy Bentham

The next 'first principle' draws on Jeremy Bentham, with his 'genius for legislation'. Bentham tried to deduce entire principles of legislation from his own first principle: the only things that people desire for their own sakes are pleasure and the avoidance of pain.[52] Private ethics teach 'how each man may dispose himself to pursue the course most conductive to his own happiness... the art of legislation teaches how a multitude of men, composing a community, may be disposed to pursue that course which upon the whole is most conducive to the happiness of the whole community, by means of motives to be applied by the legislator.'[53] Bentham's own first principle can thus be seen as a kind of egoistic hedonism.[54]

As Eric Stokes shows there was much Benthamite influence on the East India Company regime, for example on Mountstuart Elphinstone in Bombay, where 'the legislator' had in his care many multitudes of men.[55] There has been renewed interest in the thought and influence of Bentham in our own time, partly under the influence of Michel Foucault. For Foucault Bentham's 'ideal' prison, the Panopticon, is 'a figure of political technology that may and must be detached from any specific use...'; 'But the Panopticon was also a laboratory; it could be used as a machine to carry out experiments, to alter behaviour, to train or correct individuals....

The Panopticon is a privileged place for experiments on men, and for analysing with complete certainty the transformations that may be obtained from them.'[56] Inden puts it bluntly: 'India, if Bentham and Mill had their way, would become a realization of this Panopticon.'[57] We would add that India became, in the nineteenth century, the site of many 'experiments on men', including experiments in famine policy.

We need to assume some sort of philosophical 'first principle', like Bentham's egoistic hedonism, within the minds of the ruling elite, to explain the insistence on 'tests', that is ways of identifying those in need of relief, and the insistence that these 'tests' should be self-administered and deterrent. A Benthamite Poor Law, and a Benthamite famine policy, would be 'self-testing'.[58] The tests, in England, Ireland and India, involved, in various combinations, work, separation and distance. As a starting point for the development of a famine policy, a philosophy of egoistic hedonism encourages the legislator to assume the worst about the actions and motives of the hungry.

But, as in the case of Adam Smith, it is by no means certain that if the thought of Jeremy Bentham, the living man, were applied to famine policy it would lead to a policy of inaction. Though he paid lip service to the economic liberalism of Adam Smith, Bentham himself was a believer in government intervention. He even believed that governments should fix prices and guarantee a minimum wage: ' insurance against scarcity cannot be left with safety to individual exertion...'.[59]

Malthus on population

The third 'first principle' is supplied by Thomas Malthus. That there is some necessary connection between population size and food supply we would all now accept. Prefigurings of this observation have been noticed in many thinkers before Malthus.[60] The most interesting of these, for our readership here, are: Richard Cantillon (the eighteenth-century Irish, Paris-based banker), James Steuart (the eighteenth-century Jacobite Scot), and Benjamin Franklin (the American).[61] The longer-term influence of Malthus, on a variety of figures and within a variety of academic disciplines, is remarkable – the most significant influence, perhaps, is on Charles Darwin and the academic disciplines that have developed from Darwin's insights.[62]

We think it expedient to separate out the observation – about population size and food supply – from the specific historical circumstances in which Malthus wrote, and the specific spin, theoretical, ideological, or theological, that Malthus gave to the observation. For, 'unfortunately' – as Patricia James puts it – Malthus propounded a general rule, that population increases in a geometric ratio and 'subsistence', food supply, increases in an arithmetical ratio, thus producing the figures which so awed his contemporaries.[63] And Malthus brings in a theology, explicitly, in sections of his *Essay on Population* that are often treated as 'embarrassing and detachable'.[64] 'Malthus believed that fixed laws of nature constituted the only means by which God's progressive purpose could be achieved on earth.'[65] Thus 'Nature', 'Providence', the wishes of a beneficent God are inextricably linked in Malthus' own thought, and in the thought of his followers. It is with this theology in mind that they observed the arrival of famine to wipe out 'surplus' population.

Malthus cannot be ignored. Furthermore, he can be read positively. Malthus himself wrote, 'Evil exists in the world, not to create despair, but activity.'[66] John Stuart Mill saw the publication of 'Mr Malthus's Essay on Population' as a paradoxical turning point: 'only from that time has the economical condition of the labouring classes been regarded by thoughtful men as susceptible of permanent improvement.'[67] In Malthus, and in Bentham, there is – as James demonstrates – much discussion of birth control, but, in the manner of the times, couched in such terms as to often make it difficult to know what they are talking about.[68] Later in the nineteenth century the adjective 'Malthusian' would become associated with birth control policies and practices.[69] In fact, broadly, Malthus was against birth control, and Bentham in favour. (And there is a secret scandal in the youth of John Stuart Mill: in 1823, aged seventeen, he was jailed for distributing leaflets giving birth control advice.)[70]

The extent of Malthus' own interest in Ireland was, and still is, a matter of dispute.[71] His interest in India, and his influence there, are a matter of record. First, a substantial chapter on India in the *Essay on Population*. Then, in 1805 Malthus was appointed to the post of 'Professor of General History, Politics, Commerce and Finance' – in effect, the first professorship of political economy in the world – at the East India Company's new college at Haileybury. Malthus taught at Haileybury until his death in 1834.[72] William Petersen, in his over-defensive life of Malthus, says: 'For some leftist critics, the fact that Malthus was associated with the college instituted to train agents of British imperialism confirms their negative opinion of him and his works.'[73] And, indeed, Roger Wells says: 'Malthus's subsequent professorship at the College for apprentice East India Company administrators has a macabre symbolism. For Malthusian demographic logic resonates throughout the private communications of those officials, and their imperialist successors.'[74]

The influence of Malthus' theory of population on the British elite in India has, Ambirajan believes, been 'relatively neglected'.[75] But Ambirajan, and others, can demonstrate a strong 'Malthusian' bias within the British elite in India throughout the nineteenth century.[76] As far as the development of a famine policy was concerned the argument was quite circular: Malthus had specifically mentioned famine as one consequence of and cure for over-population; therefore famine was in itself evidence of over-population. There need to be no further enquiry as to cause or cure. Famine was 'Nature's' way of getting rid of the 'surplus' population. And, as Ambirajan sums up the policy, 'What is the use of saving lives when once again the people so saved would suffer later in the same way?'[77]

It might be felt, at this stage, that there is no thinker whose thought cannot, with the right degree of hypocrisy and doublethink, be used to justify unpleasant policies and actions. Certainly there is a distinct impression –

as many commentators have suggested in India, and Christine Kinealy has suggested in an Irish context – that the British ruling elite chose those elements of Smith, Bentham and Malthus that were convenient in a current crisis.[78] Yet, we have cited men, thinkers and administrators, who would have regarded themselves as clear-headed and honourable, and who, in Britain and in India, often behaved with courage and dignity. Thus histories of the women's movement will have respectful comment on John Stuart Mill. And, as we show in this chapter, there is never a time when shibboleths go unquestioned. But in the end, Ambirajan argues, 'When virtually every document relating to the formulation and execution of famine policy over a century referred to the views of Adam Smith and/or John Stuart Mill, it becomes well nigh impossible to dismiss the role of Classical economic ideas in the formation of economic policy.' Some administrators, 'goaded by their humanitarianism' may have tried to develop alternative policies, but there were not the resources or the knowledge to formulate an alternative famine policy.[79]

Malthus on rent

Before we leave Malthus on India, we need to look at another example of his influence on economic policy there. And this too identifies a 'surplus'.

Malthus' theory of rent is met, with varying degrees of enthusiasm or bafflement, throughout the history of British India. Malthus theorized that there could be only one market price for corn: that price would be based on the cost of production on the worst land that farmers thought it worthwhile to cultivate – what would later be called 'marginal land'. Corn produced on better land would command the same price, but with lower production costs:

> there would therefore be a surplus over and above the current profit on agricultural capital, and this surplus was rent. It was a gift of Providence to the owners of land better than that at the margin of cultivation, and since it arose because their fields were able to produce corn at less than the market price, a high rent could obviously not be a component part of that price; thus the landlords might receive it with a clear conscience.[80]

Malthus' observations on rent are linked with his observations on population and subsistence through the 'law' of diminishing returns: limitations on cultivation at the margins mean food supply can rise only at an arithmetical rate.

Patricia James, Malthus' most recent and sympathetic biographer, writes:

> It will be apparent to modern readers that the differential theory of rent could never have been formulated except by economists writing in early nineteenth-century Britain, where the land was almost entirely cultivated on a three-tier system practised nowhere else, except on a small scale in parts of Holland and Belgium. The work was done for wages, by labourers, directly employed by farmers, who provided the capital and made profits, while the land was owned

by proprietors who received contractual money rents, regardless of individual good or bad harvests... [81]

Malthus and James Mill became convinced that rent, or a tax on rent, or a tax on that proportion of the land's produce that could be assessed as this Providential gift, 'this surplus', was the key to the collection of revenue in British India, where, they suggested, the East India Company was the State *and* 'the landlord'. The problem was assessment. Thus, in 1828, R.K. Pringle, 'one of Malthus' best pupils while at the East India Company's college at Haileybury', began the task of assessing 'net produce' and the government 'rent' in a part of Bombay.[82] Almost immediately Pringle's system failed, as cultivators fled the land. Nonetheless the principle was established, and this form of assessed land revenue became the basis of East India Company finances, and subsequently Imperial British India's finances, throughout the century, and beyond – the government would assess a part of the land's produce as 'the surplus', and declare that this 'surplus', all or part of it, belonged rightfully to the government. This was not a tax, it was claimed; it was rent. Stokes tells us that an 1858 restatement of the 'principle' by John Stuart Mill 'was reproduced by Sir John Strachey in his book *India*; and this remained a semi-official handbook for more than twenty years after its publication in 1888.'[83] And thus, to anticipate the discussion later in this chapter, we see why the British 'government of India' was 'fortified by the opinion of the 1880 Famine Commission that the land revenue had no connexion with the famines of the seventies'.[84]

Ireland: an East India Company famine policy?

As we have seen, material about India and Ireland, and thinking about India and Ireland, are interlinked in intriguing ways. The scholar of Irish experience approaches the Indian material with an uneasy sense of familarity: thus Ó Gráda says of 'Economic Ideas and Famine Policy', Chapter 3 of Ambirajan's *Classical Political Economy and British Policy in India*, that it 'could have been written about Ireland in the 1840s.' [85] Christopher V. Hill, the scholar of India, reads Charles Trevelyan, ultimately responsible for British famine policy in Ireland, and says: 'Indeed Trevelyan's characterization of the Irish could have been lifted from numerous colonial descriptions of the population of India.'[86]

Elphinstone's dismissing of the doubts of his civil servants, Thomas and Sullivan, in 1839 Bombay has exact counterparts in Ireland when Trevelyan dismissed the doubts of Edward Twistleton, the Poor Law Commissioner in Ireland. Concerned visitors from Ireland and relief officials in Ireland were advised to read Adam Smith and Edmund Burke's *Thoughts on Scarcity*.[87] Twistleton 'eventually resigned in frustration at the frugal policies being pursued by the government...'[88] Indeed, the connections between policy in India and in Ireland are even more direct. For Charles Trevelyan was educated at Haileybury, and served the East India Company in India from 1826 to 1838. He then returned to England and in

1840 began his nineteen-year stint in the Treasury in London. In 1859 Trevelyan resumed his career in India under the newly established British imperial 'direct rule'.[89]

There is a question that should now be asked – in our experience the question has been forming in the reader's mind for some time. Since the points of contact and comparison are so many, did Ireland get an East India Company famine policy?

Ireland did not get an English famine policy. Earlier subsistence crises, in 1800, studied by Wells, and in 1817–19, studied by Post, show an interventionist famine prevention policy still strong in England at those times, though under attack.[90] Thereafter direct points of comparison are hard to find, because of the size of the catastrophe that overtook Ireland, and because of the change in official thinking signalled by the English New Poor Law of 1834. But most commentators find it difficult to believe that the British government would have, or could have, stuck to a policy of inaction if famine had appeared in England.[91]

The question – did Ireland get an East India Company famine policy? – is perhaps put in too simple a form. Certainly, a key figure like Trevelyan seems to have brought his attitudes intact from Haileybury and India. And, when Trevelyan's own account of the Irish famine, 'The Irish Crisis' in the *Edinburgh Review* of 1848, is put alongside similar documents from India throughout the early and middle parts of the nineteenth century, there are points of comparison. Thus Trevelyan expects the Irish famine to behave like an Indian famine: he expects it to last one year.[92]

The Irish famine occurred at a time when the self-confidence of the followers of 'classical political economy' was at its height. Their confidence was not based on experience: it was based on theory. India and Ireland were two places where 'political economy' influenced the powerful, or, rather, were two places where there were no counter-balancing forces – democracy, for example – to prevent the powerful from putting those policies into action. And famine policy was one of the few areas of policy where 'political economy' could be put into action because when faced by famine, 'political economy' recommended a policy of inaction. Kinealy says of famine policy in Ireland:

> That the response illustrated a view of Ireland and its people as distant and marginal is hard to deny. What, perhaps, is more surprising is that a group of officials and their non-elected advisers were able to dominate government policy to such an extent. This relatively small group of people, taking advantage of a passive establishment... were able to manipulate a theory of free enterprise...[93]

She might be talking of India. Ireland's service to India may have been simply this: the Irish Famine brought home, the fleeing Irish Famine refugees brought home – literally, brought home, to the heart of the Empire – the realities of the famine policies then in place in India.

India and Ireland

We now need to move swiftly forward, assuming that the reader knows something about events in Ireland and in India. Ireland suffered its Great Famine, 1845–50. India continued to suffer its famines. In 1857 there occurred the events that are referred to in British textbooks as the 'Indian Mutiny', or sometimes the 'Sepoy Mutiny', and in Indian histories as 'the Indian Rebellion' and sometimes 'the Red Year': a massive uprising against East India Company rule, with much vengeful cruelty on both sides.

The age of the East India Company was brought to an end and, in 1858, a form of 'direct rule' was imposed on India by London. Thus was created the need for the formal structures and the elaborate ideologies of the nineteenth-century British Empire: it was an empire that was to last less than 100 years. And the possessions in India continued to distort British foreign and economic policy.[94]

In that pre-democratic age, when the surviving princes of India were consulted little about government policy, and the people of India not at all, policy developed through debate between factions within the British ruling elite. Thus, during the post-mortems within the British elite after the Indian Rebellion of 1857, there were bitter debates about the land revenue system and the nature of property rights. Two factions can be discerned: the 'Aristocratic Reaction' or the 'Aristocratic Party', who favoured the retention of princes and the extension of landlord systems throughout India, as a buttress to British rule, and the 'Punjab Tradition' or 'Punjab School', who favoured peasant proprietorship, following the paternalistic ideals of John Lawrence. These terms were used in the 1860s.[95] In these debates comparisons with Ireland are made as a matter of course. Thus Richard Temple, a follower of John Lawrence, would write: '*Some* classes of natives look on land in the same light as English landlords do – but the *mass* of the natives regard the land as the *Irish* do. If the tenancy of land is disturbed there is apt to be the same trouble in India, as there would be in Ireland.'[96] 'Temple was not alone among the Anglo-Indians in drawing the parallel between Indian and Irish land tenures. Campbell and Mayo both perceived the danger of repeating the mistakes made in Ireland, and Salisbury, with his usual perception, came to the same conclusion during the period when he was secretary of state for India.'[97]

Similar, but not identical, divisions within the British elite can be seen in the recurring debates about famine policy. The first famine under British direct rule occurred in the North-West, 1860–61, soon followed by the devastating famine in Orissa, 1865–66. In Orissa, it is estimated, 1,364,529 people died, one fourth of the population.[98] The government stuck to the 'classical famine policy', the East India Company policy. A senior member of the government cited Trevelyan's article, 'The Irish Crisis', in the *Edinburgh Review*: 'it will explain and justify our hesitation to recommend a departure from rules and principles which para 8 of the Secretary of State's Despatch admits should not be lightly interfered with.' The Orissa famine was not unlike 'the question which so anxiously occupied the

Home Government in 1846, and which was finally dealt with by adopting measures confining their interference in Ireland to minimum.'[99]

Ambirjan comments: 'It would be difficult to conclude that Trevelyan's Irish Famine policy alone decided the Orissa Famine Policy. But it was certainly an important factor. While Trevelyan's famine policy did not endear him to the Irish people, he was nevertheless a very respected member of the Indian civil service and as such his views had considerable influence in India.'[100]

India influenced famine policy in Ireland, Ireland influenced famine policy in India. It has to be said that we have no sense that the Irish experience was studied systematically, to learn lessons for India. Individual members of the elite had different impressions of the Irish experience, and aspects of Irish experience will be cited to support one or other point of view. Thus, after the famine in Orissa, some argued that Robert Peel's importation of Indian corn during the Irish Famine offered a precedent for state interference.[101]

If a source is cited for the Irish experience it will be, as we have seen, as likely as not, 'The Irish Crisis', Charles Trevelyan's review article in the *Edinburgh Review*. Irish specialists will know that Trevelyan's article offers an incomplete and partial account of the Irish Famine. It was published in January 1848 and looks at experiences only up to November 1847.

There are two ways in which this impressionistic recall of the Irish Famine may have misled the British elite in India:

1. The Irish experience may have led the British elite in India to believe that Malthus was right. The Irish Famine, and Ireland's population history since the Famine, seemed to confirm Malthus' theory, that famine was a cure for over-population. But, if we look to recent developments in famine theory and policy, we find that 'contrary to Malthus's belief, however, recent empirical studies suggest that famines may not act as "natural population checks" at all.' Demographic crises (famine, war, epidemics) usually trigger demographic responses – 'baby booms'. Some famine studies suggest that populations recover within two decades, as if the famine had not occurred at all.[102] Thus, if over-population is a problem, famine is not a solution.

   This may explain why famine theorists listed in the opening section of this chapter could do little more than 'mention Ireland'. Impressionistic recall of the Irish experience offers few insights for those wishing to develop a famine theory and famine policy aimed at saving life, saving our species, and saving our planet. Our own view is that the specificity of Irish responses to the Famine may well offer insights: but those insights will not emerge if the Irish Famine is studied in isolation.

2. The British elite may have picked up, as the significant message from the Irish experience, the importance of emigration as a 'cure' for famine. Again, we have to recall, the logic is quite simple: famine is itself evidence of over-population, therefore remove the 'surplus' population.

Thus, during the Bengal famine of 1873–74, Richard Temple, later Lieutenant-Governor of Bengal, was appointed to oversee famine relief: he became convinced that the people should be moved to uncultivated, waste land in other parts of the region.[103] This policy, as the later 'Dufferin Report' (1888) made clear, drew on the Irish experience: 'If the idea of emigration could be popularized, so as to take hold of the people as it did in Ireland twenty-five years ago, it would be the best thing to happen...'[104]

The British ruling elite was, at this high point of empire, world wide and inter-linked. Some members of the British elite in India had had direct experience of the Famine in Ireland; some were themselves of Irish or Anglo-Irish origin. Some commentators have felt that these British administrators of Irish origin might generally have been more sympathetic to the famine-stricken of India: scholars of Ireland will know that each individual case would have to be studied on its merits.

We have already seen the example of Richard Southwell Bourke, the Earl of Mayo (1822–72), who became Viceroy in 1869. 'Irish experience led him to take a view of Indian land problems which was marked by a warm-hearted sympathy for tenant right.'[105] As a young man Mayo had first hand experience of the Famine in Ireland: his nineteenth-century biographer says that Mayo 'won for himself an honoured place among the hundreds of high-minded Irish gentlemen who tried to do their duty.'[106] On the other hand, young 'Mr Richard Bourke, MP for Kildare', Mayo before he inherited the title, is cited approvingly in Trevelyan's 'Irish Crisis'.[107] Mayo was assassinated by an Indian nationalist in 1872.

The career of Frederick Temple Blackwood, Lord Dufferin (1826–1902), took him to practically every corner of the British Empire: Governor-General of Canada, 1872–78, he became Governor-General of India in 1884.[108] As a young man Dufferin had published his own account of a journey across Ireland in the time of Famine.[109] And it might be thought that we have already seen evidence that Dufferin was influenced by his mother's poem, 'The Lament of the Irish Emigrant'.

Don't mention Ireland

In the 1860s and 1870s India was devastated by a series of famines: the North-West, 1860–61, Orissa, 1865–66, Bengal and Bihar, 1866, Madras, 1866, the North West, 1868–69, Bengal and Bihar, 1873–74, Madras, 1876–78, Bombay, 1876–77, and the North West again, 1877–78.[110] Explanations of this new, increased frequency and intensity of famine vary. Traditional Indian nationalist commentators see a direct connection between the famines and 'the almost unabated and harsh realization of the land revenue by the State...'.[111] Other commentators question this and are more inclined to take at face value British protestations of good intent.[112]

India, in this period, was like a giant Benthamite experiment in famine policy, with much dissension within the elite as to the best policy and practice. Policy swung from the extremes of the Orissa famine, 1865–66, when, as we have seen, a traditional East India Company 'classical' (or indeed 'Irish') famine policy saw 1.3 million deaths, to the Bengal and Bihar famine of 1873–74, when at a cost of about £6.5 million, almost everyone was saved.[113] (As Devereux points out, in *Theories of Famine*, it is possible to have a famine in which no one dies.)[114] Each famine in India led to further dissension within the elite, and each famine was followed by an enquiry of one sort or another.[115]

Inden, in his discussion of ideologies and 'the village', speaks of 'the desire to quarantine Ireland'.[116] In essence, in Britain, Ireland and throughout the world, arguments were being won – arguments about democracy, the use of resources, land ownership – won perhaps not rapidly enough to please radical Irish nationalists, but certainly rapidly enough to un-nerve the British elite in India.[117] There was a growing awareness of those areas of policy that could not, with safety, be left to free markets. And, in the emerging democratic age, people – perhaps 'the people' – were being asked to make judgements about the efficacy of governments. The evidence throughout the world is that the people, inevitably, chose policies on food, hunger, and famine, as the test of government.[118]

The link, between Ireland and India, was made most significantly by the Irish nationalist MP, F. Hugh O'Donnell, as he responded to the news of famines in India:

> I had a vivid impression of the criminal folly of the British Government in 1846 and 1847 in permitting the export of the rich harvests of Irish corn, while millions of the people were starving through the failure of the potato crop, which was their habitual food. As they could not get potatoes, they should have got bread. Nobody need starve. But the Manchester economists had decided otherwise in Ireland, where one-sixth of the people had to starve outright. Now it seemed to me there was to be something similar in India.[119]

In 1874, in an effort to stifle criticism of famine policies in India, the British government had published correspondence between the Viceroy and Sir George Campbell, Lieutenant-Governor of Bengal: in the published version the Viceroy's defence of the official policy was given in full; Campbell's objections were briefly summarized. O'Donnell shrewdly seized on this evidence of dissension and control within the ruling elite to make it the subject of his maiden speech in the House of Commons: 'Officialism suffered a heavy exposure. Its own procedure convicted it.'[120]

Thereafter, O'Donnell argued, Irish nationalists should speak for India in the British parliament, and for all the unenfranchised people of the Empire: 'It only wanted knowledge, courage, and skill.'[121] O'Donnell formed an alliance with Dadabhai Naoroji, the future 'Grand Old Man' of Indian nationalism, and with Ganendra Mohun Tagore. 'The inauguration of the Indian Constitutional Reform Association at Tagore's house was attended by 250 people, all Indians except O'Donnell.'[122]

Naoroji, an economic theorist, a follower of Adam Smith, was himself very concerned about the welfare and the wealth of his nation and its 'unrequited exports' to Britain. Naoroji's own book, *Poverty and un-British*

Rule in India, written at that stage when you have to use the imperialist's own rhetoric against him, argues for true British rule, and economic policies, in India.[123]

It has to be said that O'Donnell's policy, of Irish nationalist speaking for India within the British parliament, most probably did as much harm as good within the minds of the British ruling elite in India. Another Irish policy, of obstruction in parliament, attracted a great deal of opprobrium.[124] If men like O'Donnell could exploit dissension within the British elite that was one more reason for putting an end to dissension. And, within the elite, among opponents as well as defenders of the 'classical' famine policy, one more reason for not mentioning Ireland.

Cumulatively, there was by now in British India, an immense amount of knowledge about famine, its patterns, its causes, its prevention. In 1877 the Conservative government in Britain decided there must be a general inquiry, a broad-ranging Famine Commission, which would draw on that knowledge, look to the future and create a famine policy that would stick. As we have seen, and Brennan notes, the Irish experience did not figure largely in discussions among the British elite in the debates in the 1870s leading up to the creation of the Famine Commission. The plain truth is that poor India had by now provided more than enough experience for the Commission to consider – there was now no need to mention Ireland, and many reasons for not mentioning Ireland.

There were also, we think, reasons for not mentioning Malthus. Malthus' theory of population, of course, attracted controversy in his own time. As the century progressed the word 'Malthusian' became associated with debates about birth control, an issue in that time discussed with difficulty, prudery, hypocrisy, and embarrassment. Two key areas of British economic policy in India ultimately depended on the theories of Malthus: the *Essay on Population* shaped famine policy, and the theory of rent had suggested the land revenue. Yet Malthus' name all but disappears from policy discussion and public documents. In documents where we might expect to see his name we find 'Adam Smith', 'political economy', 'inevitable laws' or 'Nature', or a secondary source, 'John Stuart Mill'.

The Famine Commission, 1878–80

The key figures in the shaping of the Famine Commission were the Viceroy, Lord Lytton, and his chief adviser, Sir John Strachey: both, as Ambirajan establishes, confirmed 'Malthusians' and defenders of the 'classical famine policy'.[125] Logistics and practicalities made it fairly easy for Lytton and John Strachey to hijack the Famine Commission. London accepted their suggestion that the Commission be appointed in India, and staffed by the Indian Civil Service, the British elite. Of the nine men on the Commission, six were members of the Indian Civil Service, two were representatives of the princely states. The Commission was to be chaired by General Richard Strachey, John Strachey's brother. Lord Salisbury, in London, the Secretary of State for India, conceded all this, but insisted on at least one outsider, James Caird.

Lytton wanted a unanimous report, to bring an end to scandalous dissension and to impose his will on recalcitrant underlings. For this very reason, the researcher looks with interest at the two minority, 'Notes of Dissent' appended to the final *Report*. The first Note of 'Dissent on certain Points...' is attached to *Famine Relief*, Part I of the *Report of the Indian Famine Commission*, and it is signed by James Caird and H. E. Sullivan. The second 'Note of Dissent' is attached to *Measures of Protection and Prevention*, Part II of the *Report*: it is signed by H. E. Sullivan alone. The Irish specialist will, of course, already have been intrigued by these two names, Caird and Sullivan.

James Caird

James Caird (1816–92), was a Scot, born at Stranraer, a farmer, agricultural theorist and author. Caird first came to public attention in the late 1840s, in the controversy over the repeal of the Corn Laws. In 1849, at the request of Sir Robert Peel, Caird travelled in Ireland to report on conditions there: this report was published in 1850 as *The Plantation System, or the West of Ireland as a Field for Investment*. Peel's untimely death robbed Caird of his patron: but Caird's best known work, *English Agriculture in 1850–51*, appeared in 1852, prefaced, 'with the concurrence of his literary Executors' with a letter to Caird from Peel. *English Agriculture* is a book of advice to English farmers on survival in the new era of free markets, following the repeal of the Corn Laws. Caird was an ardent free trader, a follower of Adam Smith; he was also a radical, a supporter of Cobden and Bright.

Here, on the Indian Famine Commission, at the insistence of the British government in London, was a man with personal knowledge of Ireland in the later stages of the Irish Famine, and the author of two books on Ireland.[126] 'Caird was in the tradition of the great commentators on English agriculture: he reported fairly what he found, and he knew what he wanted to say and was not afraid to say it. We cannot in justice ask for more.' [127]

Henry Edward Sullivan

Henry Edward Sullivan (1830–1905) was born in London, the second son of John Sullivan, of the East India Company, Madras.[128] He was thus a member of one of those (almost) hereditary Indian Civil Service families.[129] When the Famine Commission was established Sullivan was a civil servant, the Collector of Trichinopoly: he was not, in the first instance, invited to serve on the Commission, though he did give evidence. In 1879 one member of the Commission had to drop out due to ill-health, and Sullivan was appointed in his place. And Caird and Sullivan forged their alliance.

There is a continuity between Sullivan's own evidence, the 'Note of

Dissent' which he co-wrote with James Caird, and elements in the final *Report* of the Famine Commission – key phrases make the transition between all three texts.

Sullivan's own evidence to the Commission lists his three starting points for the development of a famine policy:

1. The recognition of the abnormal character of the situation;
2. The consequent necessity for modifying the usual system of administration;
3. A distinct understanding that the primary object of State interference is to *save life*, and that financial considerations are *not* to be allowed to defeat that object.[130]

Sullivan's evidence must be understood as part of the debates within the British elite in India at that time. Thus, a modern famine policy would most probably not start with his first point: it would search in the normal 'character of the situation' for the reasons that make a community vulnerable to famine. But Sullivan's third point – the emphases are in the original – is, of course, a categorical refutation of the thought of Malthus as applied to famine policy, and a categorical refutation of the existing 'classical famine policy', inherited from the East India Company.

Sullivan's categorical assertion is echoed in Caird and Sullivan's joint 'Note of Dissent':

We will assume that the first object of famine administration by the British Government in India will be to save life. In all the famines on record which have occurred in India, that of Behar in 1874 is the only instance in which this object, though at an excessive cost, appears to have been satisfactorily accomplished.[131]

Sullivan is again echoed, in the more formal language of the main *Report*, signed by the entire Famine Commission. The *Report* speaks of the 'Obligation of the State to give relief in time of famine'; the *Report* specifies:

that the calamity shall be one which places it beyond the power of an individual to obtain the requisite relief or efficacious remedy otherwise than with the aid of the State... There can be no doubt that a calamity such as a famine, exceptional in its nature and arising from causes wholly beyond human control, which deprives an entire population of its customary food supply, and arrests the ordinary employments of the wage-earning classes, is one which in a country such as India wholly transcends individual effort and power of resistance. It accordingly becomes a paramount duty of the State to give all practicable assistance to the people in time of famine, and to devote all available resources to this end... We need not entangle ourselves in vain speculations as to the point in which the consequences of giving relief on some imaginary scale of magnitude would become a more grievous evil to the country than the destruction that would follow if famine were left without relief, or with relief known to be insufficient. No such alternative is at all events at present before us.[132]

We have to say that the scholar of Ireland reads such a paragraph, reads all the Famine Commission's *Report* and reads the evidence placed before the Famine Commission, with a troubled heart. Here all the arguments raised against intervention in the Irish famine are again raised – and are dismissed. And here, in the Famine Commission *Report* of 1880, only 30 years after the Irish famine, is outlined a policy whose consequences, in the long term and the short term, had it been followed in Ireland, can only be speculated about. But it is certainly a policy that would have saved lives.

Of course there is much in the Famine Commission's *Report* that is specifically about India. In the paragraph just cited the *Report* declares that 'the Government stands in the place of a landlord to the agriculturalists...' of which more later. Some Irish specialists have looked at British government expenditure in other areas – the freeing of the slaves, the Crimean War – arguing that if the government could justify such expenditure it could justify famine relief in Ireland.[133] In this chapter we have stayed within the debate on famine policy, across the British Empire. Comparison can then be made with the famines in Orissa, 1865–66, when an 'Irish' policy was followed and a fourth of the population died, and in Bengal and Bihar, 1873–74, when, as Caird and Sullivan noted, almost everyone was saved.

The defenders of the 'classical famine policy' had not changed their minds. There is what Ambirajan calls a 'striking' 'Malthusian' document: dated 24 June 1881, a confidential Memorandum on famine expenses submitted to the new Viceroy by Sir George Couper. Here, despite the Famine Commission's *Report*, is the plainest statement of the old policy, and the assumptions behind it.[134] But policy had changed. The 1880 *Report* of the Famine Commission is not in itself a turning point: it is an indication that, some time in the 1870s, a turning point was reached. Some sections of the *Report* only make sense if the reader is aware of the background, the debates and dissension within the elite, and the period of 'experimentation', the trial and error famine policies of the 1870s. Thus substantial parts of the *Report* are given over to explaining why migration should not be part of a famine policy.[135]

Caird and Sullivan

Famine specialists, like Drèze and Brennan, focus on Caird and Sullivan's two practical objections to the main *Report*'s proposals. Caird and Sullivan proposed that only the healthy should be employed on public work, and on a 'piece' system, at 'ordinary rates'. The aged and infirm should be maintained in the villages: 'food should be gratuitously supplied in their villages, on the lowest scale sufficient to maintain health, without exacting other labour than such sanitary or other light work as could be advantageously done near their homes.' 'By thus employing the capable workers, and maintaining the village organization, the distance and other tests, which proved fatal to hundreds of thousands of starving people in the last famine, would be rendered unnecessary.'[136]

Thus in the 1870s Sullivan and his colleagues had seen in action the 'tests' which the 'classical famine policy' deemed necessary to distinguish the really needy from the opportunistic – the tests of work, distance and separation. And they had found that these tests themselves caused death. Caird and Sullivan do not say this, but, of course, the 'distance test' is a kind of forced migration, and the logic of the *Report's* arguments against migration elsewhere can be applied here.

Caird and Sullivan then propose that, for an experimental period, the government store grain in inaccessible areas, where it would be immediately on hand in time of famine.[137] They explicitly quarrel with the government's 'estimated annual surplus yield of five million tons of food grain'. When you look at the day-to-day lives of the Indian people, and when famine strikes, where is this 'surplus'? In one version of his study of famine prevention in India Drèze mentions Caird and Sullivan's 'Note of Dissent' as 'one notable exception' to the belief in a food abundance in India.[138] But we detect a suggestion that Caird and Sullivan do not trust the government: given the vagaries of famine policy they want some food to stay in the villages. The government should 'do for the safety of the poorer classes what the wealthier now do for themselves.'[139] And their 'Note of Dissent' makes better sense when placed within the debates about the 'surplus' within the elite in British India. This 'surplus' is the land revenue, the Malthusian 'rent' – the gift of Providence, you will recall, the landlord's right, which, it was asserted, had no effect on prices.

This interpretation of Caird and Sullivan's joint 'Note of Dissent' is given support by the second 'Note of Dissent', signed by H. E. Sullivan alone, and appended to Part II of the *Report, Measures of Protection and Prevention.* Sullivan begins obliquely, quoting from a speech by the then Finance Minister, before the Legislative Council of India, in 1860, 20 years before: the Minister had argued that the opium revenue could 'in no sense be called a tax', the land revenue could 'only be regarded as rent'. Sullivan then proceeds to attack this view, and to attack the belief that the land revenue, or 'rent', had no effect on prices, had no effect on the resources available to the peasants of India, and could be disregarded in the planning of a famine policy.

> This idea of the Government of India being a vast landed proprietor, and the occupiers of the soil its tenants, was repeatedly brought forward in the course of our discussions, and, although opposed by me to the best of my ability, has found expression here and elsewhere in the Report. I, therefore, now place on record my reasons for dissenting from a doctrine for which I believe there is no historical foundation, which the action of the Government itself goes to disprove, and which if accepted might lead to most mischievious results.'[140]

This, from the Collector of Trichinopoly. If Sullivan's own Evidence to the Commission can be read as a categorical refutation of Malthus on famine, here is a categorical refutation of Malthus on rent.

There is another interesting thing about the first 'Note of Dissent', by Caird and Sullivan together: they mention Ireland. They mention Ireland, in a curiously oblique way, in the preamble to their 'Note of Dissent': 'The people of England can hardly realize the loss by death in the last Indian famine. Upwards of five millions of human beings, more in number than the population of Ireland, perished in that miserable time.'[141] Thus Caird and Sullivan certainly have Ireland in mind. What is more, they assume that their readership in Britain, 'the people of England' will have Ireland in mind, as the 1880 *Report* of the Indian Famine Commission is read. Caird and Sullivan use Ireland to help 'England' to 'imagine India'. In London, in 1880, an enterprising publisher issued a reprint of Charles Trevelyan's *The Irish Crisis*.[142]

Back in England, Caird reported to Parliament, as he had been asked by the Secretary of State for India, on the 'Condition of India'. The British elite in India felt constrained to attack Caird's report, at very great length. It is in his reply to that attack that James Caird makes the brief comment that cuts through 100 years of guff. Caird offers a straightforward Malthusian explanation of famine, which uses the key words 'Nature' and 'surplus'. But this follower of Adam Smith then insists that the ideology of empire cannot let matters rest there. Caird says: 'Nature herself interferes by periodically cutting down by famine the surplus population. If we rest content with this, what becomes of the boasted advantage of our rule to the people of India.'[143]

The Famine Codes

From the 1880 Famine Commission *Report* developed the famous Famine Codes.[144] The Codes were implemented in subsequent famines, and revised by further Famine Commissions. For the sequence of famines in India continued throughout the 1880s and 1890s. But, once the duty of the state to save life had been acknowledged and legitimated, then British decency, ingenuity and hard work, and a portion of India's vast resources, tackled the problems of famine prevention.

The entry on famine in the 1932 *Cambridge History of the British Empire* was written by Sir H. Verney Lovett, who had 'served through two famines, once as district officer and again as commissioner'. Note that word, 'served'. Lovett describes the Famine Codes in action in 'a stricken district'. The district officer, 'consults his copy of the provincial famine code and examines the programmes of relief works which, in obedience to its provisions, have been prepared and revised by his predecessors.' 'Scarcity' is declared. The programmes swing into action, and for each problem there is a solution. (Caird and Sullivan would have been pleased to note that the aged and infirm are helped in the villages.) Lovett's every word breathes pride in caste and a job well done: 'it will always be necessary for the state to see that the helpless and the destitute are not left to starve. But we may surely think that the day of isolated experiments and costly blunders has for ever passed. Out of failures and disappointments has come a broad, deliberate and well-tested policy, a matured and effective plan of campaign.'[145] Ireland's Famine must be placed within the pattern of the British Empire's 'isolated experiments'.

The story does not end there, of course. India's penultimate major famine under British rule occurred in 1902–03. But note that, under the Famine Codes, a famine has to be 'declared', before the preventative measures of the Codes could swing into action. In 1943 the British government in India refused to 'declare' a famine in Bengal.[146] The British Empire was, at that time, fighting a world war, in Europe, Asia and Africa, and the decision was made that resources could not be diverted from the war effort: 3 million people died in the famine in Bengal in 1943.[147] (Maybe Caird and Sullivan were wise not to rely totally on the good intentions of government.) This famine in Bengal it has been suggested, may have been a famine of the type that Adam Smith declared could not occur, a failure of supply, in part at least caused by the collusion of traders.[148]

Famines like that in Bengal in 1943 have led some famine theorists to suggest that a free press and democracy are essential parts of a famine prevention policy.[149] There has to be some procedure for 'whistle-blowing', for alerting the community to approaching danger, even if the government is unwilling to hear that message. There has to be some procedure for holding government to account.

Conclusion

The Irish Famine was but one of the nineteenth-century British Empire's many famines. The nature of the connection, between the British Empire and famine, is still a matter of debate. Some theorists see the imperialist incursion as itself a cause of famine, in imposing demands upon a community other than the one of feeding its own people and in disrupting the ordered development of that community.[150] Others see the British Empire expanding beyond its strength, and beyond its understanding. Certainly, as this chapter has shown, ideologies of understanding within the British Empire actively hindered the Empire from truly understanding the nature of the tasks it had taken on.

Within the early nineteenth-century British Empire there developed a famine policy of non-intervention, the 'classical famine policy', or 'East India Company policy', which drew on elements of the thought of Adam Smith, Jeremy Bentham, Thomas Malthus, James Mill, and John Stuart Mill. This famine policy thus connects directly with debates about the treatment of the poor, and the Poor Laws in England and in Ireland. And this famine policy reached its strongest form at the mid-point of the nineteenth century: the policy can be seen in action in Ireland, 1845-50, and Orissa, 1865-66. It was the experiences of the 1870s famines in India that gave the opponents of the 'classical famine policy' the experience, knowledge and confidence to attack that policy. That policy was attacked from within the British ruling elite in India, for example by H. E. Sullivan, and from without, for example by James Caird and F. Hugh O'Donnell. This chapter has demonstrated the influence of the Irish experience, sometimes indirect, sometimes direct, on policy in India in the 1860s and 1870s and on the explorations of the Famine Commission. It is from the 1880 Famine Commission *Report*, with all its faults and limitations, that twentieth-century thinking about famine policy flows.

The Irish Famine occupies a peculiar privileged place in the discourse of famine, a place not really justified by the strengths of the research literature – though this is changing. Ireland's Famine, at the mid-point of the nineteenth century, so physically and politically close to the heart of the British Empire, does have a pivotal place in the developing understanding of the patterns of famine. Famine theorists want to mention Ireland, drawing on 'common knowledge', but they do little more than *mention* Ireland. It may be that there is a fear that what are usually seen as the 'lessons' of the Irish Famine – that famine cures over-population, and that emigration cures famine – might mislead more than enlighten. The key texts are, in the latter part of the nineteenth century, Charles Trevelyan's *Edinburgh Review* article, 'The Irish Crisis', and, in the latter part of the twentieth century, Cecil Woodham-Smith's, *The Great Hunger*. Both are unsatisfactory, for different reasons. Trevelyan's article is a statement of the 'classical famine policy', with all its ideological and theological underpinnings. Woodham-Smith's book sees the Irish Famine in isolation, and, for that reason, distorts our understanding of it.

The Irish experience was in some ways like, and in other ways unlike, experience of famine elsewhere. We need to understand this, and understand how the Irish Famine fits into the patterns of famine. Otherwise the Irish understanding of the Irish experience will become, in turn, isolated from the experiences of the rest of the world. In our world, we know, we must look to the famines of the twenty-first century, and plan our policies now.[151] It is possible to have a famine in which no one dies.

Notes

1. The first draft of this chapter was written by Patrick O'Sullivan in consultation with Richard Lucking. That draft was then much revised, in the main by Patrick O'Sullivan, after further discussion between the co-authors. The co-authors thank those who commented on early drafts of this chapter, especially colleagues within the University of Bradford, and Cormac Ó Gráda, Janet Nolan and Lance Brennan.
2. Stephen Devereux, *Theories of Famine*, Harvester Wheatsheaf, Hemel Hempstead, London & New York, 1993, p. 71, citing Amartya Sen, 'The food problem: theory and policy', *Third World Quarterly*, Vol. 4, 3, July 1982, p. 456.
3. Cecil Woodham-Smith, *The Great Hunger*, Hamish Hamilton, London, 1962, and many times reprinted.
4. John W. Warnock, *The Politics of Hunger*, Methuen, London & New York, 1987, p. xi, p. xv.
5. Warnock, *Politics of Hunger*, p. xv.
6. Though Warnock's Preface is not referenced he does mention Woodham-Smith, p. xii. Some of the information Warnock gives as fact does not coincide with information given by Woodham-Smith and other writers about the Irish Famine. Thus Warnock, p xii, says of the Irish Famine: 'The results are well known. Within ten years 2 million people starved to death and another two million people emigrated.' These figures are not those given by Woodham-Smith, p. 411, and would not be supported by recent writers on the Irish Famine.

7. Michelle Burge McAlpin, *Subject to Famine: Food Crises and Economic Change in Western India, 1860–1920*, Princeton University Press, Princeton, 1983, pp. 6–7.

8. Jean Drèze and Amartya Sen, *Hunger and Public Action*, Clarendon Press, Oxford, 1989, pp. 21–2.

9. Drèze and Sen, *Hunger and Public Action*, p. 90.

10. Megan Vaughan, *The Story of an African Famine: Gender and Famine in Twentieth-Century Malawi*, Cambridge University Press, Cambridge, 1987, p. 15.

11. R. Dudley Edwards and T. Desmond Williams, *The Great Famine: Studies in Irish History, 1845–52*, Browne & Nolan, Dublin, 1956. A helpful reprint by Lilliput Press, Dublin, 1994, has an Introduction by Cormac Ó Gráda.

12. Thus, W. R. Aykroyd, *The Conquest of Famine*, Chatto & Windus, London, 1974, an optimistic book from a more optimistic era, as its title indicates, cites Edwards and Williams, p. 30.

13. Woodham-Smith, *Great Hunger*, p. 75, p. 165. As we see later, Note 42, this perception was available to the economist, David Ricardo, writing in 1822, before the great Irish Famine.

14. Drèze and Sen, *Hunger and Public Action*: the discussion of 'Intra-household redistribution' is on pp. 79-81. The reference to Cormac Ó Gráda, is in Note 39, p. 80, hidden among references to some 10 studies of other famines. Discussion of gender should also figure in discussion of food distribution within households: see, for example, Vaughan, *An African Famine*, and J. R. Behrman, 'Intra-household allocation of nutrients and gender effects: a survey of structural and reduced-form estimates', in S. R. Osmani, *Nutrition and Poverty*, Clarendon Press, Oxford, 1992.

15. Christopher V. Hill, 'Philosophy and reality in Riparian South Asia: British famine policy and migration in colonial North India', *Modern Asian Studies*, Vol. 25, 2, 1991, p. 264. Hill is here citing Anand A. Yang, *The Limited Raj: Agrarian Relations in Colonial India, Saran District, 1793–1920*, University of California Press, Berkeley, 1989, and Yang is drawing on Albert O. Hirschman, *Exit, Voice and Loyalty: Responses to Decline in Firms, Organisations and States*, Harvard University Press, Cambridge, 1970.

16. Christopher V. Hill, 'British famine policy and migration', pp. 266–7.

17. 'In the wake of the First World War, both Ireland and Finland were prised away from the empires that had long coveted them.'; Cormac Ó Gráda, *Ireland: A New Economic History, 1780–1939*, Clarendon Press, Oxford, 1994, p. 208.

18. See Richard G. Robbins Jr., *Famine in Russia 1891-92: The Imperial Government's Response to a Crisis*, Columbia University Press, New York & London, 1975; Devereux, *Theories of Famine*, has a section on the famine in the Netherlands in 1944, pp. 159 ff.

19. '...as an economy evolves, individual action is no longer a sure means of achieving individual objectives. It was, above all, Albert Hirschman and Amartya Sen who demonstrated that such objectives can best be achieved either by collective action or by tying individual action to a moral code of behaviour, a "richer" code than the mercantile moral code of which Smith and the classical economists spoke, in the sense that, besides honesty and trust, it includes benevolence.' Ernesto Screpanti & Stefano Zamagni, *An Outline of the History of Economic Thought*, Clarendon Press, Oxford, p. 361.

20. Perry Anderson, *English Questions*, Verso, London & New York, 1992, p. 279.

21. Jean Drèze, 'Famine Prevention in India', in Jean Drèze and Amartya Sen (eds),*The Political Economy of Hunger, Volume II: Famine Prevention*, Clarendon Press, Oxford, 1990, p. 20. The quotation is from the *Report of the Indian Famine*

Commission, HMSO, London, 1880, p. 31. (Hereafter, Famine Commission, *Report*).

The three volumes of Drèze and Sen (eds), *Political Economy of Hunger*, published by the Clarendon Press (Volume I, *Entitlement and Well-Being*, 1990, Volume II, *Famine Prevention*, 1990, Volume III, *Endemic Hunger*, 1991), bring together much thought and research based on conferences and a research programme based at the World Institute for Development Economics Research (WIDER), Helsinki. Some of the papers in Drèze and Sen, *Political Economy of Hunger*, had previously been published as individual WIDER pamphlets, and sometimes these earlier versions differ from the version published in Drèze and Sen. For an example see Note 138 below.

22. Drèze, 'Famine prevention in India', p. 20. Limitations of space forbid our extending the discussion here to consideration of famine in Africa.

23. Lance Brennan, 'The development of the Indian Famine Codes: personalities, policies and politics', in Bruce Currey and Graeme Hugo (eds), *Famine as a Geographical Phenomenon*, Reidel, Dordrecht, 1984, pp. 92–3.

24. Brennan, 'Indian Famine Codes', p. 93.

25. Christine Kinealy, *This Great Calamity: The Irish Famine, 1845–52*, Gill & Macmillan, Dublin, 1994, p. 23.

26. It is for this reason, of course, that the work of Sen on famine and food 'entitlement' connects with the study of the history of the poor, the working class, dearth, famine and death in England and throughout Europe. We have found Roger Wells review article, 'E.P. Thompson, *Customs in Common* and Moral Economy', *Journal of Peasant Studies*, Vol. 21, No. 2, January 1994, a most helpful outline of these connections. See also John Walter and Roger Schofield (eds), *Famine, Disease and the Social Order in Early Modern Society*, Cambridge University Press, Cambridge, 1989, whose first chapter, by Walter and Schofield themselves, 'Famine, disease and crisis in early modern society', is an excellent introduction to the work of Andrew Appleby, mentioning Sen (p. 32). Appleby's work has had surprisingly little influence on research into Irish famines, but the connections are there: see Walter and Schofield on 'the ecology of famine', p. 22.

27. Stephen Devereux, *Theories of Famine*, p. 5.

28. S. R. Osmani, *Food and the History of India – an 'Entitlement' Approach*, World Institute for Development Economic Research [WIDER], Helsinki, 1988, pp. 44–5.

29. Warnock, *Politics of Hunger*, p. 110. See pp. 108–12 for his section on the increase in the number of famines under British rule, part of a more general chapter on the European impact on Asia.

30. 'Throughout the nineteenth century, Mill's *History* remained the hegemonic textbook of Indian history. Later Indologists have either (wittingly or not) reiterated his constructs of India or they have (directly or indirectly) written their accounts as responses to it.' 'Mill, who had written his *History* in the hope of making money on its sales, succeeded not only in that; he obtained a post with the East India Company (as did his son, the more famous John Stuart) in 1819, eventually becoming Examiner of Correspondence in 1830.' Ronald Inden, *Imagining India*, Blackwell, Oxford, 1990, p. 165, p. 45. That second point is worth stressing: James Mill wrote his *History* before becoming an employee of the East India Company.

Eric Stokes, *The English Utilitarians and India*, Clarendon Press, Oxford, 1959, sees James Mill – rather than his 'more famous' son, John Stuart Mill – as the key figure in transmitting utilitarian influences to the British elite in India, and the key figure in shaping and defending East India Company economic policy. In fairness, as Stokes points out (p. 53), one of Mill's main aims in the *History* was to dispel the 'silly sentimental admiration of oriental despotism which had marked the early thinkers of the Enlightment.' – Voltaire, for example.

31. This point is made quite independently, in a quite different context, by Megan Vaughan, *An African Famine*, p. 59: 'The neo-Malthusian theory employed in explaining the 1949 famine refers implicitly to some "natural" state of affairs existing in pre-colonial times, when there was assumed to be a balance between population and resources... What is clear, however, is that by the late nineteenth century, when the first Europeans arrived, the economy and society of this area had undergone rapid transformation, and that the scene which greeted the first European arrivals was anything but "natural". Not only was population distribution very skewed (an important factor when Europeans started to alienate land), but the area was most probably experiencing an absolute population decline.'

32. David Washbrook, 'Economic depression and the making of "traditional" society in colonial India, 1820–1855', *Transactions of the Royal Historical Society*, Sixth Series, III, London, 1993, p. 237.

33. The scholar of Irish cultural history will at once place Inden's *Imagining India* alongside David Cairns and Shaun Richards, *Writing Ireland: Colonialism, Nationalism and Culture*, Manchester University Press, Manchester, 1988.

34. B. M. Bhatia, *Famines in India*, Asia Publishing House, Bombay, 1967, pp. 7–8.

35. S. Ambirajan, *Classical Political Economy and British Policy in India*, Cambridge University Press, Cambridge, 1978, p. 64. Roger Wells sees these subsistence crises in England as the impetus to Thomas Malthus' development of the 'Theory of population': Roger Wells, *Wretched Faces: Famine in Wartime England, 1763–1801*, Alan Sutton, Gloucester, 1988.

36. Famine Commission, *Report*, p. 31.

37. Ambirajan, *Classical Political Economy*, p. 72. The quotation is from Elphinstone's Minute, dated 17 February 1839, where Elphinstone also cites Edmund Burke. See also, for example, J. S. Narayan Rao, 'Adam Smith in India', in Hirosgi Mizuta and Chuhei Sugiyama (eds), *Adam Smith: International Perspectives*, Macmillan, Basingstoke & London, 1993, p. 264. Ambirajan later, pp. 81-2, cites Thomas' and Sullivan's Notes and Minutes: their argument is essentially about the applicability of Adam Smith to India. For further remarks on John Sullivan see Note 129 below.

38. Amartya Sen, 'Food, economics and entitlements', in Drèze and Sen, *Entitlement and Well-Being*, Volume 1 of *The Political Economy of Hunger*, p. 45.

39. J. S. Narayan Rao, 'Adam Smith in India', p. 265.

40. Adam Smith concludes 'Of Colonies', Chapter VII of Book IV of *The Wealth of Nations* thus: 'Such exclusive companies, therefore, are nuisances in every respect; always more or less inconvenient to the countries in which they are established, and destructive to those which have the misfortune to fall under their government.' See p. 137, Volume 2 of the readily available Everyman edition, Adam Smith, *The Wealth of Nations*, with an Introduction by Edwin R. A. Seligman, Dent & Sons, London, 1910, and many times reprinted. *The Wealth of Nations* first appeared in 1776–78.

41. Alexander Bain, *James Mill: A Biography*, Kelley, New York, 1967 (reprint of first edition, Longmans, Green & Co., London, 1882), p. 348.

42. When scholars of Indian subsistence crises need to quote the 'classical economists' on British knowledge and policies the quotations will, as likely as not, refer to Ireland. See, Amartya Sen, 'Food economics and entitlements', in Drèze and Sen (eds), *Political Economy of Hunger*, Volume 1, *Entitlement and*

Well-Being, p. 40. Sen here wants to demonstrate that the classical economists were aware that famines could arise when there was no shortage of food – and he quotes Ricardo on Ireland. The quotation is from a speech that Ricardo wrote for delivery in Parliament in 1822, though he did not, in the event make the speech: Ricardo objects to the views of 'an honourable gentleman' who sees 'a manifest contradiction' in the news that 'people are dying for want of food in Ireland, and the farmers are said to be suffering from superabundance': 'Where was the contradiction in supposing that in a country where wages were regulated mainly by the price of potatoes the people should be suffering the greatest distress if the potato crop failed and their wages were inadequate to purchase the dearer commodity corn. From whence was the money to come to enable them to purchase the grain however abundant it might [be] if its price far exceeds that of potatoes…'. As Sen observes, the 'honourable gentleman' has confused, as many people do, supply with command. Ricardo thus anticipates Sen's 'entitlement' approach to food crises. Ricardo also anticipates the Famine in Ireland.

43. 'Of the wages of labour', Chapter VIII, of Book I of Smith, *The Wealth of Nations*, p. 65, Volume 1 of the Everyman edition.

44. 'Digression concerning the Corn Trade and Corn Laws', part of 'Bounties', Chapter V of Book IV of Smith, *The Wealth Of Nations*, p. 26, p. 38, Volume 2 of the Everyman edition.

45. Sen, 'Food, economics and entitlement', p. 43, p. 44. Here, on p. 44, is one of the places where Sen cites the Wollo Famine of 1973, Bangladesh in 1984, and 'most spectacularly' the 'Irish famines' as examples of the fact that 'food often does move *out of* the famine-stricken regions to elsewhere…'.

46. Sen, 'Food, economics and entitlement', p. 45.

47. Indeed, at times in the drafting of this chapter, we felt tempted to resort to the typographic devices of the semiotic theorists, writing 'Adam Smith' when we meant Adam Smith the person, <Adam Smith> when we mean the writings of Adam Smith, and even <<Adam Smith>> when we mean the writings and thought of Adam Smith, as interpreted and sometimes put into action, or inaction, by the East India Company and the British Empire in India.

48. S. Ambirajan, *Classical Political Economy and British Policy in India*, Cambridge University Press, Cambridge, 1978, p. 72.

49. Patricia James, *Population Malthus: His Life and Times*, Routledge & Kegan Paul, London, 1979, p. 174.

50. Penderel Moon, *The British Conquest and Dominion of India*, Duckworth, London, 1989, p. 486.

51. Eric Roll, *A History of Economic Thought*, Faber and Faber, London, new and revised edition 1992, p. 511.

52. William Thomas, *Mill*, Oxford University Press, Oxford, 1985, p. 21, notes that Macaulay thought that this 'first principle' was a tautology: 'it merely amounted to saying that a man would rather do what a man would rather do'. It might – to return to our discussion earlier – give a parent 'pleasure' to go hungry and give what food there is to the children: there is an example of precisely that in Roger J. McHugh, 'The Famine in Irish oral tradition', in Edwards & Williams (eds), *The Great Famine*, p. 404.

53. Bentham cited in Thomas, *Mill*, p. 6.

54. We suggest this formulation (derived from standard philosophy textbooks and, for example, from Thomas, *Mill*, p. 6) because ideas like 'utilitarianism', or 'the greatest happiness of the greatest number', do not come to grips with the use made of the thought of Jeremy Bentham by policy makers. Thomas, *Mill*, p. 6, comments: 'The principle of utility (from which the popular name

of the whole outlook rather confusingly derives) embraced both an ethical and a psychological theory.'

55. Stokes, *English Utilitarians and India*, p. 149. Elphinstone planned to build a Panopticon-style prison on Bombay Island (Stokes, p. 325).

56. Michel Foucault, *Discipline and Punish*, translated by Alan Sheridan, Pantheon, New York, 1977, cited in Inden, *Imagining India*, p. 168.

57. Inden, *Imagining India*, p. 168.

58. These reflections are suggested by Brennan, 'Indian Famine Codes', p. 92.

59. Bentham, cited in Thomas, *Mill*, p. 19.

60. James, *Population Malthus*, p. 103 onwards.

61. Eric Roll, *Economic Thought*, p. 109, p. 111. On Steuart and Franklin see James, *Population Malthus*, pp. 103–05.
    On Cantillon see Antoin E. Murphy, 'Richard Cantillon – an Irish banker in Paris', *Hermathena*, No. CXXXV, Winter 1983; Richard Cantillon, *Essai sur la Nature du Commerce en Général*, edited with a translation by Henry Higgs, MacMillan & Co., for the Royal Economic Society, London, 1931: this edition reprints the 1881 essay by W. Stanley Jevons, 'Richard Cantillon and the Nationality of Political Economy'. Jevons says (p. 347) of Cantillon's Chapter XV: 'The chapter is simply Malthus's celebrated Essay, condensed by anticipation into twenty-seven pages. But I am not aware that Malthus ever saw the book and should think it very unlikely that he knew anything about it.' Jevons also points out (p. 346) that Adam Smith misquotes Cantillon.

62. Darwin is quite clear about the stimulus that Malthus gave to his thought: 'In October 1838 I happened to read for amusement "Malthus on Population" and being well prepared to appreciate the struggle for existence which everywhere goes on from long-continued observation of the habits of animals and plants it at once struck me that under these circumstances favourable variations would tend to be preserved, and unfavourable ones to be destroyed... Here then I had at last got a theory by which to work.' And, in *The Origin of Species*, Darwin writes: 'It is the doctrine of Malthus applied with manifold force to the whole animal and vegetable kingdoms; for in this case there can be no artificial increase of food, and no prudent restraint from marriage.' See Mark Ridley, *A Darwin Selection*, Fontana, London, 1994, p. 12, p. 89. And you will find a section on Malthus at the beginning of every ecology textbook.

63. James, *Population Malthus*, p. 62. Two rigorous explorations of Malthus' theory, within two different disciplines, are Joel Mokyr, *Why Ireland Starved*, Allen & Unwin, London, 1983, Chapter 3 (on its application to Ireland), and Alec Fisher, *The Logic of Real Arguments*, Cambridge University Press, Cambridge, 1988, Chapter 3 (on its internal coherence as a work of philosophy).

64. Donald Winch, *Malthus*, Oxford University Press, Oxford, 1987, p. 18.

65. Winch, *Malthus*, p. 34.

66. Winch, *Malthus*, p. 34; James, *Population Malthus*, p. 67.

67. James, *Population Malthus*, p. 109.

68. James, *Population Malthus*, p. 61, p. 109, p. 375.

69. Rosanna Ledbetter, *A History of the Malthusian League, 1877-1927*, Ohio State University Press, Columbus, 1976.

70. James, *Population Malthus*, p. 368; Ledbetter, *Malthusian League*, p. 7

71. James, *Population Malthus*, pp. 142–59. See also Cormac Ó Gráda, 'Malthus and the pre-famine economy', *Hermathena*, No. CXXXV, Winter 1983.

72. James, *Population Malthus*, p. 173.

73. William Petersen, *Malthus*, Heineman, London, 1979, p. 32.

74. Roger Wells, 'E.P. Thompson, *Customs in Common* and Moral Economy', pp. 283–4.

75. S. Ambirajan, 'Malthusian population theory and Indian famine policy in the nineteenth century', *Population Studies*, Vol. 30, No. 1, 1976, p. 5.
76. Ambirajan, 'Malthusian population theory'; Simon Commander, 'Malthus and the theory of "unequal powers": Population and Food Production in India, 1800–1947', *Modern Asian Studies*, Vol. 20, No. 4, 1986.
77. Ambirajan, 'Malthusian population theory', p. 5.
78. Kinealy, *This Great Calamity*, p. 8.
79. Ambirajan, *Classical Political Economy and India*, p. 100.
80. James, *Population Malthus* p. 279. See also the discussion in Stokes, *English Utilitarians and India*, Chapter II, 'Political economy and the land revenue', especially p. 87, p. 90.
81. James, *Population Malthus*, pp. 279–80. Malthus' theory of rent was opposed by his contemporary, David Ricardo, in Chapter XXXII, 'Mr. Malthus's Opinions on Rent', of *The Principles of Political Economy and Taxation*: 'Mr Malthus's proposition is much too universal...' (see p. 275, of Ricardo, *Principles of Political Economy*, with an Introduction by Donald Winch, Everyman, London, 1973). And Patricia James believes that the theory effectively disproved by Richard Jones, Malthus' successor at Haileybury (James *Population Malthus*, pp. 283–4).
82. McAlpin, *Subject to Famine*, p. 109.
83. Stokes, *English Utilitarians and India*, p. 137. Of the early twentieth century British administrators in India Stokes says (p. 139), 'It was they who upheld most faithfully the ideas of James Mill and the early Benthamites, and it was fitting that the rent theory should find among them its last convinced adherents.' In fact it is difficult to judge quite how convinced any of the British elite in India were by the 'theory of rent': they were interested in extracting revenue, and the 'theory of rent' provided a rationale.
84. Stokes, *English Utilitarians and India*, p. 138.
85. Cormac Ó Gráda, *The Great Irish Famine*, Macmillan, Basingstoke and London, 1989, p. 77, speaking of S. Ambirajan, *Classical Political Economy and India*. The Irish specialist will immediately put Ambirajan, *Classical Political Economy*, and Stokes, *English Utilitarians and India*, alongside R. D. Collison Black, *Economic Thought and the Irish Question*, Cambridge University Press, Cambridge, 1960.
86. Christopher V. Hill, 'Famine policy and migration in South Asia', p. 267. Hill records that Trevelyan 'felt that Ireland's "greatest evil" was not scarcity but "the selfish, perverse and turbulent character of the people" ': Hill's source is Miller, *Emigrants and Exiles*, p. 283.
87. Kinealy, *This Great Calamity*, p. 53, pp. 248–9; Ó Gráda, *Ireland: A New Economic History*, p. 193; Jennifer Hart, 'Sir Charles Trevelyan at the Treasury', *English Historical Review*, LXXV, 1960. Edmund Burke can be cited to support intervention in time of 'famine', as opposed to 'scarcity' (Thomas P. O'Neill, 'The organisation and administration of relief, 1845–52', in Edwards and Williams, *The Great Famine*, p. 259).
88. Kinealy, *This Great Calamity*, p. xviii.
89. Hart, 'Sir Charles Trevelyan'.
90. Roger Wells, *Wretched Faces: Famine in Wartime England, 1763–1803*, Alan Sutton, Gloucester, 1988; John D. Post, *The Last Great Subsistence Crisis in the Western World*, Johns Hopkins University Press, Baltimore, 1977, draws attention to a distinctively English traditional, interventionist famine policy. Hill, 'Famine policy and migration in South Asia', p. 272, feels that one cause of problems within British famine policy in Bengal in 1873-74 was 'the Eurocentrism exemplified in the use of the Irish model. Any attempt to copy the "solution" to the Irish famine ignored the societal and environmental phe-

nomena of the Bengal Presidency.' Hill offers a most interesting essay, making many connections between the Indian and the Irish experiences: but we think it unwise to describe 'the Irish model' as 'Eurocentric'.

91. Mokyr, *Why Ireland Starved*, pp. 291–2; Kinealy, *This Great Calamity*, pp. 351–2; Cormac Ó Gráda, *Ireland: A New Economic History*, p. 191. Ó Gráda gives the example of the Lancashire 'cotton famine' in the 1860s, which prompted subsidized loans of £1.5 d and the relaxation of the Poor Laws.

92. Trevelyan, 'The Irish Crisis', *Edinburgh Review*, Vol. 87, No. CLXXV, 1848, pp. 229-320, speaks, p. 229, of 'the great Irish famine of 1847', and concludes, p. 320, that 'the deep and inveterate root of social evil... has been laid bare by a direct stroke of an all-wise and all-merciful Providence...'.

93. Kinealy, *This Great Calamity*, p. 359.

94. The British always had problems running India at a profit – hence the importance of the Indian opium harvest and the export of opium to China. But large scale accounting procedures disguise the extent to which specific groups benefited from the British Empire. 'Much, no doubt, remains to be said concerning the relationship between Empire and economics. But perhaps, when all is said and done, Cecil Rhodes came closest to summing the whole thing up when he said, not totally in jest, that imperialism was nothing more than philanthropy plus 5 per cent! But philanthropy for whom? It appears that imperialism can best be viewed as a mechanism for transferring income from the middle to the upper classes... the Elites and the colonies with responsible government were clear winners; the middle class, certainly, and the dependent Empire, probably, were losers. A strange kind of philanthropy – socialism for the rich, capitalism for the poor.' Lance E. Davis and Robert A. Huttenback, *Mammon and the Pursuit of Empire: The Economics of British Imperialism*, Cambridge University Press, Cambridge, abridged edition 1988, p. 279.

95. C. R. G. Hambly, 'Richard Temple and the Punjab Tenancy Act of 1868', *English Historical Review*, LXXIX, 1964, p. 47, p. 49.

96. Cited in Hambly, 'Richard Temple', p. 61.

97. Hambly, 'Richard Temple', p. 61.

98. Ambirajan, *Classical Political Economy and India*, p. 74, p. 76; Brennan, 'Famine Codes', p. 94.

99. Minutes and Reports, 1867, cited in Ambirajan, *Classical Political Economy and India*, p. 79.

100. Ambirajan, *Classical Political Economy and India*, p. 79, Note 72.

101. Ambirajan, *Classical Political Economy and India*, p. 84.

102. Devereux, *Theories of Famine*, p. 48–9.

103. Christopher V. Hill, 'British famine policy and migration', p. 268.

104. 'Report on the Condition of the Lower Classes of Population in Bengal', 1888, commonly known as the 'Dufferin Report', cited in Hill, 'British famine policy and migration', p. 267. We have to add that emigration was offered as the solution to *every* problem in nineteenth-century Britain.

105. Hambly, 'Richard Temple', pp. 62–3.

106. William Wilson Hunter, *The Earl of Mayo*, Clarendon Press, Oxford, 1892, p. 35.

107. Trevelyan, 'The Irish Crisis', p. 315.

108. Nicholas Flood Davin, *The Irishman in Canada*, Irish University Press, Shannon, 1969 (reprint of first edition of 1877), is dedicated to Dufferin and (p. 662 onwards) concludes with high praise for Dufferin as Governor-General of Canada.

109. Lord Dufferin and the Hon. G. F. Boyle (Earl of Glasgow), *Narrative of a Journey from Oxford to Skibbereen During the Year of the Irish Famine*, Parker, Oxford,

1847. Dufferin maintained an interest in Irish issues: see, for example, his *Irish Emigration and the Tenure of Land in Ireland*, Willis, Sotheran & Co., London, 1867 (abridged edition, John Falconer, Dublin, 1870.)

110. Brennan, 'Indian Famine Codes', p. 95.

111. A. K. Banerji, *Aspects of Indo-British Economic Relations, 1858–1898*, Oxford University Press, Bombay, 1982, p. 6.

112. For example, McAlpin, *Subject to Famine*, pp. 217–18.

113. Brennan, 'Indian Famine Codes', pp. 94–5. There were 23 famine-related deaths in Bengal.

114. Devereux, *Theories of Famine*, pp. 17–18.

115. Brennan, 'Indian Famine Codes', p. 95.

116. Inden, *Imagining India*, p. 142. See also Clive Dewey, 'Images of the village community: a study in Anglo-Indian Ideology', *Modern Asian Studies*, Vol. 6, No. 3, 1972, especially p. 317 onwards.

117. Thus Dewey, 'Images of the village community', p. 317, sees the Irish Land Act of 1881 as alarming property-owners everywhere and forcing a re-think by British elite theorists of the Indian village.

118. For example, Robbins, *Famine in Russia*, says (p. 176): 'the famine was the beginning of the end for Imperial Russia... . The autocracy had always been justified because it had made Russia a powerful, modern nation. The disaster of 1891–92 gave the lie to that claim. The great states of Europe did not suffer famine; only backward, colonial lands like China, Ireland, and India starved.'

119. F. Hugh O'Donnell, *A History of the Irish Parliamentary Party*, Longmans, Green & Co., London, 1910, Volume 1, p. 104.

120. O'Donnell, *Irish Parliamentary Party*, Volume 1, p. 105.

121. O'Donnell, *Irish Parliamentary Party*, Volume 1, p. 105.

122. Mary Cumpston, 'Some early Indian Nationalists and their allies in the British Parliament, 1851–1906', *English Historical Review*, LXXVI, 1961, p. 297.

123. Rao, 'Adam Smith in India', p. 268. See Dadabhai Naoroji, *Poverty and un-British Rule in India* , Ministry of Information and Broadcasting, Government of India, Delhi, 1962 (Original edition: Swan Sonneschian, London, 1901). On a plan to elect Naoroji to a Home Rule seat in Ireland see: O'Donnell, *Irish Parliamentary Party*, Michael Davitt, *The Fall of Feudalism in Ireland*, Harper, London, 1904, p. 447; Cumpston, 'Early Indian Nationalists', p. 285.

124. 'The association of Indian nationalism with Irish torment did not aid the Indian cause in parliament.' – Cumpston, 'Early Indian Nationalists', p. 286.

125. Ambirajan, 'Malthusian population theory', p. 6, p. 9.

126. James Caird, *The Plantation Scheme, or the West of Ireland as a Field for Investment*, Blackwood & Sons, Edinburgh & London, 1850; *The Irish Land Question*, Longmans & Co., London, 1869. Caird is cited approvingly by E. R. R. Green, 'Agriculture', in Edwards and Williams, *The Great Famine*, pp. 119–20.

127. G. E. Mingay, 'Introduction to the Second Edition', in James Caird, *English Agriculture in 1850–51*, Frank Cass, London, 1968, p. xxvii (original edition 1852). There is an entry on Caird in the DNB.

128. There is a brief entry on Henry Edward Sullivan in *Who Was Who, 1897–1916*.

129. John Sullivan, Henry Edward's father, is most probably the same John Sullivan mentioned in Note 37 above, so we may have here a family tradition of opposition to the harsher famine policy. But this is a question that requires detailed archival research, and the archivist of the East India Company urges caution: 'It is difficult to distinguish between J. Sullivan and J. Sulivan, and between John Stewart Sulivan and John Sullivan. Both of the latter were in the Madras Civil Service about the same time.' Samuel Charles Hill, *Catalogue of*

the *Home Miscellaneous Series of the India Office Records*, HMSO, London, 1927, p. 660. Further, in some standard histories, 'John Sullivan is confused with his uncle Laurence Sulivan,' the Director of the East India Company (C. H. Philips, *The East India Company, 1784–1834*, Manchester University Press, Manchester, 1940, p. 102). In British records in this period 'Sulivan', with one 'l', usually, but not always, indicates a member of the Cornish family, whose Irish origins lie in the early eighteenth century.

130. H. E. Sullivan's Evidence, Famine Commission, *Accounts & Papers*, Vol. LXXI, Part III, Government of India, London, 1881, p. 380. The emphasis is in the original.

131. Caird and Sullivan, 'Note of Dissent', p. 64.

132. Famine Commission, *Report*, pp. 34–5.

133. Mokyr, *Why Ireland Starved*, p. 292; Kinealy, *This Great Calamity*, p. 351; Cormac Ó Gráda, *Ireland: A New Economic History*, p. 191.

134. 'If we are to secure that a class of men – so low in intellect, morality, and possessions, the retention of which makes life valuable, as to be absolutely independent of natural population checks – shall be protected from every cause, such as famine or sickness, which tends to restrain their numbers by an abnormal mortality, they must end up by eating every other class in the community.' Couper's confidential Memorandum, dated 24 June 1881, cited in Ambirajan, 'Malthusian population theory', p. 9. Ambirajan notes that Couper not only believed in these ideas but also used them in administering the 1878 famine in the North West.

135. Famine Commission, *Report*, Part I, pp. 61–2, Part II, 179–81. Granted that there are limitations to the Famine Commission's *Report*, these sections and subsequent developments in famine theory should cause us to question whether the link between famine and emigration, so strong in Irish historiography, is as clear-cut as is often assumed. See also Ambirajan, 'Malthusian population theory', pp. 12–13.

136. Caird and Sullivan, 'Note of Dissent', p. 65; Brennan, 'Indian Famine Codes', p. 103.

137. Caird and Sullivan, 'Note of Dissent', p. 67.

138. The Drèze paper, 'Famine prevention in India', in Drèze and Sen, Volume II, *Famine Prevention*, 1990, was first published as Jean Drèze, *Famine Prevention in India*, WIDER, Helsinki, 1988. In that Drèze WIDER pamphlet there is the reference, in Note 11, p. 11, to the Caird and Sullivan 'Note of Dissent' cited here: this reference is missing from the version of the Drèze paper published in the Drèze and Sen volume.

139. Caird and Sullivan, 'Note of Dissent', p. 67.

140. Sullivan, 'Note of Dissent', Part II of the *Report of the Famine Commission, Measures of Protection and Prevention*, HMSO, London, 1880, p. 183, p. 184. See also Bhatia, *Famines in India*, pp. 32–3.

141. Caird and Sullivan, 'Note of Dissent', p. 64

142. Charles Trevelyan, *The Irish Crisis*, Macmillan, London, 1880.

143. See 'Mr. Caird's Report on the Condition of India', Parliamentary Papers, LIII, 1880, pp. 3–16, the Government of India's rejoinder, pp. 16–43 (this has seven signatories, including Lytton and John Strachey), and Caird's Reply, pp. 43–6: the quotation is from p. 45 of Caird's Reply.

144. The Commission itself did not draw up a Famine Code; a draft code was developed by Charles Elliot, the Commission's secretary, in line with the majority findings and his own experiences in the North West and in Mysore, then circulated for comment. See Brennan, 'Indian Famine Codes', p. 91, pp. 106–07. For a critical survey of the Famine Codes in action, from 1880 to the

present, see Drèze, 'Famine Prevention in India'.

145. Sir H. Verney Lovett, 'The development of Famine Policy', in H. H. Dodwell (ed.), *The Cambridge History of the British Empire*, Volume V, *The Indian Empire 1858–1918*, Cambridge University Press, Cambridge, 1932, p. 304, p. 305, p. 313.

146. Drèze, 'Famine prevention in India', p. 33,

147. Devereux, *Theories of Famine*, p. 70; Drèze and Sen, *Hunger and Public Action*, p. 5. Paul Greenough, *Prosperity and Misery in Modern Bengal, 1943–1944*, Oxford University Press, Oxford, 1982, is a very distressing account of that famine.

148. A. Sen, *Poverty and Famines*, Clarendon Press, Oxford, 1981, p. 165.

149. See, for example, N. Ram, 'An independent press and anti-hunger strategies: the Indian experience', in Drèze and Sen (eds), *Entitlement and Well-Being*; Drèze and Sen, *Hunger and Public Action*, p. 278.

150. Warnock, *Politics of Hunger*, Chapter 5, 'The European impact on Asia', p. 107 onwards. This is the argument developed and applied to the Irish context by Raymond Crotty, *Ireland in Crisis: A Study of Capitalist Colonial Undevelopment*, Brandon, Dingle, 1986.

151. Some who read this chapter in draft asked, at this stage, for a word of hope. Drèze and Sen, *Hunger and Public Action*, is a good starting point; and we recommend two books by Colin Tudge, *The Famine Business*, Faber and Faber, London, 1977, and *Future Cook: A Taste of Things to Come*, Mitchell Beazley, London, 1980.

Index

The reader's attention is drawn to the indexer's note on page 222 of *Patterns of Migration*, Volume 1 of *The Irish World Wide*.

Cumulative series index

The reader's attention is once again drawn to the indexer's note on page 222 of *Patterns of Migration*, Volume 1 of *The Irish World Wide*. However, note that in this Cumulative Series Index the contents of specific chapters are only briefly indexed under their main headings: for detailed lists of chapter contents readers should continue to use the indexes to the separate volumes.

Readers are reminded of the patterns within the 6 volumes of *The Irish World Wide*. Volume 1 offers a series of case studies, Volume 2 continues that pattern with a series of case studies linked to theoretical chapters. Volume 3 focuses on culture and artistic activity, Volume 4 focuses on women, Volume 5 on religion, and Volume 6 on the Irish Famine.

The Cumulative Series Index absorbs the six separate indexes to the 6 volumes of *The Irish World Wide*. Within the Cumulative Series Index volume numbers are given in **BOLD**. Within complex entries citations are listed in volume order, giving all the possible citations within Volume **1** before moving on to Volume **2**, and so on. Numbers in brackets after a name, thus 'Akenson, Donald Harman (**2**/4)' or 'Miller, Kerby A. (**4**/2)' indicate that this person is a contributor to *The Irish World Wide*: the first number in **BOLD** indicates the volume number of the contribution, the second number indicates the chapter number within that volume.

Wexford **1** migration to
Argentina 69, 70, origins
of Murphy family 85–87
Whately, Archbishop Robin
6 20, 158
Whitaker Anne-Maree
(5/1) **5** 11
White, Patrick **3** 126
Whiteboys **1** 111; **2** 136;
see also vigilantes
Whitman, Walt **3** 45
Whyte, John, *Interpreting
Northern Ireland* **2** 10
Wibberley, Leonard Patrick
O'Connor **3** 136
widows **4** 134–135
'Wild Geese' **1** the Irish in
European armies 36–62;
2 other birds of passage
15; **4** women 'Wild
Geese' 23–40; **5** 10
Wilde, Oscar **3** 83, 84, 107;
5 117
Wilde, William **6** 113
Williams, Raymond **3** 1,
230
Williams, W.H.A. **5** 45
Williamson, George **3** 91
Williamson, Jeffrey G. **2** 62
Wilmington, Delaware **5**
70
Wilson, Christopher P. **3**
57, 58, 60–61, 64
Winter, George **2** 128,
132–136 *passim*
Wiseman, Capel, Bishop of
Dromore **3** 103, 104
Wiseman, Cardinal
Nicholas **5** 202, 207
Wittke, Carl **2** 235, 236
'Wobblies' *see* Industrial
Workers of the World
Wodehouse, P.G. **3** 84, 97,
108
Wogan, Charles and
Jacobite cause **1** 50–51
woman **3** image of Ireland
as 122, image of
Australia as 123; **4**
ideal/ image 7, 49–50,
70, 79, 140, 160, 220, 222,
226, image of Ireland as
7; **5** Ireland as woman
133, US South as
woman 106
Women's Aid **4** 187–188
women's history **4** 11, 41,
113

women's studies **4** 4–11
women *see* Volume **4**
passim; **1** 169, 173, 179,
196–221 *passim*, 200, 210,
Argentina 77, 81, Irish
poor in England
1560–1640 21, 20, 23,
dowry 156, higher
status of Irish in
Australia 167, labour
legislation, Boston 132,
servants 21, single
(unmarried) women 81,
widow's pensions 40,
'Wild Geese' 40,
women's history xviii;
2 180, mental illness
201–225 *passim*,
especially 201, 206; **3**
cinematic 174, 175–176,
dance 18, 194, 200,
dance costumes 196,
204, 209, 213, dance
teachers 194, 196, 202,
203–207, 209, 213; **4**
absence from history 3,
6–7, 24–25, 37, 41, 113,
175, absence from
migration studies 1–2,
41, 89, 113, 131, 146, 175,
192–193, Emigrant
Advice agency 14,
168–191, emigration,
1922–71, 146–167;
female-headed
households, 131–145,
left behind 14, 31–32,
185–187, lesbian women
179, 200 *n*6, 217, 226,
Liverpool, women in
nineteenth century,
89–112, London,
middle-class women in,
201–234, pauper women
66–88, Philadelphia,
women workers in
113–130, women 'Wild
Geese' 23–40; **5** 14 and
Catholicism 187,
191–192, image of
132–133, women; **6**
135, 208, and migration,
174 181–182, 189–191;
see also deaths, Vere
Foster, gender, Irish Female
Emigration Fund,
Lerner, nuns, men,
woman, working class

Wood, Charles **6** 141, 156,
166
Woodham-Smith, Cecil, *The
Great Hunger* **6** 2, 5, 17,
18, 43, 52, 195–196, 222
Woods, Julian Tenison **5**
234–235, 238–243 *passim*,
250, death 239,
excommunication 238
Woodward, Vann **5** 94
woollen industry **6** 23
workhouse **4** 66–88 *passim*,
see also pauper women,
Poor Law
working class **1** 7, 135, 179,
193; **2** Butte, Montana
82–98 *passim*, especially
86–89, Manchester
27–51, especially 39–40,
nationalism 85–86,
94–95; **3** autobiography
154–169, cinematic
173–175
World Irish Dancing
Championships **3** 194
World Museum of Mining,
Butte **2** 5
wren **3** 91
Wright L.C. **5** 149
writing **3** 71, 72
Writing Ireland **3** 16; **4** 5

Y

Yang, Anand A. **6** 197
Yeats, William Butler **2** and
Armenia 22 *n*39; **3** 15,
83, 92, 94, 111; **5** and
Abbey Theatre 111–134
passim; **6** 5
Young, Arthur **2** 133; **3** 67,
193; **5** 188
Young England **6** 34
Young Ireland **2** 67, 153; **3**
222–223; **6** 35, 46, 115,
127, 145, 150; *see also*
Thomas Davis, Duffy,
McGee, Mitchel,
O'Doherty

Z

Zangwill, Israel, *Melting Pot*
2 155
Zen **3** 64, 65, 66, 70, 71